D1625648
GRAND CANYON
Rogers Highway
To and around SOUTH AMERICA TOURS
French Line
Cie Gle
S/S NORMANDIE
TRANSATLANTIQUE
AIR-INDIA INTERNATIONAL
HERTZ
SYSTEM
Sunshine U.S.A.
DEL WEBB'S HOTEL
SAHARA
AROUND THE WORLD IN 80 DAYS
AIR CANADA
TRANS-CANADA AIR LINES
This ite
latest d
period i
• Pho
• Visi
Disc
MAN ON THE MOON TODAY
NO GAS
I'M SORRIER
THAN YOU ARE
ROUTE
66
MURDER ON THE ORIENT EXPRESS
jetBlue
AIRWAYS
mirage
LAS VEGAS
013492665 1
EURAIL SAVERPASS
15 DAYS $230

THE AIRLINES OF THE UNITED STATES
ALASKA AIRLINES, INC.
ALL AMERICAN AVIATION, INC.
AMERICAN AIRLINES, INC.
AMERICAN EXPORT AIRLINES, INC.
BRANIFF AIRWAYS, INC.
CHICAGO AND SOUTHERN AIR LINES, INC.
COLONIAL AIRLINES, INC.
CONTINENTAL AIR LINES, INC.
DELTA AIR LINES
EASTERN AIR LINES, INC.
INLAND AIR LINES, INC.
MID-CONTINENT AIRLINES, INC.
NATIONAL AIRLINES, INC.
NORTHEAST AIRLINES, INC.
NORTHWEST AIRLINES, INC.
PAN AMERICAN AIRWAYS SYSTEM
PAN AMERICAN-GRACE AIRWAYS, INC.
PENNSYLVANIA-CENTRAL AIRLINES CORP.
TRANSCONTINENTAL & WESTERN AIR, INC.
UNITED AIR LINES, INC.
WESTERN AIR LINES, INC.

JIM HEIMANN · ALLISON SILVER

20TH CENTURY TRAVEL

100 YEARS OF GLOBE-TROTTING ADS
100 JAHRE REISEWERBUNG
100 ANS DE PUBS DE VOYAGE

TASCHEN

AMERICAN IMPATIENCE ALTERED THE TRAVEL METABOLISM: FASTER, BETTER, CHEAPER WERE THE WATCHWORDS THROUGHOUT THE CENTURY.

DIE UNGEDULD DER AMERIKANER SORGTE FÜR NACHHALTIGE VERÄNDERUNG: SCHNELLER, BESSER, BILLIGER ZIEHT SICH ALS PAROLE DURCH DAS GESAMTE JAHRHUNDERT.

L'IMPATIENCE AMÉRICAINE MODIFIA LE MÉTABOLISME DU VOYAGE : PLUS RAPIDE, PLUS EFFICACE ET MOINS CHER FURENT SES MOTS D'ORDRE TOUT AU LONG DU SIÈCLE.

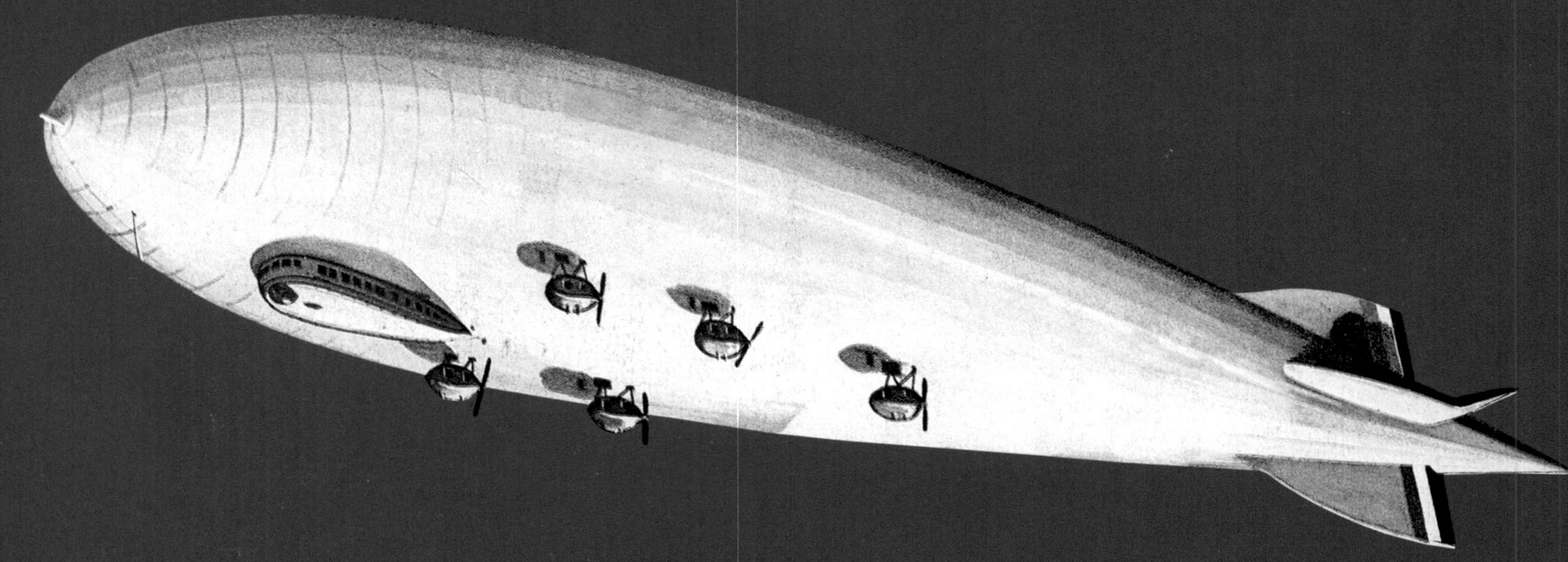

INTROD

THE REPUBLIC OF TRAVEL
DIE REISEREPUBLIK
LA RÉPUBLIQUE DU VOYAGE

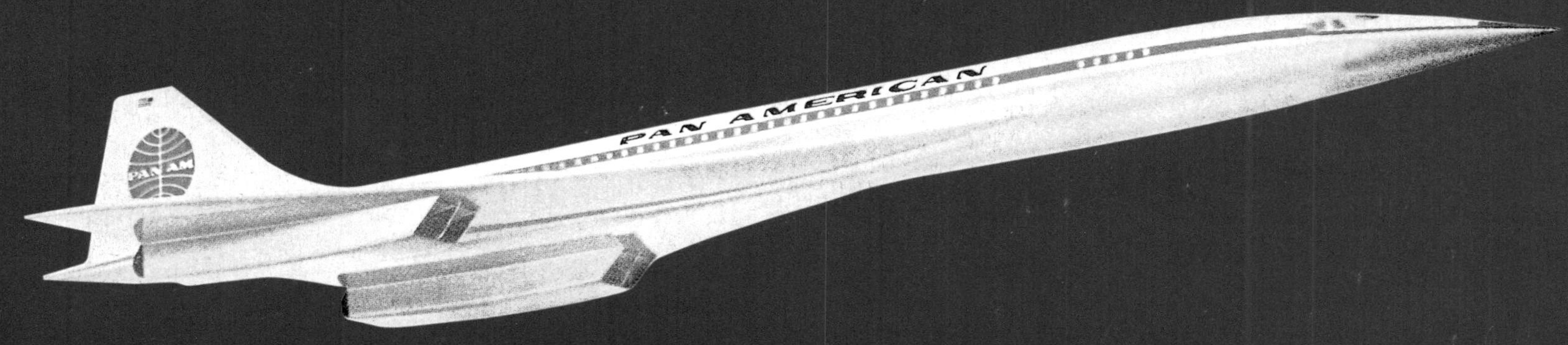

UCTION

LOZIER
"The Choice of Men Who Know"
ON touring highways, at the seashore, on the boulevard, in the mountains, at the country club,—wherever you meet people of wealth and refinement, there, in increasing numbers, you find the Lozier.
Big Six. Touring Cars $5,000, Limousines and Landaulets $6,500.
"LIGHT SIX" $3,250 to $4,450.
LOZIER MOTOR COMPANY
2403 Mack Avenue
Detroit, Michigan
Factory Branches in New York, Chicago, Boston

"WHEN ONCE YOU HAVE TASTED FLIGHT, YOU WILL FOREVER WALK THE EARTH WITH YOUR EYES TURNED SKYWARD, FOR THERE YOU HAVE BEEN, AND THERE YOU WILL ALWAYS LONG TO RETURN." —LEONARDO DA VINCI

WELL INTO THE 1950S, THE DUKE AND DUCHESS OF WINDSOR, WHITE-HOT STYLE SETTERS, WOULD CROSS THE ATLANTIC BY OCEAN LINER. They always booked the sought-after Duck Suite, three sumptuous upper-deck cabins with a gilded mural of mallards, on their favored liner, the SS *United States*. The Windsors' favorite had been the SS *Queen Mary*, but they jumped ship after the *United States* won the Blue Riband, for the fastest Atlantic crossing, on her maiden voyage, July 11, 1952. That record-breaking journey, still the fastest, took three days, 12 hours, and 12 minutes—10 hours faster than the *Queen Mary*. The Windsors had a staggering array of luggage: 118 trunks made to order from T. Anthony on Park Avenue in New York; numerous pieces from Hermes and La Maison Goyard of Paris. Myriad steamer trunks, shoe trunks, hatboxes, fitted toiletries cases, jewelry cases, document cases, even cocktail cases were par for the course on such a crossing.

The Windsors may have been style arbiters, but their travels were more mid-19th century than mid 20th—a remembrance of the grand ocean liners' potent allure in the heady age of air travel. By the late 1950s, the Jet Set was already at full throttle, taking off to Frank Sinatra's 1957 standard "Come Fly With Me." ("Just say the words, and we'll beat the birds down to Acapulco Bay.") Frank Loesser's 1960 Broadway hit *Guys and Dolls* tells of a big-time New York gambler who thinks nothing of taking a woman to dinner at his favorite restaurant—in Havana. By 1960, air travel was the very essence of glamour, epitomized in the Elizabeth Taylor—Richard Burton movie *The V.I.P.s* (1963), set in the first class lounge of the London Airport.

Prior to the 20th century, leisure travel had been the prerogative of the wealthy, the sort of people who used seasons of the year as verbs. They "summered" in a cottage in Newport, Rhode Island; "wintered" in a villa in the south of France. Only they could afford the complicated logistics of moving the mountains of luggage and armies of domestics required for lengthy stays. In the first half of the century, the very rich, as well as the celebrated, still blazed the trail. But the growing power of the middle class in postwar America changed everything. Once the rich and famous had validated a location as "the place to be," the increasing, and increasingly well-to-do, American middle class was close behind, via ever-expanding means of transportation.

The United States, after all, is a nation fueled by wanderlust. This is at the core of what it means to be an American. The country was built by people who crossed oceans to get there—then crossed the continent once they landed. You could reinvent yourself in new surroundings. Spurred on by the hope that good things awaited—just beyond the next valley or over the next hill—Americans were ever eager to "light out for the territory," as Mark Twain wrote in *Huckleberry Finn* (1844). When the Census Bureau pronounced the frontier officially "closed" in 1890, all this traveling did not stop. In fact, it increased.

Voyages of the next century, however, shifted the focus to leisure travel. American impatience altered the travel metabolism: Faster, better, cheaper were the watchwords throughout the century—as the advertisements for cruise lines, railways, and airlines can attest. Americans demanded the democratization of travel, and by century's end, they got it.

"SPEED IS THE CRY OF OUR ERA," INDUSTRIAL DESIGNER NORMAN BEL GEDDES DECLARED IN 1932, "AND GREATER SPEED, ONE OF THE GOALS OF TOMORROW." Bel Geddes said this at the height of the Machine Age—but it could well apply to any year of the century. In 1900 stagecoaches were still in use; by the century's end, a weekend trip from New York might as likely be to Prague (Czech Republic) as Quogue (Long Island). Speed mattered. In the Gilded Age finely appointed luxury liners like the RMS *Mauretania* vied to break speed records. Soon, trains developed express "flyer" routes; then, in the 1930s, aerodynamically streamlined locomotives, with names like Zephyr and Mercury, roared down the tracks.

Decade after decade, once-popular means of transportation were discarded when viewed as too slow. Stately ocean

1900

1900 Stagecoaches still in use, not fully replaced by motorbus until World War I

Postkutschen bis zum Ersten Weltkrieg noch nicht vollständig durch „Motorbusse" verdrängt

On voyage encore en diligences ; elles ne seront remplacées par les autocars qu'à partir de la Première Guerre mondiale

1901 Louis Vuitton introduces steamer bag, designed to fit inside larger trunks

Louis Vuitton präsentiert die in größere Koffer passende Dampfer-Tasche

Louis Vuitton lance le « steamer bag », un sac conçu pour tenir à l'intérieur des grandes malles

1903 Hawaii Promotion Commission uses exotic images of hula dancers to lure U.S. tourists

Hawaii Promotion Commission verwendet exotische Bilder von Hulatänzerinnen, um US-Touristen anzulocken

La Hawaii Promotion Commission se sert d'images exotiques de danseuses de hula pour attirer les touristes américains

1904 Travel photographer and lecturer Burton Holmes coins term "travelogue"

Der Reisefotograf und Präsentator Burton Holmes prägt den Begriff „Travelogue"

Le photographe de voyage et conférencier Burton Holmes forge le terme « travelogue »

◂◂ Lozier, 1912

▸▸ Hollywood By-the-Sea, Florida, 1926

liners—even the glamorous French and Cunard lines—could not compete against the speed of air travel. Luxurious long-distance trains fell by the wayside. Most of the mighty railroads declared bankruptcy by the end of the '60s. Amtrak, a government-owned corporation, was cobbled together out of the wreckage in 1971.

Air travel had been bumpy at the start. Early passengers—often celebrities seeking publicity as well as a faster trip—sought speed above all else. Windy cabins lacked temperature controls and made conversation a challenge. But in 1933, the streamlined Boeing 247 introduced soundproofing, heating, and air conditioning—and cut cross-country flights to less than 20 hours. Two years later, the Douglas DC-3 captured the nation's fancy with its shimmering, svelte aluminum body that ferried 28 passengers coast-to-coast in 15 hours.

Yet the élan of elite planes like the Pan Am Clipper did not matter when jetliners, no matter how jam-packed, halved flight time. By 1973, the supersonic Concorde cut transatlantic flights to 3.5 hours—you got there before you took off.

"A BED AND A BATH FOR A BUCK AND A HALF." WHEN IT OPENED IN 1907, HOTEL BUFFALO IN BUFFALO, NEW YORK, (later the Hotel Statler) was the first major urban hotel to offer a private bathroom with every room. Just three years before, John Jacob Astor IV's St. Regis Hotel boasted a telephone in every room, and central heating and air cooling—luxuries the millionaire hotelier and his social set enjoyed at home were now available to middle-class guests for the first time. Just as the public's impatience with the speed of travel had increased, so had its expectations for ease and comfort.

The first fully air-conditioned hotel, the Flamingo in Las Vegas, opened in 1946. Tropical breezes were one thing, but reliable air conditioning made travel to warm climates all the more enjoyable for leisure travelers. Sun-kissed beaches in Hawaii and Cuba may have called to tourists before, but with modern conveniences like air conditioning, travel boomed. By 1961, tourism revenue in Hawaii brought in more money ($161 million) than the island state's two staples—sugar and pineapples.

With these innovations, tourism was finally mass-market. The cost of an airline trip had previously been out of reach for the average American, but the prosperous postwar middle class thought the enjoyment and pleasure of travel should be available for everyone. One turning point was in 1968, when the Boeing 737 first flew. The most ordered and most produced jetliner in history, by the end of the century there were roughly 1,250 airborne at any time, with one landing or departing somewhere in the world every five seconds on average. In the 1970s, the Jet Set was no longer limited to the chic elite. It was anyone with an airplane ticket. From exotic panoramas to ancient walled cities, pristine South Sea beaches to stratified European capitals, Americans were traveling, and traveling far and wide.

BUT FOR AMERICANS, "WIDE" COULD MEAN A TRIP ACROSS THE COUNTRY AS WELL AS A TRIP AROUND THE GLOBE. Within the nation's broad expanses, the rapid acceptance of automobiles was testimony to Americans' lust to get up and go, independently. Car sales zoomed to 26.7 million in 1930, from 4,000 units sold domestically in 1900. American travelers were increasingly masters of their own destinies, going where they wanted, when they wanted.

As one of the country's first automobile dealers, Carl G. Fisher, a travel visionary, grasped Americans' love affair with cars. He saw how California, the Golden State at the end of the continent, beckoned. In 1913, Fisher conceived and developed the Lincoln Highway, the first roadway across the country, from New York to San Francisco. The next year, Fisher developed the north-south Dixie Highway, from Indianapolis to Miami. When the U.S. Congress passed the first public highways law in 1916, Fisher had paved the way—literally.

Washington ultimately constructed ribbons of wide roadways—from the creation of Route 66, the "Main Street of America," in 1926, through President Dwight D. Eisenhower's

1905

1905 Las Vegas, Nevada, founded when Union Pacific Railroad officially connects with Central Pacific line

Gründung von Las Vegas (Nevada), als die Union Pacific Railroad offiziell an die Central Pacific angebunden wird

Fondation de Las Vegas, Nevada, quand la compagnie Pacific Railroad assure officiellement la correspondance avec la ligne Central Pacific

1907 After visiting Hawaii, Jack London writes about surfer George Freeth and introduces sport to mainland

Nach einem Hawaiibesuch schreibt Jack London über den Surfer George Freeth und macht das Festland mit diesem Sport bekannt

Après une visite à Hawaï, Jack London écrit sur le surfeur George Freeth et fait connaître ce sport sur le continent

1908 President Theodore Roosevelt declares Grand Canyon U.S. National Monument; will become national park in 1919

Präsident Theodore Roosevelt erklärt den Grand Canyon zum U.S. National Monument (ab 1919 Nationalpark)

Le Président Theodore Roosevelt déclare le Grand Canyon Monument National Américain ; il deviendra un parc national en 1919

1912 RMS *Titanic*, queen of White Star Line, hits iceberg and sinks on maiden voyage; 1,517 passengers killed

Die RMS *Titanic*, das Flaggschiff der White Star Line, kollidiert auf ihrer Jungfernfahrt mit einem Eisberg und sinkt; 1517 Passagiere kommen ums Leben

Le *Titanic*, fleuron de la compagnie White Star, heurte un iceberg et sombre pendant sa croisière inaugurale ; bilan : 1517 morts

signing of the Interstate Highways Act, the largest public works project the world had ever seen, in 1956. Forget the pyramids! The initial cost estimate for interstate highways was $25 billion over 12 years; actual cost was $114 billion over 35 years. And as these roads were built, Americans filled them. Road trips may well be the national pastime. Young people took off cross-country, in search of themselves. (Consider Jack Kerouac's *On the Road*.) College students on spring break sought romance in sunny climes. (Consider Dolores Hart, George Hamilton, and Yvette Mimieux in *Where the Boys Are*.) Families journeyed to sublime destination hotels with stunning natural views. (Consider *The Shining*. Or, maybe not!) Think how American it is to go your own road—and also how incredibly fun. (Consider any Bob Hope–Bing Crosby *Road* picture—especially *Road to Morocco* or *Road to Utopia*.)

But travelers needed a place to stay on these road trips. As part of this democratization, a certain standardized level of hospitality came to be expected. One answer was motel (a combination of "motor" and "hotel") chains. When driving on a family vacation, checking into a Howard Johnson Motor Lodge or Holiday Inn would ensure clean, inexpensive, *standardized* rooms anywhere in the country. Holiday Inn started in 1952; there were 1,000 franchises by 1968. From Athens, Georgia, to Anaheim, California, the Howard Johnson's restaurant chain featured the same 28 ice cream flavors on every one of its menus across the nation.

While Howard Johnson's would become a reliable stop on the American roadside, more upscale chains like Hilton and Hyatt hotels provided little islands of America in foreign lands. In fact, the hotelier Conrad Hilton said he wanted to display the values that he believed had made America great. During the height of the Cold War, in the 1950s and '60s, Hilton saw his hotels as envoys for American values—and the U.S. government did too. With help from Washington and foreign governments, Hilton placed his hotels in Cold War capitals—where the West confronted the Soviet Bloc.

This was hotel-building with an ideological agenda. Much like the modernist embassies built during the same era, Hilton Hotels were designed to epitomize America. The structures were open and transparent, inviting to all who wanted to enter. Unlike Europe's older grand hotels, where guests walked into ornate, imposing lobbies, Hiltons featured clean lobby spaces with glass curtain-walls that allowed visitors to look through to the view beyond. "We mean these hotels as a challenge," Hilton explained, "not to the people who have so cordially welcomed us into their midst—but to the way of life preached by the Communist world." Hilton viewed his hotels as the vanguard of democracy—of a piece with the nation's desire to democratize travel.

This democratization process continued well after the Cold War ended. With the enactment of the 1978 Airline Deregulation Act, flights became more affordable—and more frequent. Going to the airport was no longer such a glamorous experience, but more and more people could afford to taxi down the runway. Americans developed this attitude with hotels as well. In the '80s, Ian Schrager, a former nightclub owner, developed the boutique hotel, an intimate hotel where anyone who checked in could feel exclusive. By the end of the '90s, the W chain and the Standard were opened as bigger, more affordable iterations—budget exclusivity.

Americans transformed the notion of travel in the 20th century. They reinvented the form, just as they had reinvented themselves throughout their history. By the century's end, travel was swifter than those present at its start could ever have dreamed. America's vast postwar middle class was peripatetic and unstoppable.

CONSIDER THE DEVELOPMENT OF THE SOUTH OF FRANCE, WHICH MORPHED RADICALLY OVER THE CENTURY—FROM AN EXCLUSIVE WINTER ENCLAVE TO A WIDELY POPULAR SUMMER PLEASURE DOME. In the early 1900s, winters were *the* season. Russian aristocrats would stop at the grand hotels for weeks at a time. The weather might be wet and somewhat chilly, but it was balmy compared to winter in St. Petersburg.

1914 Eiffel Tower, Paris's top tourist attraction, closes with onset of WWI

Der Eiffelturm, die bedeutendste Sehenswürdigkeit von Paris, wird mit Ausbruch des Ersten Weltkriegs geschlossen

La Tour Eiffel, la plus grande attraction touristique de Paris, ferme ses portes quand éclate la Première Guerre mondiale

1916 Nebraskan Joe Saunders loans out Ford Model T to traveling salesmen, starting first car rental business

Joe Saunders aus Nebraska vermietet das Model T an Geschäftsreisende; der erste Autoverleih ist geboren

Joe Saunders, habitant du Nebraska, loue des Model T aux voyageurs de commerce, lançant ainsi la première entreprise de location de voitures

1917 America enters World War I

Eintritt der USA in den Ersten Weltkrieg

Les Etats-Unis entrent dans la Première Guerre mondiale

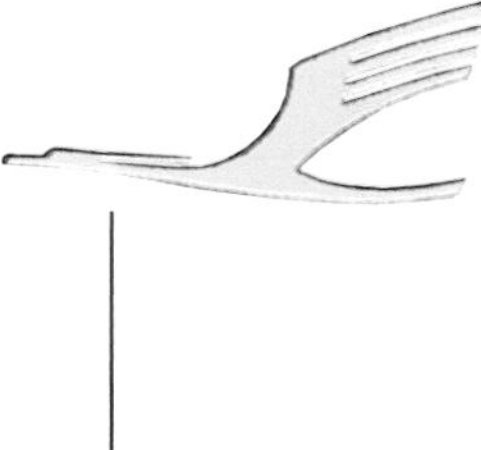

1919 Lufthansa predecessor Deutsche Luft Reederei adopts flying crane symbol; first airline to have logo

Die Deutsche Luft-Reederei, Vorläuferin der Lufthansa, präsentiert einen fliegenden Kranich; erste Airline mit Logo

La Deutsche Luft Reederei, prédécesseur de la Lufthansa, adopte le logo de la grue en vol; première compagnie aérienne à se doter un logo

"ONE'S DESTINATION IS NEVER A PLACE, BUT A NEW WAY OF SEEING THINGS." —HENRY MILLER

Enter the Jazz Age and a constellation of wealthy Americans who would forever alter the landscape: First, Cole Porter, a rich American songwriter with sophisticated European friends, decided to spend summer at Antibes in 1922. He rented a villa near the Hôtel du Cap, a landmark that closed every summer. Porter invited his close friend, Gerald Murphy, scion of the Mark Cross luggage company, and his family. By the next summer, the Murphys (the basis for Dick and Nicole Diver in F. Scott Fitzgerald's *Tender Is the Night*) convinced the Hôtel du Cap to stay open. They checked in — along with their friend Pablo Picasso and his entire family. Gertrude Stein and Alice B. Toklas stopped by. Summer in the south of France hit the social radar.

This was when suntans became fashionable, and outdoor sports like sailing, tennis, golf, and swimming beckoned women as well as men. Meanwhile, starting in 1922, getting to the south of France was easier. When the Impressionists had painted there, the area was considered exotic, even by the French. But the Train Bleu, a stylish blue metal train with gold detailing, now traveled from Paris to the Côte d'Azur every night. By 1925, when the Murphys moved into their new home, the Villa America, in Antibes, summer in the south of France was talked of around the globe. It was not only the deep blue of the sea and the sweet perfume of mimosa in the air, the entire Riviera became a vacation spot of choice for so many because it was ever easier to get there. There was a big airport in Nice, less expensive trains, better roads. Not just the rich and famous, but much of the middle class, even pensioners, decided it was worth the trip.

The Cannes Film Festival, which began the year after the end of World War II, only increased the allure. Every spring, Hollywood stars, studio moguls, and assorted beautiful people — usually literally so — jetted to the south of France. Frolicking in the surf could translate into international stardom. In 1953, a young starlet named Brigitte Bardot posed wearing only a bikini — and the world took notice. American movies constantly reminded viewers of the pleasures waiting in the south of France. (Who wouldn't want to film there?) Grace Kelly never looked so creamy or Cary Grant as suave as in Alfred Hitchcock's *To Catch a Thief* (1955). And when Kelly married Prince Rainier III of Monaco, Americans had another reason to check on the Riviera.

By the end of the century, every summer, Riviera beaches were wall-to-wall sunbathers. Travelers flocked from around the globe, whether flying in coach standby or on private jets, taking special trains or mini rental cars, docking on a cruise ship or a huge private yacht. Hotels for all budgets and all attitudes dot the coastline. The grandest hotels were no longer exclusive.

And it was Americans who led the way. This love of travel is one of America's legacies. The American travel plan — faster, easier, and democratized — set the standard for the world.

1920

1920 Automobile travel miles overtake railroad travel miles in United States

In den USA werden mit dem Auto erstmals mehr Kilometer zurückgelegt als per Bahn

Aux Etats-Unis, le nombre de kilomètres parcourus en voiture excède celui effectué en train

1922 After the RMS *Titanic* tragedy, ocean liners institute safety drills with designated life boats and life jacket training

Nach der *Titanic*-Tragödie werden auf den Linienschiffen Sicherheitsübungen mit Rettungsbooten und -westen eingeführt

Après la tragédie du *Titanic*, les compagnies transatlantiques introduisent des entraînements au maniement de canots et gilets de sauvetage

1926 Route 66, "The Main Street of America," is created, extending from Chicago to Los Angeles

Entstehung der Chicago und Los Angeles verbindenden Route 66, der „Hauptstraße Amerikas"

Création de la Route 66, « la Grand-rue de l'Amérique », entre Chicago et Los Angeles

1927 Matson Line opens its $4-million "Pink Palace of the Pacific"—The Royal Hawaiian Hotel, built in Spanish-Moorish style

Die Matson Line eröffnet mit dem 4 Mio. $ teuren The Royal Hawaiian Hotel den „Pink Palace of the Pacific", der sich im spanisch-maurischen Stil präsentiert

La Matson Line ouvre son « palais rose du Pacifique », le Royal Hawaiian Hotel, un édifice de 4 millions de dollars

+10
6 8
7 5 3
2 9 4
-10

◂ SS *Normandie* (Paul Iribe), ca. 1935

UMTRIEBIGE STILIKONEN, WÄHLTEN DER HERZOG UND DIE HERZOGIN VON WINDSOR BIS WEIT IN DIE 1950ER-JAHRE HINEIN DAS LINIENSCHIFF, UM DEN ATLANTIK ZU ÜBERQUEREN. Auf ihrem Lieblingsdampfer, der SS *United States*, buchten sie stets die begehrte Duck Suite – drei luxuriöse Oberdeckkabinen, benannt nach einem vergoldeten Wandgemälde mit Stockenten. Zuvor hatten sie die SS *Queen Mary* bevorzugt, dann aber wechselten sie das Schiff, nachdem die *United States* auf ihrer Jungfernfahrt am 11. Juli 1952 das Blaue Band für die schnellste Atlantiküberquerung gewonnen hatte. Die bis heute den Rekord haltende Reise dauerte genau drei Tage, zwölf Stunden und zwölf Minuten – zehn Stunden weniger als die der *Queen Mary*. Die Windsors reisten mit einer atemberaubenden Menge an Gepäck: allein 118 von T. Anthony von der New Yorker Park Avenue maßgefertigte Schrankkoffer und zahlreiche Gepäckstücke von Hermès und La Maison Goyard aus Paris. Myriaden von Überseekoffern, Schuhkisten, Hutschachteln, Toilettengarnituren, Schmuckkästen, Aktenkoffern und sogar Cocktailsets waren für eine solche Überfahrt nur angemessen.

Die Windsors mögen Vorreiter in Sachen Stil gewesen sein, doch ihre Reisen erinnern eher an die Mitte des 19. denn des 20. Jahrhunderts – ein Echo der Verlockungen der Ozeanriesen in einer temporeichen Ära der Flugreisen. Ende der 1950er-Jahre gab der Jetset bereits Vollgas und nahm Frank Sinatras Hit „Come Fly With Me" (1957) wörtlich („Just say the words, and we'll beat the birds down to Acapulco Bay"). Frank Loessers Broadwayhit *Guys and Dolls* (1960) erzählt von einem Kerl, der in New York illegale Glücksspiele veranstaltet und mal eben eine Frau zum Dinner in sein Lieblingsrestaurant entführt – nach Havanna. Flugreisen waren 1960 der Glamour schlechthin, versinnbildlicht in dem Kinofilm *The V.I.P.s* (*Hotel International*, 1963) mit Elizabeth Taylor und Richard Burton, mit der Erste-Klasse-Lounge des Londoner Flughafens als zentralem Schauplatz.

Vor dem 20. Jahrhundert waren Vergnügungsreisen das Vorrecht der Reichen, von Leuten, die den ganzen Sommer in einem Cottage in Newport auf Rhode Island oder den Winter in einer Villa in Südfrankreich verbrachten. Nur sie konnten sich die komplexe Logistik leisten, die für einen längeren Aufenthalt benötigten Berge von Gepäck und Heerscharen von Dienstboten zu befördern. In der ersten Hälfte des 20. Jahrhunderts gaben die Superreichen wie auch die Berühmten weiterhin den Ton an. Doch im Nachkriegsamerika sollte nun der zunehmende Einfluss der Mittelschicht die Dinge gründlich verändern. Wenn die Reichen und Berühmten einen Ort auserkoren hatten, folgte ihnen die zunehmende und zunehmend gut situierte amerikanische Mittelschicht dicht auf den Fersen, dank stetig verbesserter Transportmöglichkeiten.

Schließlich sind die Vereinigten Staaten eine Nation, die durch Wanderlust angetrieben wird, gleichsam ein Wesenszug des Amerikaners. Das Land wurde von Menschen erschlossen, die Meere überquerten, um dort anzukommen – und nach der Landung überquerten sie noch den Kontinent. Jeder konnte sich in einer neuen Umgebung quasi neu erfinden. Angetrieben von der Hoffnung, dass Gutes auf sie wartete – gleich hinter dem nächsten Tal oder jenseits des nächsten Hügels –, waren die Amerikaner stets darauf erpicht, sich „vor 'n andern [zu] verdünnisieren Richtung Territorium", wie Mark Twain 1884 in *Huckleberry Finn* schrieb. Auch als das Census Bureau das Grenzland 1890 offiziell für „geschlossen" erklärte, blieb nicht jeder an seinem Ort. Im Gegenteil.

Im folgenden Jahrhundert verlagerte sich der Schwerpunkt jedoch auf den Freizeitsektor. Dabei sorgte die Ungeduld der Amerikaner für nachhaltige Veränderungen: Schneller, besser, billiger zieht sich als Parole durch das gesamte Jahrhundert, wie die Anzeigen für Kreuzfahrten, Zug- und Flugreisen bezeugen. Die Amerikaner verlangten die Demokratisierung des Reisens. Ende des 20. Jahrhunderts war diese Forderung erfüllt.

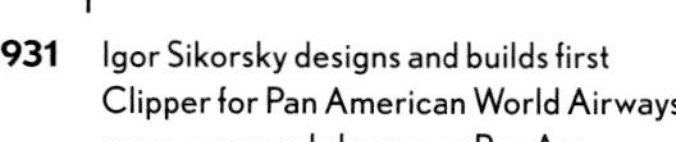

1929

1929 The hotel that defined swank, whether in Harlem or on Park Avenue, is immortalized in Irving Berlin's "Puttin' on the Ritz"

Dieses Hotel, der Inbegriff der Pracht, erlangt durch Irving Berlins Song „Puttin' on the Ritz" Unsterblichkeit

En 1929, l'hôtel parisien correspondant à l'idée que se font les Américains du grand luxe est immortalisé par le compositeur Irving Berlin dans « Puttin' on the Ritz »

1929 Worldwide Depression sets in following stock market crash

New Yorker Börsenkrach mündet in eine Weltwirtschaftskrise

La Grande Dépression sévit sur le monde entier après le krach du marché boursier

1931 Igor Sikorsky designs and builds first Clipper for Pan American World Airways, more commonly known as Pan Am

Igor Sikorsky entwirft und baut den ersten Clipper für Pan American World Airways, besser bekannt als Pan Am

Igor Sikorsky conçoit et construit le premier Clipper pour la compagnie Pan American World Airways, plus connue sous le nom de Pan Am

1932 Greta Garbo and all-star cast check into Berlin's *Grand Hotel*, Oscar-winning movie of Vicky Baum's novel

Eine Starbesetzung, allen voran Greta Garbo, checkt in der oscarprämierten Verfilmung des Romans *Menschen im Hotel* von Vicky Baum im Berliner *Grand Hotel* ein

Greta Garbo et une distribution de stars descendent au « Grand Hotel » de Berlin, Oscar du Meilleur Film

„WER EINMAL DAS FLIEGEN GEKOSTET, WIRD FÜR IMMER GEN HIMMEL BLICKEND AUF ERDEN WANDELN, DENN DORT KOMMEN WIR HER, UND DORTHIN ZURÜCKZUKEHREN WERDEN WIR IMMER ERSEHNEN." – LEONARDO DA VINCI

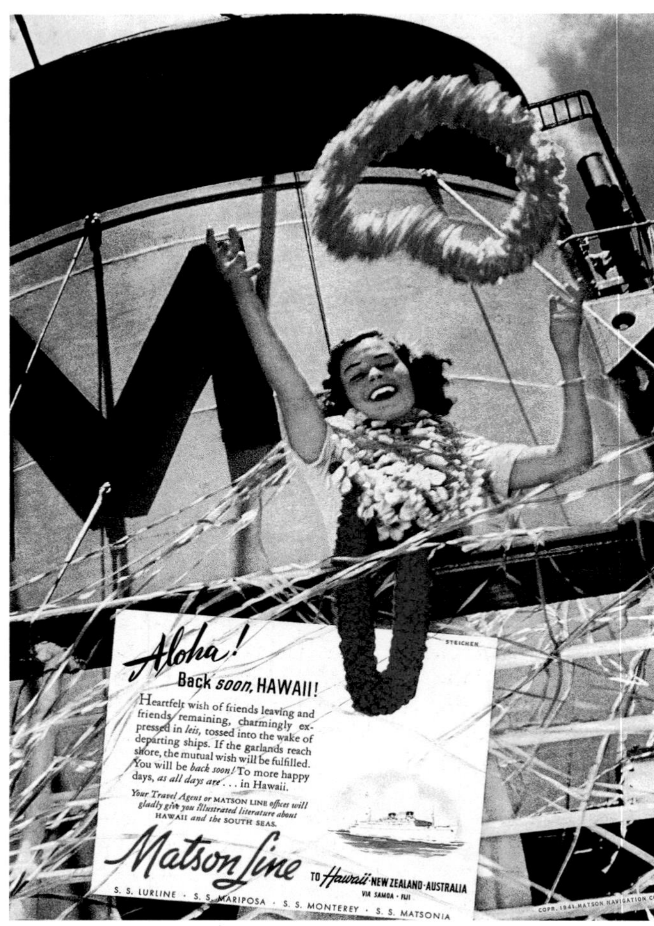

„TEMPO LAUTET DER SCHLACHTRUF UNSERER ZEIT", VERKÜNDETE DER INDUSTRIEDESIGNER NORMAN BEL GEDDES 1932, „UND MEHR TEMPO EINES DER ZIELE VON MORGEN." Bel Geddes sagte diese Worte am Gipfelpunkt des Maschinenzeitalters, doch sie könnten auf jedes Jahr in diesem Jahrhundert zutreffen. Im Jahr 1900 gab es immer noch Postkutschen, während man Ende des Jahrhunderts von New York aus übers Wochenende Quogue auf Long Island, aber auch Prag ansteuern konnte. Tempo war wichtig. Im Gilded Age (Vergoldetes Zeitalter, um 1876–1914) hatten prächtig ausgestattete Luxusliner wie die RMS *Mauretania* um neue Geschwindigkeitsrekorde gewetteifert. Bald darauf entstanden im Zugverkehr spezielle Expressverbindungen, bis in den 1930er-Jahren stromlinienförmige Loks mit Namen wie Zephyr und Mercury vorbeidonnerten.

Jahrzehnt für Jahrzehnt wurden dereinst beliebte Transportmittel wieder verworfen, wenn sie als zu langsam galten. Auch die majestätischen Linienschiffe der renommierten Reedereien French und Cunard konnten mit dem Tempo der Flugreisen einfach nicht konkurrieren. Die luxuriösen Fernzüge blieben ebenfalls auf der Strecke. Das Gros der einst mächtigen Eisenbahngesellschaften war Ende der 1960er-Jahre bankrott. Aus der Konkursmasse ging 1971 die staatseigene Amtrak hervor.

Anfangs waren Flugreisen noch eine recht holprige Angelegenheit. Viele der ersten Passagiere waren Berühmtheiten, die das Rampenlicht wie auch vor allem einen Zeitgewinn anstrebten. Die zugigen Kabinen waren nicht klimatisiert und erschwerten die Konversation. Bis dann 1933 bei der aerodynamischen Boeing 247 Schalldämmung, Heizung und Klimatisierung Einzug hielten – und ein Flug quer über die USA keine 20 Stunden mehr dauerte. Zwei Jahre später begeisterte die Douglas DC-3 mit ihrem glitzernden, grazilen Aluminiumrumpf die Nation und brachte 28 Passagiere in nur 15 Stunden von Küste zu Küste.

Flotte Flugboote wie die Pan Am Clipper spielten keine Rolle mehr, als Linienjets, seien sie auch noch so proppenvoll, die Flugzeit halbierten. Das Überschallflugzeug Concorde reduzierte 1973 einen Transatlantikflug auf dreieinhalb Stunden – man war quasi schon da, bevor man überhaupt abgehoben hatte.

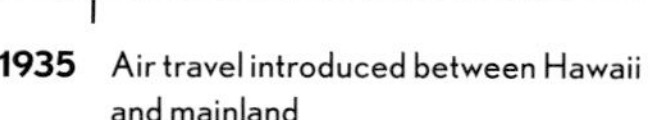

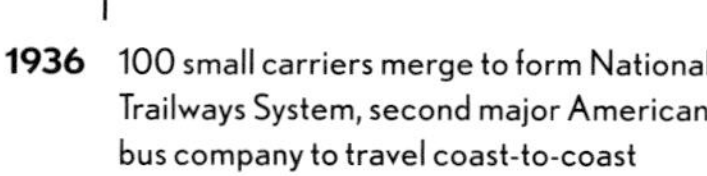

1934 Cunard and White Star merge

Fusion der Reedereien Cunard und White Star

Fusion des compagnies Cunard et White Star

1935 Air travel introduced between Hawaii and mainland

Erste Flugverbindung zwischen Hawaii und dem Festland

Premières liaisons aériennes entre Hawaï et le continent américain

1936 100 small carriers merge to form National Trailways System, second major American bus company to travel coast-to-coast

Union von 100 kleineren Transportunternehmen zu National Trailways System, der zweiten großen US-Busgesellschaft

100 petits transporteurs fusionnent pour former National Trailways System, deuxième compagnie américaine d'autocars reliant les deux côtes

1938 Industrial designer Henry Dreyfuss reinvents 20th Century Ltd., from locomotive to dinner menus, for N.Y. Central Line

Industriedesigner Henry Dreyfuss überarbeitet den 20th Century Ltd. bis zur Speisekarte für die N.Y. Central Line

Le designer industriel Henry Dreyfuss réinvente le train 20th Century Ltd. de la compagnie N.Y. Central Line, de la locomotive jusqu'aux menus du restaurant

◂ Matson Line, 1941

Foote Bros., 1945

„BETT UND BAD FÜR ANDERTHALB DOLLAR." DAS 1907 IN BUFFALO, NEW YORK, ERÖFFNETE HOTEL BUFFALO (das spätere Hotel Statler) war das erste große Stadthotel mit einem Bad für jedes Zimmer. Nur drei Jahre zuvor warb das St. Regis Hotel von John Jacob Astor IV. mit einem Telefon auf jedem Zimmer sowie Zentralheizung und Luftkühlung – Annehmlichkeiten, wie sie der Millionär und Hotelier und seinesgleichen daheim genossen, wurden nun erstmals auch den Gästen aus der Mittelschicht geboten. Die Öffentlichkeit erwartete mit wachsender Ungeduld nicht nur verkürzte Reisezeiten, sondern auch immer mehr Behaglichkeit und Komfort.

Das erste voll klimatisierte Hotel ist das 1946 eröffnete Flamingo in Las Vegas. Eine tropische Brise war ja ganz nett, doch eine zuverlässige Klimaanlage machte das Reisen in warme Klimazonen für den Freizeitmenschen doch um einiges angenehmer. Sonnenverwöhnte Strände auf Hawaii oder Kuba, seit jeher nicht ohne Reiz, erlebten dank moderner Annehmlichkeiten wie der Klimaanlage einen Aufschwung. Hawaii erzielte 1961 durch den Tourismus mehr Einnahmen (161 Mio. $) als mit seinen beiden Haupterzeugnissen Zuckerrohr und Ananas.

Dank dieser Neuerungen wurde der Tourismus schließlich zu einem Massenmarkt. Flugreisen waren für den Durchschnittsamerikaner bislang unerschwinglich, doch nach dem Krieg machte sich in der prosperierenden Mittelschicht die Ansicht breit, dieses Reisevergnügen solle niemandem versagt bleiben. Ein Wendepunkt war 1968 der Jungfernflug der Boeing 737. Von dem meistproduzierten Linienjet aller Zeiten befanden sich Ende des Jahrhunderts zu einem beliebigen Zeitpunkt rund 1250 Maschinen in der Luft, und durchschnittlich alle fünf Sekunden landete oder startete eine von ihnen irgendwo auf der Welt. In den 1970er-Jahren gehörte quasi jeder mit einem Flugticket zum Jetset. Von exotischen Panoramen bis zu alten Festungsstädten, von unberührten Südseestränden bis zu den vielschichtigen europäischen Hauptstädten – die Amerikaner reisen, und zwar weit.

DOCH FÜR DIE AMERIKANER KONNTE „WEIT" REISEN EBENSO EINEN TRIP QUER DURCHS LAND BEDEUTEN WIE EINE REISE UM DIE WELT. Angesichts der schieren Größe der Vereinigten Staaten zeugt die rasche Akzeptanz des Automobils von der Lust der Amerikaner, auf eigene Faust aufzubrechen. Der inländische Absatz schnellte von 4000 Autos im Jahr 1900 auf 26,7 Millionen Einheiten im Jahr 1930. Und die reisenden Amerikaner nahmen ihr Schicksal zunehmend selbst in die Hand, indem sie Ziel und Zeitpunkt bestimmten.

Als einer der ersten Autohändler im ganzen Land hatte Carl G. Fisher, ein Visionär des Reisens, die Liebesbeziehung der Amerikaner zu ihren Autos erfasst. Er sah, wie sehr Kalifornien, der Golden State am Ende des Kontinents, lockte. Im Jahr 1913 plante und errichtete Fisher mit dem New York und San Francisco verbindenden Lincoln Highway die erste quer durchs Land führende Trasse. Im Jahr darauf schuf er den Dixie Highway, der Indianapolis im Norden mit Miami im Süden verband. Als der U.S. Congress 1916 das erste Gesetz für öffentliche Highways verabschiedete, hatte

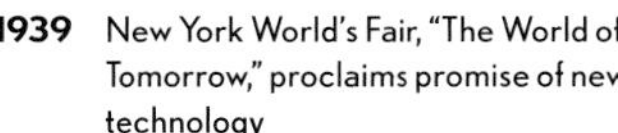

1939 New York World's Fair, "The World of Tomorrow," proclaims promise of new technology

Die New Yorker Weltausstellung „Die Welt von morgen" verheißt neue Technologien

L'Exposition Universelle de New York, « Le Monde de Demain », célèbre les promesses des nouvelles technologies

1941 Japanese bomb Pearl Harbor; U.S. enters World War II

Nach dem Angriff Japans auf Pearl Harbor treten die USA in den Zweiten Weltkrieg ein

Les Japonais bombardent Pearl Harbor ; les Etats-Unis entrent dans la Seconde Guerre mondiale

1943 Washington Statler opens; only modern urban hotel developed and built between start of Depression and end of WWII

Eröffnung des Washington Statler als einziges Stadthotel, das zwischen Wirtschaftskrise und dem Ende des Zweiten Weltkriegs errichtet wurde

Ouverture du Washington Statler, unique hôtel urbain moderne construit entre 1929 et 1945

1944 Pan American World Airways, which had resisted using air stewardesses, hires them

Pan American World Airways entscheidet sich nach anfänglichem Zögern für den Einsatz von Stewardessen

La compagnie Pan American World Airways finit par embaucher des hôtesses de l'air

CENTRAL

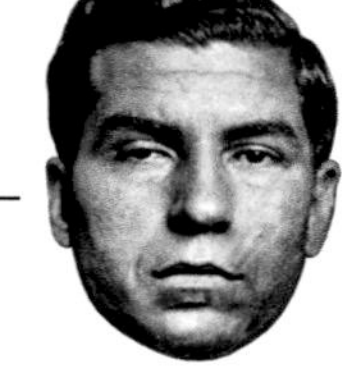

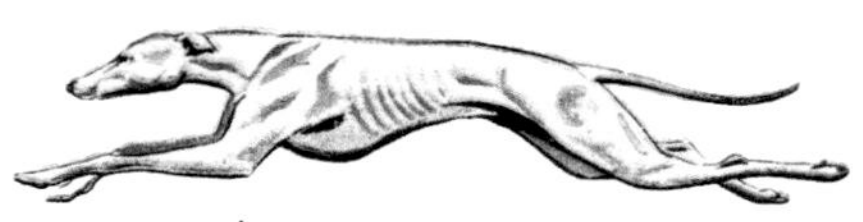

1945 Stan Kenton hit "Tampico" tells of troubles awaiting unwary tourists in Mexico

Stan Kentons Hit „Tampico" handelt von Problemen, die in Mexiko auf unvorsichtige Touristen warten

Le tube « Tampico » de Stan Kenton évoque les ennuis qui attendent les touristes imprudents au Mexique

1946 Lucky Luciano calls meeting of mobsters at Hotel Nacional in Havana to decide how to divide up Cuba

Auf Betreiben von Lucky Luciano tagen Mafiabosse im Hotel Nacional in Havanna, um Kuba unter sich aufzuteilen

Lucky Luciano organise une réunion de parrains de la mafia à l'Hotel Nacional de La Havane pour décider de « partage » de Cuba

1947 Production begins on Raymond Loewy designs of Greyhound's Silversides motorcoach; he retools dog logo as well

Produktionsstart von Greyhounds Silversides-Reisebussen nach Raymond Loewys Design, der auch das Logo überarbeitet

Lancement de la production des modèles d'autocars Silversides conçus par Raymond Loewy pour Greyhound ; le designer remanie aussi le logo de chien

1949 Under Chinese Communist regime, Shanghai's Palace and Cathay hotels merged into Peace Hotel

Unter der Herrschaft der chinesischen Kommunisten werden das Palace und das Cathay Hotel in Schanghai zum Friedenshotel vereinigt

Sous le régime communiste chinois, les hôtels Shanghai's Palace et Cathay fusionnent pour créer le Peace Hotel

◂ New York Central, 1950

▸▸ American Express Travelers Cheques, 1950

Fisher buchstäblich den Weg geebnet. Washington sorgte letztlich für ein ganzes Netz aus breiten Trassen – beginnend 1926 mit der Route 66 als „Hauptstraße Amerikas" bis zu Präsident Dwight D. Eisenhowers Unterschrift 1956 unter den Interstate Highways Act als dem weiträumigsten öffentlichen Bauvorhaben, das die Welt je gesehen hat. Was sind dagegen die Pyramiden! Für die Interstate Highways rechnete man anfangs mit Kosten von 25 Mrd. $ über zwölf Jahre, tatsächlich aber wurden es 114 Mrd. $ über 35 Jahre.

Und diese Straßen wurden von den Amerikanern rasch angenommen. Spritztouren entwickelten sich zu *dem* Zeitvertreib. Junge Leute kurvten durchs Land auf der Suche nach sich selbst – siehe Jack Kerouacs *On the Road* (*Unterwegs*). In den Frühjahrsferien suchten Studenten in sonnigen Gefilden nach Romanzen – siehe Dolores Hart, George Hamilton und Yvette Mimieux in *Where the Boys Are* (*Dazu gehören zwei*). Familien fuhren zu erlesenen Landhotels mit faszinierenden Naturpanoramen – siehe *The Shining* (*Shining*), oder vielleicht besser nicht! Wie amerikanisch ist es doch, seinen eigenen Weg zu wählen, und Spaß macht es auch – siehe einen der sieben *Road-to*-Filme mit Bob Hope und Bing Crosby, – speziell *Road to Morocco* (*Der Weg nach Marokko*) oder *Road to Utopia* (*Der Weg nach Utopia*).

Doch auf diesen Autotouren musste man auch irgendwo übernachten können. Immer mehr Menschen konnten verreisen, und zugleich erwartete man einen gewissen Beherbergungsstandard. Eine Antwort war das Motel – ein Kunstwort aus „Motor" und „Hotel". Und wer mit der ganzen Familie in eine der Howard Johnson's Motor Lodges oder ein Holiday Inn eincheckte, konnte überall im Land mit sauberen, preiswerten und *standardisierten* Zimmern rechnen. Das erste Holiday Inn wurde 1952 eröffnet; 1968 gab es bereits 1000 Franchisenehmer. Und auf jeder Speisekarte bot die Restaurantkette Howard Johnson's die gleichen 28 Eissorten an, sei es in Athens, Georgia, oder in Anaheim, Kalifornien.

Während Howard Johnson's zu einem verlässlichen Haltepunkt wurde, boten gediegenere Hotelketten wie Hilton und Hyatt im Ausland kleine Inseln des Amerikanischen. In der Tat hatte der Hotelier Conrad Hilton den Wunsch ausgesprochen, seine Hotels mögen jene Werte repräsentieren, die seiner Ansicht nach Amerika groß gemacht haben. Auf der Höhe des Kalten Kriegs in den 1950er- und 1960er-Jahren sah Hilton in seinen Hotels Botschafter der amerikanischen Werte – und die US-Regierung nicht minder. Unterstützt durch Washington und ausländische Regierungen, platzierte Hilton seine Hotels in den Kapitalen des Kalten Kriegs – dort, wo der Westen dem Sowjetblock gegenüberstand.

Mit den Hotels verfolgte man eine konkrete Ideologie, denn ganz wie die in der gleichen Zeit entstehenden modernistischen Botschaftsgebäude sollten auch die Hilton-Hotels ein Sinnbild Amerikas verkörpern. Die Gebäude präsentierten sich offen, transparent und einladend. Anders als die älteren Grandhotels in Europa, wo der Gast ein prunkvolles, imposantes Foyer betrat, gab es nun einen aufgeräumten Eingangsbereich hinter gläsernen Vorhangfassaden, die nichts verbargen. „Wir sehen diese Hotels als Herausforderung", erläuterte Hilton, „nicht für die Menschen, die uns in ihrer Mitte so herzlich willkommen geheißen haben, sondern für die von der kommunistischen Welt gepredigte Lebensweise." Hilton betrachtete seine Hotels als Speerspitze der Demokratie – nicht zu trennen von dem Bestreben der Nation, das Reisen zu demokratisieren.

Dieser Demokratisierungsprozess ging weit über das Ende des Kalten Kriegs hinaus. Mit Erlass des Airline Deregulation Act 1978 wurden die Flüge bezahlbarer – und auch häufiger. Die Fahrt zum Flughafen büßte etwas von ihrem einstigen Glamour ein, denn immer mehr Menschen konnten es sich leisten, auch tatsächlich abzuheben. Ähnliches geschah mit den Hotels. In den 1980er-Jahren schuf der einstige Nachtclubbesitzer Ian Schrager mit dem Boutiquehotel ein intimes Hotel, das jedem Gast ein Gefühl der Exklusivität vermittelte. W-Hotels und Standard entstanden Ende der 1990er-Jahre als größere, preiswertere Abwandlungen – exklusiv für den kleinen Geldbeutel.

1950 American GIs returning from the Pacific popularize Hawaiian shirts

Die aus dem pazifischen Raum heimkehrenden GIs machen das Hawaiihemd populär

De retour du Pacifique, les G.I. américains popularisent les chemises hawaïennes

1951 Travel to desert playground Palm Springs, California, shoots up with air conditioning now ubiquitous

Rasante Zunahme von Reisen in die Wüstenoase Palm Springs, Kalifornien, dank der inzwischen allgegenwärtigen Klimaanlagen

Le tourisme explose à Palm Springs dans le désert de Californie grâce à l'air conditionné, désormais omniprésent

1954 Conrad Hilton buys Statler chain for $111 million, largest price for real-estate venture since Louisiana Purchase

Conrad Hilton erwirbt die Hotelkette Statler für 111 Mio. $ – das teuerste Grundstücksgeschäft seit dem Kauf von Louisiana

Conrad Hilton rachète la chaîne d'hôtels Statler pour 111 millions de dollars, le prix le plus élevé payé pour un projet immobilier depuis la Vente de la Louisiane

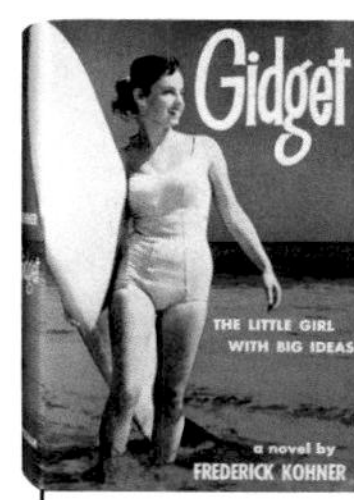

1957 Publication of *Gidget* and later film and TV show export Southern California surf culture to world

Der Roman *Gidget*, später gefolgt von Spielfilmen, exportiert die Surfkultur Südkaliforniens in die ganze Welt

La publication du livre *Gidget*, suivie d'une adaptation cinématographique (*Un Amour de Vacances*), exporte la culture surf californienne dans le monde entier

„DAS ZIEL IST NIEMALS EIN ORT, SONDERN EINE NEUE ART, DIE DINGE ZU SEHEN.“ – HENRY MILLER

Die Amerikaner veränderten die Definition des Reisens im 20. Jahrhundert. Sie erfanden eine neue Form, so wie sie sich während ihrer gesamten Geschichte immer wieder neu erfunden hatten. Gegen Ende des Jahrhunderts reiste man flotter, als man sich um 1900 je erträumt hätte. In der Nachkriegsära zeigte sich die große amerikanische Mittelschicht rastlos und unaufhaltbar.

MAN DENKE ETWA AN DIE TOURISTISCHE ERSCHLIESSUNG DER FRANZÖSISCHEN RIVIERA, DIE SICH IM LAUF DES JAHRHUNDERTS VON EINER EXKLUSIVEN WINTERENKLAVE IN EINEN ÜBERAUS BELIEBTEN SOMMERHIT VERWANDELTE. Anfang des 20. Jahrhunderts war der Winter *die* Saison. Russische Aristokraten quartierten sich gleich für Wochen in den Grandhotels ein. Auch wenn sich das Klima feucht und recht kühl gestaltete, so war das noch heimelig, verglichen mit dem Winter in St. Petersburg.

Vorhang auf für die Ära des Jazz und ein Grüppchen betuchter Amerikaner, die die Szenerie nachhaltig verändern sollten: Cole Porter, ein reicher amerikanischer Komponist und Liedtexter mit erlauchten europäischen Freunden, beschloss 1922, den Sommer in Antibes zu verbringen. Er mietete eine Villa unweit des Hôtel du Cap, ein Wahrzeichen, das jeden Sommer seine Pforten schloss. Porter lud seinen engen Freund Gerald Murphy ein, Spross der Lederwarenkette Mark Cross, nebst Familie. Im nächsten Sommer gelang es den Murphys (die F. Scott Fitzgerald zu Dick und Nicole Diver in *Zärtlich ist die Nacht* inspirierten), dass das Hôtel du Cap offen blieb. Und sie checkten ein – zusammen mit ihrem Freund Pablo Picasso und seiner gesamten Familie. Auch die Schriftstellerin Gertrude Stein und ihre Partnerin Alice B. Toklas schauten vorbei. Ein Sommer in Südfrankreich, das war es doch!

Inzwischen galt Sonnenbräune als schick, und Freiluftaktivitäten wie Segeln, Tennis, Golf und Schwimmen sprachen Frauen wie Männer an. Und ab 1922 konnte man auch immer bequemer nach Südfrankreich gelangen. Als die Impressionisten noch dort gemalt hatten, galt die Region sogar den Franzosen als exotisch. Nun aber gab es Le Train Bleu, einen blauen Luxuszug mit metallenen Schlafwagen und goldener Verzierung, der jede Nacht Paris mit der Côte d'Azur verband. Als die Murphys 1925 ihr neues Heim, die Villa America, in Antibes bezogen, redete man überall auf der Welt von einem Sommer in Südfrankreich. Es waren nicht allein das tiefblaue Meer und der süßliche Duft der Silberakazien, nein, die gesamte Riviera wurde zu einem gefragten Reiseziel, weil man es immer leichter erreichen konnte – es gab einen großen Flughafen in Nizza, preiswertere Züge und bessere Straßen. So machten sich neben den Reichen und Berühmten auch zahlreiche Menschen aus der Mittelschicht auf den Weg, Pensionäre nicht ausgenommen.

Das Filmfestival von Cannes, ein Jahr nach Ende des Zweiten Weltkriegs gestartet, machte die Sache noch reizvoller. Hollywoodstars, Studiobosse und diverse Schönheiten jetteten (meist ist dies wörtlich zu nehmen) jedes Frühjahr nach Südfrankreich. In der Brandung herumzutollen verhieß internationalen Ruhm. Ein Starlet namens Brigitte Bardot posierte 1953 im Bikini – und die Welt nahm Notiz. Amerikanische Kinofilme erinnerten das Publikum immer wieder an die in Südfrankreich wartenden Freuden. Grace Kelly wirkte nie so frisch und Cary Grant nie so weltmännisch wie in Alfred Hitchcocks *To Catch a Thief* (*Über den Dächern von Nizza*, 1955). Und als Kelly Fürst Rainier von Monaco III. heiratete, hatten die Amerikaner noch einen Grund, die Riviera anzusteuern.

Gegen Ende des Jahrhunderts hatten sich die Strände der Riviera im Sommer bis zum Überquellen mit Sonnenanbetern gefüllt. Die Gäste strömten aus der ganzen Welt herbei, sei es per Charterflug oder im Privatjet, mit dem Sonderzug oder im gemieteten Kleinstwagen, auf einem Kreuzfahrtschiff oder an Bord einer riesigen Privatjacht. Hotels für jeden Geldbeutel und Anspruch zieren die Küste. Die besten Hotels waren nicht länger exklusiv.

Und es waren Amerikaner, die vorangingen. Diese Liebe zum Reisen gehört einfach zu ihrem Wesen. Und der amerikanische Fahrplan – schneller, leichter, für alle – wurde weltweit zum Standard.

1957 Last gasp of grand cruise ships – Deborah Kerr and Cary Grant fall in love on ocean liner in *An Affair to Remember*

Letzter Seufzer der großen Schiffe: In *Die große Liebe meines Lebens* verlieben sich Deborah Kerr und Cary Grant auf einem Luxusdampfer

Dernier soupir des paquebots de croisière : idylle de Deborah Kerr et Cary Grant à bord d'un paquebot dans *Elle et Lui*

1958 Mike Todd's star-packed version of the Jules Verne novel *Around the World in 80 Days* soars into movie theaters

Mike Todds hochkarätig besetzte Verfilmung von Jules Vernes Roman *In 80 Tagen um die Welt* lässt die Kinokassen klingeln

La version du roman de Jules Verne *Le Tour du Monde en 80 Jours* produite par Mike Todd avec une distribution de stars déferle dans les salles de cinéma

1958 American Express, whose traveler's checks have toured with American tourists since 1891, debuts charge card

American Express, dessen Travellerschecks die Amerikaner seit 1891 begleiten, präsentiert die erste Kundenkreditkarte

American Express, dont les « traveller's checks » voyagent avec les touristes américains depuis 1891, lance sa carte de paiement

1959 Hotel del Coronado in San Diego, California, stands in for Florida resort in *Some Like It Hot*

Das Hotel del Coronado im kalifornischen San Diego fungiert in *Manche mögen's heiß* als Florida-Resort

Censé se dérouler en Floride, le film *Certains l'Aiment Chaud* est en fait tourné à l'Hotel del Coronado de San Diego, en Californie

B00,000,000
Anywhere, the date
U.S. DOLLAR TRAVELERS CHEQUE
John Traveler
American Express Company
$20
Anyone
IN UNITED STATES
Twenty Dollars
John Traveler

◂ American Airlines, 1950

VERS LE MILIEU DES ANNÉES 50, LE DUC ET LA DUCHESSE DE WINDSOR, LES RÉFÉRENCES EN MATIÈRE D'ÉLÉGANCE À CETTE ÉPOQUE, TRAVERSAIENT L'ATLANTIQUE EN BATEAU. Sur leur paquebot préféré, le SS *United States*, ils réservaient toujours la très convoitée Duck Suite composée de trois somptueuses cabines ornées d'une fresque de canards sauvages dorée à l'or fin. Si leur bateau de prédilection était auparavant le *Queen Mary*, le *United States* avait gagné leurs faveurs en décrochant le Ruban Bleu le 11 juillet 1952, pendant leur voyage de noces, pour la traversée la plus rapide de l'Atlantique. Cette transatlantique à vitesse record, encore jamais battue, dura trois jours, 12 heures et 12 minutes, soit 10 heures de moins que le *Queen Mary*. Les Windsor voyageaient avec un nombre de bagages impressionnant: 118 malles fabriquées sur commande par la boutique T. Anthony de Park Avenue à New York, ainsi qu'une multitude de sacs de chez Hermès à Paris et de La Maison Goyard. Tous ces malles, boîtes à chaussures, cartons à chapeaux, trousses de toilette, coffres à bijoux, porte-documents et même coffrets à cocktail étaient de mise pour une telle traversée.

Les Windsor dictaient l'élégance du moment, mais leur façon de voyager rappelait plutôt celle du milieu du XIXe siècle, comme une réminiscence de l'élégance et de la puissance des grands paquebots alors que s'ouvrait l'ère enivrante du voyage aérien. A la fin des années 50, la jet-set fendait déjà les cieux à toute allure, décollant au son du standard «Come Fly With Me» (1957) de Frank Sinatra («Just say the words, and we'll beat the birds down to Acapulco Bay.»). *Guys and Dolls*, la comédie musicale à succès de Broadway signée Frank Loesser, mettait en scène un parieur new-yorkais trouvant parfaitement normal d'emmener une femme à dîner dans son restaurant préféré ... à La Havane. En 1960, le voyage en avion représentait l'essence même du glamour, comme l'a incarné le couple Elizabeth Taylor/Richard Burton dans le film *Hôtel International* (1963) qui se déroule dans le salon VIP de l'aéroport de Londres.

Avant le XXe siècle, voyager pour le plaisir était l'apanage des classes aisées, de ceux qui conjuguaient les saisons de l'année comme des verbes. Ils passaient l'été dans un cottage à Newport, dans le Rhode Island, et l'hiver dans une villa du sud de la France. Seuls ces privilégiés pouvaient s'offrir la logistique complexe impliquée par le déplacement des montagnes de bagages et des armées de domestiques nécessaires à ces longs séjours. Pendant la première moitié du siècle, les riches et les célébrités avaient ouvert la voie, mais dans l'Amérique d'après-guerre, le pouvoir croissant de la classe moyenne fit tout changer. Dès que les plus privilégiés avaient validé tel ou tel endroit comme «the place to be», la classe moyenne américaine, toujours plus nombreuse et plus aisée, les suivait de près grâce à des moyens de transport en constant développement.

Après tout, les Etats-Unis sont nés du désir de découvrir le monde. Ce désir se trouve au cœur de la définition de l'Américain. Le pays a été construit par des gens qui ont traversé des océans pour l'atteindre, puis tout un continent après avoir débarqué. Dans un nouvel environnement, il était possible de se réinventer. Motivés par l'espoir que, juste après la prochaine vallée ou derrière la prochaine colline, de bonnes choses les attendaient, les Américains étaient toujours plus impatients «d'éclairer le territoire», comme l'a écrit Mark Twain dans *Les Aventures de Huckleberry Finn* (1884). Le Bureau du Recensement eut beau déclarer la frontière officiellement «fermée» en 1890, cela n'éteignit en rien cette passion du voyage. En fait, cela ne fit que l'attiser.

Les voyages du XXe siècle s'orientèrent toutefois davantage vers le loisir. L'impatience américaine modifia le métabolisme du voyage: plus rapide, plus efficace et moins cher furent ses mots d'ordre tout au long du siècle, comme en témoignent les publicités des compagnies de croisières, ferroviaires et aériennes. Les Américains exigeaient la démocratisation du voyage, et obtinrent gain de cause à la fin du siècle.

1960

1960 First year that Hawaiian tourism brings in more money than pineapples or sugar—$161 million

Der Tourismus bringt Hawaii mit 161 Mio. $ erstmals mehr Geld ein als Ananas oder Zuckerrohr

Première année où le tourisme rapporte plus à Hawaï que les ananas et le sucre : 161 millions de dollars

1961 Rat Pack hits Las Vegas—Frank Sinatra, Dean Martin, and Sammy Davis Jr. film *Ocean's 11* at the Sahara Hotel

Das Rat Pack landet in Las Vegas: Frank Sinatra, Dean Martin und Sammy Davis Jr. drehen im Sahara Hotel

Le Rat Pack fait un tabac à Las Vegas : Frank Sinatra, Dean Martin et Sammy Davis Jr. tournent dans *L'Inconnu de Las Vegas* à l'hôtel Sahara

1961 Cold War divide in Europe deepens; border between East and West Berlin closes with construction of Berlin Wall

Der Bau der Berliner Mauer vertieft die mit dem Kalten Krieg einhergehende Teilung Europas

Renforcement du rideau de fer en Europe ; la frontière entre Berlin-Est et Berlin-Ouest est matérialisée par la construction du Mur de Berlin

1962 Eero Saarinen designs swooping TWA Terminal at New York's Idlewild Airport

Eero Saarinen kreiert den geschwungenen TWA-Terminal für den New Yorker Idlewild Airport

Eero Saarinen conçoit le terminal futuriste de la TWA à l'aéroport Idlewild de New York

«CELUI QUI A VOLÉ MARCHERA TOUJOURS SUR LA TERRE AVEC LE REGARD TOURNÉ VERS LE CIEL, CAR IL Y A GOÛTÉ ET VOUDRA TOUJOURS Y RETOURNER.» – LÉONARD DE VINCI

«LA VITESSE EST LE MOT D'ORDRE D'AUJOURD'HUI», DÉCLARA LE DESIGNER INDUSTRIEL NORMAN BEL GEDDES EN 1932, «ET PLUS DE VITESSE, L'UN DES OBJECTIFS DE DEMAIN». L'ère des machines vivait alors son apogée, mais une telle affirmation pourrait s'appliquer à n'importe quelle année du siècle. En 1900, on voyageait encore en diligence; à la fin du siècle, on quittait New York en avion pour un week-end à Prague (République Tchèque) ou Quogue (Long Island). La vitesse avait son importance. Pendant la seconde moitié du XIXe siècle, les paquebots de luxe aménagés avec raffinement comme le RMS *Mauretania* rivalisaient pour battre des records de vitesse. Les chemins de fer ne tardèrent pas à créer des itinéraires «express». Dans les années 1930, des locomotives aérodynamiques baptisées Zephyr ou Mercury filaient à toute allure sur les rails.

D'une décennie à l'autre, les moyens de transport les plus populaires étaient ensuite délaissés dès qu'ils paraissaient trop lents. Les majestueux transatlantiques, même les paquebots français si glamour et ceux de la compagnie Cunard, ne pouvaient pas lutter face à la vitesse des voyages en avion. Les trains de luxe empruntés pour parcourir de longues distances restèrent au bord du chemin. La plupart des puissantes compagnies ferroviaires se déclarèrent en faillite à la fin des années 1960. Amtrak, entreprise appartenant à l'Etat, fut sauvée de justesse de la banqueroute en 1971.

Au début, les vols en avion étaient très chahutés. Les premiers passagers aériens – souvent des célébrités en quête de publicité et de rapidité – recherchaient avant tout la vitesse. Balayées de courants d'air, les cabines ne possédaient pas de système de régulation thermique et rendaient difficile toute conversation. En 1933, les voyageurs découvrirent le Boeing 247 aux lignes fuselées et équipé d'une isolation phonique, du chauffage et de l'air conditionné. Il réduisit les vols d'un bout à l'autre du pays à une durée inférieure à 20 heures. Deux ans plus tard, le Douglas DC-3 enflamma l'imagination des Américains grâce à son fuselage élancé et scintillant d'aluminium, d'autant plus qu'il était capable de transporter 28 passagers d'une côte à l'autre en 15 heures.

Néanmoins, la fougue des avions d'élite comme le Pan Am Clipper fit pâle figure quand les avions courrier

1964

1964 First ride of Japanese bullet train, Tokaido Shinkansen

Jungfernfahrt des japanischen Hochgeschwindigkeitszugs Tokaido Shinkansen

Lancement du Tokaido Shinkansen, train à grande vitesse japonais

1964 New York World's Fair proves "It's a Small World After All"

Die New Yorker Weltausstellung bestätigt ihr Motto „Eigentlich ist die Welt doch klein"

«Le Monde est petit», proclame la Foire Internationale de New York

1965 Laurance Rockefeller opens luxe Mauna Kea Beach Hotel on Hawaii's Kona-Kohala Coast

Laurance Rockefeller eröffnet das luxuriöse Mauna Kea Beach Hotel an Hawaiis Kona-Kohala-Küste

Laurance Rockefeller ouvre le luxueux Mauna Kea Beach Hotel sur la côte Kona-Kohala de Hawaï

1966 Howard Hughes moves into Wilbur Clark's Desert Inn in Las Vegas, which he buys, with four other casinos

Howard Hughes zieht in Wilbur Clarks Desert Inn in Las Vegas, das er zusammen mit vier weiteren Kasinos aufkauft

Howard Hughes s'installe à Las Vegas dans l'hôtel Desert Inn de Wilbur Clark. Il finit par le racheter, ainsi que quatre autres casinos

◂ Greyhound, 1965

Southwest Airlines, 1971

à réaction, même pleins à craquer, divisèrent par deux le temps de vol. En 1973, le Concorde supersonique réduisit les vols transatlantiques à une durée de 3h30 : on arrivait à destination avant même d'avoir décollé.

« A BED AND A BATH FOR A BUCK AND A HALF. » LORS DE SON OUVERTURE EN 1907, L'HOTEL BUFFALO (rebaptisé plus tard l'Hotel Statler) **DE BUFFALO, ETAT DE NEW YORK,** fut le premier grand hôtel urbain à proposer une salle de bains séparée dans chaque chambre. A peine trois ans plus tôt, le St. Regis Hotel de John Jacob Astor IV se targuait d'offrir un téléphone dans toutes les chambres, ainsi que le chauffage central et la climatisation : les luxes dont l'hôtelier millionnaire et ses pairs de la haute société profitaient chez eux étaient désormais mis pour la première fois à la disposition des clients de la classe moyenne. L'impatience du public concernant la vitesse du voyage avait grandi de pair avec ses attentes en termes de bien-être et de confort.

Le Flamingo de Las Vegas, premier hôtel entièrement climatisé, ouvrit ses portes en 1946. Certes, les voyageurs de loisirs appréciaient les brises tropicales, mais un système d'air conditionné fiable rendait les destinations au climat chaud d'autant plus attrayantes. Si les plages ensoleillées de Hawaï et de Cuba attiraient déjà les touristes, le confort moderne offert par la climatisation fit exploser l'industrie du voyage. En 1961, les revenus du tourisme (161 millions de dollars) rapportèrent plus à Hawaï que le sucre et les ananas, les deux principales ressources de l'Etat insulaire.

Grâce à de telles innovations, le tourisme devint enfin un marché de masse. Avant, l'Américain lambda ne pouvait pas se permettre de voyager en avion, mais la classe moyenne prospère de l'après-guerre estimait que le divertissement et le plaisir du voyage devaient être accessibles à tous. Le premier vol du Boeing 737 en 1968 marqua un grand tournant. C'est l'avion de ligne le plus commandé et le plus produit de l'histoire aéronautique. A la fin du siècle, on comptait environ 1250 Boeing 737 en vol simultanément, avec en moyenne un décollage ou un atterrissage toutes les cinq secondes dans le monde. Dans les années 1970, le club des voyageurs aériens n'était plus réservé à l'élite. Il accueillait parmi ses membres toute personne munie d'un billet d'avion. Des panoramas exotiques aux anciennes cités fortifiées, des plages vierges des mers du Sud aux villes européennes changées d'histoire, les Américains voyageaient, toujours plus loin et dans le monde entier.

QU'IL S'AGISSE DE VOYAGER À L'AUTRE BOUT DU PAYS OU L'AUTRE BOUT DU MONDE, LE MOT « LOIN » REVÊT DIVERSES SIGNIFICATIONS POUR LES AMÉRICAINS. Sur l'immense territoire national, l'adoption rapide de l'automobile refléta le désir de partir à l'aventure en toute liberté.

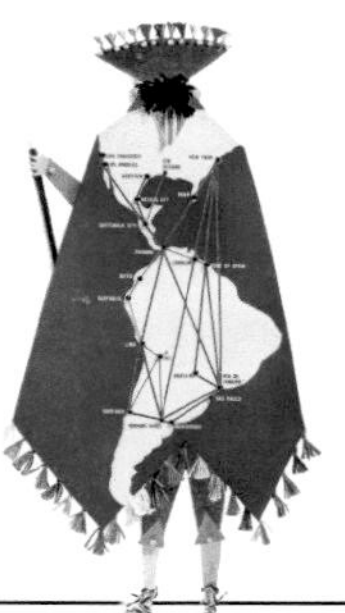

1967 Latin American carrier Panagra merges with Braniff

Die lateinamerikanische Fluggesellschaft Panagra fusioniert mit Braniff

La compagnie aérienne sud-américaine Panagra fusionne avec Braniff

1968 American Airlines introduces curbside baggage check

American Airlines führt die Gepäckaufgabe am Straßenrand ein

American Airlines introduit les comptoirs d'enregistrement de bagages

1969 Neil Armstrong and Buzz Aldrin first humans to walk on Moon

Neil Armstrong und Buzz Aldrin betreten als erste Menschen den Mond

Neil Armstrong et Buzz Aldrin sont les premiers hommes à marcher sur la Lune

1970 First commercial flight of Boeing 747 jumbo jet, which holds passenger capacity record for rest of century

Erster kommerzieller Flug der Boeing 747 (Jumbojet), die den Sitzplatzrekord für den Rest des Jahrhunderts verteidigen kann

Premier vol commercial du « jumbo jet » Boeing 747, qui conserve le record de capacité d'accueil de passagers jusqu'à la fin du siècle

American Airlines, 1971

En 1930, les ventes de voitures atteignirent 26,7 millions d'unités, contre seulement 4000 en 1900. Les voyageurs américains étaient toujours plus maîtres de leur destin. Ils allaient où ils voulaient, quand ils voulaient.

Figurant parmi les premiers concessionnaires automobiles du pays, le visionnaire du voyage Carl G. Fisher misa sur l'histoire d'amour des Américains avec leurs voitures. Il comprit tout le pouvoir d'attraction de la Californie, ce « Golden State » aux confins du continent. En 1913, Fisher conçut et fit construire le Lincoln Highway, première route transcontinentale reliant New York à San Francisco. L'année suivante, il lança les travaux du Dixie Highway nord-sud entre Indianapolis et Miami. Quand le Congrès américain vota les premières lois sur les autoroutes publiques en 1916, Fisher avait déjà – littéralement – ouvert la voie. Washington finit par faire construire de nombreuses et larges routes, de la Route 66, « Grand-rue de l'Amérique », en 1926, à la signature par le Président Eisenhower

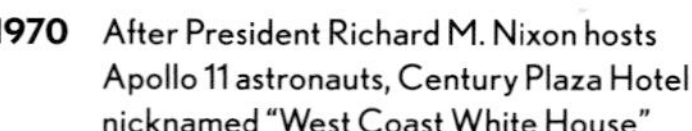

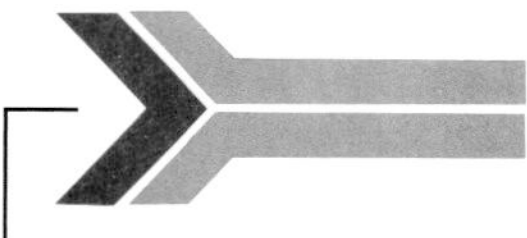

1970 After President Richard M. Nixon hosts Apollo 11 astronauts, Century Plaza Hotel nicknamed "West Coast White House"

Präsident Richard M. Nixon empfängt die Astronauten von Apollo 11 im Century Plaza Hotel, Spitzname „Weißes Haus der Westküste"

Nixon y ayant reçu les astronautes d'Apollo 11, le Century Plaza Hotel est surnommé « la Maison Blanche de la Côte Ouest »

1971 With private rail lines on brink of bankruptcy, U.S. creates nationally funded Amtrak

Da die privaten Bahngesellschaften fast bankrott sind, gründet die US-Regierung die mit Bundesmitteln finanzierte Amtrak

Alors que les compagnies ferroviaires privées sont au bord de le faillite, le gouvernement américain fonde la compagnie publique Amtrak

1973 Energy shortage leads to gasoline lines and skyrocketing airfares

Die Energiekrise führt zu Schlangen an den Tankstellen und lässt die Preise für Flugtickets in die Höhe schnellen

La crise pétrolière provoque de longues files d'attente devant les stations essence et voit monter en flèche le prix des billets d'avion

1977 The Hotel Cala di Volpe, Prince Aga Khan IV's voluptuous hotel, appears in James Bond movie *The Spy Who Loved Me*

Das Hotel Cala di Volpe, Eigentümer ist Prinz Aga Khan IV., erscheint in dem Bond-Film *Der Spion, der mich liebte*

L'Hotel Cala di Volpe, le somptueux établissement du Prince Aga Khan IV, sert de décor au film *L'Espion qui m'aimait* de la saga James Bond

«UNE DESTINATION N'EST JAMAIS UN LIEU, MAIS UNE NOUVELLE FAÇON DE VOIR LE MONDE.» – HENRY MILLER

de l'Interstate Highways Act en 1956, le plus grand projet de travaux publics que le monde eût jamais connu. Oubliez les pyramides! Le devis initial pour ces autoroutes inter-Etats s'élevait à 25 milliards de dollars sur 12 ans; en fin de compte, les travaux coûtèrent 114 milliards de dollars sur 35 ans. Les Américains investirent ces routes au fur et à mesure de leur construction. D'ailleurs, le voyage en voiture constitue sans doute leur passe-temps préféré. Les jeunes traversaient le pays à la recherche d'eux-mêmes (comme en parle Jack Kerouac dans *Sur La Route*). Les étudiants en quête de romance passaient les vacances de Pâques au soleil (comme dans le film *Where the Boys Are* avec Dolores Hart, George Hamilton et Yvette Mimieux). Les familles voyageaient vers de sublimes destinations touristiques et séjournaient dans des hôtels offrant des vues spectaculaires sur la nature (comme dans *Shining*... ou peut-être pas!). Imaginez comme il est typiquement américain de suivre son propre chemin, et si amusant aussi (comme dans n'importe quel film de la saga *En Route* avec Bob Hope et Bing Crosby, notamment *En Route pour le Maroc* ou *En Route pour l'Alaska*).

Ces voyageurs automobiles avaient cependant besoin d'endroits où dormir. Dans le cadre de cette démocratisation, on en vint à attendre un certain standard d'hospitalité. L'une des réponses fut apportée par les chaînes de motels (la contraction de «moteur» et de «hôtel»). Quand une famille voyageait en voiture, descendre dans un Howard Johnson's Motor Lodge ou un Holiday Inn lui assurait des chambres propres, bon marché et *standardisées* partout à travers le pays. Fondée en 1952, la chaîne Holiday Inn comptait déjà 1 000 enseignes en 1968. D'Athens, Géorgie, à Anaheim, Californie, la chaîne de restaurants Howard Johnson's proposait les mêmes 28 parfums de glace d'une carte de restaurant à l'autre.

Alors qu'Howard Johnson's allait devenir une enseigne digne de confiance le long des routes américaines, des chaînes plus haut de gamme comme les hôtels Hilton et Hyatt reproduisirent de petits îlots d'Amérique dans les pays étrangers. En fait, l'hôtelier Conrad Hilton affirma que ses hôtels devaient refléter les valeurs qui, selon lui, avaient fait la grandeur de l'Amérique. En pleine Guerre Froide, dans les années 1950 et 1960, Hilton considérait ses hôtels comme autant d'ambassadeurs des valeurs américaines – et le gouvernement américain le pensait aussi. Avec l'aide de Washington et des gouvernements étrangers, Hilton installa ses hôtels dans les capitales de la Guerre Froide, là où l'Occident affrontait le Bloc soviétique.

Ces projets hôteliers visaient un but idéologique. Comme les ambassades modernistes construites à la même époque, les hôtels Hilton étaient conçus pour symboliser l'Amérique. Leurs structures étaient ouvertes, transparentes et accueillantes pour tous ceux qui souhaitaient y entrer. Contrairement aux grands hôtels européens plus anciens, où les clients pénétraient dans des halls imposants et richement décorés, ils se distinguaient par des volumes épurés et des parois en verre permettant aux visiteurs de regarder à travers. «Pour nous, ces hôtels sont un défi», expliquait Hilton. «Non pas envers ceux qui nous ont si cordialement accueillis sur leur territoire, mais envers le mode de vie prêché par le monde communiste». Hilton considérait ses hôtels comme l'avant-garde de la démocratie, des pions placés par son pays pour démocratiser le voyage.

Ce processus de démocratisation se poursuivit bien après la fin de la Guerre Froide. Avec le vote de l'Airline Deregulation Act en 1978, les voyages en avion devinrent plus abordables, et plus fréquents. Si se rendre à l'aéroport n'avait plus rien de glamour, un nombre croissant de personnes pouvait se permettre de rouler sur le tarmac. Les Américains développèrent la même attitude envers l'hôtellerie. Dans les années 1980, Ian Schrager, ancien propriétaire de boîtes de nuit, inventa le concept de «boutique hotel», un hôtel à l'ambiance feutrée où chaque client a l'impression de bénéficier d'un traitement exclusif. A la fin des années 1990, la chaîne W et le Standard ouvrirent leurs portes sous forme de copies plus grandes et plus abordables: le luxe version économique.

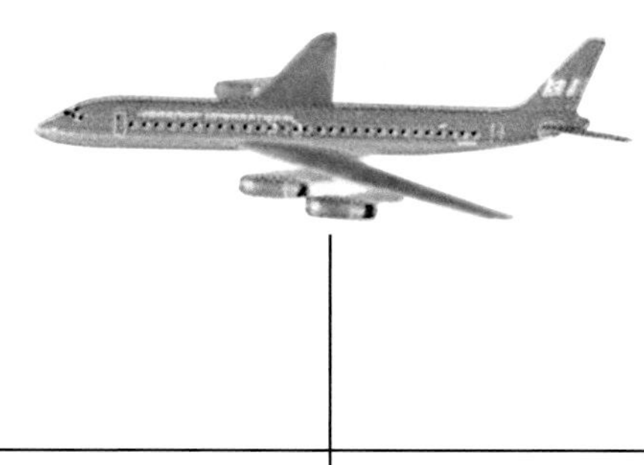

1982 Braniff International Airways closes shop

Braniff International Airways schließt die Pforten

La compagnie Braniff International Airways dépose le bilan

1984 With inexpensive screen printing widely available, T-shirts becoming popular tourist souvenir

Die weite Verbreitung des preiswerten Siebdruckverfahrens macht das bedruckte T-Shirt zu einem beliebten Souvenir

Les impressions bon marché par sérigraphie font le succès du «T-shirt souvenir» auprès des touristes

1986 *The Love Boat* TV series docks after nine years at sea, but Princess Cruises more popular than ever

Die Fernsehserie *The Love Boat* wird nach neun Jahren eingestellt, doch Princess Cruises ist beliebter denn je

Si la série télé *La Croisière s'amuse* est arrêtée au bout de neuf ans, la compagnie Princess Cruises n'a jamais eu autant de succès

1988 Amanpuri, flagship of Aman Resorts, small luxury hotels emphasizing natural surroundings, opens in Phuket, Thailand

Die Aman Resorts sind kleine, um natürliche Umgebung bemühte Luxushotels. Ihr Flaggschiff, das Amanpuri, öffnet im thailändischen Phuket seine Pforten

Ouverture de l'Amanpuri – fleuron d'Aman Resorts, petits hôtels de luxe dans de superbes cadres naturels – à Phuket en Thaïlande

Au XXe siècle, les Américains ont transformé l'idée du voyage. Ils en ont réinventé la forme, tout comme ils n'ont cessé de se réinventer eux-mêmes au cours de leur histoire. A la fin du siècle, le voyage était devenu plus rapide que ce dont ses pionniers n'auraient jamais rêvé. La vaste classe moyenne de l'Amérique d'après-guerre était nomade et intrépide.

LE SUD DE LA FRANCE OFFRE UN BON EXEMPLE D'UN TEL DÉVELOPPEMENT. CETTE ANCIENNE ENCLAVE HIVERNALE DE LUXE S'EST RADICALEMENT MÉTAMORPHOSÉE AU COURS DU SIÈCLE, AU POINT DE DEVENIR UN PARADIS ESTIVAL EXTRÊMEMENT POPULAIRE. Au début des années 1900, l'hiver était *la saison*. Les aristocrates russes séjournaient plusieurs semaines d'affilée dans les grands hôtels. Même s'il pleuvait et faisait un peu froid, le climat leur semblait doux par rapport aux rigueurs de l'hiver russe.

Pendant les Années Folles, une myriade d'Américains fortunés devait à jamais transformer le paysage: en 1922, Cole Porter, riche compositeur américain aux amis européens sophistiqués, décida de passer l'été à Antibes. Il loua une villa près de l'Hôtel du Cap, une adresse de référence qui fermait chaque été. Porter invita son ami proche Gerald Murphy, héritier du bagagier Mark Cross, avec sa famille. L'été suivant, les Murphy, le couple qui inspira les personnages de Dick et Nicole Diver à F. Scott Fitzgerald dans *Tendre Est la Nuit*, persuadèrent l'Hôtel du Cap de rester ouvert. Ils s'y installèrent avec leur ami Pablo Picasso et tous les siens. Gertrude Stein et Alice B. Toklas y descendirent aussi. Les vacances d'été dans le sud de la France venaient d'apparaître sur le radar de la jet-set.

C'est à cette époque que les bains de soleil devinrent à la mode et que la voile, le tennis, le golf et la natation séduisirent les femmes comme les hommes. Dès 1922, il était plus facile de rejoindre le sud de la France. Quand les Impressionnistes venaient y peindre, même les Français considéraient cette région comme « exotique », mais l'élégant Train Bleu effectuait désormais chaque nuit la liaison Paris/Côte d'Azur. En 1925, quand les Murphy s'installèrent dans la Villa America, leur nouvelle maison à Antibes, le monde entier ne parlait plus que des étés dans le sud de la France. Ce n'était pas que le bleu profond de la mer et le doux parfum du mimosa. Toute la Côte d'Azur devint une destination de prédilection pour de très nombreuses personnes car il était de plus en plus facile de s'y rendre. Il y avait un grand aéroport à Nice, des trains moins chers, de meilleures routes. Tout le monde décida que ça valait le déplacement, non seulement les riches et les célébrités, mais aussi une bonne partie de la classe moyenne, même les retraités.

Le Festival du Film de Cannes, créé un an après la fin de la Seconde Guerre mondiale, ne fit qu'augmenter l'attrait de la région. Chaque printemps, les stars d'Hollywood, les patrons des studios et tout un assortiment de « beautiful people » – généralement au sens propre du terme – s'envolaient pour le sud de la France. On pouvait devenir une vedette internationale simplement en folâtrant dans les vagues. En 1953, une jeune starlette nommée Brigitte Bardot posa en bikini devant les photographes, et son nom fit le tour du monde. Les films américains ne cessaient de rappeler aux spectateurs les plaisirs qui les attendaient dans le sud de la France (qui n'aurait pas envie de tourner un film là-bas?). Grace Kelly ne fut jamais plus délicieuse et Cary Grant plus suave que dans *La Main au Collet* d'Alfred Hitchcock (1955). Et quand Grace Kelly épousa le Prince Rainier III de Monaco, les Américains eurent une autre bonne raison d'aller visiter la Riviera.

A la fin du siècle, les plages de la Côte d'Azur étaient bondées d'estivants serrés comme des sardines. Les voyageurs arrivaient des quatre coins du globe, qu'ils volent en classe éco ou à bord de jets privés, roulent dans des trains supplémentaires ou de minuscules voitures de location, fassent une escale pendant une croisière ou débarquent d'un énorme yacht. La côte fourmille d'hôtels adaptés à tous les budgets et tous les styles. Les meilleurs hôtels ne sont plus réservés à l'élite.

Et ce, grâce aux Américains. Accélérer, simplifier et démocratiser le voyage: l'objectif américain a défini la norme mondiale.

1990

1990 A tycoon (Richard Gere) and a hooker (Julia Roberts) pair up at Regent Beverly Wilshire Hotel in *Pretty Woman*

Ein Finanzmogul (Richard Gere) und eine Prostituierte (Julia Roberts) finden in *Pretty Woman* im Regent Beverly Wilshire Hotel zueinander

Pretty Woman – un homme d'affaires (Richard Gere) et une prostituée (Julia Roberts) au Regent Beverly Wilshire Hotel

1994 First non-smoking transatlantic flight on American Airlines

Erster transatlantischer Nichtraucherflug von American Airlines

Premier vol transatlantique non fumeur d'American Airlines

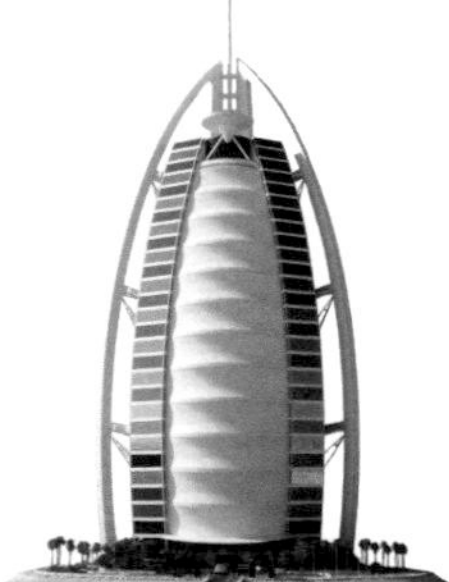

1994 Construction begins on Burj Al Arab in Dubai, tallest freestanding hotel in world

Baubeginn des Burj Al Arab in Dubai, des höchsten frei stehenden Hotels der Welt

Début de la construction de la tour Burj Al Arab à Dubaï, le plus haut hôtel privé du monde

1999 The Standard Hotel opens on Sunset Strip in West Hollywood; live models behind check-in are talk of town

Eröffnung des Standard Hotel am Sunset Strip in West-Hollywood; in der ganzen Stadt verbreitet sich die Kunde von den Livemodels hinter dem Empfangsschalter

Le Standard Hotel ouvre sur le Sunset Strip dans West Hollywood; les mannequins derrière la réception défrayent la chronique

WHEN GUESTS WALKED INTO A PALATIAL HOTEL IN PARIS... THEY STAYED THE SEASON, NOT THE WEEK.

QUAND LES CLIENTS DESCENDAIENT DANS UN PALACE PARISIEN ... ILS N'Y PASSAIENT PAS QU'UNE SEMAINE, MAIS TOUTE UNE SAISON.

WENN EIN GAST EIN FEUDALES PARISER HOTEL BETRAT, DANN BLIEB ER NICHT EINE WOCHE, SONDERN DIE GANZE SAISON.

1900

CHECKING IN

EINCHECKEN

LA VIE DE PALACE

–1919

◂ Hotel St. Francis, 1904

Pacific Mail, ca. 1916

AT THE TURN OF THE CENTURY, LEISURE TRAVEL WAS A LUXURY, THE RECREATION OF CHOICE FOR THE VERY RICH. JOURNEYS COULD BE FASHIONABLY EDUCATIONAL, LIKE A GRAND TOUR OF EUROPE, or exotically sybaritic, like a stay in a North African casbah. In the first decade of the new century, a grand procession of Beaux Arts hotels opened around the globe. When guests checked in to a palatial hotel in Paris or a vast Victorian Saracenic pile in Cairo, they entered a world of opulence. They stayed the season, not the week.

These stately hotels sought to outshine each other. The Hôtel des Bains, a monumental resort that helped make sunbathing acceptable, opened on the Venice Lido in 1900. In 1903, the massive Taj Mahal Hotel opened in Bombay. The next year, John Jacob Astor IV built the $5.5-million St. Regis in New York. Soon, the Palace Hotel debuted on the Bund in Shanghai, the Ritz in London, the Adlon in Berlin, the Plaza Hotel in New York, and the Hotel Excelsior in Rome. Each staked its claim as "greatest hotel in the world."

Out West, Americans built their own version of a grand hotel — sprawling rustic lodges made of natural, local materials, developed by public and private interests. President Theodore Roosevelt, an ardent conservationist, pushed the federal government to create national parks, including the Grand Canyon. Yet it was Western railroads, eager for passengers, that built the picturesque destination hotels. The influential 1904 Old Faithful Inn, built by the Northern Pacific Railroad in Yellowstone National Park, featured a vast seven-story lobby made entirely of logs. The next year, the Atchison, Topeka and Santa Fe Railway opened El Tovar, a grand lodge at the southern rim of the Grand Canyon. It was owned and run by Fred Harvey, who built the Harvey House restaurants into the first national chain and brought the same meticulous service to the hotel. It did what it was designed to do: dramatically increase tourism in the area.

When Europe beckoned, Gilded Age travelers embarked on grand ships. The Hamburg-American Line was most popular, and its *Deutschland* won the Blue Riband in 1900 for the fastest voyage across the Atlantic — five days, 15 hours, five minutes. Travel to Hawaii blossomed as well. In 1902, the Matson Navigation Company, which steamed between Hawaii and the mainland, opened the Moana, the first hotel on Waikiki Beach. Jack London's 1907 magazine article about the Hawaiian surfer George Freeth introduced that sport to the mainland. By 1908, William Matson had built the steamship *Lurline*, named for his daughter, to carry freight and 51 passengers. Hawaii was on its way to becoming a major travel destination.

Yet, one of the decade's biggest attractions was not an exotic locale, but the 1904 St. Louis World's Fair. More than 20 million visitors from around the globe saw the Louisiana Purchase Exposition. The newfangled ice cream cone was a crowd favorite. This large turnout signaled that U.S. travel destinations appealed to the growing middle class. Democratization of travel had begun.

1900

1900 Hôtel des Bains opens; Thomas Mann writes *Death in Venice* after 1911 stay there

Eröffnung des Hôtel des Bains; Thomas Mann verfasst *Der Tod in Venedig*, nachdem er 1911 dort abgestiegen war

Ouverture de l'Hôtel des Bains ; Thomas Mann écrira *La Mort à Venise* après y avoir séjourné en 1911

1901 Visitors astounded as Pan American Exposition in Buffalo, New York, uses electricity generated by Niagara Falls, 25 miles away

Die Pan American Exposition in Buffalo, New York, verwendet von den 40 km entfernten Niagarafällen generierten Strom und verblüfft damit die Besucher

La Pan American Exposition de Buffalo, Etat de New York, est alimentée en électricité par les Chutes du Niagara situées à 40 km

1901 New York Central debuts overnight 20th Century Limited train from New York to Chicago

New York Central führt mit dem Zug 20th Century Limited die erste Nachtstrecke zwischen New York und Chicago ein

La compagnie New York Central lance le train de nuit « 20th Century Limited » qui relie New York à Chicago

1902 First science fiction film, and one of earliest movies, *A Trip to the Moon* imagines flight beyond Earth

Die Reise in den Mond, der erste Science-Fiction-Film und einer der frühesten Filme überhaupt, träumt von einem Vorstoß zum Erdtrabanten

Le Voyage dans la Lune, l'un des premiers films et le premier de science-fiction met en scène une expédition spatiale

Southern Pacific, 1904

▸ Hamburg-American Line, 1911

ONCE HENRY FORD STARTED SELLING HIS MODEL T IN 1908, IT REVOLUTIONIZED THE WAY AMERICANS APPROACHED TRAVEL. At the dawn of the 1910s, trains provided 95% of all intercity transportation in the United States. By the decade's close, automobile travel miles surpassed railroad miles.

Yet throughout the 1910s, trains seemed in a golden era, moving ever faster and more comfortably. The California land boom, for one, created huge demand. Cited for its cheap land and endless sunshine, California was also considered exotic and fascinating by Easterners. In 1912, a leading Hawaiian surfer, Duke Kahanamoku, emerged as the worldwide envoy for the sport, giving demonstrations on Southern California beaches. The fact that the young movie industry settled there was also alluring.

Travelers flocked to the Golden State. The Atchison, Topeka and Santa Fe responded, in 1911, with Santa Fe de-Lux service. Flyers roared express to California, for $25 more than the standard ticket price. Two years later, the Sante Fe Line tried a new form of advertising—billboards. Demand only increased.

But there was an enticing alternative: the automobile. And when it comes to car travel, all roads lead to Carl G. Fisher, an entrepreneur infatuated by automobiles, auto racing, and land development. Later in the century, Fisher would dream of dazzling resorts in Miami Beach, Florida, and Montauk, New York, but he was practical enough to realize you first needed roads to get there. So, in 1913, he developed the first cross-country roadway, the Lincoln Highway, beating the U.S. Congress's first public highways legislation by three years.

While land travel was on the rise, ocean travel faced rocky shoals. Ocean liners had grown ever more glorious each passing year. But on April 14, 1912, the RMS *Titanic*, queen of the White Star Line and the largest passenger steamship, hit an iceberg and sank on its maiden voyage. It was one of the deadliest peacetime maritime disasters—1,517 passengers were killed (including hotelier John Jacob Astor IV), and only 706 survived. Then, with the onset of World War I in 1914, passenger travel plummeted. Many sumptuous liners, like the Hamburg-American Line's *Vaterland*, the largest ship afloat, were refitted as troop ships. Passenger travel slumped even more after the RMS *Lusitania*, part of the Cunard Line, was torpedoed by a German U-boat in 1915. It sank in 18 minutes, and of the 1,959 people aboard, 1,198 died.

Yet ocean travel did see advances when the Panama Canal, dubbed "the 13th labor of Hercules," opened in 1914. Travel by ship between New York and San Francisco was cut by more than half—to 11,000 km (6,000 miles), from 25,900 km (14,000 miles). The new canal was celebrated with the Panama-Pacific International Exposition in San Francisco in 1915. This world's fair signaled the host city's rebirth after the devastating 1906 earthquake. One exhibit, built by Henry Ford, featured an assembly line. It produced cars three hours a day, six days a week. This was so popular that the line of visitors waiting to see it never seemed to shorten.

1903

1903 Wright Brothers' first flight at Kitty Hawk, North Carolina

Erster Flug der Gebrüder Wright in Kitty Hawk, North Carolina

Premier vol des frères Wright à Kitty Hawk, Caroline du Nord

1903 Horatio Nelson Jackson and dog Bud make first transcontinental car journey

Horatio Nelson Jackson unternimmt mit seinem Hund Bud die erste transkontinentale Autoreise

Horatio Nelson Jackson et le chien Bud effectuent le premier voyage transcontinental en voiture

1904 Hotel St. Francis opens in San Francisco, but soon destroyed in 1906 earthquake

Eröffnung des Hotel St. Francis in San Francisco, das jedoch durch das Erdbeben von 1906 zerstört wird

L'Hotel St. Francis ouvre à San Francisco, avant d'être détruit par le tremblement de terre de 1906

1904 Old Faithful Inn opens in Yellowstone National Park, influences all rustic grand hotels

Eröffnung des Old Faithful Inn im Yellowstone National Park als wegweisendes Beispiel für ein rustikales Grandhotel

Ouverture de l'Old Faithful Inn dans le Parc National de Yellowstone, hôtel qui influencera la conception de tous les grands pavillons hôteliers rustiques

HAMBURG-AMERICAN LINE

VATERLAND

◂ Hamburg-American Line, 1914

Great Northern Steamship Line, 1904

VERGNÜGUNGSREISEN WAREN UM 1900 PURER LUXUS, DIE VON DEN WIRKLICH REICHEN BEVORZUGTE ART DER ERHOLUNG. DIE REISEN KONNTEN, WIE ES DAMALS SCHICK WAR, PÄDAGOGISCH WERTVOLL SEIN WIE EINE BILDUNGSREISE DURCH EUROPA oder aber in Exotik schwelgen wie der Aufenthalt in einer nordafrikanischen Kasba. In der ersten Dekade des neuen Jahrhunderts entstanden überall auf der Welt zahlreiche „Beaux Arts"-Hotels. Wer in ein feudales Hotel in Paris oder einen viktorianisch-sarazenischen Prachtbau in Kairo eincheckte, betrat eine opulente Welt. Und er blieb nicht eine Woche, sondern die ganze Saison.

Jedes dieser Prachthotels wollte das Beste sein. Das Hôtel des Bains, eine monumentale Anlage, die das Sonnenbaden salonfähig machte, öffnete im Jahr 1900 seine Pforten auf dem Lido von Venedig, 1903 folgte das wuchtige Taj Mahal Hotel in Bombay. Im Jahr darauf baute John Jacob Astor IV. für 5,5 Mio. $ das St. Regis in New York. Kurz danach kamen das Palace Hotel auf dem Bund in Schanghai, das Ritz in London, das Adlon in Berlin, das Plaza Hotel in New York und das Hotel Excelsior in Rom. Jedes von ihnen beanspruchte eine weltweite Spitzenstellung.

Weit im Westen schufen die Amerikaner ihre eigene Version eines „Grandhotels" – ausufernde rustikale Lodges aus natürlichen, lokalen Materialien, finanziert mit öffentlichen und privaten Mitteln. Präsident Theodore Roosevelt, ein leidenschaftlicher Naturschützer, drängte die nationale Regierung zur Einrichtung von Nationalparks, darunter auch der Grand Canyon. Die pittoresken Landhotels verdanken sich indes der auf mehr Fahrgäste bedachten Eisenbahngesellschaft Western Railroads. Das stilbildende, 1904 von der Northern Pacific Railroad im Yellowstone National Park errichtete Old Faithful Inn bestach mit einer gewaltigen siebenstöckigen Lobby in Blockbauweise. Im Jahr darauf eröffnete die Atchison, Topeka and Santa Fe Railway das El Tovar, eine große Lodge am Südrand des Grand Canyon. Eigentümer und Betreiber war Fred Harvey, der die Harvey House Restaurants zur ersten landesweiten Restaurantkette ausgebaut hatte und deren untadeligen Service nun auf den Hotelsektor übertrug. Der Plan ging auf, denn die regionalen Besucherzahlen schnellten in die Höhe.

Amerikaner, die sich im Gilded Age von Europa angelockt fühlten, gingen an Bord eines der großen Dampfer. Am beliebtesten war die Hamburg-Amerika-Linie (HAPAG), deren *Deutschland* 1900 das Blaue Band für die schnellste Atlantiküberquerung gewann – fünf Tage, 15 Stunden und fünf Minuten. Reisen nach Hawaii waren ebenfalls gefragt. Zwischen Hawaii und dem Festland verkehrend, eröffnete die Matson Navigation Company 1902 mit dem Moana das erste Hotel von Waikiki Beach. Jack Londons 1907 erschienener Zeitschriftenartikel über den hawaiianischen Surfer George Freeth machte auch die Landratten mit diesem Sport bekannt. Und 1908 lief William Matsons nach seiner Tochter benanntes Dampfschiff *Lurline* vom Stapel, das Fracht plus 51 Passagiere beförderte. Hawaii war auf dem besten Weg, ein gefragtes Reiseziel zu werden.

Doch zu den größten Attraktionen dieser Dekade zählte nicht ein exotischer Schauplatz, sondern die Weltausstellung von 1904 in St. Louis. Mehr als 20 Millionen Menschen aus aller Welt besuchten die Louisiana Purchase Exposition. Das neumodische Eishörnchen entwickelte sich zum Publikumsmagneten. Die wachsende Mittelschicht fand an inländischen Reisezielen Gefallen. Die Demokratisierung des Reisens hatte begonnen.

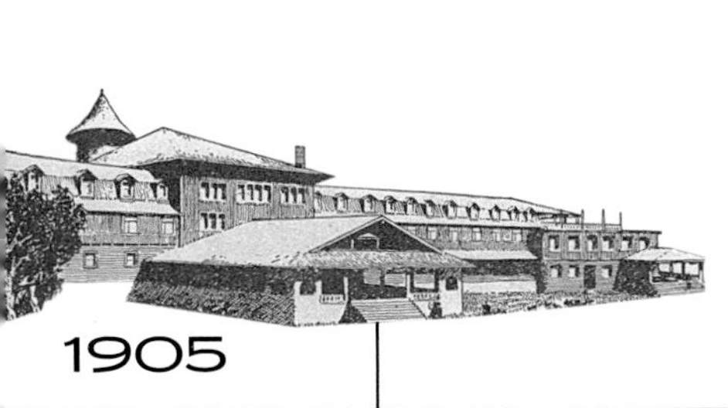

1905

1905 El Tovar, grand resort lodge at south rim of Grand Canyon, opens, dramatically increasing tourism to area

Die Eröffnung des El Tovar, einer großen resortartigen Lodge am Südrand des Grand Canyon, führt zu einem drastischen Anstieg des regionalen Tourismus

Avec l'ouverture d'El Tovar, grand pavillon hôtelier sur la bordure sud du Grand Canyon, le tourisme explose dans la région

1907 Hotel Buffalo debuts as first major urban hotel with bath in each room

Hotel Buffalo als erstes großes Stadthotel mit Bad für jedes Zimmer

Ouverture de l'Hotel Buffalo, le premier grand hôtel urbain avec salle de bains dans chaque chambre

1908 Cunard's *Mauretania* wins Blue Riband for fastest Atlantic crossing and holds it for 22 years

Cunards *Mauretania* gewinnt das Blaue Band für die schnellste Atlantiküberquerung und kann es 22 Jahre verteidigen

Le *Mauretania* de la compagnie Cunard remporte le Ruban Bleu pour la traversée la plus rapide de l'Atlantique et le conserve pendant 22 ans

1908 Henry Ford's new Model T democratizes road travel in America

Henry Fords neues Model T demokratisiert das Reisen mit dem Auto in den USA

La nouvelle Model T d'Henry Ford démocratise le voyage en voiture aux Etats-Unis

SOBALD HENRY FORD 1908 SEIN MODEL T ANGEBOTEN HATTE, VERWANDELTE SICH DIE AUFFASSUNG DER AMERIKANER VOM REISEN GRUNDLEGEND. Um 1910 sorgten Züge noch für 95% aller Transporte zwischen den Städten. Gegen Ende des Jahrzehnts wurden die Eisenbahnkilometer indes von den Autokilometern übertroffen.

Dennoch war dieses Jahrzehnt eine Blütezeit der Eisenbahn. Eine immense Nachfrage entstand etwa durch den Bauboom in Kalifornien. Das wegen seiner niedrigen Grundstückspreise und des endlosen Sonnenscheins gerühmte Kalifornien wirkte auf die Menschen im Osten zudem exotisch und faszinierend. Duke Kahanamoku, einer der besten Surfer von Hawaii, trat 1912 als weltweiter Botschafter seines Sports auf und gab Kostproben an den Stränden von Südkalifornien. Verlockend war auch, dass sich die noch junge Filmindustrie hier niedergelassen hatte.

Die Reisenden strömten in den Golden State. Bereits 1911 reagierte die Bahngesellschaft Atchison, Topeka and Santa Fe mit dem „Santa Fe de Lux"-Service. Für einen Zuschlag von nur 25 $ donnerten Schnellzüge nach Kalifornien. Zwei Jahre darauf versuchte es die Santa Fe mit einer neuen Art der Werbung: Reklametafeln.

Es gab jedoch eine verführerische Alternative: das Auto. Und beim Thema Autoreisen führen gleichsam alle Straßen zu Carl G. Fisher, einem Unternehmer mit einem Faible für Autorennen und Landerschließung. Später würde Fisher von prächtigen Resorts in Miami Beach und Montauk, New York, träumen, doch ihm war klar, dass man zunächst einmal Straßen brauchte, um dorthin zu gelangen. Mit dem Lincoln Highway entwickelte er 1913 die erste Überlandtrasse und kam damit den ersten Gesetzen für öffentliche Highways um drei Jahre zuvor.

Während das Reisen zu Lande einen Aufschwung nahm, hatten die Reedereien schwer zu kämpfen. Bisher waren jedes Jahr immer prachtvollere Linienschiffe vom Stapel gelaufen. Dann aber kam der 14. April 1912: Die RMS *Titanic*, Flaggschiff der White Star Line und größtes Passagierschiff der Welt, kollidiert auf ihrer Jungfernfahrt mit einem Eisberg und geht unter. Dies war eines der verheerendsten Seeunglücke in Friedenszeiten – 1517 Passagiere und Besatzungsmitglieder kamen um, und nur 706 überlebten. Als 1914 der Erste Weltkrieg ausbrach, gingen die Passagierzahlen in den Keller. Viele Luxusliner wie HAPAGs *Vaterland*, das größte Schiff der Meere, wurden für den Truppentransport umgerüstet. Das Passagieraufkommen ging noch stärker zurück, nachdem die RMS *Lusitania* der Cunard Line 1915 von einem deutschen U-Boot torpediert worden war.

Positiv war indessen die Eröffnung des Panamakanals im Jahr 1914. Eine Schiffsreise von New York nach San Francisco verkürzte sich fortan um mehr als die Hälfte – von 25 900 auf 11 000 Kilometer. Den neuen Kanal feierte man 1915 mit der Panama-Pacific International Exposition in San Francisco. Diese Weltausstellung kündete von der Wiedergeburt der gastgebenden Stadt nach dem verheerenden Erdbeben von 1906. Ausgestellt wurde auch ein von Henry Ford stammendes Montageband, das drei Stunden täglich und sechs Tage pro Woche Autos ausspuckte und derart populär war, dass die Schlange der Besucher niemals kürzer zu werden schien.

1909

1909 With travel becoming more accessible to the middle class, luggage begins to lighten up

Reisen werden auch für die Mittelschicht erschwinglich, und das Gepäck wird allmählich leichter

Alors que le nouveau siècle bat son plein et que le voyage devient plus accessible à la classe moyenne, les bagages commencent à s'alléger

1910 Kaiser Wilhelm II stays at Zurich, Switzerland's Baur au Lac, built facing lake rather than town—new idea for hotels at the time

Aufenthalt von Kaiser Wilhelm II. im Zürcher Hotel Baur au Lac, das – damals ungewöhnlich – dem See zugewandt ist

L'Empereur Guillaume II séjourne à l'hôtel Baur au Lac de Zurich en Suisse, un établissement construit face au lac et non face à la ville : un concept alors inédit en hôtellerie

1912 1,517 passengers killed when RMS *Titanic* sinks – including John Jacob Astor IV, hotelier; only 706 survive

Untergang der RMS *Titanic*; 1517 Passagiere kommen ums Leben, darunter der Hotelier John Jacob Astor IV., bei nur 706 Überlebenden

1517 passagers meurent dans le naufrage du *Titanic*, dont l'hôtelier John Jacob Astor IV ; seules 706 personnes survivent

1912 Women begin to do more than just go for a dip in the ocean; they go swimming with men

Die ersten Frauen mischen sich unter die männlichen Schwimmer, anstatt wie bisher nur im seichten Wasser zu planschen

Au bord de la mer, les femmes ne se contentent plus de timides bains de pieds ; elles se mettent à nager, comme les hommes

CREOLE

◂ Austrian Lloyd, 1912

La Reserve de Nice, ca. 1910

AU DÉBUT DU SIÈCLE DERNIER, VOYAGER POUR LE PLAISIR ÉTAIT UN LUXE. LES VOYAGES POUVAIENT ÊTRE À LA FOIS INSTRUCTIFS ET TRÈS À LA MODE, COMME LE GRAND TOUR D'EUROPE, ou d'un exotisme sybaritique, tel un séjour dans une casbah d'Afrique du Nord. Pendant la première décennie du nouveau siècle, un grand nombre d'hôtels style Beaux-arts ouvrit ses portes à travers le monde entier. Quand les clients descendaient dans un palace parisien ou un immense hôtel de style victorien et mauresque au Caire, ils pénétraient dans un univers d'opulence. Ils n'y passaient pas qu'une semaine, mais toute une saison.

Ces splendides hôtels cherchaient tous à s'éclipser les uns les autres. L'Hôtel des Bains, un édifice monumental qui contribua à rendre les bains de soleil acceptables, ouvrit sur le Lido de Venise en 1900. En 1903, l'impressionnant Taj Mahal Hotel était inauguré à Bombay. L'année suivante, John Jacob Astor IV fit construire le St. Regis à New York pour un montant de 5,5 millions de dollars. Tous furent rapidement suivis par le Palace Hotel du Bund de Shanghai, le Ritz à Londres, l'Adlon à Berlin, le Plaza Hotel à New York et l'Excelsior à Rome. Chacun se targuait d'être « le meilleur hôtel du monde ».

Outre-atlantique, les Américains inventèrent leur propre version du grand hôtel: des complexes tentaculaires composés de pavillons rustiques construits dans des matériaux naturels locaux à l'aide de participations publiques et privées. Le Président Theodore Roosevelt incita le gouvernement fédéral à créer des parcs nationaux, notamment celui du Grand Canyon. Ce furent néanmoins les compagnies de chemins de fer de l'Ouest, avides de passagers, qui construisirent ces pittoresques hôtels. Bâti par la Northern Pacific Railroad dans le Parc National de Yellowstone, l'influent Old Faithful Inn de 1904 comprenait un vaste hall de sept étages entièrement construit de rondins de bois. L'année suivante, la compagnie ferroviaire Atchison, Topeka and Santa Fe Railway inaugura El Tovar, un grand pavillon situé sur la bordure sud du Grand Canyon. Il appartenait à Fred Harvey, qui fit de ses restaurants Harvey House la toute première chaîne nationale et soigna les prestations

hôtelières, avec l'effet escompté : l'essor de tourisme dans la région.

Pour se rendre en Europe, les voyageurs du « Gilded Age » embarquaient à bord de navires grandioses. Le paquebot *Deutschland* de la Hamburg-American Line remporta le Ruban Bleu en 1900 pour la traversée la plus rapide de l'Atlantique en cinq jours, 15 heures, cinq minutes. Le tourisme à Hawaï prospérait aussi. En 1902, la Matson Navigation Company qui effectuait la liaison entre Hawaï et le continent ouvrit le Moana, le premier hôtel de Waikiki Beach. Les Américains découvrirent le surf dans l'article de Jack London paru en 1907 sur le surfeur hawaïen George Freeth. En 1908, William Matson fit construire son bateau vapeur *Lurline,* ainsi baptisé en hommage à sa fille, pour transporter du fret et 51 passagers. Hawaï allait s'imposer comme une grande destination touristique.

L'une des plus grandes attractions de la décennie ne fut toutefois pas un lieu exotique, mais l'Exposition Universelle de 1904 à Saint-Louis qui accueillit plus de 20 millions de visiteurs venus du monde entier. Les tout nouveaux cônes gaufrés utilisés pour la dégustation des crèmes glacées firent fureur auprès du public. Les destinations touristiques américaines attiraient la classe moyenne en plein essor. La démocratisation du voyage venait de commencer.

1912

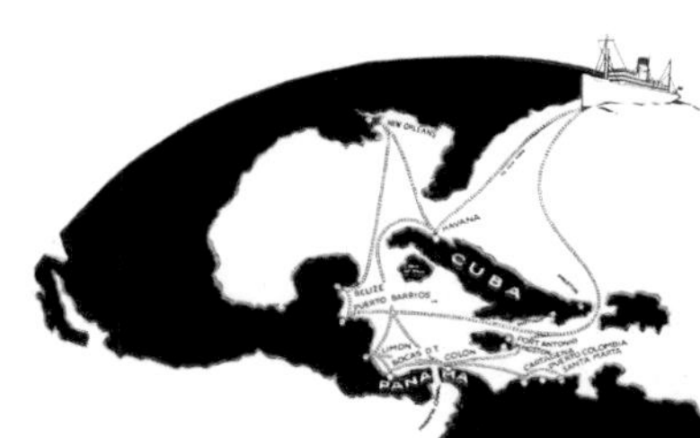

1912 Hawaiian Duke Kahanamoku acts as surfing ambassador, giving demonstrations in California before swimming in Olympics

Duke Kahanamoku wirbt für das Surfen und demonstriert vor seiner Olympiateilnahme als Schwimmer sein Können

En donnant des démonstrations de surf en Californie avant de nager aux Jeux Olympiques, le Hawaïen Duke Kahanamoku devient l'ambassadeur de son sport

1913 Great White Fleet of United Fruit Company grows to meet to U.S. demand for travel to Latin America

Die „Große Weiße Flotte" der United Fruit Company reagiert auf die US-Nachfrage nach Reisen nach Mittelamerika

Le Great White Fleet de la United Fruit Company répond à la demande des Américains en voyages aux Caraïbes et en Amérique Centrale

1913 Gustave Eiffel devises metal framing for the large dome of Hôtel Negresco in Nice, France

Gustave Eiffel entwirft das Metallgerüst für die große Kuppel des Hôtel Negresco in Nizza

Gustave Eiffel invente la structure en métal du grand dôme de l'Hôtel Negresco de Nice

1914 Opening of Panama Canal; cuts voyage between New York and California by more than half

Eröffnung des Panamakanals, der die Reise von New York nach Kalifornien um mehr als die Hälfte verkürzt

Ouverture du Canal de Panama, qui réduit de moitié le trajet par bateau entre New York et la Californie

Hôtel Riviera, 1912

▸ North German Lloyd, 1909

LORSQUE HENRY FORD LANÇA LA MODEL T EN 1908, LA FAÇON DE VOYAGER DES AMÉRICAINS CHANGEA. A l'aube des années 1910, le train représentait 95 % de la totalité du trafic interurbain aux Etats-Unis. Dix ans plus tard, on voyageait davantage par la route que par le rail.

Toujours plus rapides et plus confortables, les trains connurent leur âge d'or de 1910 à 1920. La ruée vers la Californie, entre autres, contribua au boom des voyages ferroviaires. Recherchée pour ses terres bon marché et son soleil éternel, la Californie fascinait les habitants de l'Est. En 1912, le grand surfeur hawaïen Duke Kahanamoku devint l'ambassadeur mondial de son sport en s'y adonnant sur les plages de Californie du Sud. L'installation de la jeune industrie du cinéma en Californie rendit cet Etat d'autant plus attirant.

Les voyageurs se précipitèrent vers le « Golden State ». La compagnie de chemins de fer Atchison, Topeka and Santa Fe réagit dès 1911 en introduisant le service Santa Fe de Lux : pour seulement 25 dollars de plus que le prix d'un billet standard, on pouvait rejoindre la Californie par voie « express ». Deux ans plus tard, la ligne de Sante Fe testa une nouvelle forme de publicité : les panneaux d'affichage. La demande ne fit qu'augmenter.

La voiture restait toutefois séduisante. Et en matière de voyage automobile, toutes les routes mènent à Carl G. Fisher, homme d'affaires passionné de voitures et d'aménagement foncier. Fisher imaginera des hôtels éblouissants à Miami Beach en Floride et à Montauk dans l'Etat de New York, mais il possédait suffisamment de bon sens pour savoir qu'il fallait d'abord des routes. En 1913, il fit donc construire la première route transcontinentale du pays, le Lincoln Highway, avec trois ans d'avance sur les premières lois sur les autoroutes publiques des Etats-Unis.

Alors que le voyage terrestre se développait, les compagnies maritimes naviguaient en eaux troubles. Le 14 avril 1912, le *Titanic*, fleuron de la White Star et plus grand bateau vapeur destiné au transport de passagers, heurta un iceberg et sombra pendant sa croisière inaugurale. Ce fut l'une des catastrophes maritimes les plus mortelles jamais connues en temps de paix : 1517 morts (dont l'hôtelier John Jacob Astor IV) pour seulement 706 survivants. Avec le début de la Première Guerre mondiale en 1914, le trafic de voyageurs continua de chuter. De nombreux paquebots somptueux, comme le *Vaterland* de la Hamburg-American Line, plus grand navire à flot, furent reconvertis pour le transport de troupes. Le trafic de passagers toucha le fond quand le *Lusitania*, membre de la Cunard Line, fut torpillé par un U-boat allemand en 1915. Il coula en 18 minutes, et sur les 1959 personnes à bord, 1198 périrent.

Les voyages en paquebot connurent pourtant une embellie quand le Canal de Panama, surnommé « le 13e travail d'Hercule », fut inauguré en 1914. La durée de la traversée de New York à San Francisco fut ainsi plus que divisée par deux, passant de 11 000 à 5900 kilomètres. Le nouveau canal fut célébré à l'occasion de l'Exposition internationale Panama-Pacific de San Francisco en 1915, qui annonçait la renaissance de sa ville hôte après le terrible tremblement de terre de 1906. L'un des stands, construit par Henry Ford, présentait une ligne de montage qui produisait des voitures trois heures par jour, six jours par semaine. Elle remporta un tel succès que la file d'attente de visiteurs ne désemplit pas.

1915

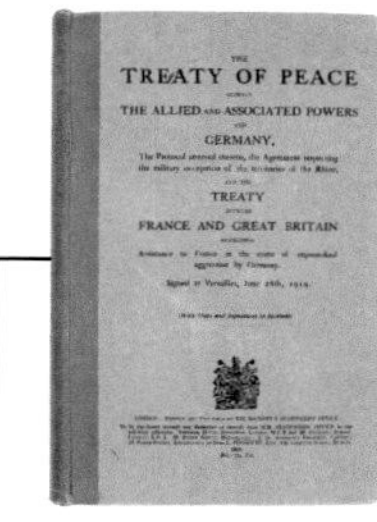
TREATY OF PEACE
THE ALLIED AND ASSOCIATED POWERS
GERMANY,
TREATY
FRANCE AND GREAT BRITAIN

1915 Cunard's RMS *Lusitania* torpedoed by German U-boat and sinks in 18 minutes; of 1,959 people aboard, 1,198 die

Cunards RMS *Lusitania* wird durch ein deutsches U-Boot torpediert und sinkt innerhalb von 18 Minuten; 1198 der 1959 Menschen an Bord kommen um

Torpillé par un U-boat allemand, le *Lusitania* de la Cunard sombre en 18 minutes ; sur les 1959 personnes à bord, 1198 périssent

1917 King Constantine I. of Greece and family move into Grand Hotel National, in Lucerne, Switzerland, for 2 years

Der griechische König Konstantin I. zieht mitsamt Familie für zwei Jahre ins Luzerner Grand Hotel National

Le Roi Constantin de Grèce et sa famille s'installent pendant deux ans au Grand Hotel National de Lucerne en Suisse

1918 Grand dame Art Nouveau hotel Gellert Spa and Bath opens in Budapest, Hungary

Eröffnung des im Sezessionsstil errichteten Gellert Hotel und Bad in Budapest

L'hôtel Gellert, la « grande dame » de l'architecture Art Nouveau, ouvre avec thermes et bains à Budapest en Hongrie

1919 At close of WWI, preparation for Treaty of Versailles completed at Trianon Palace Hotel in Versailles

Abschluss der Vorbereitungen des Friedensvertrags von Versailles im Trianon Palace Hotel in Versailles

À la fin de la Première Guerre mondiale, la préparation du Traité de Versailles est finalisée à l'hôtel Trianon Palace de Versailles

NORD AMERIKA
NEW YORK
LONDON
BREMEN
Antwerpen
PARIS
Cherbourg
Coruña
Marseille
St. Vincent
AFRIKA
SÜD AMERIKA

NEW YORK
NEW ORLEANS
BY
WATER
For HEALTH or PLEASURE
The Southern Pacific Morgan line steamers "Proteus," "Comus" and "Excelsior" sail regularly between New York and New Orleans, leaving New York on Saturdays and New Orleans on Wednesdays, making the trip in five days without stops
FOLLOW THE COURSE OF THE GULF STREAM
Information at all offices of the
SOUTHERN PACIFIC COMPANY

◂ Southern Pacific, 1903

Cunard, 1911

In addition to transatlantic voyages, Cunard Lines offered Mediterranean cruises and voyages on the Adriatic. These ships often had a different configuration, with fewer first-class accommodations than those used for ocean journeys.

Neben transatlantischen Reisen offerierte Cunard Lines Mittelmeerkreuzfahrten und Adriatouren. Diese Schiffe waren oft anders aufgeteilt und besaßen weniger Erste-Klasse-Kabinen als die Ozeandampfer.

Outre les voyages transatlantiques, la compagnie Cunard proposait des croisières en Méditerranée et dans l'Adriatique sur des bateaux présentant une configuration différente et moins de cabines de première classe, contrairement aux navires dédiés aux transatlantiques.

CUNARD
AQUITANIA
S.S."AQUITANIA"

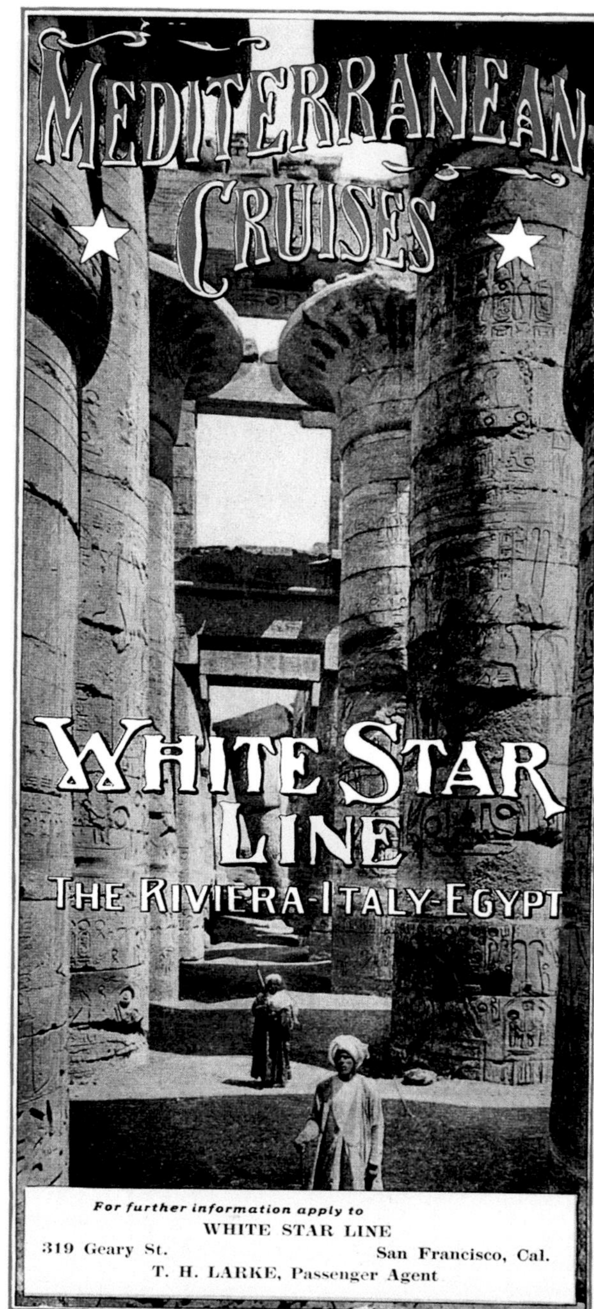

◄ Cunard, ca. 1914

The Cunard Line aimed for speed, leaving luxury to White Star. But the SS *Aquitania* was the "White Star Cunarder," nicknamed "Ship Beautiful." She was sister to the ill-fated *Lusitania* and the *Mauretania*, which won the Blue Riband for fastest Atlantic crossing in 1906 and held it 22 years.

Der Cunard Line ging es ums Tempo. Den Luxus überließ man der Reederei White Star. Doch die SS *Aquitania* war der „White Star von Cunard" alias „Ship Beautiful". Sie war das Schwesterschiff der unglückseligen *Lusitania* und der *Mauretania*, die 1906 das Blaue Band für die schnellste Atlantiküberquerung gewann und 22 Jahre lang verteidigte.

Laissant le luxe à la White Star, la compagnie Cunard faisait de la vitesse sa priorité. Son paquebot *Aquitania*, surnommé « le beau bateau », n'avait pourtant rien à envier à ceux de la White Star. C'était l'un des navires jumeaux de l'infortuné *Lusitania* et du *Mauretania*, qui remporta le Ruban Bleu pour la traversée la plus rapide de l'Atlantique en 1906, un titre qu'il conserva pendant 22 ans.

White Star Line, 1913

White Star Line, 1914

California
THE OLD AND
THE NEW WAY
The NEW way is by the SOUTHERN PACIFIC, Sunset Route Express Trains, equipped with latest Pullman Drawing-Room Sleepers, Combination Library, Observation and Buffet Cars, Dining and Chair Cars, a veritable "Hotel on Wheels" with clean Motive Power, Oil-Burning Locomotives, no dirt, dust or cinders, traversing the sugar plantations and rice fields of quaint Louisiana, the historic cities of the great State of Texas, through the interesting states of Arizona and New Mexico, on to the "Road of a Thousand Wonders," to the Garden of the World, the "Italy of America," CALIFORNIA. Connections made at San Francisco with magnificent new steamers of the Pacific Mail Steamship Company for Honolulu, China, Japan, Philippines and Round the World. For all information apply to any agent of
Southern Pacific
NEW YORK, N. Y. 349 Broadway 1 Broadway
BALTIMORE, MD. Baltimore, and Hanover Sts.
CHICAGO, ILL. 120 Jackson Boulevard
LOS ANGELES, CAL. 600 South Spring St.
ATLANTA, GA. 124 Peachtree St.
NEW ORLEANS, LA. Magazine and Natchez Sts.
BOSTON, MASS. 170 Washington St.
PHILADELPHIA, PA. 632 Chestnut St.
CINCINNATI, OHIO 53 East Fourth St.
SAN FRANCISCO, CAL Ferry Building
HOUSTON, TEXAS Main and Franklin Sts.
SYRACUSE, N. Y. 212 West Washington St.
HAMBURG, GERMANY "Amerikahaus," Ferdinand Strasse

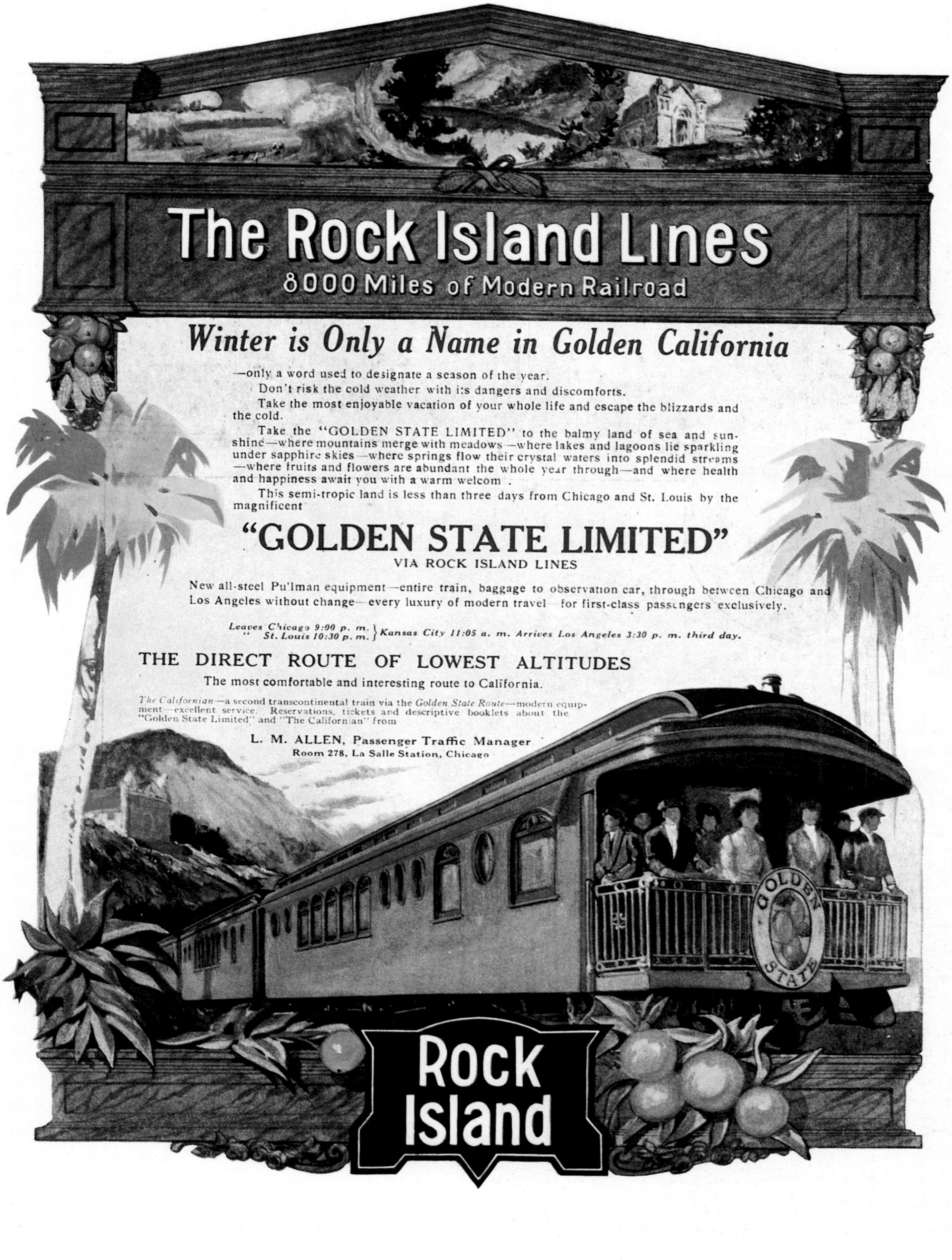

The Rock Island Lines

8000 Miles of Modern Railroad

Winter is Only a Name in Golden California

—only a word used to designate a season of the year.

Don't risk the cold weather with its dangers and discomforts.

Take the most enjoyable vacation of your whole life and escape the blizzards and the cold.

Take the "GOLDEN STATE LIMITED" to the balmy land of sea and sunshine—where mountains merge with meadows—where lakes and lagoons lie sparkling under sapphire skies—where springs flow their crystal waters into splendid streams—where fruits and flowers are abundant the whole year through—and where health and happiness await you with a warm welcom .

This semi-tropic land is less than three days from Chicago and St. Louis by the magnificent

"GOLDEN STATE LIMITED"

VIA ROCK ISLAND LINES

New all-steel Pullman equipment—entire train, baggage to observation car, through between Chicago and Los Angeles without change—every luxury of modern travel—for first-class passengers exclusively.

Leaves Chicago 9:00 p. m.
" St. Louis 10:30 p. m. } *Kansas City 11:05 a. m. Arrives Los Angeles 3:30 p. m. third day.*

THE DIRECT ROUTE OF LOWEST ALTITUDES

The most comfortable and interesting route to California.

The Californian—a second transcontinental train via the *Golden State Route*—modern equipment—excellent service. Reservations, tickets and descriptive booklets about the "Golden State Limited" and "The Californian" from

L. M. ALLEN, Passenger Traffic Manager
Room 278, La Salle Station, Chicago

GOLDEN STATE

Rock Island

◂ Southern Pacific, 1907

The Rock Island Lines, 1915

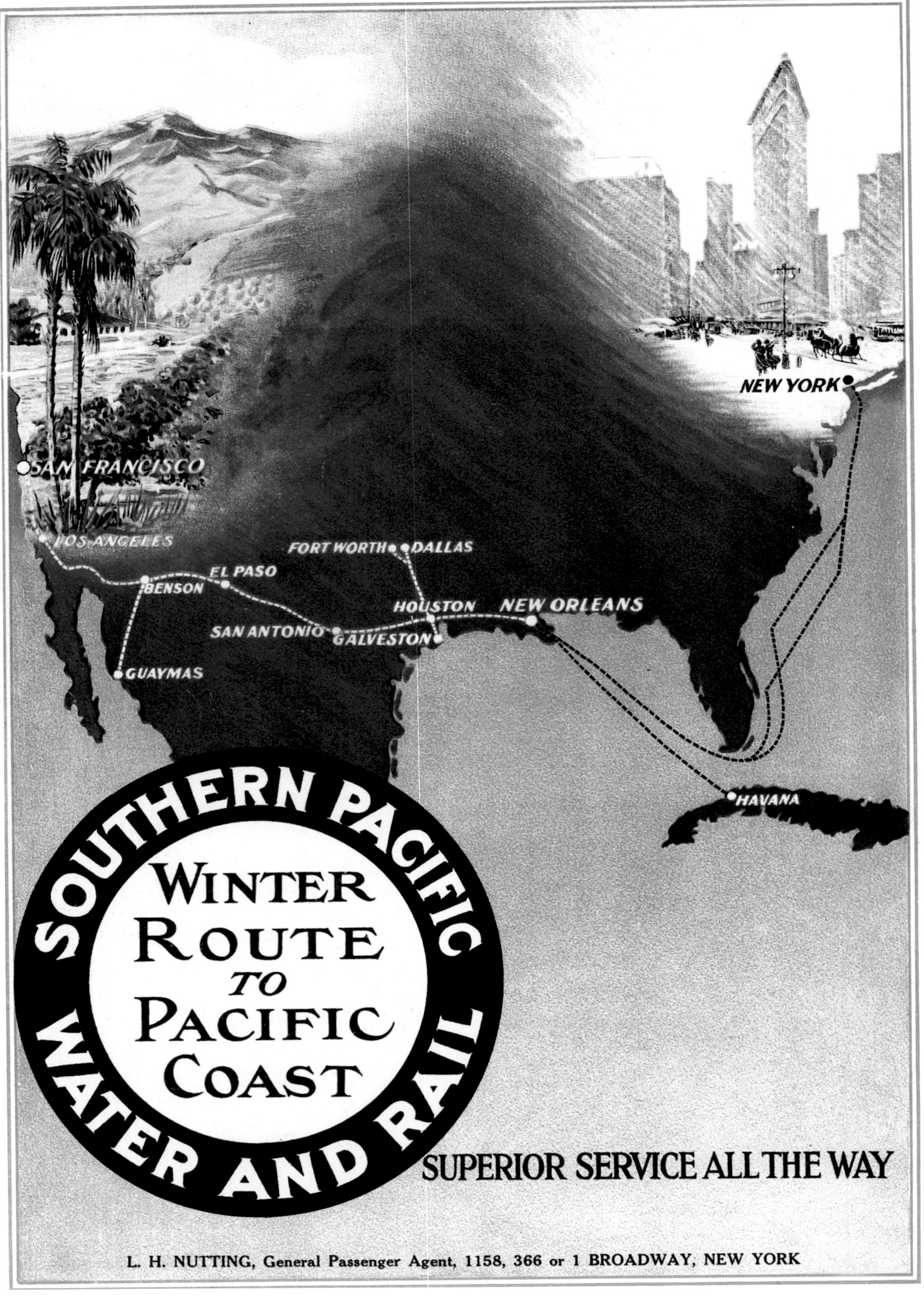

Southern Pacific, 1910

Lamport & Holt Line, ca. 1912

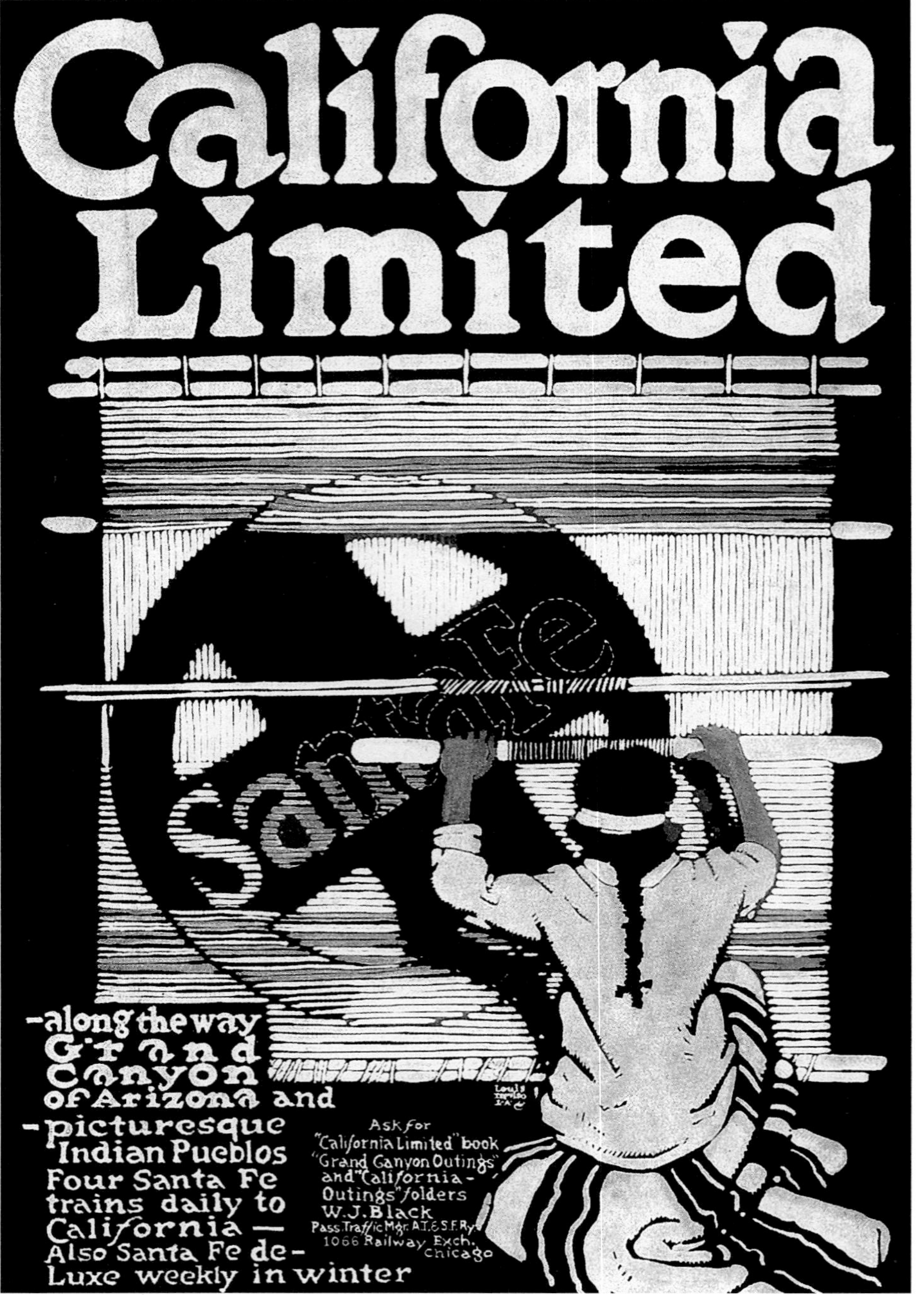

California Limited
Santa Fe
-along the way Grand Canyon of Arizona and
-picturesque Indian Pueblos
Four Santa Fe trains daily to California —
Also Santa Fe de-Luxe weekly in winter
Ask for "California Limited" book "Grand Canyon Outings" and "California-Outings" folders
W.J. Black
Pass. Traffic Mgr. A.T. & S.F. Ry.
1066 Railway Exch. Chicago

Santa Fe Railway, 1916

The Sante Fe Railway created a series of influential campaigns that adroitly blended its corporate image with the routes traveled. Artists captured the romance of the Southwest, blending the Indian and Spanish heritage into an alluring ad. Even before the Indian chief logo was devised, there was an identifiable brand.

Santa Fe Railway schuf eine Reihe einflussreicher Werbekampagnen, die das eigene Image mit den bedienten Routen geschickt vermengten. Künstler fingen die Romantik des Südwestens ein und vereinigten das indianische mit dem spanischen Erbe in einer verlockenden Anzeige. Noch bevor man das Logo mit dem Indianerhäuptling erfand, war dies bereits eine unverwechselbare Marke.

La compagnie Sante Fe Railway lança une série de campagnes marquantes qui mêlaient adroitement son image institutionnelle avec son offre d'itinéraires. Des artistes saisirent le romantisme du sud-ouest américain en fusionnant son héritage indien et espagnol dans une publicité très attrayante. Bien avant la création du logo de chef indien, la marque était déjà reconnaissable.

▸ Southern Pacific, 1910

SEATTLE
TACOMA
PORTLAND
SAN FRANCISCO
LOS ANGELES
COLTON
YUMA
BENSON
TO MEXICO
EL PASO
SAN ANTONIO
HOUSTON
NEW ORLEANS
NEW YORK
Through Storyland to Sunset Seas
Southern Pacific Sunset Route
Trains of Superior Equipment
Sleepers, Diners, Chair, Observation, Library, Smoking Cars
Oil Burning Locomotives, Rock Ballast Roadbed
Automatic Electric Block Signals
DINING CAR SERVICE BEST IN THE WORLD
For Literature Address
L. H. NUTTING, G. E. P. A., 366 OR 1158 OR 1 BROADWAY, NEW YORK
READ "SUNSET," THE MAGAZINE OF THE WEST. NEWSSTANDS, FIFTEEN CENTS
PRESBREY CO. N.Y.

53

See the Apache Trail
En route to or from
CALIFORNIA
This marvelous motor side trip which has just been opened through Arizona's National Reserve is possible only if you choose the
Southern Pacific—Sunset Route
New Orleans Los Angeles San Diego San Francisco
Eight magic hours of sightseeing in Oldest America—stupendous canyons, ancient cliff dwellings, picturesque copper camps and the famous Roosevelt Dam.
The Sunset Limited and other splendid trains afford daily service at No Extra Fare. Read the story of the Apache Trail in this issue of TRAVEL.
GENERAL OFFICES:
New York City 366 Broadway
San Francisco Flood Building
New Orleans Metropolitan Bank Building
Houston Southern Pacific Building

◂ Southern Pacific, 1916

Great Northern Pacific S. S. Company, 1916

The Hawaii Promotion Committee was started in 1903 to help entice tourists to the tropical isles. By the teens, surfing was one its most successful exports, largely popularized by Hawaiian swimming champion Duke Kahanamoku. While en route to the 1912 Olympics, Duke brought the island sport to America by giving surfing demonstrations as well as swimming demonstrations on Southern California beaches. He won multiple medals in swimming, but his surfing élan captured America's attention.

Das 1903 gegründete Hawaii Promotion Committee diente dem Zweck, mehr Touristen auf die tropischen Inseln zu locken. Schon 1910 zu einem der Exportschlager geworden, hatte der hawaiianische Schwimm-Champion Duke Kahanamoku das Surfen sehr popular gemacht. Auf dem Weg zur Olympiade 1912 brachte Duke den bisher auf Hawaii beschränkten Sport in die USA, indem er an den Stränden Südkaliforniens Kostproben seiner Surf- und auch Schwimmkünste gab. Als Schwimmer gewann er zahlreiche Medaillen, doch es war sein Surfstil, der die Menschen in den Bann zog.

Le Hawaii Promotion Committee fut créé en 1903 pour faire venir les touristes dans l'archipel tropical. Auprès des adolescents, l'une de ses exportations les plus plébiscitées fut le surf, popularisé par le champion de natation hawaïen Duke Kahanamoku. En route pour les Jeux Olympiques de 1912, Kahanamoku importa ce sport insulaire en Amérique en donnant des démonstrations de surf et de natation sur les plages de Californie du Sud. Il a remporté de nombreuses médailles de natation, mais l'Amérique se souvient surtout de ses prouesses de surfeur.

Santa Fe Railway, 1916

United Fruit Company Steamship Service, 1916

United Fruit Company Steamship Service, 1914

► United Fruit Company Steamship Service, 1912

The United Fruit Company began taking passengers with cargos of bananas in Latin America in 1907. It increased passenger counts, and ships, throughout the 1910s. The ships were dubbed the Great White Fleet, after the white armada that President Theodore Roosevelt sent around the globe to display U.S. sea power.

Die United Fruit Company begann 1907, im Verkehr nach Lateinamerika neben Bananen auch Passagiere zu befördern. Die Anzahl der Passagiere wie auch der Schiffe nahm in dem Jahrzehnt stetig zu. Dies war die „Große Weiße Flotte", benannt nach der „weißen Armada", die Präsident Theodore Roosevelt als Zeichen der Seemacht USA rund um den Globus entsandt hatte.

En 1907, la United Fruit Company commença à transporter des passagers en Amérique Latine avec ses cargos de bananes. Le nombre de passagers et de navires augmenta tout au long des années 1910. Sa flotte fut surnommée la « Great White Fleet » après que le Président Theodore Roosevelt a eu envoyé son armada blanche faire le tour du monde pour afficher la puissance de la marine américaine.

►► Panama California San Diego Exposition, 1915

The Panama California Exposition in San Diego, California, celebrated the city as first U.S. port of call on the Pacific north of the year-old Panama Canal. A New York architect, Bertram Goodhue, devised the fair's Spanish baroque style, which led to California's affection for Spanish colonial revival architecture. Earlier fairs had been neoclassical.

Die Panama California Exposition in San Diego, Kalifornien, feierte diese Stadt als ersten angelaufenen US-Hafen im Pazifik nördlich des erst ein Jahr alten Panamakanals. Der von dem New Yorker Architekten Bertram Goodhue kreierte spanisch-barocke (und nicht wie sonst neoklassizistische) Ausstellungsstil begeisterte die Kalifornier für spanisch-neokoloniale Architektur.

L'exposition Panama-California de San Diego en Californie mit la ville à l'honneur en tant que premier port d'escale américain du Pacifique au nord du Canal de Panama, ouvert un an plus tôt. Le style hispano-baroque de l'exposition, conçue par l'architecte new-yorkais Bertram Goodhue, suscita l'engouement des Californiens pour l'architecture néocoloniale espagnole. Auparavant, ce genre d'expositions se tenait dans des bâtiments de style néoclassique.

UNITED FRUIT COMPANY
STEAMSHIP SERVICE
SAILINGS OF
THE GREAT
WHITE FLEET
BETWEEN
NEW YORK,
BOSTON,
PHILADELPHIA,
BALTIMORE,
NEW ORLEANS
— AND —
JAMAICA, PANAMA,
COLOMBIA, COSTA RICA,
GUATEMALA, HONDURAS,
NICARAGUA
CONNECTING FOR
PACIFIC COAST PORTS OF
COLOMBIA, ECUADOR,
PERU, CHILE,
MEXICO & CENTRAL AMERICA
From New York, Boston, Philadelphia,
Baltimore, New Orleans.
SUBJECT TO CHANGE WITHOUT NOTICE.
This sailing list shows the times when steamers may be expected to sail from and arrive at the several ports, but their sailing or arrival at the time stated is not guaranteed, nor will the United Fruit Company hold itself responsible for any delay or consequences arising therefrom.
The time of connecting transportation lines is shown only for the convenience of the public. The Company will not be responsible for any errors or changes which may occur.

San Diego

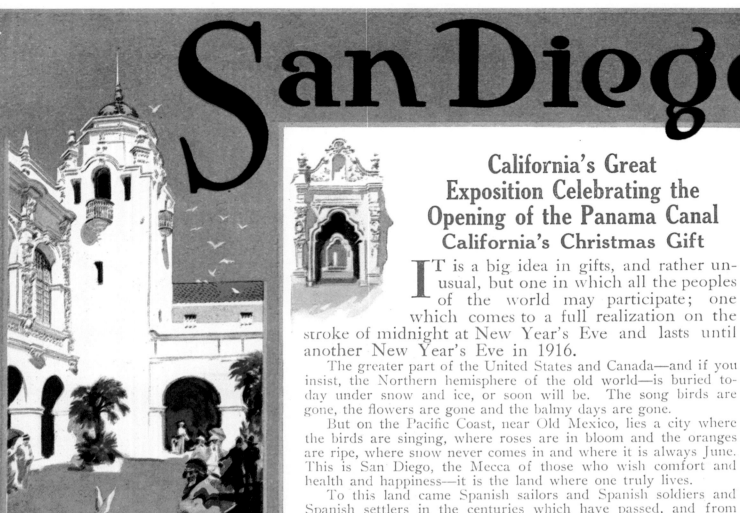

California's Great Exposition Celebrating the Opening of the Panama Canal
California's Christmas Gift

IT is a big idea in gifts, and rather unusual, but one in which all the peoples of the world may participate; one which comes to a full realization on the stroke of midnight at New Year's Eve and lasts until another New Year's Eve in 1916.

The greater part of the United States and Canada—and if you insist, the Northern hemisphere of the old world—is buried today under snow and ice, or soon will be. The song birds are gone, the flowers are gone and the balmy days are gone.

But on the Pacific Coast, near Old Mexico, lies a city where the birds are singing, where roses are in bloom and the oranges are ripe, where snow never comes in and where it is always June. This is San Diego, the Mecca of those who wish comfort and health and happiness—it is the land where one truly lives.

To this land came Spanish sailors and Spanish soldiers and Spanish settlers in the centuries which have passed, and from their life sprang the traditions which still rule their arts and architecture and romance.

And in that Spanish atmosphere of mission and cathedral, of quiet patio and gay fiesta, has been built San Diego's Exposition Beautiful.

THE PLAZA AS

Panama California Exposition

Five hundred miles to the north lies San Francisco, where during the greater part of 1915 will be held another Exposition, also celebrating the opening of the Panama Canal, presenting to the world many features differing from the Exposition Beautiful—the two supplementing one another.

When California celebrates, the Golden State's enthusiasm requires two outlets.

This Is the West of Your Country

It is a West in which you find a civilization that pre-dates that of pre-historic Egypt; it is the Great West of the Grand Canyon, the Yosemite, the Yellowstone, the Painted Desert, the Great Trees; the Great West that is old, yet young. It is the West that you should see, and 1915 is the time for you to see it.

Throughout 1915 the San Diego Exposition Beautiful will be open, offering a gorgeous landscape of unchanging verdure, set with the flashing crimson and gold and purple of the Southwest coast, offering a dreamy renaissance of old Spain, with caballero and troubadour and señorita dwelling in the quaint balconies and plazas and patios of this magic city.

This is California's gift for 1915 for all the year. It cannot quite be delivered to your door on Christmas morning, but your nearest ticket agent will tell you all about it.

PANAMA-CALIFORNIA EXPOSITION SAN DIEGO 1915

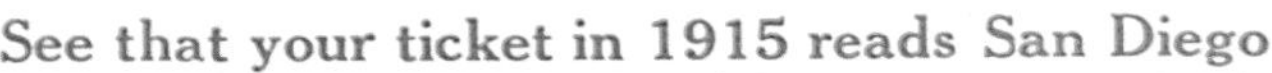

See that your ticket in 1915 reads San Diego

1915 All the Year

"Oh! España, como mi joven, corazon por ti latia en tiempos pasados."
—*Longfellow.*

"How much of my young heart, O Spain, Went out to thee in days of yore?"
—*Longfellow.*

1915 All the Year

IT APPEARS TODAY

COPYRIGHT 1914 CHARLES DANIEL FREY

FOLLOWING THE DEVASTATION OF WORLD WAR I, THE LOST GENERATION WAS READY FOR A GOOD TIME.

NACH DEN VERWÜSTUNGEN DES ERSTEN WELTKRIEGS WOLLTE ES DIE LOST GENERATION BESSER HABEN.

APRÈS LES RAVAGES DE LA PREMIÈRE GUERRE MONDIALE, LA « GÉNÉRATION PERDUE » EUT ENVIE DE S'OFFRIR DU BON TEMPS.

1920

CHASING THE SUN
SONNENHUNGRIG
LA RUÉE VERS LE SOLEIL

-1929

1323
NY 1925
9C-2170

◄ *Scientific American*, 1925

Glacier National Park, 1921

IN HER BEST-SELLING NOVEL *GENTLEMEN PREFER BLONDES* (1925), ANITA LOOS SATIRIZED THE TRAVELS OF AMERICANS with a tale of two showgirls, Lorelei Lee, an enterprising gold-digger, and her friend, Dorothy, on a grand tour of Europe. As Lorelei describes the voyage: "I always love the ocean. I mean I always love a ship and I really love the *Majestic* because you would not know it was a ship because it is just like being at the Ritz."

Following the devastation of World War I, the Lost Generation was ready for a good time. Flappers and sheiks of the Jazz Age moved to a fast, syncopated beat. The literary smart set joked with a knowing patter—especially the Algonquin Round Table, the famed clique of successful young writers who lunched at New York's Algonquin Hotel.

Sumptuous ocean liners attracted passengers during this giddy era. Despite Prohibition, Americans would drink once a ship entered international waters. The French Line (Compagnie Générale Transatlantique) was the most exclusive and desirable. Its stunning *Ile de France* had the first entirely art deco interior. Throughout the decade, French Line passenger counts and revenues soared. It had 91,000 passengers in 1928, up from 20,000 in 1919.

American society was changing. There was a sense of freedom in the air, a kicking over of traces. Automobiles offered young people escape from the restrictions of their parents and communities. Women's emancipation only *started* with winning the vote in 1920. Jazz babies shortened their skirts, smoked in public, wore makeup, and frequented speakeasies. *Jazz*, after all, was often used as a slang term for sex. Sunbathing was all the rage. Travelers followed the sun from the tropics to the south of France, which was best reached by the exclusively first-class Train Bleu.

Hawaiian beaches called. The Matson Line opened the stunning "Pink Palace of the Pacific," the Royal Hawaiian Hotel, in 1927. This $4-million Spanish-Moorish confection was a dream of a tropical hotel, as imagined by the prominent New York architects Warren and Wetmore.

Meanwhile, railroads, seeking to maintain ridership, presented the Golden State as the new Eden. Absent during the war, advertising for trains came roaring back in the '20s, and long-distance travel statistics held firm throughout the decade. The Southern Pacific hired artist Maurice Logan for an ad campaign of iconic Western images. His first series had no trains—just a sun-kissed beauty sitting on a California beach, or riding a mule in Yosemite. In 1926, Hernando Villa designed the Santa Fe's distinctive logo, a proud Indian chief in a war bonnet, and it became the railroad's most indelible image.

In Florida, the developer Carl G. Fisher saw a mangrove swamp and envisioned the playground of Miami Beach. During a freezing New York winter, Fisher installed a sign in Times Square that flashed, "It's June in Miami." With the easy credit of the decade, the Florida land boom was on. But a devastating 1926 hurricane started deflating land values. Well before the 1929 crash, Florida's bubble had popped.

1920

1920 Spotlight hits Hawaii as world tour of Edward, Prince of Wales, stops at Matson Line's Moana Hotel

Alles blickt nach Hawaii, als Edward, Prince of Wales, auf seiner Weltreise im Moana Hotel der Matson Line absteigt

Hawaï se retrouve sous les projecteurs quand la tournée mondiale d'Edward, Prince de Galles, fait halte au Moana Hotel de la compagnie Matson Line

1923 Longtime winter hot spot Hôtel du Cap in Antibes stays open for summer; Gertrude Stein and Alice B. Toklas visit Pablo Picasso

Der Winter-Hotspot Hôtel du Cap in Antibes bleibt im Sommer geöffnet; Gertrude Stein besucht Pablo Picasso

L'Hôtel du Cap à Antibes, villégiature hivernale de choix, reste ouvert tout l'été ; Gertrude Stein et Alice B. Toklas rendent visite à Pablo Picasso

1924 *A Passage to India*, E.M. Forster's novel about cultural differences separating British schoolmistress and an Indian doctor

E.M. Forster veröffentlicht seinen Roman *Auf der Suche nach Indien* über die eine britische Lehrerin und einen indischen Arzt trennenden kulturellen Unterschiede

Un Passage vers L'Inde, roman d'E. M. Forster sur le fossé culturel entre une institutrice anglaise et un médecin indien

1925 First motel – or motorist's hotel – built in San Luis Obispo, California

Erstes Motel – oder „motorist's hotel" – im kalifornischen San Luis Obispo errichtet

Construction du premier motel – ou hôtel pour automobilistes – à San Luis Obispo, Californie

► Furness Prince Cruise Line, 1929

Royal Hawaiian Hotel, ca. 1927

IN IHREM ROMANBESTSELLER *GENTLEMEN PREFER BLONDES* VON 1925, EINER SATIRE AUF DIE REISEN DER AMERIKANER, ERZÄHLT ANITA LOOS VON ZWEI SHOWGIRLS – der unternehmungslustigen, aufs Geld versessenen Lorelei Lee und ihrer Freundin Dorothy – auf einer Bildungsreise durch Europa. Lorelei beschreibt die Reise so: „Das Meer mochte ich schon immer. Also, ich mag Schiffe, und die *Majestic* mag ich wirklich, denn man würde gar nicht merken, dass es ein Schiff ist, denn es ist dort wie im Ritz."

Nach den Verwüstungen des Ersten Weltkriegs wollte es die Lost Generation besser haben. Die literarischen Cliquen tauschten ihre Insiderwitze aus, speziell der Algonquin Round Table, ein legendärer literarischer Zirkel erfolgreicher junger Autoren, die im New Yorker Algonquin Hotel regelmäßig zu Mittag aßen.

Luxuriöse Linienschiffe verloren dennoch nicht ihren Reiz. Trotz Prohibition sprachen die Amerikaner dem Alkohol zu, sobald sich ein Schiff in internationalen Gewässern befand. Exklusivste und gefragteste Reederei war die French Line (Compagnie Générale Transatlantique). Ihre fantastische *Ile de France* besaß das erste vollständige Art-déco-Interieur. Buchungszahlen und Einnahmen schnellten nach oben, von 20 000 Passagieren 1919 auf 91 000 im Jahr 1928.

In den Vereinigten Staaten vollzog sich ein sozialer Wandel. Ein Gefühl der Freiheit lag in der Luft, eine radikale Abkehr vom Vergangenen. Autos ermöglichten den jungen Leuten eine Flucht vor den Einschränkungen ihrer Eltern. Das Erstreiten des Wahlrechts im Jahr 1920 war nur der *Startschuss* für die Emanzipation der Frau. Die „Jazz Babys" kürzten die Röcke, rauchten, trugen Make-up und hockten in Kneipen. *Jazz* benutzte man oft als Slangausdruck für Sex. Sonnenbäder waren der Hit. Man reiste der Sonne entgegen – von den Tropen bis nach Südfrankreich, das man am besten mit dem luxuriösen Le Train Bleu erreichte.

Auch die Strände von Hawaii lockten. Die Matson Line eröffnete 1927 den „Pink Palace of the Pacific", das Royal Hawaiian Hotel. Diese 4 Mio. $ teure spanisch-maurische Kreation war ein Traum von einem Tropenhotel, wie ihn sich die Architekten Warren und Wetmore ausgedacht hatten.

Um ihr Fahrgastaufkommen zu wahren, präsentierten die Eisenbahngesellschaften den Golden State als das neue Eden. Werbung für Bahnreisen, die es während des Kriegs nicht gegeben hatte, feierte in den 1920er-Jahren eine schwungvolle Wiedergeburt, sodass sich die Langstreckenstatistik gut behaupten konnte. Die Southern Pacific gewann den Maler Maurice Logan für eine Anzeigenkampagne mit ikonenhaften Bildern vom Westen. In der ersten Serie gab es gar keine Züge – nur eine von der Sonne geküsste Schönheit an einem kalifornischen Strand oder auf einem Esel in Yosemite. Hernando Villa entwarf 1926 das markante Logo der Santa Fe: einen stolzen Indianerhäuptling, der zum unauslöschlichen Sinnbild der Eisenbahn wurde.

In Florida erblickte der Baulöwe Carl G. Fisher einen Mangrovensumpf und träumte vom Tummelplatz Miami Beach. Mitten in einem bitterkalten New Yorker Winter warb Fisher mit einer Leuchtreklame auf dem Times Square: „In Miami ist es Juni". Angesichts leicht erhältlicher Kredite boomte das Grundstücksgeschäft in Florida. Nach einem verheerenden Hurrikan begannen die Grundstückspreise 1926 jedoch wieder zu fallen. Lange vor dem Börsenkrach von 1929 war die Blase namens Florida geplatzt.

1926 In wake of hurricane, Florida land boom goes bust

Ein Hurrikan bereitet den in Florida florierenden Grundstücksgeschäften ein Ende

À la suite d'un ouragan, la bulle immobilière de Floride explose

1926 First run of the Chief—Santa Fe Lines' Chief deluxe limited train running from Chicago to Los Angeles

Erste Fahrt des Luxuszugs Chief der Santa Fe Lines von Chicago nach Los Angeles

Lancement du train Chief Deluxe de la compagnie Chief-Santa Fe Lines entre Chicago et Los Angeles

1926 Dude Ranchers Association founded in Cody, Wyoming, in response to popular interest in travel to American West

Dude Ranchers Association als Reaktion auf das große Interesse an Reisen in den Westen der USA gegründet

Fondation de la Dude Ranchers Association à Cody, Wyoming, en réponse à l'intérêt de la population pour les voyages dans le Grand Ouest américain

1927 Elsa Maxwell retained by Prince of Monaco to create principality's social cachet as summer resort

Der Fürst von Monaco beauftragt die Gesellschaftsjournalistin Elsa Maxwell, das Fürstentum zum gefragten Sommerresort zu machen

Le Prince de Monaco demande à Elsa Maxwell de promouvoir sa principauté comme une destination estivale exclusive

◂ *World Traveler*, 1923

Hôtel du Cap, 1923

▸▸ Hawaii Tourist Bureau, 1929

DANS SON BEST-SELLER DE 1925 *LES HOMMES PRÉFÈRENT LES BLONDES*, ANITA LOOS SE MOQUAIT DE LA FAÇON DE VOYAGER DES AMÉRICAINS À TRAVERS L'HISTOIRE DE DEUX DANSEUSES DE REVUE, Lorelei Lee, une croqueuse de diamants pleine d'audace, et son amie Dorothy, parties pour une grande tournée d'Europe. Lorelei décrit le voyage en ces termes: «J'ai toujours adoré la mer. J'ai toujours aimé les bateaux, et si j'aime vraiment le *Majestic*, c'est parce qu'on n'a pas l'impression d'être sur un bateau, on se croirait au Ritz».

Après les ravages de la Première Guerre mondiale, la «génération perdue» eut envie de s'offrir du bon temps. Les garçonnes et les rois de l'ère du jazz dansaient sur des rythmes endiablés tandis que l'intelligentsia littéraire plaisantait avec esprit et répartie, notamment dans le Cercle d'Algonquin, célèbre clique de jeunes écrivains à succès qui se retrouvaient pour déjeuner à l'hôtel Algonquin de New York.

Les paquebots somptueux attirèrent de nouveau les voyageurs. Fuyant la Prohibition, les Américains se mettaient à boire dès que leur bateau pénétrait dans les eaux internationales. La Compagnie Générale Transatlantique était la plus luxueuse et la plus demandée. Son impressionnant *Ile de France* fut le premier paquebot aménagé dans le style Art Déco. Tout au long des années 1920, le nombre de passagers et les revenus de la compagnie explosèrent. En 1928, elle transporta 91 000 passagers, contre 20 000 en 1919.

La société américaine changeait aussi. Grâce à la voiture, les jeunes pouvaient échapper aux contraintes imposées par leurs parents et leurs communautés. L'émancipation des femmes ne *démarra* qu'avec leur droit de vote en 1920. Les jazzeuses raccourcirent leurs jupes, fumaient en public, se maquillaient et fréquentaient les bars clandestins. La dernière mode était au bronzage. Les voyageurs suivaient le soleil, des Tropiques au sud de la France, de préférence à bord du Train Bleu.

Les plages de Hawaï faisaient envie. En 1927, la Matson Line ouvrit l'impressionnant Royal Hawaiian Hotel, surnommé le «palais rose du Pacifique». Cet édifice hispano-mauresque de 4 millions de dollars symbolisait l'hôtel tropical de rêve tel que l'avaient imaginé les grands architectes new-yorkais Warren et Wetmore.

Parallèlement, les compagnies de chemins de fer, toutes désireuses de conserver leur leadership, présentèrent la Californie comme le nouvel Eden. Absentes pendant la guerre, les publicités pour les trains firent un retour fracassant dans les années 1920, et les statistiques des trajets longue distance se maintinrent fermement tout au long de la décennie. La compagnie Southern Pacific recruta l'artiste Maurice Logan pour concevoir une campagne publicitaire composée d'images symbolisant l'Ouest. Sur la première série, on ne voyait même pas de train, juste une beauté bronzée allongée sur une plage californienne ou chevauchant un mulet à Yosemite. En 1926, Hernando Villa imagina un logo original pour la ligne Santa Fe, un chef indien fièrement couronné d'une parure de plumes qui devint le symbole le plus indélébile de la compagnie.

Le promoteur immobilier Carl G. Fisher découvrit la mangrove de Floride et imagina Miami Beach. Pendant un hiver glacial à New York, il fit installer sur Times Square un panneau clignotant qui proclamait «C'est le mois de juin à Miami». Comme il était alors très facile d'obtenir un crédit, la Floride connut un boom immobilien, mais en 1926, un ouragan dévastateur commença à faire chuter la valeur des terres. La bulle de Floride éclata bien avant le crash de 1929.

1927

1927 Maiden voyage of SS *Ile de France*, luxury ocean liner designed by Emile-Jacques Ruhlmann for French Line

Jungfernfahrt des von Emile-Jacques Ruhlmann für die French Line entworfenen Kreuzfahrtschiffs SS *Ile de France*

Croisière inaugurale de l'*Ile de France*, luxueux paquebot conçu par Emile-Jacques Ruhlmann pour la Compagnie Générale Transatlantique

1928 Tango bursts from backstreets of Buenos Aires, Argentina; Paris swoons over singer Carlos Gardel

Der Tango macht sich aus den Hinterhöfen von Buenos Aires, Argentinien, hörbar; Paris wird vom Sänger Carlos Gardel verzaubert

Le tango déferle sur le monde depuis les rues de Buenos Aires, Argentine ; Paris se pâme devant le chanteur Carlos Gardel

1929 Agua Caliente resort in Tijuana, Mexico, opens racetrack; Hollywood celebrities head south of border

Einweihung der Rennbahn des Agua Caliente Resort im mexikanischen Tijuana; zahlreiche Hollywoodstars hüpfen über die Grenze

L'Agua Caliente Resort de Tijuana, Mexique, ouvre un circuit automobile ; les célébrités d'Hollywood s'y pressent

1929 Aviatrix Amelia Earhart promotes passenger airline service; with Charles Lindbergh founds Transcontinental Air Transport

Amelia Earhart, eine frühe Befürworterin von Passagierflügen, gründet zusammen mit Charles Lindbergh die Transcontinental Air Transport

L'aviatrice Amelia Earhart promeut les vols de passagers et fonde la Transcontinental Air Transport avec Lindbergh

"Most Sublime of All Earthly Scenes"

Grand Canyon National Park

So world travelers say of this colossal chasm, more than a mile deep, more than two hundred miles long, and twelve miles wide, filled with magnificent rock temples aflame with changing colors. See it this summer from the loftier North Rim, reached through the enchanting Kaibab National Forest with its thousands of deer, by a 5-day, all-expense Union Pacific motor bus tour that also includes

Zion National Park
Bryce Canyon *Cedar Breaks*
Kaibab Forest *Prismatic Plains*

Easy to reach. Low summer fares. Through Pullmans to Cedar City, Utah, the gateway. Escorted tours. Comfortable lodges. A wonderful vacation itself or a memorable side trip en route to Yellowstone or the Pacific Coast. Season June 1 to October 1.

The Zion-Grand Canyon Red Book tells all. Ask for it.

Address nearest representative or General Passenger Agent, Dept. 124, at Omaha, Neb. : Salt Lake City, Utah : Portland, Ore. : Los Angeles, Calif.

UNION PACIFIC

THE OVERLAND ROUTE

◄ Union Pacific Railroad, 1927

Travels to national park destination hotels and their breathtaking views increased in the '20s. The stunning Ahwahnee Hotel in Yosemite National Park opened in 1927, after two years of construction that required the most complicated trucking effort of its day.

In den 1920er-Jahren steuerte man immer häufiger die in Nationalparks gelegenen Landhotels mit ihren atemberaubenden Ausblicken an. Das prächtige Ahwahnee Hotel im Yosemite National Park wurde 1927 eröffnet – nach zweijähriger Bauzeit mit der kompliziertesten Transportlogistik jener Tage.

Dans les années 1920, les touristes affluaient dans les hôtels des parcs nationaux pour profiter de leurs panoramas époustouflants. L'impressionnant Ahwahnee Hotel du Parc National de Yosemite ouvrit en 1927, après deux années de construction qui nécessitèrent l'effort de camionnage le plus complexe de l'époque.

Union Pacific Railroad, 1925

Sacred to the Indian
The Great White Throne, Zion National Park, held in awe as the abode of the Great Spirit.

The long hidden splendors of Zion National Park, Bryce Canyon and Cedar Breaks are yours

Here, in Southern Utah, are flaming canyons and jewelled amphitheatres painted in incredible colors by sun magic and the wizardry of wind and water. Here, too, is a lingering frontier of empurpled distances with quaint Mormon villages, Indians, wild horses, extinct volcanoes and mysterious cliff dwellings.

Season May 15 to October 15

Inaccessible a few years ago except to a few adventurous Americans, the Union Pacific has now made it possible to see it in comfort by providing sleeping car service, regular motor tours and the latest style of National Park lodges and dining rooms.

The trip is a memorable vacation adventure in itself, or may be made in connection with tours to Salt Lake City, Yellowstone National Park or the Pacific Coast.

Ask about low round trip summer fares.

Send For Free Booklet In *Natural Colors*
It is the only way we can tell you of the unbelievable coloring of this unique land; also contains complete practical information.

Address nearest Union Pacific Representative or General Passenger Agent at Omaha, Neb. :-: Salt Lake City, Utah :-: Portland, Ore. :-: Los Angeles, Cal.

Union Pacific

◄ *World Traveler*, October 1923

Railroads saw the Golden State as the way to maintain high ridership, since a bevy of travelers followed the sun to California in the '20s. Al Jolson, the biggest star of his day, recorded the 1924 hit "California, Here I Come." It sounded like one long ad: "Where bowers of flowers bloom in the spring!"

Die Bahngesellschaften setzten auf den Golden State, um ihr hohes Fahrgastaufkommen zu wahren, denn in den 1920er-Jahren folgte ein ganzer Schwarm von Reisenden der Sonne nach Kalifornien. Al Jolson, der größte Gesangsstar seiner Zeit, nahm 1924 den Hit „California, Here I Come" auf. Er klang wie eine lange Werbeanzeige: „Where bowers of flowers bloom in the spring!"

Les compagnies de chemins de fer voyaient dans le « Golden State » un moyen de conserver un nombre maximum de passagers, car dans les années 1920, beaucoup de voyageurs suivaient le soleil jusqu'en Californie. Al Jolson, la plus grande star de son époque, enregistra le tube « California, Here I Come » en 1924. On aurait dit une longue réclame publicitaire : « Where bowers of flowers bloom in the spring! » (« Là où des berceaux de fleurs éclosent au printemps ! »)

All-Year Club of Southern California, 1929

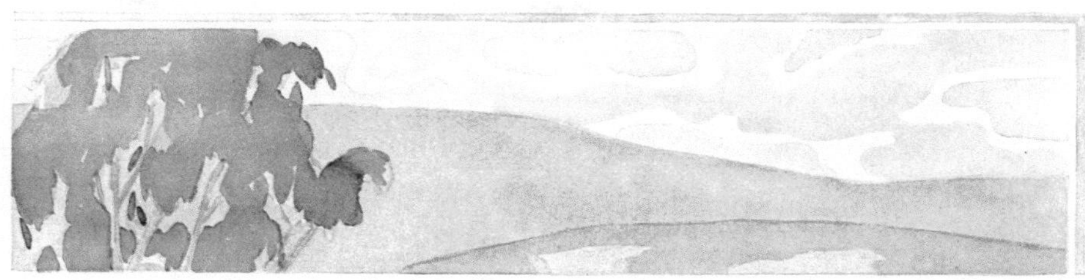

CALIFORNIA

WHEN your gorgeous autumn days are graying into winter... and that cold November twilight comes . . . well, winter's on the way . . .

Soon smart society is on the move, winging westward to the blue Pacific... to California, America's gay Riviera... playground of the world!

Come either to Los Angeles or San Francisco... and this whole enchanted land is at your feet—a land of sunshine and flowers, of highways that roll away like magic carpets through the mountains, along the sea... through fascinating, colorful cities . . . stately redwood forests. All California is your playground, infinitely varied... polo and golf, and five o'clock tea in the patio... starry nights, with the slumberous roar of the surf. A land of sunny loveliness, June-like days—in California.

Los Angeles and its Hollywood, Pasadena and Beverly Hills, gay words . . . to the travel-wise . . . then San Diego, with Agua Caliente just over the border. And for good stylish loafing, which science calls heliotherapy, heed the call of the desert! Palm Springs... or Death Valley, with its enthralling beauty and vast brooding expanse of sand and silence... back to the ocean again at Santa Barbara, another favorite of the smart world.

San Francisco—flavor of Naples and Paris. Center of a brilliant social season... charming, cosmopolitan, sophisticated. Nearby, you'll find paradise made fashionable at Monterey and Del Monte . . . Yosemite and Tahoe a night away, and just to the north the great Redwood Empire... duck and quail shooting, steelhead and salmon fishing . . . the kinds you read about in sport magazines.

Golf—all up and down the coast memorable green courses welcome you, from Eureka to Coronado and out on Catalina, 25 miles off shore.

California requests the pleasure of your company this fall and winter. Bring the youngsters—the schools are good.

Books picturing California will be sent on request. Write either of these organizations.

CALIFORNIANS, INC.
SEC. 1811. 703 MARKET STREET, SAN FRANCISCO

ALL-YEAR CLUB OF SOUTHERN CALIFORNIA
SEC. R-11. 1151 SO. BROADWAY, LOS ANGELES

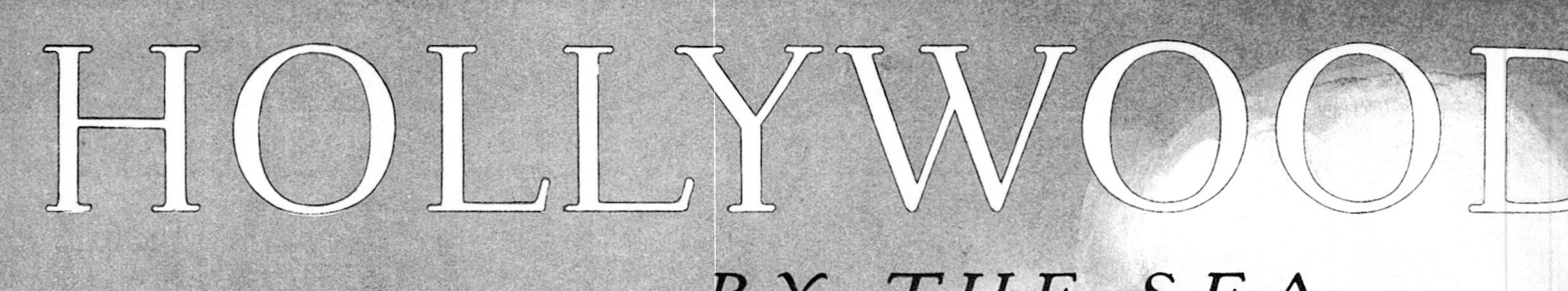

BY-THE-SEA

The gay Broad Walk along the ocean's edge passes directly in front of the Hollywood Hotel.

Enjoy Your

HOLLYWOOD BY-THE-SEA lends itself to gaiety outdoor recreation in variety such as you sel find in a summer vacation land. From morning evening Hollywood's guests make merry on Beach Broad Walk—in surf and Casino pool—on fis grounds and golf course—in yachts and motor craft

At night, when myriad lights transform the ocean f into a great white way, Caesar La Monaca's Hollyw Band adds to the enjoyment of the merry crowds— the music of Arnold Johnson's famous orchestra quic dancing feet, as cool sea breezes freshen bodies tired f the sports of the day . . . .

In dining rooms and lobbies of brilliant hotels, at

HOLLYWOOD RESORT AND INDUSTRIAL BOARD

On the Ocean • • On the Florida East Coast Railr

in FLORIDA
Swim here in the great pool of the Bathing Casino—or in the surf and sea, as you prefer.
cation Here
lendid Country Club, on the roof garden of the Holly-
ood Hotel on the Beach, or outdoors under the stars,
e accumulated cares of workday life magically fall away
d hearts are light again . . . . .
acation days are always fair at Hollywood By-the-Sea,
d nights are always cool. Here vacation dreams really
me true. The gaiety that every normal life craves and
e glow of health that only the great outdoors can give,
vait you here—whether your stay be brief or permanent.
uxurious, hospitable hotels will add to the pleasure and comfort
your visit. Special low cost Hollywood summer excursions
ake possible a trip to this seaside wonderland on a very mod-
ate vacation budget. Just sign and mail the coupon for com-
ete information.
W. YOUNG, President · Hollywood, in Florida
· On the Dixie Highway
Hollywood summer excursions by boat and rail offer wonderful vacation opportunities. Mail this coupon for full information.
YOUR SUMMER VACATION
MAIL THIS COUPON TODAY
HOLLYWOOD RESORT AND INDUSTRIAL BOARD
Hollywood, in Florida
Please mail me full information about low cost summer excursions to Florida, with free illustrated folders.
Name
Street
City
State

ARISTOCRATS OF THE SEA
With a background of fine traditions and nautical lineage, and a foreground of modern standards, White Star, Red Star and Atlantic Transport ships traverse the ocean lanes, the aristocrats of the sea. . . . Chosen by the fashionables because they are correct—by confirmed travelers for their inimitable service and comfort—by students, artists and economical vacationists because of their delightful TOURIST Third Cabin accommodations.
Ships for every purse and plan.
No. 1 Broadway, N. Y. Offices and agents everywhere.
WHITE STAR LINE
RED STAR LINE · ATLANTIC TRANSPORT LINE
INTERNATIONAL MERCANTILE MARINE COMPANY

Hollywood By-the-Sea, Florida, 1925 ◂◂

Developer Joseph Young planned his Hollywood By-the-Sea down to its boardwalk and business district. Young's version of his "Dream City" was on the ocean—not inland like its West Coast namesake. Started in 1920, it flourished during the Florida boom, with 36 apartment buildings, almost 2,500 houses, and 252 commercial buildings by 1926.

Joseph Young plante sein Hollywood-By-the-Sea von der Uferpromenade bis zum Einkaufsviertel. Youngs „Traumstadt" lag allerdings am Meer und nicht im Binnenland wie ihr Namensvetter von der Westküste. Die 1920 gegründete Siedlung profitierte vom Floridaboom; 1926 besaß sie 36 Wohnblocks, fast 2500 Häuser und 252 Geschäftsgebäude.

Le promoteur immobilier Joseph Young imagina tous les détails de son Hollywood By-the-Sea, jusqu'à sa promenade en front de mer et son quartier d'affaires. La « ville de rêve » de Young se trouvait au bord de la mer, et non dans les terres comme son homonyme de la Côte Ouest. Lancé en 1920, le projet prospéra pendant le boom immobilier de Floride et comptait 36 immeubles résidentiels, près de 2500 maisons et 252 immeubles commerciaux dès 1926.

Cunard, 1929

International Mercantile Marine Company, 1928

▸ *Life*, 1927

Life
Tourists' Number
August 18 1927
Price 15 cents

Travel
SEPTEMBER
1 9 2 4
35 cents a c
$4.00 a y

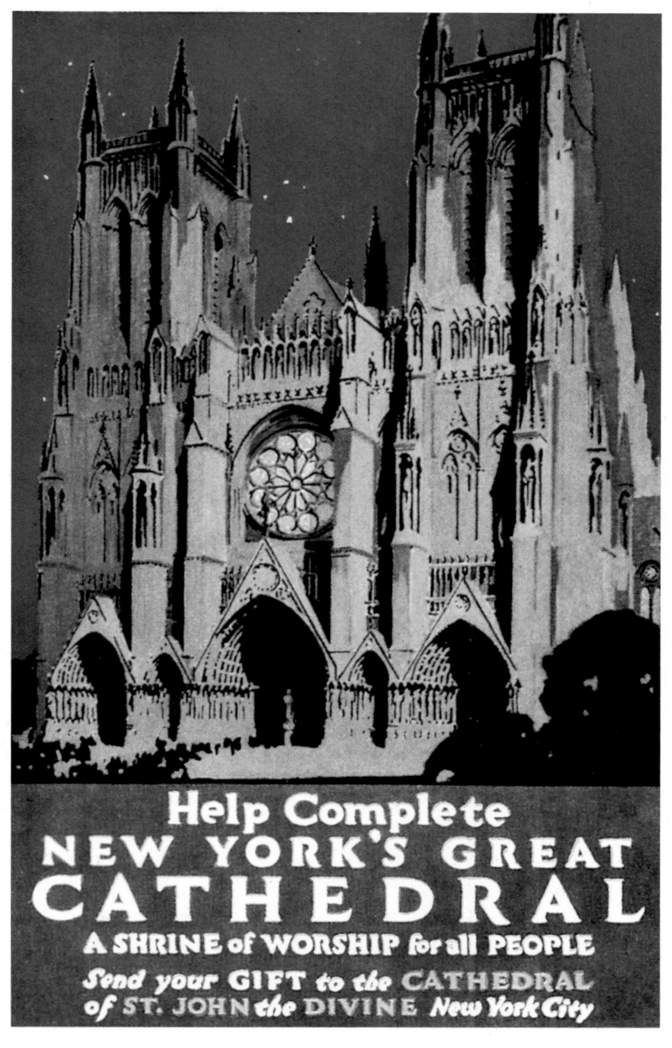

◂ *Travel*, 1924

In the race between cars and trains, automobile travel miles surpassed train travel by 1920. Railroads fought back with express "flyers" that offered exclusive first-class service. But, by 1930, there were 26.7 million cars, one for every 4.5 people, in the United States, an amazing increase from 4,000 in 1900.

Im Wettrennen zwischen Auto und Zug hatte das Auto hinsichtlich der zurückgelegten Kilometer 1920 erstmals die Nase vorn. Die Bahngesellschaften konterten mit schnellen „Flyers", die einen exklusiven Erste-Klasse-Service boten. Doch in den Vereinigten Staaten gab es 1930 bereits 26,7 Millionen Autos, rund 22 pro 100 Einwohner, ein immenser Zuwachs gegenüber nur 4000 im Jahr 1900.

Dans la course entre trains et voitures, la route l'emporta sur le rail en kilomètres parcourus en 1920. Les compagnies ferroviaires réagirent en lançant des trains express exclusivement première classe. En 1930, on comptait 26,7 millions de voitures aux Etats-Unis, soit une pour 4,5 personnes, contre seulement 4 000 en 1900.

New York Central, 1926

Cathedral of St. John the Divine, 1925

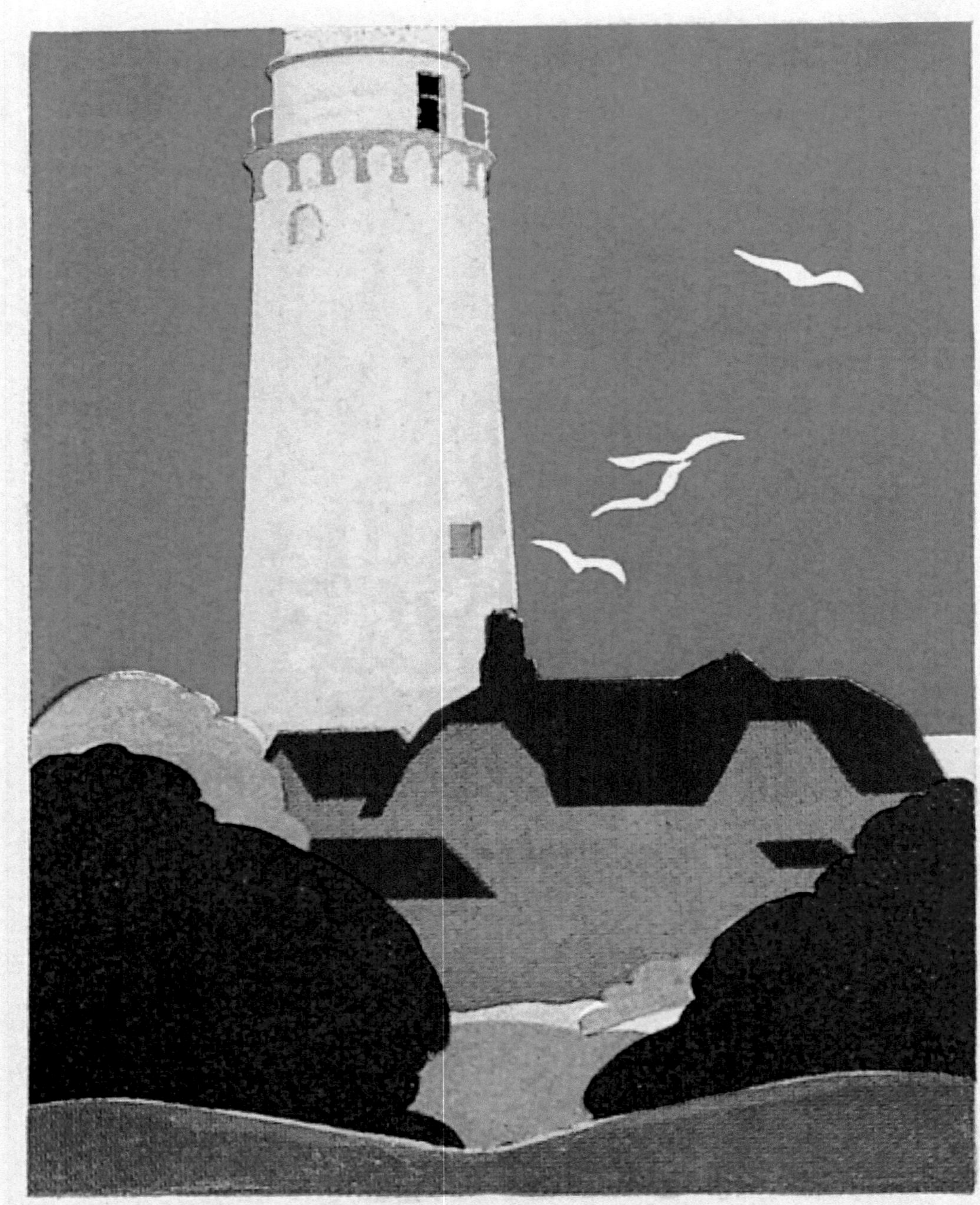

Chicago Illinois Rail, 1925

North Shore Line, 1925

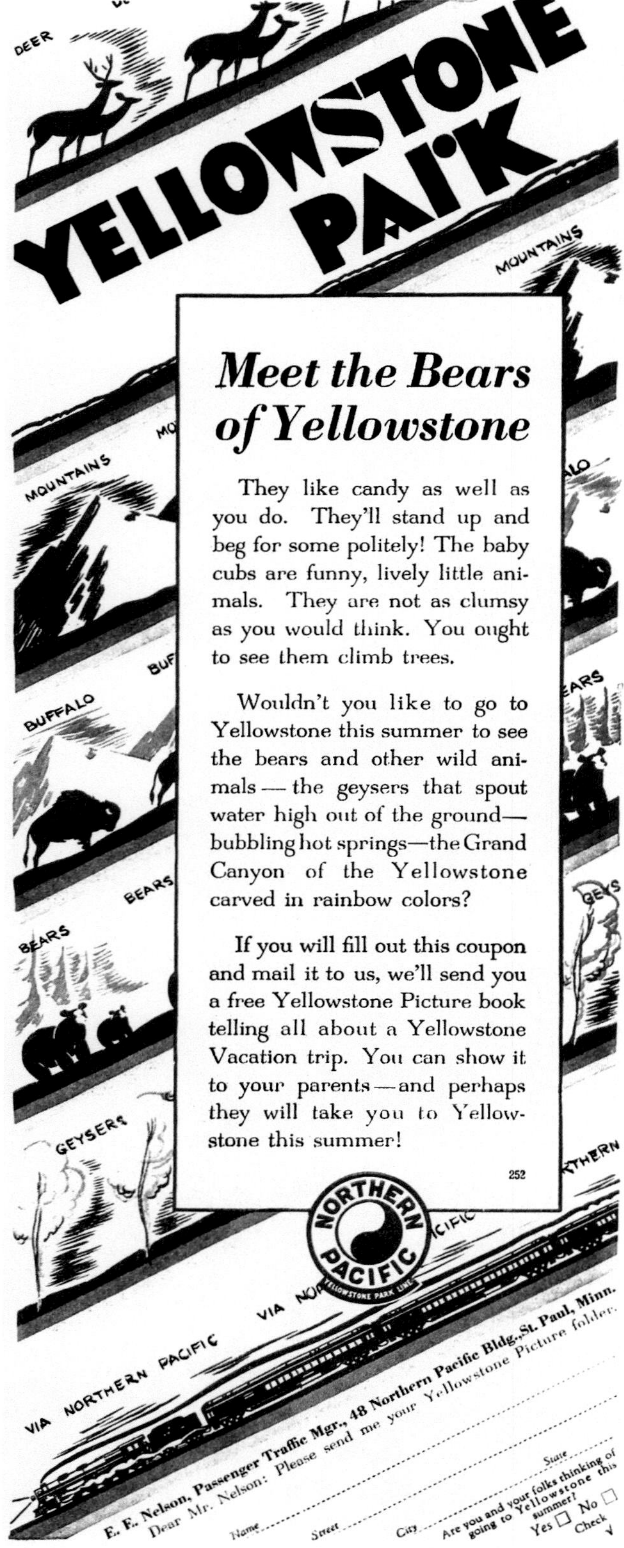

YELLOWSTONE PARK
DEER
MOUNTAINS
BUFFALO
BEARS
GEYSERS
Meet the Bears of Yellowstone
They like candy as well as you do. They'll stand up and beg for some politely! The baby cubs are funny, lively little animals. They are not as clumsy as you would think. You ought to see them climb trees.
Wouldn't you like to go to Yellowstone this summer to see the bears and other wild animals — the geysers that spout water high out of the ground—bubbling hot springs—the Grand Canyon of the Yellowstone carved in rainbow colors?
If you will fill out this coupon and mail it to us, we'll send you a free Yellowstone Picture book telling all about a Yellowstone Vacation trip. You can show it to your parents — and perhaps they will take you to Yellowstone this summer!
252
NORTHERN PACIFIC
YELLOWSTONE PARK LINE
VIA NORTHERN PACIFIC
E. E. Nelson, Passenger Traffic Mgr., 48 Northern Pacific Bldg., St. Paul, Minn.
Dear Mr. Nelson: Please send me your Yellowstone Picture folder.
Name
Street
City
State
Are you and your folks thinking of going to Yellowstone this summer?
Yes ☐ No ☐
Check ✓

Burlington Route, 1923

Northern Pacific Railway, 1929

► South Shore Line Trains, 1926

HOMEWARD BOUND
by SOUTH SHORE LINE

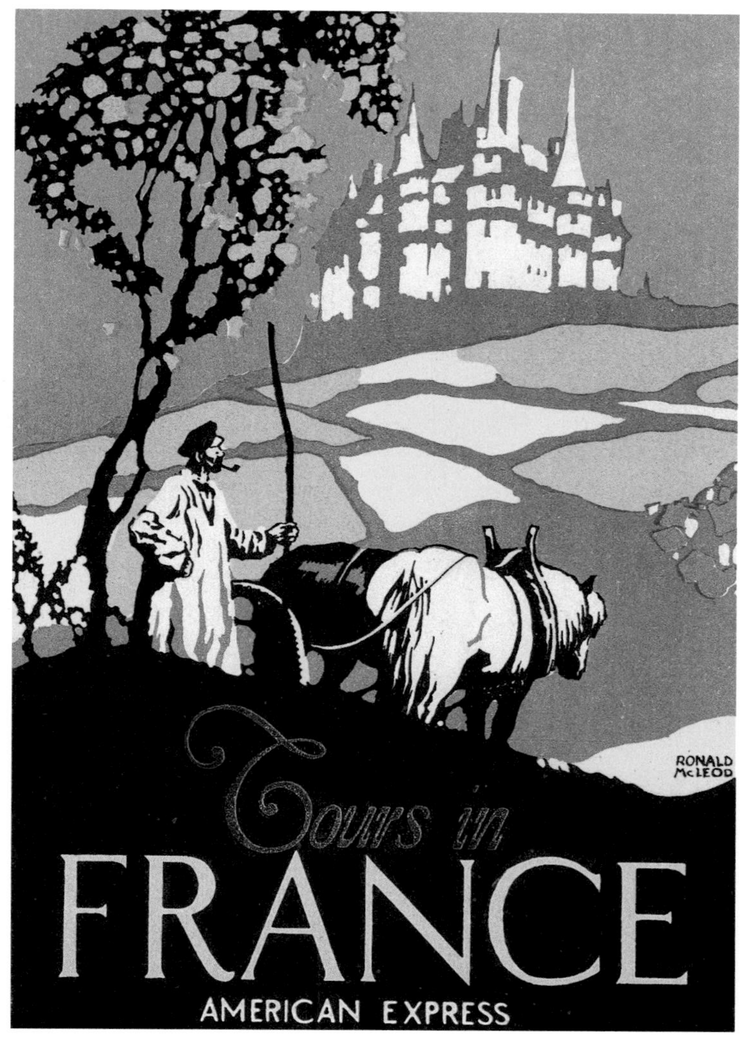

◂ *National Motorist*, 1929

The membership magazine of the Automobile Club of America reflects the decade's passion for sunbathing. Before the 1920s, fair skin was one hallmark of a "lady," since workers labored under the hot sun. But in the Industrial Age, workers went into factories. Fashion reversed—a sun-kissed complexion was desirable.

Die Mitgliederzeitschrift des Automobile Club of America bezeugt die aufkommende Begeisterung fürs Sonnenbaden. Bis etwa 1920 war helle Haut gleichsam das Gütesiegel einer „Lady", in Abgrenzung von den im Freien tätigen Arbeitern. Im Industriezeitalter indes ging man zum Arbeiten in die Fabrik, und die Mode kehrte sich um, sodass man nun einen von der Sonne verwöhnten Teint anstrebte.

Le magazine des membres de l'Automobile Club of America reflète la passion des bains de soleil qui naquit dans les années 1920. Auparavant, une lady digne de ce nom se devait de garder le teint pâle pour se différencier de la classe ouvrière qui travaillait sous un soleil de plomb, mais les ouvriers ayant rejoint les usines depuis la Révolution Industrielle, la mode s'inversa. La tendance était désormais au bronzage.

American Express, 1926

American Express, 1927

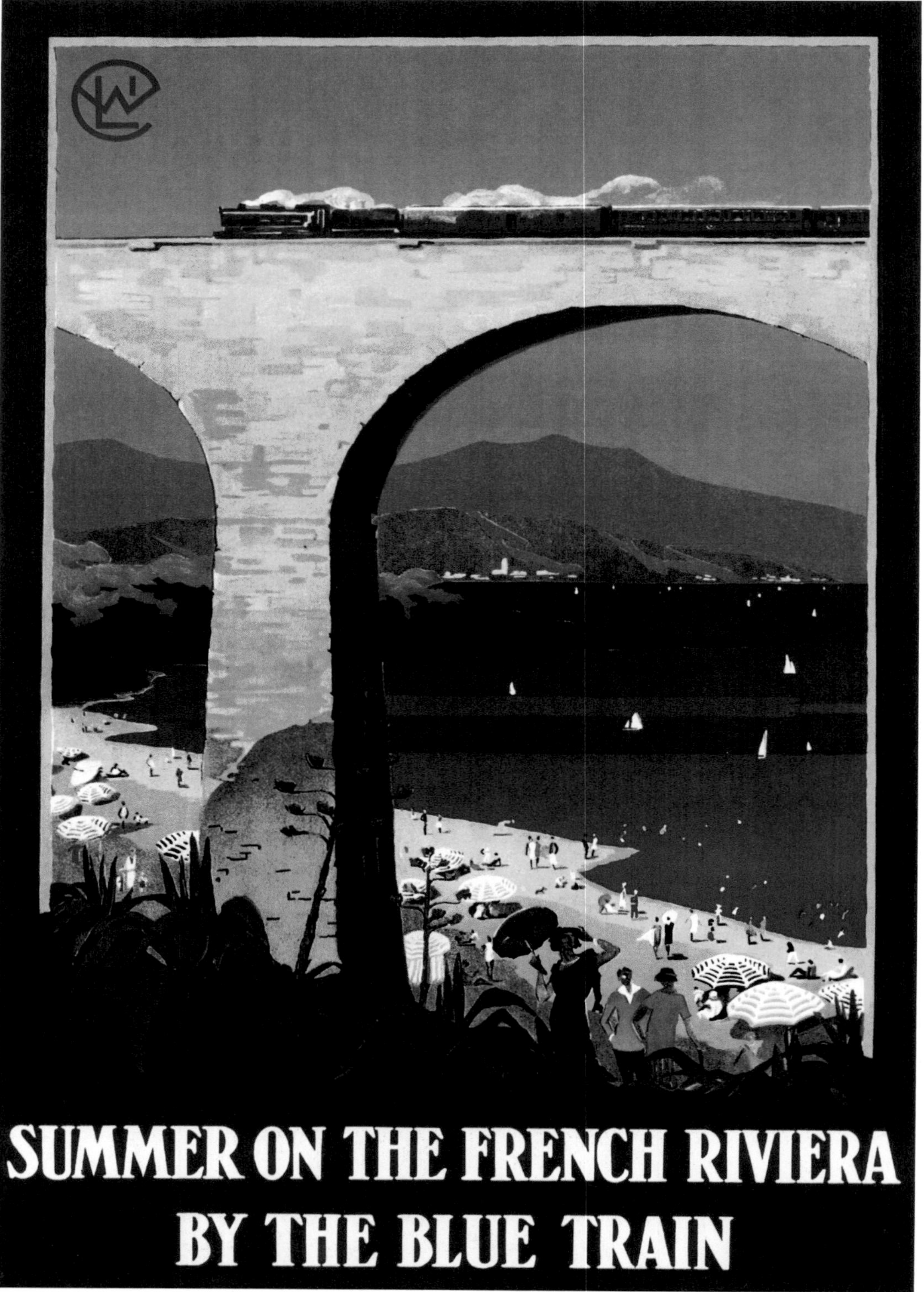

South of France, 1928

Starting in 1922, the Train Bleu made the journey to the south of France as hot as the destination. This "train of paradise" seemed like one big party, for all 80 passengers had connecting luxury compartments. It inspired a Diaghilev ballet, with story by Jean Cocteau and costumes by Coco Chanel.

Ab 1922 verkehrend, machte Le Train Bleu die Reise nach Südfrankreich so aufregend wie das Ziel selbst. Die Fahrt mit dem „Paradieszug" glich einer großen Party, denn für sämtliche 80 Fahrgäste gab es miteinander verbundene Luxusabteile. Der Zug inspirierte Diaghilew zu einem Ballett mit Libretto von Jean Cocteau und Kostümen von Coco Chanel.

Lancé en 1922, le Train Bleu ralliait le sud de la France, qui était alors la destination à la mode. Ce « train paradisiaque » ressemblait à un grand salon mondain sur roues, les compartiments de luxe des 80 passagers étant communicants. Cela inspira un ballet à Diaghilev, avec livret de Jean Cocteau et costumes de Coco Chanel.

► Cannes, ca. 1925

PERI
ÉTÉ CANNES HIVER

—and a Great Exposition

ANCIENT MOORISH TEMPLES . . . Magnificent "Castles in Spain" . . . land of Romance—Play . . . Wonder places all, where time has lent its graceful charm to enchant you!

Travelling in Spain is like a wonderful dream . . . the wonders of history parading before your eyes!

And you may live amidst this historical grandeur, this romance—in modern comfort—at moderate cost!

Visit the great "International Exposition of Barcelona" and see the greatest collection of art, science and industry of all times. Housed in buildings that took eight years to build and at a cost of $22,000,000. Spain has perfectly blended her own architecture, centuries old, with all that is beautiful in the "Moderne."

Spain—Barcelona—should be on your itinerary for your tour in 1929.

[Barcelona—Paris, 23 hours . . . London, 30 hours . . . Berlin, 39 hours. Motor Tours on 40,000 miles of hard surface roads! Rail transportation reduced.]

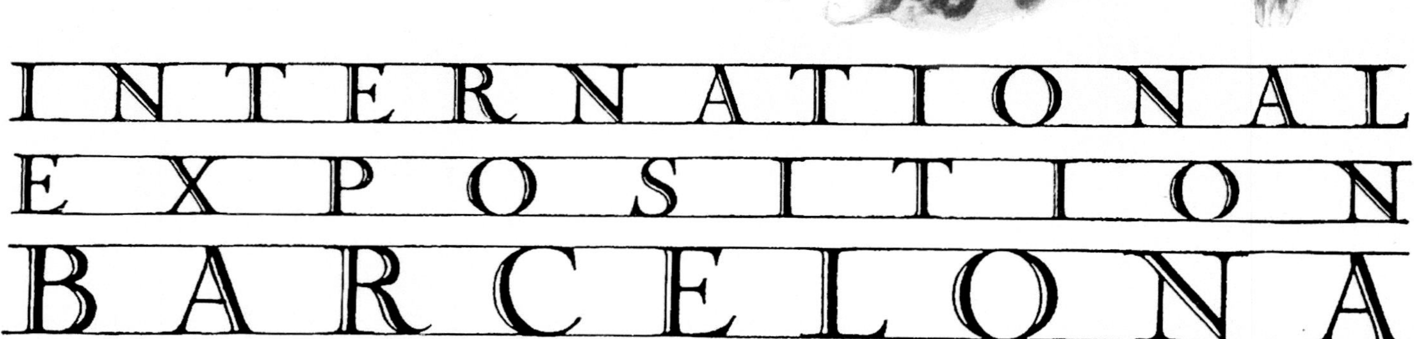

May to December

1 9 2 9

For further information address any Tourist Bureau, or M. Ventura, American Delegate, Steinway Hall, 113 West 57th Street, New York City

DELIGHTFUL DURBAN

CHARMINGLY different, this gem-like Riviera in the Garden Province of South Africa . . . Gay, colorful, joyful Durban . . . Here health and pleasure prosper in a setting of sparkling sunshine, zestful climate, the amazing blue of the Southern sky, the dancing waters of the Indian ocean.

Luxurious hotels overlook spacious stretches of beach and a beautiful harbor alive with white-bellied sails of pleasure craft, with warships, whalers, windjammers . . . Delightful golf and yachting clubs . . . Sailing, sea bathing, surfing, angling, polo, cricket, horse-racing, motoring, high-class concerts, theatres . . . all catering happily to the lovers of sport, recreation, leisure.

Durban's attractions provide an exquisite interval in a tour of South Africa's many wonders . . . Matchless Victoria Falls . . . Zimbabwe's mysterious ruins . . . Kimberley's famous diamond mines . . . Marvelous Cango Caves . . . The gold mines of the Rand . . . Drakensberg Mountains . . . The Valley of a Thousand Hills . . . The great Kruger Big Game Preserve . . . and Historic Good Hope, the "Cape Beautiful."

Send for fully illustrated booklet to

SOUTH AFRICAN GOVERNMENT RAILWAYS
11 Broadway, New York City

OSHKOSH "Chief" TRUNKS

Hotchkotch? . . . Oochkooch? "Better to be guilty of mispronunciation than travel with anything less than the best trunk in the world." That's what hundreds of experienced French travelers say who have a perfectly terrible time pronouncing the name "OSHKOSH."

THE TRUNK *in the picture is an Oshkosh "Chief" Wardrobe. The name "Chief" means the best trunk that Oshkosh knows how to make. The people of Mars may have discovered how to produce a better trunk than this, but they haven't told anyone on earth about it yet. A handsome descriptive booklet, "The Chief of Trunks," is free. For a copy, address the Oshkosh Trunk Company, 445 High Street, Oshkosh, Wisconsin.*

◂ International Exposition Barcelona, 1929

South African Government Railways, 1929

During the 1920s, the French Riviera became the place to go during the summer. Here, South African Government Railways wants some of these flocks of tourists to head to a Riviera farther south—in Durban, South Africa.

In den 1920er-Jahren wurde die französische Riviera zum bevorzugten Sommerziel. In dieser Anzeige versucht die staatliche südafrikanische Eisenbahngesellschaft einen Teil dieser Touristenscharen an eine weiter südlich gelegene Riviera zu locken – nach Durban in Südafrika.

Pendant les années 1920, la Côte d'Azur devint le dernier endroit à la mode pour passer l'été. Ici, la compagnie South African Government Railways tente de faire descendre ces foules de touristes bien plus au sud, à Durban, en Afrique du Sud.

Oshkosh Trunks, 1926

Travel in the early '20s usually meant extended stays and formal dinners. Travelers needed trunks—often several. Oshkosh was noted for well-made pieces—this ad might be a sly reference that it was the "Louis Vuitton of America." Top of its line was the Chief, made of waterproof duck cloth. In 1927, as travel patterns shifted, Oshkosh began making smaller hand luggage.

Reisen bedeutete Anfang der 1920er-Jahre meist einen längeren Aufenthalt und förmliche Diners. Hierzu benötigte man einen Schrankkoffer – oft gleich mehrere. Womöglich birgt diese Anzeige der für ihre gute Qualität bekannten Firma Oshkosh einen unterschwelligen Hinweis auf ihren Status eines „Louis Vuitton von Amerika". Beim Topmodell „Chief" bot imprägniertes Segeltuch zusätzlichen Schutz. Als sich das Reiseverhalten änderte, begann Oshkosh 1927 mit der Fertigung von Handgepäck.

Au début des années 1920, le voyage était en général synonyme de longs séjours et de dîners chics. Les voyageurs avaient souvent besoin de plusieurs malles. Oshkosh se distingua par ses produits de bonne facture : cette publicité sous-entend peut-être que la marque était le « Louis Vuitton d'Amérique ». Le Chief, son produit le plus haut de gamme, était en toile imperméable. En 1927, quand la façon de voyager évolua, Oshkosh se mit à fabriquer des bagages à main plus petits.

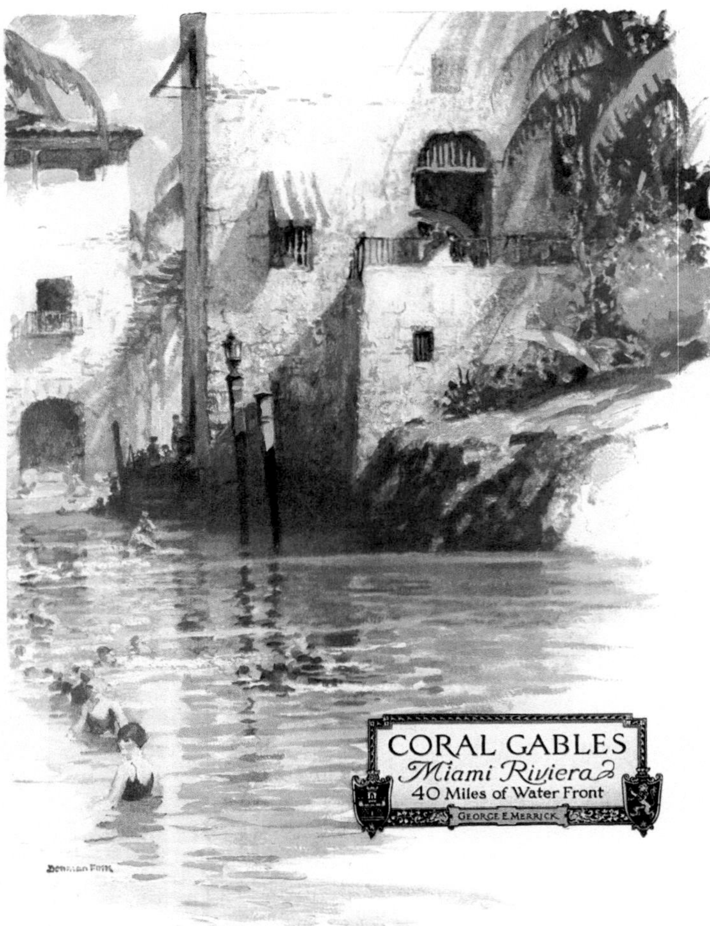

Coral Gables, Florida, 1926

Coral Gables, influenced by the City Beautiful movement, was envisioned by the developer George Merrick in the languid Mediterranean revival style. Propelled by the Florida boom, $7 million in land was sold, 65 miles of roads constructed, and more than 600 homes built between the town's inception in 1921 and incorporation in 1925.

Beeinflusst durch die „City Beautiful"-Bewegung, ist Coral Gables eine Kreation des Städteplaners George Merrick im lässigen Stil des Mediterranean Revival. Angetrieben durch den Boom in Florida, wurden zwischen den ersten Anfängen 1921 und der Stadtgründung 1925 Land für 7 Mio. $ verkauft sowie 100 Straßenkilometer und mehr als 600 Häuser gebaut.

Influencé par le mouvement urbaniste City Beautiful, le projet Coral Gables au style néo-méditerranéen langoureux est né de l'imagination du promoteur immobilier George Merrick. Sous l'impulsion du boom immobilier de Floride, la vente de terrains s'eleva à 7 millions de dollars, 105 kilomètres de routes furent construits et plus de 600 maisons bâties entre la création de la ville en 1921 et son incorporation en 1925.

Coral Gables, Florida, 1925

▸ Coral Gables, Florida, 1926

CORAL GABLES

Miami Riviera

40 Miles of Water Front

GEORGE E MERRICK

Society's Winter Paradise.... Hawaii

CORAL SANDS gleam today with gay Cosmopolites lured from the far reaches of the earth. The throbbing colors of Deauville, Cannes, famed watering places of the world, merge with the lavish tints of the South Seas › › › their glistening greens and tropic golds and the million shifting shades between. The sparkle of Continental smartness is on great hotels that jewel the shore at Waikiki › › › Everywhere is the zest of anticipation › › › the vibrant thrill that marks the pre-holiday season in the Paradise Isles.

¶ Sophisticates enticed by the bizarre have opened the season each year a little earlier. They have come to know the rapture of Christmas under a velvet sky › › › windows ablaze in the palaces of departed Hawaiian Kings › › › clear-throated carols ascending to pendant stars that glow like orbs of fire through the fronds of swaying palms › › › They come in the mellow beauty of autumn to linger until languorous spring bursts into the crashing colors of Hawaiian summer › › › For them winter is only a fiction › › › They know tonight the miracle of a moon of molten silver pouring its translucent sheen over majestic mountains and dancing waters › › › the haunting harmony of sobbing steel-guitars and plaintive voices that rise and fall on vagrant breezes that drift in from the sea.

¶ They have learned that Hawaii is just a *few days* away › › › a land of enchantment at the end of a blissful interlude of sun and sea and sky on luxurious liners as proud as any that float. They know it as the magic place where shimmering rainbows drape verdant golf courses › › › where friendly beach-boys weave native hats or conquer racing waves, erect on charging surf-boards › › › where sporty denizens of the deep lurk in constant challenge to the mettle of the ardent fisherman, or idle days may be dreamed away in tropic bowers still primitive and unspoiled.

¶ You can go from any of the four great gateways of the Pacific in four to six days, according to the liner selected. And you do not have to bother with passports or other formalities. Hawaii is an integral part of the United States—as much so as your own State.

The Hawaii Tourist Bureau

San Francisco, Calif.
1119 Monadnock Building
MATSON Line *from* San Francisco
Portland and Seattle

535 Fifth Ave. - - - - - - - - - - New York
140 So. Dearborn - - - - - - - - - Chicago
215 Market St. - - - - - - - San Francisco
723 W. Seventh St. - - - - - - Los Angeles
1805 Elm St. - - - - - - - - - Dallas, Texas
1319 Fourth Ave. - - - - - - - - - - Seattle
82½ Fourth St. - - - - - - Portland, Ore.

Los Angeles, Calif.
655T Chamber of Commerce Building
LASSCO Line *from* Los Angeles
in Southern California

730 So. Broadway - - - - - - - Los Angeles
521 Fifth Ave. - - - - - - - - - - - New York
119 W. Ocean Ave. - - - - - - - Long Beach
140 So. Dearborn - - - - - - - - - - Chicago
685 Market St. - - - - - - - - San Francisco
213 E. Broadway - - - - San Diego, Calif.
609 Thomas Bldg. - - - - - - Dallas, Texas

Any travel agent will gladly give you full particulars and arrange your bookings

◄ *Sunset*, 1929

Hawaii Tourist Bureau, 1929

REST IN BERMUDA
The rest and quiet for which your soul longs, await you here. Bermuda is a haven of peace, for it is almost alone in allowing no automobiles, railroads and street cars, and it is blessed with the world's most equable climate.
The winter temperature averages between 60° and 70°.
Unique as a rest resort, Bermuda also offers rare recreation the year 'round—unexcelled golf, tennis, bathing, sailing, fishing, riding, driving, cycling, sightseeing among natural marvels. The sea gardens, magical caves, natural arches, cathedral rocks, and marine grottos, vie in interest with the lavish displays of exotic flowers, the rare trees and plants, the white coral roads, the pink beaches, and the 17th-century homes and gardens.
Two days from New York—no passports. Excellent hotels and boarding places, and furnished cottages. Booklet from the Furness Bermuda Line, 34 Whitehall Street, New York, The Royal Mail Steam Packet Company, 26 Broadway, New York, any travel bureau, or
THE BERMUDA TRADE DEVELOPMENT BOARD
250 Park Avenue, New York
(A Department of the Bermuda Government, which has authorizied the pubication of this advertisement.)

Those who have crossed more than once invariably choose their ship with care

S. S.
RELIANCE
ALBERT BALLIN

AND OTHER SPLENDID STEAMERS

S. S
RESOLUTE
DEUTSCHLAND

UNITED AMERICAN LINES
(HARRIMAN LINE)
joint service with
HAMBURG AMERICAN LINE

Write for fascinating travel booklet P. Q.

39 BROADWAY, NEW YORK
171 W. RANDOLPH ST., CHICAGO
230 CALIFORNIA ST., SAN FRANCISCO

◄ Bermuda Trade Development Board, 1925

United American Cruise Line, 1924

CUNARD
WEST INDIES
CRUISES

S. S. CALIFORNIA
Jan. 19 *and* Feb. 23, 1929

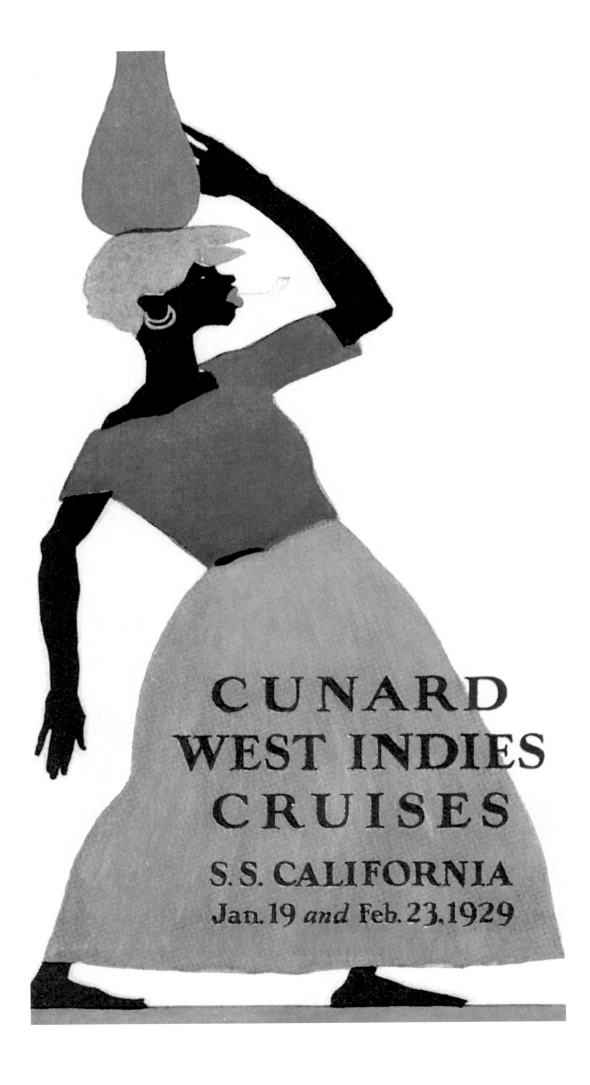

◂ Cunard, 1929

Cuban National Tourist Commission, 1929

Havana was known as the "Paris of the Caribbean." During Prohibition it rivaled Miami as a tourist center, for Cuba's legal alcohol was only a short hop from many big East Coast cities. Cuba also offered something more: Its colonial past signaled a promise of sultry and voluptuous experiences.

Während der Prohibition machte Havanna, das „Paris der Karibik", Miami als Touristenmagnet Konkurrenz, denn Kubas legaler Alkohol war von vielen Großstädten an der Ostküste nur einen Katzensprung entfernt. Doch Kuba bot noch mehr: Seine koloniale Vergangenheit verhieß sinnenfrohe Ausschweifungen.

La Havane passait pour être le « Paris des Caraïbes ». Pendant la Prohibition, elle concurrençait Miami en tant que centre touristique car Cuba, où la consommation d'alcool était autorisée, ne se trouvait qu'à un saut de puce de nombreuses grandes villes de la Côte Est. L'île avait aussi autre chose à offrir : son passé colonial était une promesse d'expériences sensuelles et voluptueuses.

HAVANA

Here's a trip abroad – not far away – not too expensive

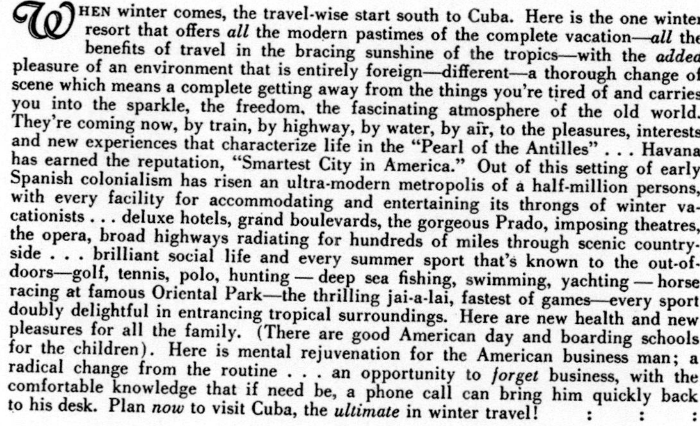

WHEN winter comes, the travel-wise start south to Cuba. Here is the one winter resort that offers *all* the modern pastimes of the complete vacation—*all* the benefits of travel in the bracing sunshine of the tropics—with the *added* pleasure of an environment that is entirely foreign—different—a thorough change of scene which means a complete getting away from the things you're tired of and carries you into the sparkle, the freedom, the fascinating atmosphere of the old world. They're coming now, by train, by highway, by water, by air, to the pleasures, interests and new experiences that characterize life in the "Pearl of the Antilles" . . . Havana has earned the reputation, "Smartest City in America." Out of this setting of early Spanish colonialism has risen an ultra-modern metropolis of a half-million persons, with every facility for accommodating and entertaining its throngs of winter vacationists . . . deluxe hotels, grand boulevards, the gorgeous Prado, imposing theatres, the opera, broad highways radiating for hundreds of miles through scenic countryside . . . brilliant social life and every summer sport that's known to the out-of-doors—golf, tennis, polo, hunting — deep sea fishing, swimming, yachting — horse racing at famous Oriental Park—the thrilling jai-a-lai, fastest of games—every sport doubly delightful in entrancing tropical surroundings. Here are new health and new pleasures for all the family. (There are good American day and boarding schools for the children). Here is mental rejuvenation for the American business man; a radical change from the routine . . . an opportunity to *forget* business, with the comfortable knowledge that if need be, a phone call can bring him quickly back to his desk. Plan *now* to visit Cuba, the *ultimate* in winter travel! : : :

For information, etc., any travel bureau, any railroad, steamship or airplane ticket office or the National Tourist Commission, Havana.

◂ The St. Charles Hotel, 1923

La Fonda Inn, 1927

Your stop in China takes you back 1000 years

By HARRY A. FRANCK*

"Go-as-you-please" tours Round the World under this unique plan. The only way really to see what you want to see at your own option. Stop where you wish. Continue when you choose. Your ticket permits two years for the complete trip, or aboard one liner, circle the globe in 110 days. Your fare, including meals and accommodations aboard ship, as low as $1250 Round the World.

Every fortnight a President Liner sails from Seattle for Japan, China, Manila and Round the World.

Every week a similar liner sails from Los Angeles and San Francisco for Honolulu, Japan, China and Manila. Then onward on fortnightly schedules to Malaya, Ceylon—with easy access to India—Egypt, Italy, France, New York.

Fortnightly sailings from New York via Havana and Panama to California. Thence Round the World.

Palatial Liners, they are broad of beam, steady and comfortable. Spacious decks. Luxurious public rooms. A swimming pool. Outside rooms with beds, not berths. A cuisine famous among world travelers.

* World Traveler and Author of "A Vagabond Journey Around the World," "Wandering in Northern China," "East of Siam."

"CHINA, a world in itself. An ancient civilization that has come down to us almost intact. It is as if the social life of the pre-Christian era had been shifted into neutral and placed in a museum, not as a dead world's junk but still teeming with life, that we might see how our remote ancestors lived. For with all its recent furor to overtake the procession of what we perhaps mistakenly call modern progress, the great land of half a billion people is still essentially in the hand-making and barter stage . . .

"You cannot, of course, even if you try, miss Shanghai, where to cross the street separating the foreign concessions from the native city will instantly carry you back a thousand years. Thence great foreign steamers will take you up the Yang Tze Kiang, the "River Son of the Sea," if you like; modern trains to Peking. inimitable among world's cities. There is only one Peking. Charm of ancient ways, a culture and social deportment quite as advanced as ours, yet so different that it has won for the West the term "barbarian." Street-straddling arches like the materialization in permanent form of some extravaganza, hundreds of thousands of men and boys trotting between the shafts of vehicles bearing hundreds of thousands of others on many a strange errand . . . pages would not suffice merely to catalogue the incredibly quaint, the thrilling, the wonder producing sights—and sounds—to be found within those triple gigantic walls that surround what was long the Forbidden City . . ."

Harry A. Franck

COMPLETE INFORMATION FROM ANY STEAMSHIP OR TOURIST AGENT

DOLLAR STEAMSHIP LINE AND AMERICAN MAIL LINE

DOLLAR STEAMSHIP LINE · AMERICAN MAIL LINE

25 AND 32 BROADWAY . . . NEW YORK
604 FIFTH AVE. . . . . NEW YORK
210 SO. SIXTEENTH ST. . . . PHILADELPHIA
177 STATE ST. . . . BOSTON, MASS.
110 SOUTH DEARBORN ST. . . CHICAGO, ILL.
514 W. SIXTH ST. . . LOS ANGELES, CALIF.
ROBERT DOLLAR BLDG. . SAN FRANCISCO
1005 CONNECTICUT N. W. . WASH., D. C.
DIME BANK BLDG. . . . . DETROIT
UNION TRUST ARCADE . CLEVELAND, OHIO
152 BROADWAY . . . PORTLAND, ORE.
21 PIAZZA DEL POPOLO . . ROME, ITALY
11 BIS RUE SCRIBE . . PARIS, FRANCE
22 BILLITER STREET E. C. 3 . . LONDON
4TH AT UNIVERSITY . . SEATTLE, WASH.
909 GOVERNMENT ST. . . VICTORIA, B. C.
517 GRANVILLE ST. . VANCOUVER, B. C.
YOKOHAMA KOBE SHANGHAI
HONG KONG MANILA

Dollar Steamship Line and American Mail Line, 1929

Intrepid explorers could still brave the unknown in the 1920s, and travelers were eager to follow their adventures. Often literally so. Tourists seeking an escape from modern life could steam to the Far East. This ad invokes China as some sort of ultra-exotic theme park.

In den 1920er-Jahren gab es für kühne Forscher noch Unbekanntes zu ergründen, und die Menschen folgten ihren Abenteuern mit Begeisterung. Oft sogar wörtlich. Touristen, die eine Auszeit vom modernen Leben suchten, konnten in den Fernen Osten schippern. Diese Anzeige sieht China als eine Art extrem exotischen Freizeitpark.

Dans les années 1920, les explorateurs intrépides pouvaient encore braver l'inconnu et les voyageurs mourraient d'envie de marcher sur leurs pas, littéralement. Les touristes désireux d'échapper à la modernité pouvaient rejoindre l'Asie en bateau vapeur. Cette publicité présente la Chine comme une sorte de parc à thème ultra exotique.

► French Line, 1924

The French Line was celebrated as the most exclusive and sumptuous fleet. Its mystique increased in 1927, with the maiden voyage of the acclaimed *Ile de France*, which had dazzling art deco interiors designed by Emile-Jacques Ruhlmann. By decade's end, the French Line carried the lion's share of transatlantic first-class passengers.

Die French Line galt als die exklusivste und den meisten Luxus bietende Flotte. Verstärkt wurde der Mythos 1927 durch die Jungfernfahrt der gefeierten *Ile de France* mit ihrem fantastischen Art-déco-Interieur von Emile-Jacques Ruhlmann. Am Ende der Dekade beförderte die French Line den Löwenanteil der Transatlantikpassagiere erster Klasse.

La Compagnie Générale Transatlantique était considérée comme la plus luxueuse et la plus somptueuse. Le mythe grandit encore en 1927 lors de la croisière inaugurale du célèbre *Ile de France* aux éblouissants intérieurs Art Déco conçus par Emile-Jacques Ruhlmann. A la fin des années 1920, la « French Line » s'octroyait la part du lion du transport transatlantique de passagers en première classe.

►► Cunard, 1927

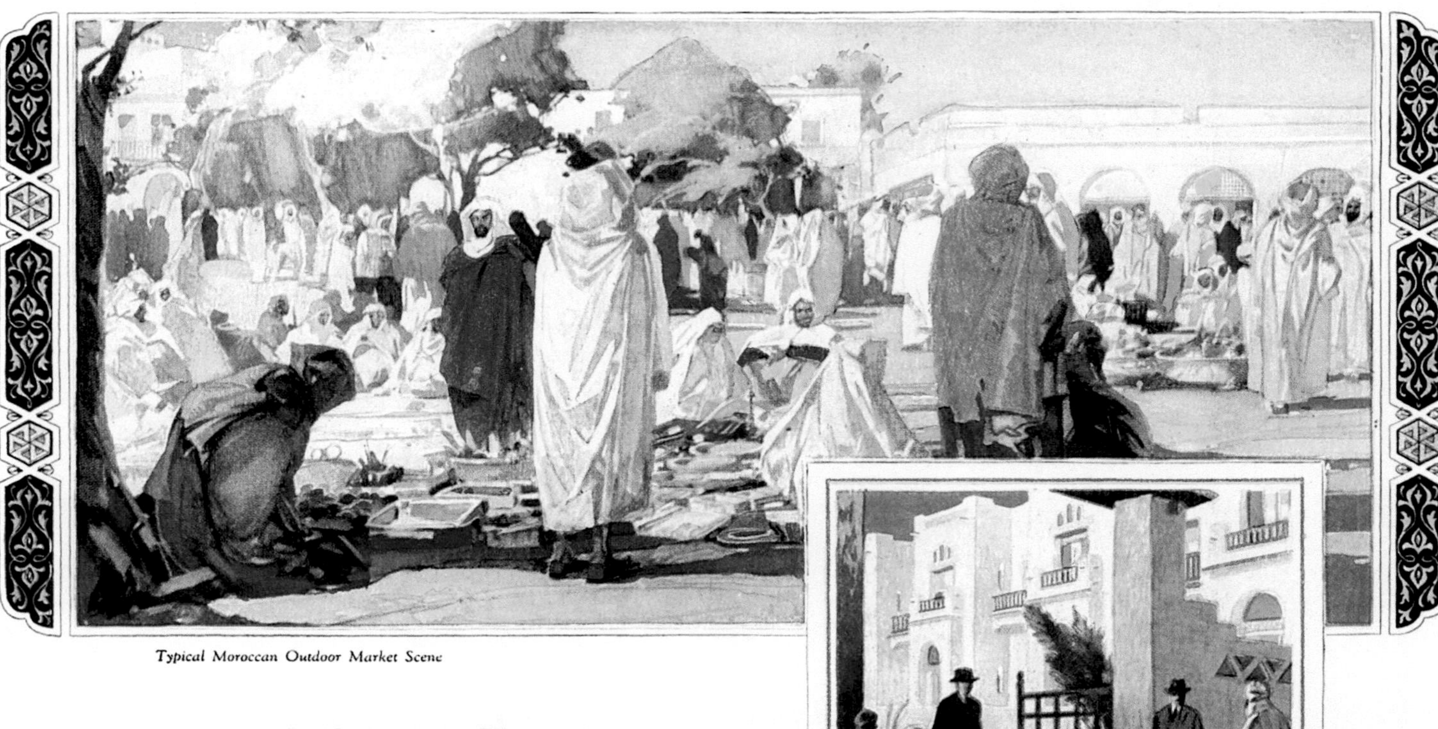

Typical Moroccan Outdoor Market Scene

Exterior of Transatlantique Hotel at Biskra

Along the White Roads above the Mediterranean

DON'T you wish sometimes that life weren't so conventional? Wouldn't you like to slip back a thousand years and find a strange, white city, basking in topaz sunshine above a sapphire sea — a city with all the color in the world adrift in its narrow streets?

Wouldn't you like to sit in a cool blue and white courtyard in Algiers while a sand diviner tells your fortune? Wouldn't you like to wander past the twisted red and black pillars of the Street of the Perfumers in Tunis? Wouldn't you like to mount a mule and go slowly, slowly, down a reed-roofed street in Fez, with the sunshine filtering through in wide gold squares?

Wouldn't you like to watch the Ouled Nails, the only women who can wander with unveiled faces, go out from their red-striped tents to dance on the hearts of men?

Wouldn't you like to buy rose-pink embroideries in Sale, rich old rugs, squares of glazed turquoise tiling like mermaids' jewels, high-backed crimson saddles with winking brass mountings—and even a bit of candy from the bronze pirate who cries with such musical pathos, "Oh Allah, Allah, send me many people with sweet teeth" . . . . ?

All this only twenty-six hours from Europe, and Europe six days from America! You step on board a French Liner in New York and are under French Line management until you see the Statue of Liberty again. Steamships, hotels, motor cars to run you right out into the Sahara. All guaranteed by those red funnels with black tops that stamp the service sterling. . . . . In the meantime, drop a line for information. The booklets are a trip in themselves.

Compagnie Générale Transatlantique, 19 State Street, New York

"Oh Allah, Allah, send me many people with sweet teeth," cry the Algerian market venders

Offices and agencies in principal cities of Europe and the United States

a
m
b
c
d
l
e
f
CU
WEST
CR
19

RD
DIES
ES
28
h

HENRY DREYFUSS RECONCEIVED EVERY ELEMENT—FROM LOCOMOTIVE TO DINNER CHINA, DOWN TO THE SUGAR-CUBE WRAPPERS.

HENRY DREYFUSS ERFAND QUASI ALLES NEU – VON DER LOK ÜBER DAS TAFELGESCHIRR BIS ZUM WÜRFELZUCKERPAPIER.

HENRY DREYFUSS EN RECONÇUT CHAQUE ÉLÉMENT, DE LA LOCOMOTIVE À LA VAISSELLE EN PORCELAINE, EN PASSANT PAR LES SACHETS DE SUCRE.

1930

STREAMLINING THE JOURNEY
LOB DER STROMLINIE
VOYAGE ET PROGRÈS TECHNOLOGIQUE

-1939

◂ Bermuda, 1934

Greyhound, 1938

OUT OF THE FINANCIAL MAELSTROM OF THE GREAT DEPRESSION CAME A BELIEF IN THE POWER OF PURE DESIGN. "Brute force," said the industrial design luminary Raymond Loewy, "can have a very sophisticated appearance, almost of great finesse, and at the same time be a monster of power."

As leading industrial designers honed the shape of trains — transforming them down to the cocktail shakers — they also sped trains up. The first lightweight, streamlined train, the Union Pacific Railroad's City of Salinas (or M-10,000) left the station in February 1934. Months later, the elegant Burlington Zephyr had its first run, zooming to Chicago for the Century of Progress Exposition. Henry Dreyfuss redesigned every aspect of the New York Central Line's Mercury in 1936. But this was only a dress rehearsal for his overhaul of the 20th Century Limited. He reconceived every element — from locomotive to dinner china, down to the sugar-cube wrappers — on the deluxe, streamlined train that sped from New York to Chicago in 16 hours. Meanwhile, the Pennsylvania Railroad commissioned Raymond Loewy to redesign the GG1 electric locomotive in 1936. His torpedo-shaped S-1 for the Broadway Limited dazzled visitors to the 1939 New York World's Fair.

The Union Pacific Railroad's owner, Averell Harriman, on the other hand, wanted more than just a train designed — he wanted to create the destination. In 1936 he opened the Sun Valley Lodge, the first U.S. ski resort. A mix of Hollywood royalty and actual royalty hit the slopes in Ketchum, Idaho.

Airplane travel also took off in the '30s. In 1930, Boeing introduced air stewardesses, to make travel more congenial. The next year, Igor Sikorsky designed and built the first Clipper for Pan American World Airways. These flying boats, which could land on water, offered an opulent ride at an opulent price. For example, the price from San Francisco to Manila was $1,710 round trip in 1937 — more than many people then earned in a year. Meanwhile, the popular new Douglas DC-3 captured the nation's fancy with its shimmering, streamlined aluminum body, soundproofed cabins, ventilation ducts, upholstered seats, and high cruising altitude. As many as 28 passengers could soar coast-to-coast in 15 hours — the first airplane to turn a profit carrying only passengers.

Flying, however, only accounted for 7.6% of the long-distance travel market in 1936 — early airplane passengers were roughing it in pursuit of speed. At the other end of the luxury spectrum was the SS *Normandie*, the biggest, swiftest, most sophisticated vessel afloat, which first set sail in 1935. This French Line ship had an innovative hull design by Vladimir Yourkevitch, for a smoother voyage. But it was the art deco and streamline moderne interiors by leading French artists like Jean Dunand, Raymond Subes, and Jean Dupas that held the public's attention.

These luxuries — available, it is true, only to first-class passengers — and the many technological advances made travel better despite the severe economic turbulence. That sense of hope carried into the 1939 New York World's Fair. Its theme, "The World of Tomorrow," was sunny and optimistic about the transportation wonders to come.

1931 Waldorf Astoria opens in New York; last major hotel planned in U.S. before stock market crash

Eröffnung des Waldorf Astoria in New York als letztes großen Hotel, das in den USA vor dem Börsenkrach geplant wurde

Ouverture du Waldorf Astoria à New York, le dernier grand hôtel américain dont la construction avait été planifiée avant le krach boursier

1931 Greyhound Corporation formed; by 1936 will be first bus company with routes across U.S.

Gründung der Greyhound Corporation, die 1936 als erste Busgesellschaft ein flächendeckendes Streckennetz offerierte

Création de Greyhound Corporation : dès 1936, elle s'impose comme la première compagnie d'autocars proposant des itinéraires à travers tous les Etats-Unis

1932 Hertz opens first airport-based U.S. car rental franchise, at Chicago's Midway

Hertz eröffnet auf dem Chicagoer Midway Airport die erste Autovermietung an einem Flughafen

À l'aéroport Midway de Chicago, Hertz ouvre la première franchise américaine de location de voitures dans les aéroports

1932 Marlene Dietrich in *Shanghai Express*: "It took more than one man to change my name to Shanghai Lily"

Marlene Dietrich in *Shanghai Express*: „Es brauchte mehr als nur *einen* Mann, um mich in Shanghai Lily zu verwandeln"

« Il a fallu plus d'un homme pour me rebaptiser Shanghai Lily », dit Marlene Dietrich dans *Shanghai Express*

DAS FINANZDESASTER DER WELTWIRTSCHAFTSKRISE HATTE ZUR FOLGE, DASS MAN AN DIE WIRKUNG REINER FORMEN ZU GLAUBEN BEGANN. „Rohe Gewalt“, so Raymond Loewy, die Lichtgestalt des Industriedesigns, „kann sehr raffiniert wirken, fast von großer Finesse und doch zugleich vor Kraft strotzend.“

Während führende Industriedesigner die Konturen der Züge glätteten (und sie bis hinab zu den Cocktailshakern verwandelten), wurden die Züge automatisch schneller. Der erste dieser leichten, stromlinienförmigen Züge war der ab Februar 1934 verkehrende City of Salinas (oder M-10 000) von Union Pacific Railroad. Wenige Monate später trat der elegante Burlington Zephyr seine erste Fahrt an, indem er nach Chicago zur Weltausstellung „A Century of Progress“ raste. Henry Dreyfuss überarbeitete 1936 den Mercury der New York Central Line in sämtlichen Details. Doch dies war nur die Generalprobe für seine Generalüberholung des 20th Century Limited. Für diesen stromlinienförmigen Luxuszug, der in 16 Stunden von New York nach Chicago flitzte, erfand Dreyfuss quasi alles neu – von der Lok über das Tafelgeschirr bis zum Würfelzuckerpapier. Ebenfalls im Jahr 1936 wurde Raymond Loewy von Pennsylvania Railroad beauftragt, der Elektrolok GG1 ein neues Design zu verpassen. Und 1939 verblüffte seine torpedoförmige S-1 für Broadway Limited die Besucher der Weltausstellung in New York.

Averell Harriman, Eigentümer der Union Pacific Railroad, wollte mehr als einen neu designten Zug, er wollte ein Reiseziel kreieren. 1936 eröffnete er mit der Sun Valley Lodge das erste Skiresort der USA. Prominente jeglicher Provenienzen frequentierten die Hänge in Ketchum, Idaho.

Auch Flugreisen nahmen in den 1930er-Jahren einen Aufschwung. Boeing präsentierte 1930 die ersten Stewardessen, um das Reisen angenehmer zu gestalten. Igor Sikorsky baute ein Jahr später den ersten Klipper für Pan American World Airways. Diese Flugboote (sie können auf dem Wasser landen) boten einen opulenten Trip zu einem opulenten Preis. So zahlte man 1937 für ein Rückflugticket von San Francisco nach Manila 1710 $ – mehr als viele damals in einem Jahr verdienten. Derweil begeisterte die neue Douglas DC-3 die Nation mit ihrem glitzernden stromlinienförmigen Alurumpf, schallgedämmten Kabinen, Lüftungsdüsen, gepolsterten Sitzen und großer Reiseflughöhe. In nur 15 Stunden gelangten 28 Passagiere von Küste zu Küste – im ersten Flugzeug, das mit der ausschließlichen Personenbeförderung Profit machte.

Flugreisen machten 1936 jedoch nur 7,6 % des Langstreckenmarktes aus. Am anderen Ende des Luxussegments begegnen wir mit der 1935 in Dienst gestellten SS *Normandie* dem größten, schnellsten und fortschrittlichsten Schiff der Zeit. Wladimir Yourkewitsch hatte diesem Passagierdampfer der French Line einen innovativen Rumpf verpasst, der eine ruhigere Fahrt ermöglichte. Nachhaltigen Eindruck hinterließen indes die Art-déco- und Streamline-Moderne-Interieurs von führenden französischen Künstlern wie Jean Dunand, Raymond Subes und Jean Dupas.

Dieser allerdings nur den Passagieren der ersten Klasse gebotene Luxus sowie die zahlreichen technologischen Fortschritte machten das Reisen trotz der schweren ökonomischen Turbulenzen angenehmer. Auch die Weltausstellung 1939 in New York zeugte von Hoffnung, denn sie gab unter dem Thema „Die Welt von morgen“ einen optimistischen Ausblick auf die künftigen fantastischen Verkehrsmittel.

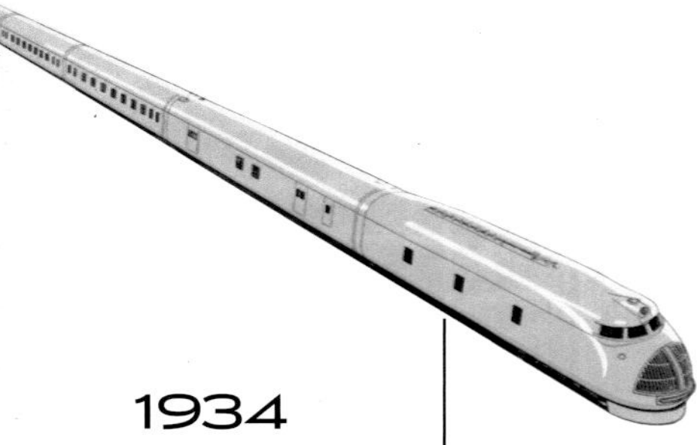

1934

1934 Union Pacific Railroad's M-10,000 is first lightweight, streamlined train; together with Zephyr, reenergizes train travel

Als erster leichter Zug verleiht der M-10 000 von Union Pacific Railroad mit dem Zephyr den Bahnreisen neuen Schwung

Le M-10 000 de l'Union Pacific Railroad est le premier train léger et aérodynamique ; aux côtés du Zephyr, il redonne un nouvel élan au voyage en train

1935 New SS *Normandie* is biggest, fastest, most sophisticated vessel afloat, with innovative hull by Vladimir Yourkevitch

Mit ihrem innovativen Rumpf von Wladimir Yourkewitsch ist die neue SS *Normandie* das größte und schnellste Schiff der Zeit

Le nouveau *Normandie*, le navire le plus grand, le plus rapide et le plus sophistiqué alors à flot, présente une coque innovante conçue par Vladimir Yourkevitch

1935 Glen Martin designs flying boats – the M-130, or China Clipper; Norman Bel Geddes redesigns interiors for Pan Am

Glen Martin entwirft Flugboote wie M-130 oder China Clipper; Norman Bel Geddes überarbeitet für Pan Am die Interieurs

Glen Martin invente des bateaux volants – le M-130, ou le China Clipper ; Norman Bel Geddes reconçoit les intérieurs des appareils de la Pan Am

1937 Hindenburg disaster, killing 36 people, essentially ends passenger travel by dirigible

Die Hindenburg-Katastrophe mit 36 Toten bedeutet letztlich das Ende für Reisen per Luftschiff

La catastrophe du Hindenburg, 36 morts, met quasiment un terme au transport de passagers par dirigeable

◄ Italian Line, 1934

Californians Inc., 1937

►► Thompson Products, 1935

LE MAELSTRÖM FINANCIER DE LA GRANDE DÉPRESSION ENGENDRA UNE GRANDE CONFIANCE DANS LE POUVOIR DU DESIGN ÉPURÉ. « La force brute », déclara le visionnaire du design industriel Raymond Loewy, « peut avoir un aspect très sophistiqué, voire extrêmement raffiné, tout en étant un monstre de puissance ».

Quand les grands designers industriels aiguisaient la forme des trains – les transformant dans leurs moindres détails jusqu'aux shakers à cocktail – ils en accéléraient aussi la vitesse. Le City of Salinas (ou M-10 000) d'Union Pacific Railroad, premier train léger et aérodynamique, fut lancé en février 1934. Quelques mois plus tard, l'élégant Burlington Zephyr vivait son baptême du rail en filant vers Chicago pour l'exposition « Un Siècle de Progrès ». Henry Dreyfuss reconçut chaque aspect du Mercury de la New York Central Line en 1936, un exploit surpassé par la transformation qu'il imposa au 20th Century Limited. Il réinventa le moindre élément de ce train aérodynamique de luxe qui reliait New York à Chicago en 16 heures, de la locomotive à la vaisselle en porcelaine, en passant par les sachets de sucre. En 1936, la compagnie Pennsylvania Railroad demanda à Raymond Loewy de reconcevoir la locomotive électrique GG1. En 1939, la S-1 en forme de torpille qu'il inventa pour le Broadway Limited éblouit les visiteurs de l'Exposition Universelle de New York.

Quant à Averell Harriman, propriétaire de l'Union Pacific Railroad, il ne se contenta pas d'inventer un train : il créa une destination. En 1936, il inaugura Sun Valley Lodge, la toute première station de sports d'hiver du pays. Un mélange d'élite hollywoodienne et de têtes couronnées déferla alors sur les pistes enneigées de Ketchum, Idaho.

Les années 1930 virent aussi décollage du voyage aérien. En 1930, Boeing recruta des hôtesses de l'air pour rendre les voyages plus agréables. L'année suivante, Igor Sikorsky conçut et construisit le premier Clipper pour la compagnie Pan American World Airways. Ces « bateaux volants » capables de se poser sur l'eau proposaient des voyages de luxe à prix exorbitants. Par exemple, l'aller-retour San Francisco/ Manille coûtait 1710 dollars en 1937, un montant supérieur au salaire annuel de l'Américain moyen. Pendant ce temps, le

nouveau Douglas DC-3 enflamma l'imagination du pays grâce à son fuselage en aluminium scintillant, ses cabines insonorisées, ses conduits d'aération, ses sièges rembourrés et sa haute altitude de croisière. Capable de transporter 28 passagers d'une côte à l'autre en 15 heures, ce fut le premier avion à devenir rentable en transportant seulement des passagers.

En 1936, les vols en avion ne représentaient toutefois que 7,6 % du marché des voyages longue distance. Sur le marché du luxe, le *Normandie*, navire le plus grand, le plus rapide et le plus sophistiqué alors à flot, effectua sa première traversée en 1935. Le paquebot français possédait une coque innovante conçue par Vladimir Yourkevitch pour voyager plus confortablement. Ce furent toutefois ses intérieurs Art Déco modernes et épurés signés par de grands artistes français comme Jean Dunand, Raymond Subes et Jean Dupas qui retinrent l'attention du public.

Tous ces luxes – certes uniquement accessibles aux passagers de première classe – et les nombreux progrès technologiques améliorèrent les conditions de voyage en dépit de sévères turbulences économiques. Ce sentiment d'espoir se refléta lors de l'Exposition Universelle de New York en 1939. Son thème, « Le Monde de Demain », rayonnait d'optimisme quant aux futures merveilles de l'industrie du transport.

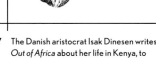

1937 San Francisco's iconic Golden Gate Bridge opens to the public

Einweihung der Golden Gate Bridge, des neuen Wahrzeichens von San Francisco

Ouverture au public du Golden Gate Bridge, l'emblème de San Francisco

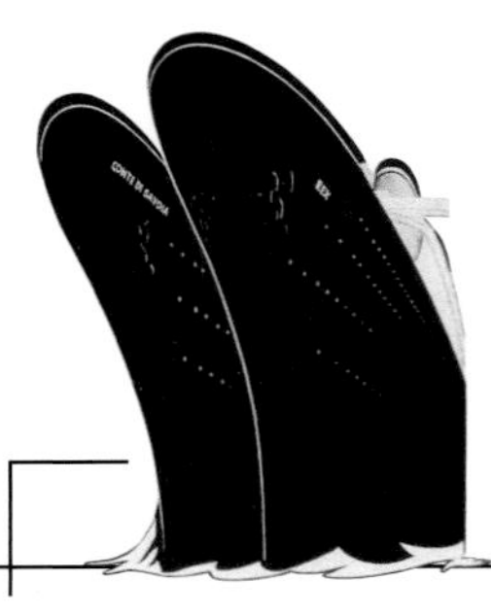

1937 Italian Line acquires SS *Rex* and SS *Conte di Savoia*; this ad is essence of haute deco, but their interiors are grandly classical

Die Italian Line erwirbt die SS *Rex* und SS *Conte di Savoia*; trotz Anzeige im Haute-Déco-Stil im Innern aber klassisch

La Società di Navigazione italienne achète le *Rex* et le *Conte di Savoia* ; contre toute attente, les intérieurs des navires restent très classiques

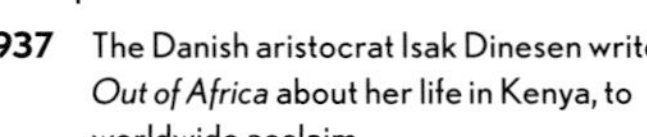

1937 The Danish aristocrat Isak Dinesen writes *Out of Africa* about her life in Kenya, to worldwide acclaim

Die dänische Aristokratin Tania Blixen erlangt Weltruhm mit dem Roman *Afrika, dunkel lockende Welt* über ihr Leben in Kenia

L'aristocrate danoise Isak Dinesen, alias Karen Blixen, écrit *La Ferme Africaine*. Ce livre racontant sa vie au Kenya est plébiscité dans le monde entier

1939 World War II begins

Ausbruch des Zweiten Weltkriegs

Début de la Seconde Guerre mondiale

Southern California, 1934

► Southern California, 1935

The biggest movie stars of the '30s were exquisitely aerodynamic. Actresses like Marlene Dietrich, Claudette Colbert, and Carole Lombard had such hollowed cheekbones and sharply sculpted jaws that they could have posed for the hood ornaments on fancy, super-chic 1930s cars. The kind few people were buying, except in movies.

Auch die größten Filmstars der 1930er-Jahre waren überaus aerodynamisch. Schauspielerinnen wie Marlene Dietrich, Claudette Colbert und Carole Lombard besaßen derart hohle Wangen und markante Kinnpartien, dass sie als Kühlerfiguren der tollsten Schlitten jener Zeit hätten posieren können. Von der Art, wie sie sich kaum jemand zulegte, außer in den Kinofilmen.

Les plus grandes stars de cinéma des années 1930 étaient d'une beauté aérodynamique. Des actrices comme Marlene Dietrich, Claudette Colbert et Carole Lombard avaient les joues tellement creuses et les mâchoires si sculptées qu'elles auraient pu inspirer les décors de capots des voitures de luxe super chic de la décennie. Du genre que peu de gens achetaient, sauf dans les films.

HOLLYWOOD *alone is worth the trip*

A BRILLIANT premiere in Hollywood. At intermission, the smart world fills the forecourt. Celebrities from the four corners of the earth. A scene you'll remember the rest of your life . . .

But the studios and the stars are just one part of this many-sided Southern California vacation. Tomorrow you're aquaplaning on a mile-high lake, deep in the pine forest. Next day, basking on a sandy beach or sailing to Catalina's palm-fringed shore.

Each day, new adventures. Golf, racing, tennis, polo—all in fascinatingly unfamiliar surroundings. Interesting cities: Los Angeles, Pasadena, Long Beach, Glendale, Beverly Hills, Pomona, Santa Monica. Flowers, orange groves, vineyards. Secluded resorts. Missions the Spanish Padres built . . . the peace and mystery of "Mother Mexico."

Give yourself this stimulating *change* this summer. You can do it easily even in a 2-weeks vacation, and costs are ridiculously low. Remember too, summer days in Southern California are rainless, and you'll sleep under blankets at night.

Free automatic trip planner

Your Southern California trip plans itself through this unique new book which gives you the whole story from the time you leave home till you're back again: What to see and do, over 100 pictures, maps, itemized cost schedules, etc. . . impartial information not available elsewhere.

ALL-YEAR CLUB OF SOUTHERN CALIFORNIA

Come to California for a glorious vacation. Advise anyone not to come seeking employment, lest he be disappointed; but for tourists, the attractions are unlimited.

SOUTHERN CALIFORNIA

All-Year Club of Southern California, Div. C-4, 1151 So. Broadway, Los Angeles, Calif.

Send me *free* book with complete details (including costs) of a Southern California vacation. Also send free routing by ☐ auto, ☐ rail, ☐ plane, ☐ bus, ☐ steamship. Also send free booklets about counties checked: ☐ Los Angeles, ☐ Santa Barbara, ☐ Orange, ☐ Inyo, ☐ Riverside, ☐ San Diego, ☐ Ventura, ☐ Imperial, ☐ Mission Trails, ☐ San Bernardino.

Name ______________ *Street* ______________

City ______________ *State* ______________

NEW ADVENTURE
A view of Sydney harbor . . . evoking admiration for Australia and the youthful vitality of its young civilization . . . playing . . . building . . . achieving a new order on the world's oldest continent. Strange contrasts—almost within sound of today's busy traffic—unique survivals of human and animal life found in no other part of the world. A voyage to this South Seas continent offers a *new adventure.*
Join a Matson *"South Pacific Cruise" personally escorted all-inclusive-cost—to Australia! via Hawaii! Samoa! Fiji! New Zealand!* Never before in travel! A 46-day cruise from California, *every month of the year.* No more than 5 days between ports. Smart elegance of magnificent liners..."Mariposa" or "Monterey"...emphasizing your enjoyment of the voyage. Similar attractive fares if you travel independently. ☆ *Your travel agent is an authority, see him for information, or any of our offices.*
The OCEANIC STEAMSHIP COMPANY
MATSON LINE
New York, 535 Fifth Ave. · Chicago, 230 No. Michigan Ave. · San Francisco, 215 Market St. · Los Angeles, 730 So. Broadway · Seattle, 814 Second Ave. · Portland, 327 Southwest Pine St.

Isles of Repose

FOR VETERANS OF THE FAIR

When you've "done" the World's Fair, and you feel pretty well "done" yourself, come to this nearby tranquil retreat, Bermuda.

Nothing occurs with rush or clatter in this coral Arcady next door. Life is thrilling enough at bicycle pace. Motor traffic is banned by a humane Parliament, along with smoke-belching chimneys, fumes, and like disturbers of the peace.

Here, in this land of fun and flowers, is the balm for all your sorrows (including hay-fever). Even the climate beguiles you. Forever pleasant, it offers year-round indulgence in your favourite sports . . . golf . . . sailing . . . game fishing . . . tennis . . . bathing on rose-tinted beaches.

As a fillip to the Fair, nothing could be more fitting than a sojourn in this spot so beautifully strange.

BERMUDA IS NEAR THE NEW YORK WORLD'S FAIR . . . BY SEA OR BY AIR — Luxury liners travel from New York to Bermuda in 40 hours . . . a round-trip total of nearly 4 days of shipboard life. Sailings from Boston, too. • Splendid new transatlantic planes now take off from New York and Baltimore, Maryland, and descend at Bermuda 5 hours later . . . an enchanting experience in the sky. • A wide choice of accommodations is provided by Bermuda's many hotels and charming cottages. • No passport or visa is required.

Bermuda
PLEASURE ISLAND

FOR BOOKLET: *Your Travel Agent, or The Bermuda Trade Development Board, 30 Rockefeller Plaza, N.Y.C., or Victory Bldg., Toronto.*

DARK TANS for Fair People

Now that you're here for the New York World's Fair, it would be a shame to miss seeing Bermuda. This coral isle is within 40 hours of New York by sea . . . and only 5 by air.

Here, to Bermuda, come sun-worshippers from all the world, to pilgrimage on beaches of pinkish coral sand. They are gathered there this very morning.

Observe their pleasant ritual: Lying relaxed, they face the sun (you can see the effect of these devotions in the golden bronze of their skins). They sip long, cold drinks. They discourse lightly on the excellence of Bermuda golf . . . the low price of English and continental goods . . . the fun of bicycling to formal dances . . . the magnificence of the view from St. David's and Gibb's Hill Lighthouses.

Surely, you owe it to yourself to see this enchanting and colourful spot before you return from the Fair.

BERMUDA IS WITHIN EASY REACH OF THE NEW YORK WORLD'S FAIR

YOU CAN GO BY SEA OR BY AIR — Luxury liners travel from New York to Bermuda in 40 hours . . . a round-trip total of nearly 4 days of shipboard life. Sailings from Boston, too. ● Splendid new transatlantic planes now take off from New York and Baltimore, Maryland, and descend at Bermuda 5 hours later . . . an enchanting experience in the sky. ● A wide choice of accommodations is provided by Bermuda's many hotels and charming cottages. ● No passport or visa is required for Bermuda.

Bermuda
PLEASURE ISLAND

FOR BOOKLET: Your Travel Agent, or The Bermuda Trade Development Board, 30 Rockefeller Plaza, New York City, or Victory Building, Toronto.

◂ Matson Line, 1934

Bermuda, 1939

Bermuda, 1940

French Line, 1934

This French Line ad describes the voyage as being "sybaritic," for the company's sumptuous first-class luxuries were heralded. Even in 1934, when the Great Depression was crushing the world economy, wealthy travelers sought out this line—and a subsidy from the French government helped keep it afloat.

Diese Anzeige der French Line spricht von einer „schwelgerischen" Reise, um die in der ersten Klasse gebotenen Annehmlichkeiten zu verkünden. Ungeachtet der Weltwirtschaftskrise entschieden sich betuchte Reisende noch 1934 für diese Reederei, die durch Finanzspritzen des französischen Staates über Wasser gehalten wurde.

Cette publicité pour la « French Line » présente le voyage comme « voluptueux » pour vendre le luxe première classe de la compagnie. Même en 1934, alors que l'économie mondiale souffrait de la Grande Dépression, les voyageurs fortunés plébiscitaient cette compagnie. Le gouvernement français lui octroya une subvention pour la garder à flot.

▶ French Line, 1931

Lady in Waiting

MONTAGE CREATED FOR THE FRENCH LINE BY HALICKA, PARIS

She might have served at the court of Versailles, this femme de chambre from Brittany. Pleasant and deft and courteous, she invents a hundred little unobtrusive attentions to make life a luxurious affair. For she is bred, through long apprenticeship, in the French Line tradition of service. ● Every voyager on France-Afloat is accorded such devotion as Royalty itself enjoys. Merely to wish is to be obeyed. There is a whole regiment of attentive stewards and stewardesses . . . who not only speak English, but seem actually to interpret one's unspoken whims. And every attendant, from the four-foot page-boys to the maître d'hôtel, is concerned, personally and intimately, with life's amenities. ● How could a French Line crossing be anything but Sybaritic? The food, for example, is considered by connoisseurs to be the flower of French cuisine . . . and it is served with an engaging and appropriate grandeur. (Enter caviar . . . cupped by the claws of a life-size eagle sculptured in gleaming ice!) Everything about France-Afloat . . . the atmosphere, the appointments, the company . . . contributes to a thoroughly successful crossing. ● May we point out that in spite of its many luxuries, a French Line passage costs no more? Any travel agent will be glad to arrange your booking . . . and there is no charge to you for his services. . . . French Line, 19 State Street, New York City.

French Line

PARIS. June 9 and 30. July 21. August 11 and 30. September 18. October 6 • **ILE DE FRANCE.** June 16. July 7 and 28. August 18. September 8 and 29. October 20 • **LAFAYETTE.** June 13. July 3. August 25. September 15 • **CHAMPLAIN.** June 2 and 23. July 15. August 4. September 22

RACKETS and riveters . . . cross-town traffic and subways . . . brownstone fronts with basement entrances . . . conferences and conventions and sales charts . . . six o'clock friends and parlor games . . . aren't you in your soul of souls fed up with them?

The sulphur and molasses season is at hand. Now is the time when executives come back from lunch wondering why nothing tastes good any more. Now is the time, also, when smart people give themselves a taste of good salt air and a few weeks abroad.

"Seymour," they say (if their budget includes a Seymour), "get out the trunks. We're off on the Vasty Deep." Or if, like most of us, they have no Seymour, they just pack a few bags, hail a taxi, and say: "Pier 57, North River."

And presto! the moment they set foot on deck, they're in France! . . . Bronzed and mustachioed tars, whose Breton forefathers saw America before Columbus . . . well-trained English-speaking servants within call . . . all is well-ordered for these fortunate travelers. They speed eastward . . . eating marvelous food . . . basking . . . walking . . . dancing . . . and in general doing whatever they darn well please. And they step ashore feeling already a different person altogether!

Ask your travel agent about voyaging on France Afloat . . . and as the skyline vanishes from view, wave your hand, sniff the salt breeze, and say: "Good-bye to all that!" The French Line, offices in the larger cities of the United States and Canada, or at 19 State Street, New York City.

French Line

ILE DE FRANCE, April 8, April 30 • • LAFAYETTE, April 16, May 21 • • DE GRASSE, April 5, May 10 • •
ROCHAMBEAU, April 30 • • PARIS, May 14 • • • FRANCE (West Indies Cruise, April 8), April 22, May 27

Lido Entertains at Sea
Engaging little groups . . . on open-air verandahs . . . or around a sunny, outdoor pool. Wherever they gather, Lido's distinguished guests are entertained with deft and gracious skill.
For superb luxury . . . for the matchless freedom of the Southern Route's world-famous "outdoor-life-at-sea" . . . and for congenial fellow-travelers—on your trip to Europe—go Lido!
Choose the Rex or gyro-stabilized Conte di Savoia for speed . . . or, for a more leisurely crossing, select the Roma, Saturnia or Vulcania. Consult your TRAVEL AGENT or Italian Line, 624 Fifth Ave., New York. Offices in Philadelphia, Boston, Cleveland, Chicago, Los Angeles, San Francisco, New Orleans, Montreal, Toronto.
Italian Line

Winter takes a Lido holiday

LIDO DECK—Conte di SAVOIA

WINTER goes a-summering on the Southern Route! Though the calendar wears a frosty look, it knows no power to change the bright skies, the blue waters, the friendly temperatures . . . as your Italian liner approaches mid-ocean, skirts the Azores, pauses at Gibraltar and moves serenely on into the placid Mediterranean.

"Lido" takes command! Thanks to the beneficent weather . . . and thanks many times over to the design and construction of Lido ships . . . your Winter crossing is transformed into a beach-revel of warmth and sunshine. For this is the *open-air* way to all Europe, especially in the cold months. Board the great Rex, the gyro-stabilized Conte di Savoia or the charming Roma, for an express voyage. Or treat yourself to the leisurely nine or ten port itinerary of the popular Vulcania or Saturnia . . . if you can afford the time to *see more* on your way to Europe.

In either case, be sure to pack your favorite beach-robe and sandals!

The Thermometer Tells the Story! . . . 69° is a fairly normal noon temperature on a typical Southern Route crossing . . . though it may be freezing at home. Ask your Travel Agent for our illustrated weather-map booklet giving comparative statistics: "Why It's Called the Mild Southern Route".

The leading **TRAVEL AGENTS** *in your city are our representatives. Consult them freely—their services are gratis. Or apply to our nearest office: New York, Philadelphia, Boston, Cleveland, Chicago, Los Angeles, San Francisco, New Orleans, Montreal, Toronto.*

THE CONTE DI SAVOIA . . . MIDNIGHT!

THE miraculous Southern Route sun has gone down . . . and the scene changes utterly. Instead of beach slacks . . . it's "white tie and tails". Instead of deck tennis, fencing, traps . . . it's music and champagne . . . or Asti Spumante, if you prefer to "do as the Romans do", as you probably will. For of course this is an Italian ship, offering all the warmth and subtlety of Italy's wines and table delicacies as well as those of other countries. Daytime Lido brought first fame to the Italian Line, with its sweeping play-decks and pools. Lido after dark brings the crowning mark of elegance to your Wintertime outdoor crossing. Choose the great Rex, the gyro-stabilized Conte di Savoia, or the charming Roma, for an express voyage. Or enjoy the more leisurely route of the Vulcania or Saturnia, with their eight or nine extra ports to entertain you on the way. All are true Lido leaders . . . by day or night!

The leading **TRAVEL AGENTS** *in your city are our representatives. Consult them freely—their services are gratis. Or apply to our nearest office: New York, Philadelphia, Boston, Cleveland, Chicago, Los Angeles, San Francisco, New Orleans, Montreal, Toronto.*

ITALIAN LINE

◄ Italian Line, 1939

Italian Line, 1938

Italian Line, 1937

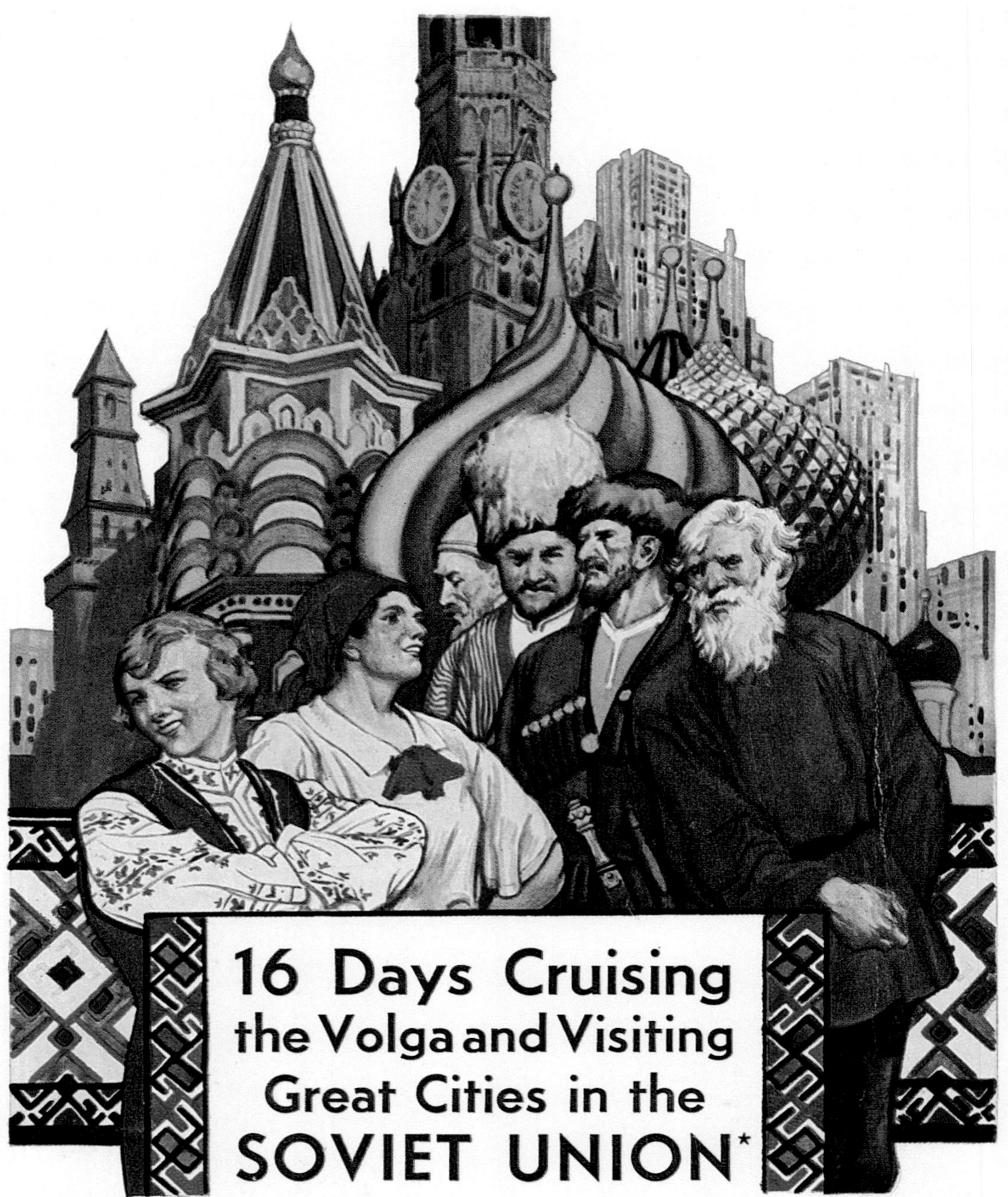
16 Days Cruising
the Volga and Visiting
Great Cities in the
SOVIET UNION*

An experience that will give you a trip of remarkable contrasts ranging from Tartar villages to the new social and industrial planning of vital Soviet cities. *Leningrad* with its palaces and museums . . . *Moscow* with its tremendous activities . . . *Nizhni-Novgorod* with its ancient romance and huge modern projects . . . 4 days on the mighty Volga following the course of many nationalities, traditions, and cultures . . . *Stalingrad* with its gigantic metal and tractor works . . . and then by return train to *Moscow*.

INTOURIST provides everything—hotels, meals, all transportation, sightseeing, theatre tickets, Soviet visa, and the services of English-speaking guides.

Other tours of unusual interest: *Moscow and Leningrad*, 5 days, $70; 7 days, $85. *Caucasus and Crimea*, 24 days, $240 up; *Volga, Caucasus and Crimea*, 30 days, $300 up. *Caucasus and Georgia*, 20 days, $200 up. Three tours to *Turkestan*. Industrial Tours.

★ $192 for two together, Second Class; $240 for one alone. Greatly reduced rates for groups of three and four together.

Write for General Booklet X4. INTOURIST, Inc., 261 Fifth Avenue, New York • 304 N. Michigan Boulevard, Chicago • 756 S. Broadway, Los Angeles. • *Or see your own travel agent.*

TRAVEL IN THE SOVIET UNION

Intourist, Inc., 1935

► *Travel*, ca. 1930

Hawaii WILL LIVE IN YOUR HEAR
forever
Matson Line TO Hawaii
NEW ZEALAND • AUSTRALIA • via SAMOA • FIJI
Complete details of exhilarating Matson South Pacific voyages may be secured from all Travel Agents or Matson Line—Oceanic Line, New York, Chicago, San Francisco, Los Angeles, San Diego, Seattle, Portland.
Hawaiian hotel reservations at the beautiful Royal Hawaiian and Moana at Waikiki may now be made when you book steamer passage. An added convenience for Matson travelers.
S. S. LURLINE • S. S. MARIPOSA • S. S. MONTEREY • S. S. MALOLO
Hawaii's floral beauty photographed in natural

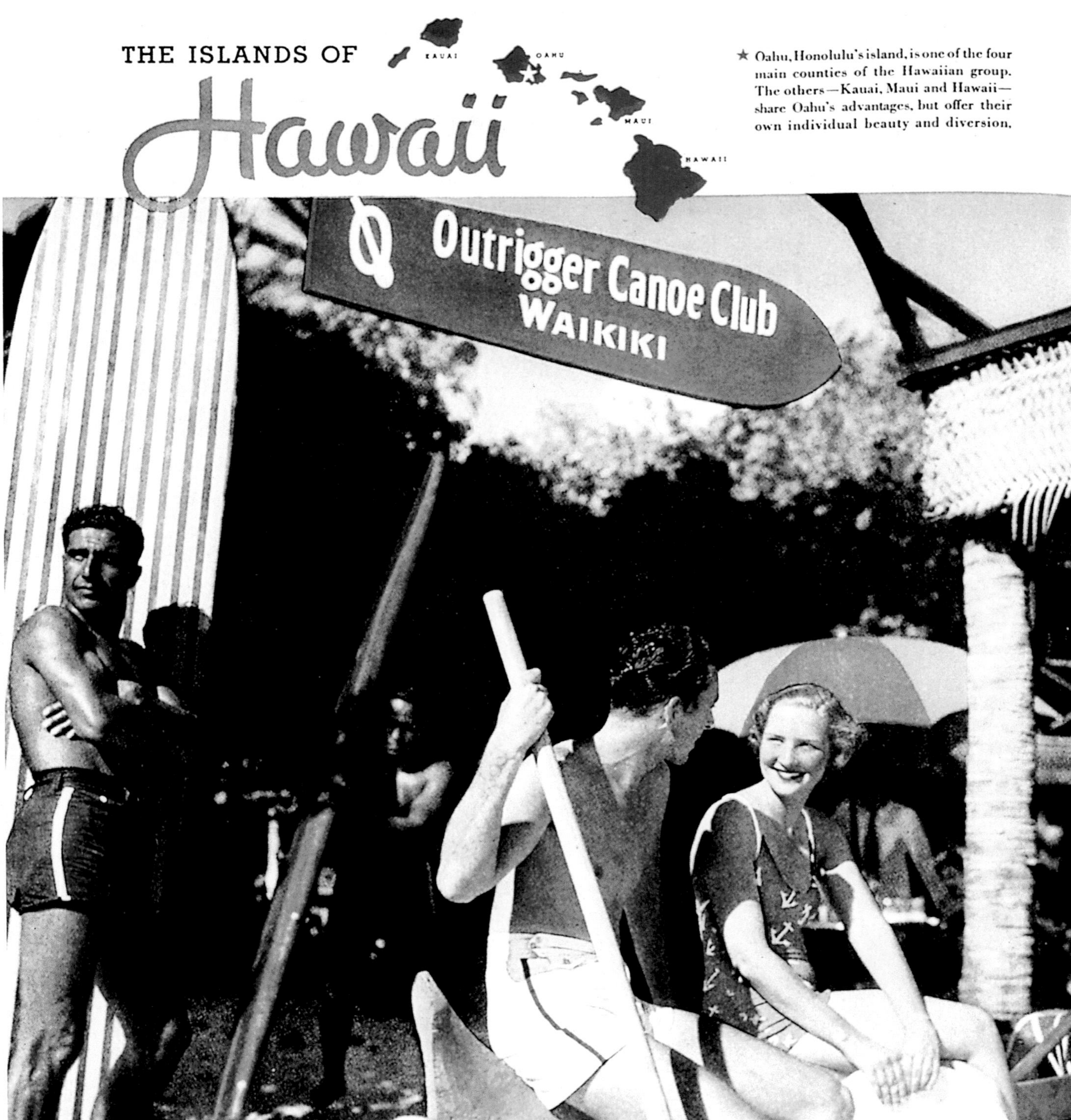

THE ISLANDS OF
Hawaii
KAUAI
OAHU
MAUI
HAWAII
★ Oahu, Honolulu's island, is one of the four main counties of the Hawaiian group. The others—Kauai, Maui and Hawaii—share Oahu's advantages, but offer their own individual beauty and diversion.
Outrigger Canoe Club
WAIKIKI

ROBERT MACK COPYRIGHT HAWAII TOURIST BUREAU 1936

★ *At play in Honolulu. Natural color photograph taken in Hawaii*

Waikiki—*the world's most famous beach is only part of Hawaii's great diversity!* All of her islands are rimmed by superb beaches . . . white sands, black sands, "barking" sands . . . shaded by slanting coco-palms, washed by lazy surf. You may swim in perfect comfort at any time by clock or calendar . . . midnight or noon . . . January or June!

Behind her shorelines, high-speed motor-roads wind through verdured canyons . . . past plantation-lands . . . and climb to the inspiring summits of great volcanoes.

Behind her gaiety and varied pleasures is *Hawaii, the community*, modern and American. A community of fine schools . . . lovely homes . . . *shops that are fashion centers.* A land of boundless energy . . . imparting to all an unique joy of living.

When *you* turn westward to these isles like no other place in the world . . . let us know your sailing-date, that we may welcome you . . . with scented necklaces fresh woven from our native flowers . . . the Aloha *lei* greeting, proud tradition of Hawaii! Nowhere else does a community say "how-do-you-do" with such sincerity and grace. *Write us by all means.*

From routine to rapture is an instant change! Swift, luxurious steamships sailing from Los Angeles, San Francisco or Vancouver, B. C. speed over this glorious sea-way in less than five days. Our booklet, "Nearby Hawaii" and "Tourfax" bulletin contain complete information, invaluable in planning your visit. Free, from your railway, steamship, or travel agent, or Hawaii Tourist Bureau, 40 Main Street, San Francisco, Calif.; 722 West Olympic Boulevard, Los Angeles, Calif.

This Bureau, with headquarters at 765 Bishop Street, in Honolulu, is a non-profit organization, maintained by

THE PEOPLE OF HAWAII

to enable you to obtain accurate information on any subject concerning the entire Territory of Hawaii, U. S. A.

◂ Matson Line, 1938

Hawaii Tourist Bureau, 1936

The American Way.. of getting places!
☆ The amazing speed and superb comfort of Flagship travel and the dependability of American's nation-wide day-and-night service provide a striking example of the American public *getting what it wants*. There are many who are not yet aware of the extent, the economy or the convenience of air travel. To these people, regular Flagship patrons say: "Fly once, and you'll fly always!" Call your Travel Agent today for Flagship schedules and fares. Or phone the nearest office of American Airlines, Inc.
AMERICAN AIRLINES Inc.
ROUTE OF THE FLAGSHIPS
AMERICAN AIRLINES INC.
SYSTEM MAP

American Airlines, 1939

► American Airlines, 1939

By the end of the '30s, airplanes had begun to change the nation's travel plans. Air passengers no longer had to rough it, since planes now offered a far smoother ride, as well as temperature control, soundproofing, and stewardesses. This wealthy businessman might well have been a likely passenger.

Im ganzen Land sah sich das Reiseverhalten ab Ende der 1930er-Jahre durch das Flugzeug zunehmend beeinflusst. Flugreisende mussten nun nicht mehr einiges einstecken, denn die neuen Maschinen boten einen weitaus ruhigeren Flug sowie Temperaturregulierung, Schalldämmung und Stewardessen. Dieser betuchte Geschäftsmann könnte durchaus als Passagier infrage gekommen sein.

A la fin des années 1930, l'avion avait commencé à modifier les projets de voyage des Américains. Les passagers aériens n'avaient plus à voyager à la dure, car les avions étaient désormais plus confortables, insonorisés, équipés du chauffage, de la climatisation et même d'hôtesses de l'air. Ce riche homme d'affaires aurait fait un passager tout à fait crédible.

►► Pennsylvania Railroad, 1938

The Pennsylvania Railroad brought in the leading designer Raymond Loewy to overhaul its *Broadway Limited*. He placed a streamlined sheath on the S1 locomotive, detailed with five horizontal bands of gold. When his sleek interiors and remarkable exterior were revealed in 1938, the public gasped—and hurried aboard.

Pennsylvania Railroad beauftragte den führenden Designer Raymond Loewy mit der Neugestaltung des *Broadway Limited*. Loewy gönnte der Lok S1 eine stromlinienförmige, mit fünf waagerechten Goldstreifen verzierte Verkleidung. Als man 1938 das elegante Interieur und beachtliche Exterieur präsentierte, hielten die Menschen den Atem an – und eilten an Bord.

La compagnie Pennsylvania Railroad fit appel au grand designer Raymond Loewy pour métamorphoser son train *Broadway Limited*. Il entoura la locomotive S1 d'un revêtement aérodynamique décoré de cinq rayures horizontales dorées. Quand ses intérieurs épurés et son extérieur remarquable furent dévoilés en 1938, le public en resta bouche bée – et se précipita à bord.

Here I am -- the fellow who said he would never fly!
"If I'd thought it was anything like this, I'd have been flying long ago! Here I am, enjoying undreamed-of travel comforts, seeing beauty I never knew existed, saving days of time! It's not costing me a penny more, but I'm sure getting more!"
Most everyone who flies has at one time said: "I'll never fly!" But wisdom whispered: "Don't be too sure. It's a big thing! Better try it and see." And so they flew . . . and alighted from their first flights, elated, discoverers of a new world! You, too, have only to fly to know that travel by air is a reality for thousands every day and night the whole year around, and that the sooner you adopt flying, the sooner you catch up with other modern-day folks! American Airlines, Inc., Dept. E-20, 20 North Wacker Drive, Chicago.
Serving America's Major Cities From Coast to Coast

PENNSYLVANIA RAILROAD PRESENTS

A FLEET OF MODE

HERE'S THE FLEET OF MODERNISM!
(Standard Time)

BROADWAY LIMITED

Lv. New York	5:00 P.M.
Lv. Philadelphia	6:20 P.M.
Ar. Chicago	8:00 A.M.
Lv. Chicago	3:30 P.M.
Ar. Philadelphia	7:09 A.M.
Ar. New York	8:30 A.M.

THE GENERAL

Lv. New York	3:40 P.M.
Lv. Philadelphia	5:09 P.M.
Ar. Chicago	7:50 A.M.
Lv. Chicago	3:15 P.M.
Ar. Philadelphia	8:01 A.M.
Ar. New York	9:30 A.M.

LIBERTY LIMITED

Lv. Washington	5:10 P.M.
Lv. Baltimore	5:55 P.M.
Ar. Chicago	8:35 A.M.
Lv. Chicago	3:10 P.M.
Ar. Baltimore	8:02 A.M.
Ar. Washington	8:50 A.M.

"SPIRIT OF ST. LOUIS"

Lv. New York	5:15 P.M.
Lv. Philadelphia	6:38 P.M.
Lv. Washington	5:30 P.M.
Ar. St. Louis	12:42 P.M.
Lv. St. Louis	12:15 P.M.
Ar. Washington	9:55 A.M.
Ar. Philadelphia	8:24 A.M.
Ar. New York	9:50 A.M.

All trains air-conditioned. P.R.R. Luxury Coaches and Improved Section Sleepers on all trains except the all-room Pullman train — Broadway Limited.

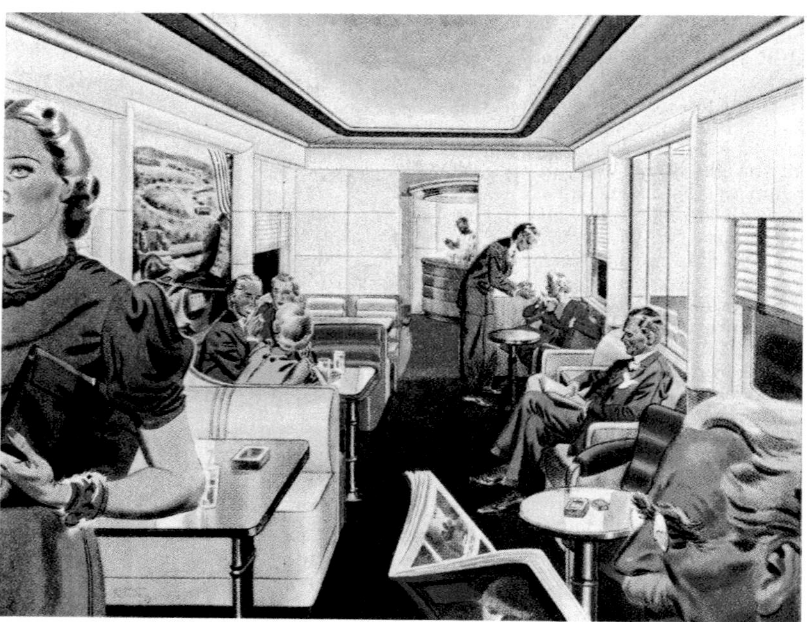

Bar Lounge: Designed in collaboration with the Pullman Company by Raymond Loewy, creator of smart modern interiors. Interestingly placed divans . . conversation corners in richly cushioned fabrics . . low broad upholstered settees . . venetian blinds . . a magnificent mural, facing long triple-panelled mirrors . . a fan-wise bar within easy hail. Soft shades predominate in the color scheme and lighting which are soothing, not flamboyant.

Master Suites (on Broadway and Liberty Limiteds) Something entirely new in private accommodations. Twc rooms, not one. The first, a handsome lounge in sof colors, with radio and other modern furnishings (at night twin beds); the second, a private bathroom with shower

ISM
Observation Cars: Here the designer's art is conspicuously evident. Crescent-shaped divans . . low tabourets . . deep carpeting . . lounge chairs informally arranged, the lighting soft but radiant. The whole effect distinctively casual, as in a smart club. A richly appointed buffet adjoins the main lounge. Anything missing? Yes, the open observation platform. Now it is glass-enclosed luxury!
BROADWAY
LIMITED
P U L
M E T R
INTO SERVICE WEDNESDAY, JUNE 15, 1938, LED BY A NEW AND FINER
BROADWAY LIMITED
First All-Room Train in History . . Daily Between New York and Chicago . . 16 Hours!
CK TRAINS are reborn—a whole fleet of them. nt innovations in comfort and style. Even car s and dimensions change. All this, achieved by ration of Pennsylvania Railroad and Pullman any engineers and Raymond Loewy, noted designer.
's all yours to enjoy in air-conditioned travel on lvania Railroad routes uniting New York, Phila- a, Baltimore, Washington and other leading cities Chicago and St. Louis.
w types of private accommodations, a wider than ever before available on any train. In ad- to new versions of drawing rooms, compart- double bedrooms, you now have . . the Master Suite, the Roomette, the Duplex. Each has a definite individuality, and all have nice soft beds—6 feet, 5 inches long—and private toilet facilities.
Nor is that all. New personality is given the fleet leader . . *Broadway Limited*. Staffed with valet, barber, manicurist, maid and train secretary, this leader becomes an all-room Pullman train. Privacy for every passenger. New-style diners, too—excitingly different. Faster schedule also—New York to Chicago in 16 hours!
Coupled with the new electrified mileage east of Harrisburg, this *Fleet of Modernism* now makes travel on the Pennsylvania Railroad even more attractive than ever before. Enjoy it!
Roomettes give you a private little world of your own. Comfortably compact, this accommodation provides . . personal toilet and washing facilities, illuminated mirror, enclosed wardrobe and, at night, a full-length bed which dips down at your finger's touch.
BY DAY *a cheery sitting room*
BY NIGHT *a cozy bedroom*
ennsylvania Railroad

◂ Hawaii Tourist Bureau, 1932

This ad promises that you can leave your troubles behind, for Hawaii was indeed far away. But after Amelia Earhart's first solo flight between Hawaii and California in 1935, air travel developed. Franklin D. Roosevelt was the first president to visit Hawaii, staying at Matson's luscious Royal Hawaiian Hotel in 1934.

Diese Anzeige verspricht, dass man seine Sorgen zurücklassen kann, denn Hawaii war in der Tat weit entfernt. Doch Amelia Earharts erster Alleinflug 1935 von Hawaii nach Kalifornien bildete gleichsam den Startschuss für die Flugreisen. Franklin D. Roosevelt besuchte 1934 als erster US-Präsident Hawaii und übernachtete in Matsons reizendem Royal Hawaiian Hotel.

Cette publicité promettait que vous pouviez laisser vos soucis loin derrière vous, puisque Hawaï se trouvait littéralement très loin. En 1935, après le premier vol en solitaire d'Amelia Earhart entre Hawaï et la Californie, les liaisons aériennes se développèrent. Franklin D. Roosevelt fut le premier Président à visiter Hawaï. Il séjourna au splendide Royal Hawaiian Hotel de la compagnie Matson en 1934.

Dollar Steamship Lines, 1935

Christmas Present

A happy, carefree cruise Round the World . . . designed to your order . . . starting whenever you choose . . . taking 85 days to two years.

Visits to 21 Fascinating Ports PHILIPPINE DUGOUT AND VINTAS

Exciting days and nights in the great cosmopolitan ports of Cuba and Panama, California, Hawaii, Japan, China, the Philippines, Malaya, India, Egypt, Italy, and France . . . 14 fascinating far-flung countries.

Low Shore Costs INDIA HAS BRAND NEW THRILLS

Ask your own Travel Agent for all details. Or write Dollar Steamship Lines, 604 Fifth Avenue, New York; 110 South Dearborn Street, Chicago; 311 California Street, San Francisco. Offices in other principal cities.

Luxurious Living ALONG THE SUNSHINE ROUTE

World-famed President Liners have broad play-decks and an outdoor swimming pool . . . every stateroom outside (with real twin beds) . . . menus made up from the best the whole wide world affords.

Stopovers and Sidetrips Anywhere PEKING SIDETRIP

Weekly sailings from New York, Los Angeles and San Francisco allow stopovers and sidetrips anywhere en route . . . continuation on the next or another of these world's only regular-world-cruising ships.

Round the World

CRUISES TO ORDER

COST JUST $854 FIRST CLASS

•

DOLLAR
Steamship Lines

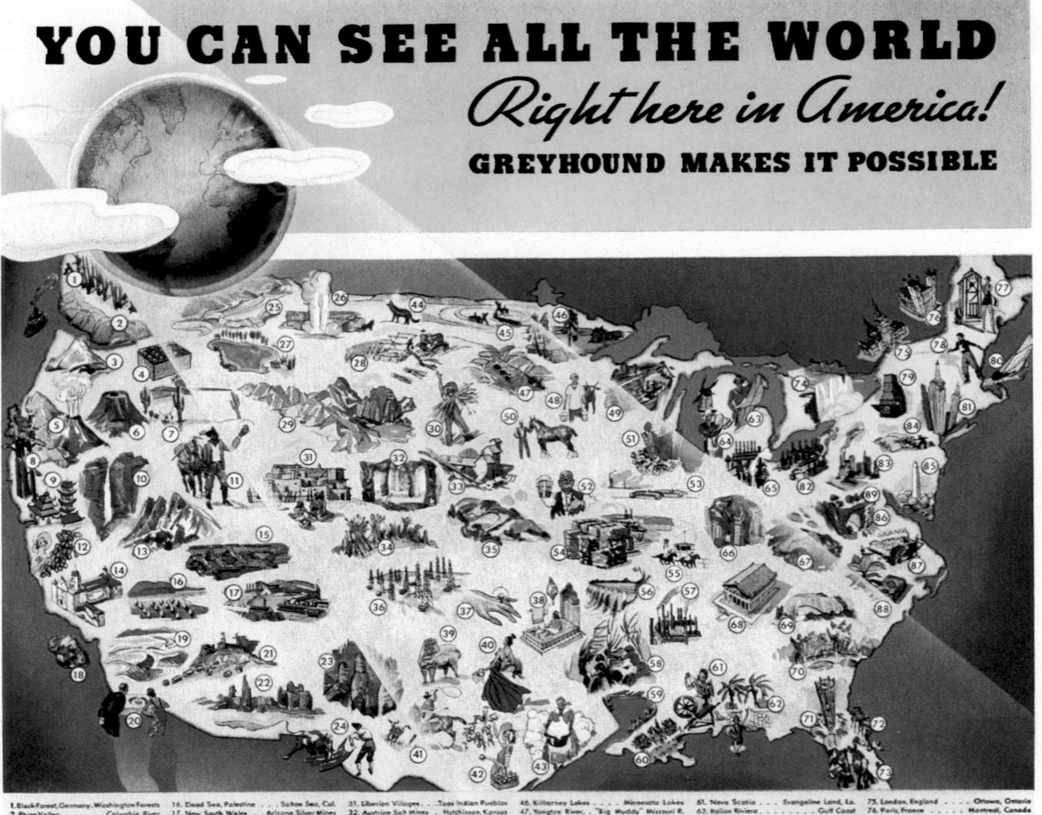

1. Black Forest, Germany . Washington Forests
2. Rhine Valley . . . . . . Columbia River
3. Mt. Fujiyama, Japan . Mt. Hood, Oregon
4. Normandy, France . . . Oregon Apples
5. Mt. Vesuvius . . . . . . Mt. Lassen, Cal.
6. Lake Bracciano, Italy . Crater Lake, Ore.
7. Arabian Deserts . . . . Nevada
8. Australian Trees . . Cal. Giant Redwoods
9. China . . . . . San Francisco Chinatown
10. Sutherland Falls, N. Z. . . . Yosemite Falls
11. Transvaal, S. Africa . Nevada Gold Mines
12. Vineyards of Italy . . . . . Fresno, Cal.
13. Himalaya Mts. . . . . Sierra Nevada Mts.
14. Old Spain . . . . . California Missions
15. Petra, Arabia . . . Grand Canyon, Ariz.
16. Dead Sea, Palestine . . . Salton Sea, Cal.
17. New South Wales . . Arizona Silver Mines
18. Isle of Capri . . . . Catalina Island
19. Sahara Desert . . . . . Yuma Sand Dunes
20. Monte Carlo . . . . Agua Caliente
21. Egypt (near Cairo) . . Ariz. Petrified Trees
22. Inca Temples, Peru . . Casa Grande, Ariz.
23. Arlsburg Grotto, Austria . Carlsbad Caverns
24. Spanish Bull Fights . . . . Juarez, Mexico
25. Alaska . . . . . . Glacier National Park
26. New Zealand Geysers . . . . Yellowstone
27. Issyk Kul, Russia . . . . . Great Salt Lake
28. Australia . . . . . . Dakota Wheat Fields
29. Swiss Alps . . . . . . Rocky Mt. Nat. Park
30. Odessa, Russia . . . Kansas Wheat Fields
31. Liberian Villages . . . Taos Indian Pueblos
32. Austrian Salt Mines . Hutchinson, Kansas
33. Bolivia, Lead & Zinc Mines . . Joplin, Mo.
34. South Africa . . . . . Kansas Kafir Corn
35. Cheviot Hills, England . . Missouri Ozarks
36. Baku, Russia . . . . . Amarillo Oil Fields
37. Kimberley, Africa . Arkansas Diamond Mines
38. Baden-Baden, Germany . Hot Springs, Ark.
39. Astrakhan, Russia . Texas, (karakul sheep)
40. Monterrey, Mex. . . . San Antonio, Texas
41. Argentine Pampas . . . . . Texas Ranges
42. Sicily, Orange Groves . Rio Grande Valley
43. Nile Valley, Egypt . . . . . Texas Cotton
44. Russian Steppes . . . . . Montana Plains
45. Gellivare, Sweden . Hibbing Iron Mines
46. Killarney Lakes . . . . Minnesota Lakes
47. Yangtze River, . "Big Muddy" Missouri R.
48. Holland Dairies . . . Wisconsin Dairies
49. Defile des Ecrots, France . Wisconsin Dells
50. Brussels, Belgium . Kansas City (horse show)
51. Buenos Aires, Argentina. Chicago Stock Yards
52. Munich, Germany . . . St. Louis Breweries
53. Brooklands, England . Indianapolis Speedway
54. Cairo, Egypt . . . . Memphis (cotton port)
55. Epsom Downs, England . Churchill Downs, Ky.
56. Dnieper Project, Russia . . Muscle Shoals
57. Birmingham, England . Birmingham, Ala.
58. Cuban Sugar Cane . . . . Louisiana
59. Kiel Canal, Germany . Houston Ship Canal
60. Marseilles, France . . . . . New Orleans
61. Nova Scotia . . . Evangeline Land, La.
62. Italian Riviera . . . . Gulf Coast
63. Yokohama, Japan . Belding Silk Mills, Mich.
64. Holland . . . . . Holland, Mich. (tulips)
65. Citroen Auto Plants, Paris . . Detroit, Mich.
66. Fingal's Cave, Scotland . Mammoth Cave, Ky.
67. Scotch Highlands . . . Great Smoky Mts.
68. Parthenon, Greece . . Parthenon, Nashville
69. India (Jain Colossus) . Atlanta, Ga. (Stone Mt.)
70. Tuileries Gardens, Paris . Magnolia Gardens, Charleston, S. C.
71. Bruges, Belgium . Bok Carillon Tower, Fla.
72. Waikiki, Hawaii . . . . Florida Beaches
73. Malay Tropics . . . . Florida Everglades
74. Victoria Falls, S. Africa . . . Niagara Falls
75. London, England . . . . Ottawa, Ontario
76. Paris, France . . . . . Montreal, Canada
77. Brighton Beach, Eng. . . Bar Harbor, Maine
78. St. Moritz, Switzerland . . Lake Placid, N. Y.
79. Jena, Germany . Rochester, N.Y., (cameras)
80. Hull, England . . Gloucester, Mass. (fishing)
81. All Nations . . . . New York City
82. The Ruhr, Germany . . . . Cleveland, O.
83. The Saar, Germany . . . . Pittsburgh, Pa.
84. Belleau Wood, France . Gettysburg, Nat. Park
85. Jap. Cherry Blossoms . . Washington, D. C.
86. Pont d'Arc, France . . . Natural Bridge, Va.
87. Lancashire, Eng. . . . Piedmont Textile Mills
88. Turkey . . . . Carolinas (tobacco)
89. English Fox Hunting . Virginia Hunt Clubs

The whole world is at your finger-tips! Strange and thrilling scenes from every foreign land—interesting people, customs, and industries of every nation—all are found right here within the borders of America—and all can be reached in short, pleasant trips by Greyhound bus.

This unusual map cannot begin to tell the story. You will at once think of other places right in your home state, which can as easily be compared with foreign scenes, natural and man-made wonders, mountains, lakes, rivers . . . they count up into thousands! The cost of reaching them by Greyhound is exceedingly low—far less than operating even a small private automobile, yet comfort, safety and convenience of schedules are exceptional. Why not plan your *round-the-world-cruise-at-home* for this very summer?

PRINCIPAL GREYHOUND INFORMATION OFFICES

CLEVELAND, OHIO . . . . E. 9th & Superior
PHILADELPHIA, PA . . . . Broad St. Station
CHICAGO, ILL. . . . . 12th & Wabash
NEW YORK CITY . . . . Nelson Tower
BOSTON, MASS. . . . . 230 Boylston St.
WASHINGTON, D. C., 1403 New York Ave., N. W.
DETROIT, MICH. . . . . Tuller Hotel
CINCINNATI, OHIO . . . . 109 East 7th St.
CHARLESTON, W. VA., 1101 Kanawha Valley Bldg.
SAN FRANCISCO, CALIF. . . Pine & Battery Sts.
FORT WORTH, TEX. . . . . . 8th & Commerce Sts.
MINNEAPOLIS, MINN. . . . 509 6th Ave., N.
LEXINGTON, KY. . . . . 801 N. Limestone
NEW ORLEANS, LA. . . . . 400 N. Rampart St.
MEMPHIS, TENN. . . . . 146 Union Ave.
RICHMOND, VA. . . . . . . 412 East Broad St.
WINDSOR, ONT. . . . . 1004 Security Bldg.
LONDON, ENG., A. B. Reynoldson, 49 Leadenhall St.

MAIL THIS FOR INFORMATION, PICTORIAL FOLDERS

Send this coupon to Greyhound information office nearest your home (listed at left), for complete information on any trip you may plan. We will give rates, suggest routes, enclose informational folder. Jot down the city or place you wish to visit, on margin below. No obligation. Paste the coupon on a penny post card if you wish.

Name ________________

Address ________________

City ________________ SP6

Greyhound, 1935

► Greyhound, 1932

Buses were considered a good alternative to trains. One of the Depression's biggest movies acknowledged this. Claudette Colbert stars as a runaway heiress in *It Happened One Night* (1934). She meets a reporter (Clark Gable) on the bus from Florida to New York. Love and many Oscars ensue.

Der Bus galt als eine gute Alternative zum Zug – so auch in einem der größten Kinoerfolge jener Zeit: *It Happened One Night* (*Es geschah in einer Nacht*, 1934) mit Claudette Colbert als Erbin auf der Flucht, die im Bus von Florida nach New York einem Reporter (Clark Gable) begegnet. Liebe und zahlreiche Oscars folgten.

Le bus était considéré comme une bonne alternative au train, comme le prouve l'un des plus grands films de la Dépression. Dans *New York-Miami* (1934), Claudette Colbert incarne une héritière en fuite qui rencontre un reporter (Clark Gable) dans un bus reliant la Floride à New York. S'ensuivirent une célèbre histoire d'amour et de nombreux Oscars.

Over the  King's Highway

—we roll . . seeing the Golden State by Greyhound . . . old Missions, blue Pacific, guardian mountains, giant trees

A STRANGE cavalcade halts in the shade of lordly oaks . . stalwart Spaniards in glittering armor and polished helmets. At their right, sun-flooded hills . . . at their left, the flashing blue Pacific. Their black-bearded captain glances back along the path . . . "A brave trail we are breaking, Cavaliers!" he shouts. "We will call it El Camino Real—the Royal Road—in honor of our King!"

That was 163 years ago. Today, the thousands who travel California's Mission Trail, by Greyhound Bus, find that it has truly earned its proud title. This broad paved road extends northward from San Diego through Los Angeles* and Santa Barbara to San Francisco's Golden Gate . . . revealing old Spanish Missions, shining Monterey Bay, giant redwood trees whose sheer height takes the breath. Greyhound Lines offer not merely the best way to travel anywhere in California, but also the most interesting way to reach Pacific Coast points from anywhere in the Nation. It is the only public transportation with a half-dozen optional routes from ocean to ocean . . . and from Canadian cities to Mexico.

This is the restful, time-saving way for short trips, too. Greyhound buses are healthfully warmed by Tropic-Aire heaters. Exceptionally comfortable chairs recline to any desired position for relaxation or sleep. Frequent rest and lunch stops are scheduled on every trip . . . terminals are right downtown.

45,000 miles of Greyhound routes cover the United States. They will serve you best on business trips, week-end visits or winter excursions to California, colorful Southwest, Gulf Coast, Florida. And remember—every ticket means a substantial saving!

Above—Tinted photograph of Santa Barbara Mission—one of the most beautiful and well-preserved of them all. *At right*—A glimpse of the Pacific through graceful palms. Greyhound offers a delightful 3-Day Tour of the Mission Trail between Los Angeles and San Francisco.

* By all means, come to the Olympic Games at Los Angeles, July 30th to August 14th, this year. And see the Rodeo at Salinas, July 20th to 24th . . . . a rip-roaring flashback to cowboy days!

GREYHOUND *Lines*

These Greyhound Lines Serve the Whole Nation . . . .

CENTRAL-GREYHOUND
E. 11 St. & Walnut Ave., Cleveland, Ohio

PENNSYLVANIA-GREYHOUND
Broad St. Station, Philadelphia, Pa.

ATLANTIC-GREYHOUND
601 Virginia St., Charleston, W. Va.

EASTERN-GREYHOUND
Nelson Tower, New York City

PACIFIC-GREYHOUND
9 Main St., San Francisco, Calif.

PICKWICK-GREYHOUND
917 McGee St., Kansas City, Mo.

CAPITOL-GREYHOUND
405 American Bldg., Cincinnati, O.

RICHMOND-GREYHOUND
42 E. Broad St., Richmond, Va.

NORTHLAND-GREYHOUND
509 6th Ave., N., Minneapolis, Minn.

SOUTHLAND-GREYHOUND
Pecan & Navarro Sts., San Antonio, Tex.

SOUTHEASTERN-GREYHOUND
Lexington, Kentucky

CANADIAN GREYHOUND
1004 Security Bldg., Windsor, Ont.

MAIL THIS TODAY

Send this coupon to the nearest Greyhound office, listed at left, for attractive pictorial booklets on California ☐, or 32 page booklet, "America's Scenic Highways" ☐. Any other information desired:

____

Name______________________________

Address______________________________ SP-2

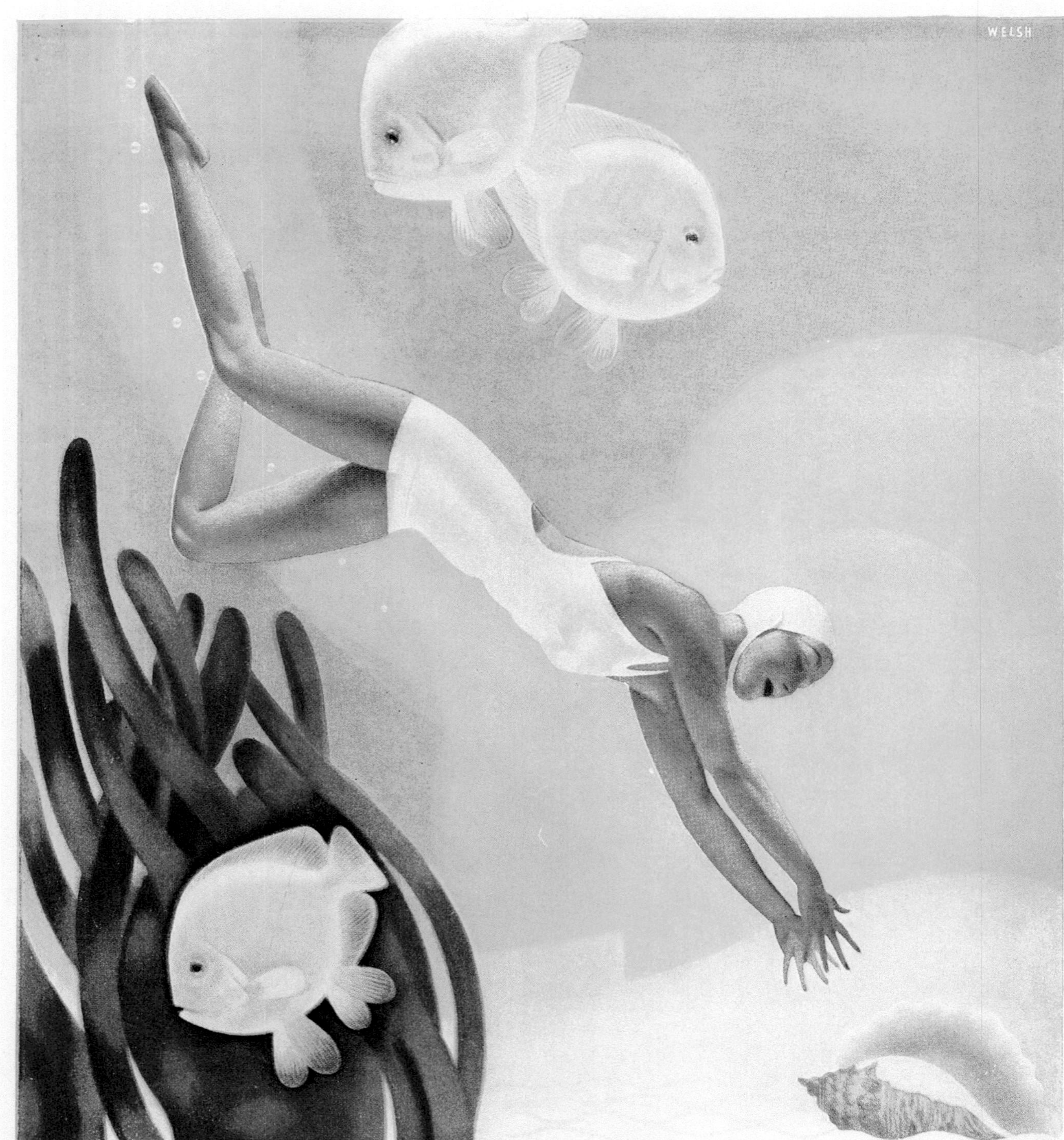

TRAVEL AT REDUCED RATES TO YOUR FAVORITE

SUMMER RESORT

IN Pullman SAFETY & COMFORT

Pullman-Standard, 1937

WELSH
TRAVEL AT REDUCED RATES TO YOUR FAVORITE
SUMMER RESORT
IN Pullman SAFETY & COMFORT

Pullman-Standard, 1937

AMERICA ON PARADE

SKY CHIEF SKY QUEEN SKY MASTER SUN RACER

SKY KING SKY EMPRESS

Every day and every night scores of passengers on TWA are gaining new appreciation of America's beauty. They thrill to the spectacle of California—are speechless at the splendor of Grand Canyon from the sky. The whole colorful West—Sky City of Acoma, Inscription Rock, Boulder Dam, Enchanted Mesa, Painted Desert—delight beyond all expectation. Even the fertile farmlands of the Mississippi Basin are surprisingly interesting. And the approach to New York, the world's greatest city, presents a view that cannot be surpassed.

On business or pleasure, by day or by night, your flight across America via TWA will seem all too short. Douglas Skyliners on all schedules, each equipped with Gyro-Pilots and Automatic Stabilizers, assure smooth, steady, comfortable flight. Call any TWA office, Pennsylvania R. R., or leading hotels and travel bureaus.

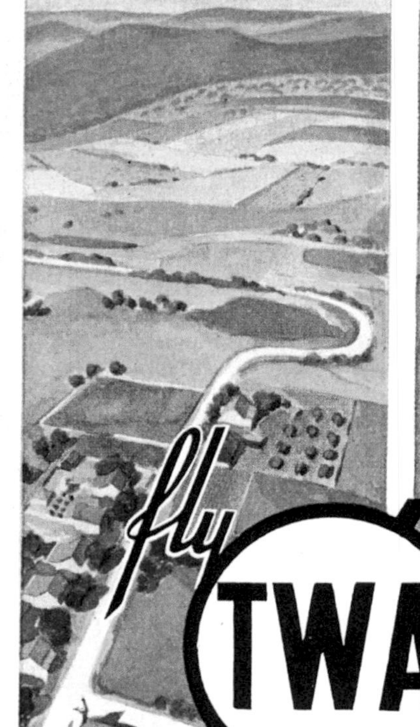

fly **TWA**

THE *Lindbergh* LINE

SAN FRANCISCO
Grand Canyon
ALBUQUERQUE
LOS ANGELES
WINSLOW
AMARILLO
WICHITA
KANSAS CITY
TWIN CITIES
ST. LOUIS
INDIANAPOLIS
CHICAGO
DETROIT
COLUMBUS
PITTSBURGH
NEW YORK
BOSTON
PHILADELPHIA
WASHINGTON

TRANSCONTINENTAL & WESTERN AIR, INC.

FASTEST
SHORTEST
. . . COAST
TO COAST

◂ TWA, 1935

SS *Normandie*, French Line (Albert Sébille), 1935

This shimmering jewel of the French Line was the fastest and biggest ship at sea. Her lavish art deco and streamline moderne interiors, by leading French artists like Raymond Subes and Jean Dupas, captured the sophisticated travelers' fancy. The vast first-class dining room featured 12 lighting pillars by Lalique.

Dieses funkelnde Juwel der French Line war das schnellste und größte Schiff der Zeit. Verschwenderische Art-déco- und Streamline-Moderne-Interieurs von führenden französischen Künstlern wie Raymond Subes und Jean Dupas fanden Anklang bei den kultivierten Passagieren. Der gewaltige Speisesaal erster Klasse glänzte mit zwölf Lichtsäulen von Lalique.

Ce joyau éblouissant de la Compagnie Générale Transatlantique était le bateau le plus grand et le plus rapide du monde. Signés par des artistes français tels Raymond Subes et Jean Dupas, ses intérieurs Art Déco somptueux, modernes et épurés enflammèrent l'imagination des voyageurs les plus raffinés. L'immense salle à manger de première classe comptait 12 piliers d'éclairage en cristal de Lalique.

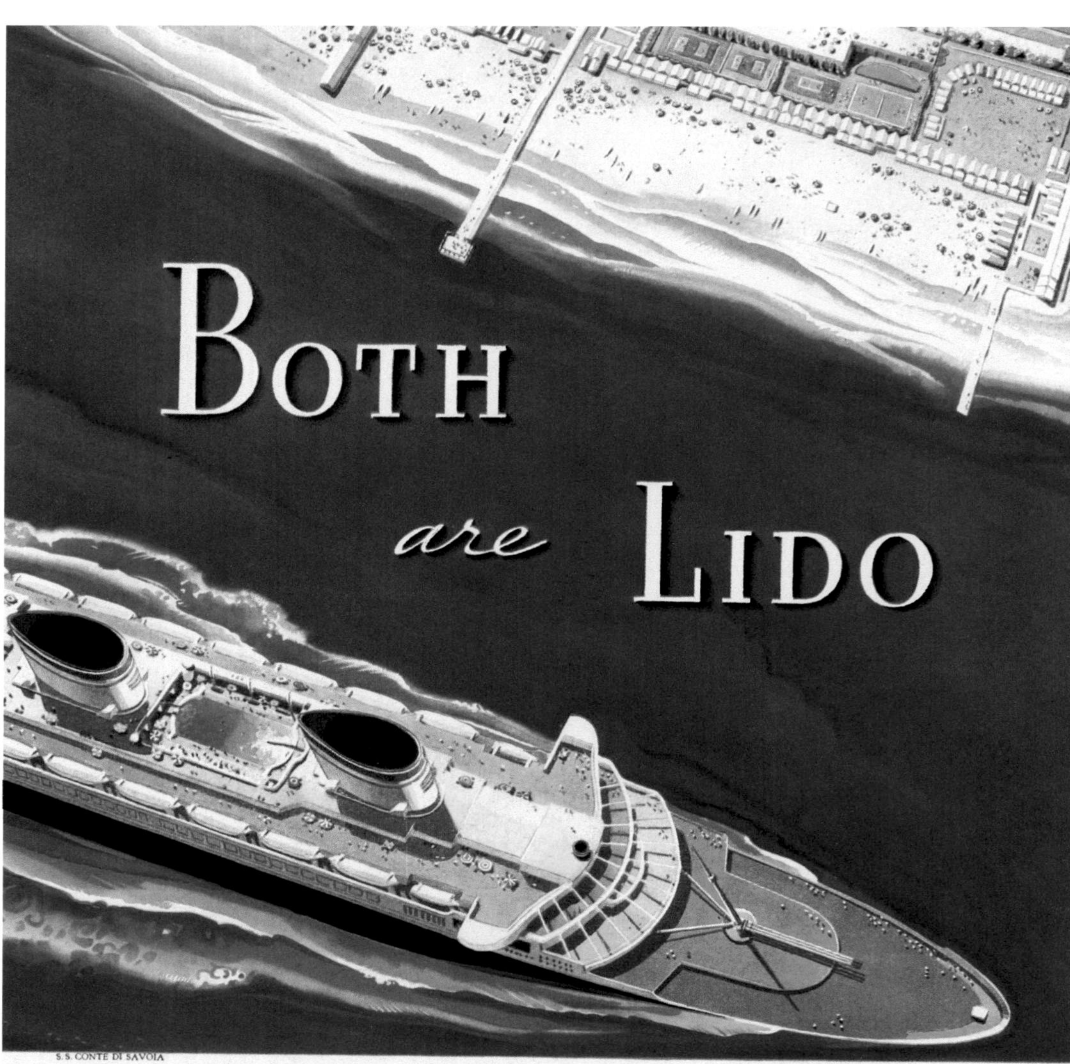

The Lido of Venice . . . and the Lido of Italian liners . . . are sisters under the sun! The famed strip of golden, warm sands, splashed by the turquoise of the Adriatic and set off by the glories of Venice across the Lagoon . . . sees its splendor, its color, its charm, its *Lido life* mirrored on the sweeping decks of the super-liners Rex and Conte di Savoia . . . leaders of the equally famed Italian Line fleet!

Smart Europe flocks to Venice's Lido "in season". Smart America more and more is flocking to the Italian Line's Lido in *all* seasons—because of the outdoor delights, the mildness, the serene comforts of the Southern Route crossing, at any time of the year.

Soon you will be going abroad again. This time, give your trip the added glamour of a Lido crossing . . . and the added 1000 miles or more of Mediterranean cruising at no added cost. There are two ways to go—a direct, express crossing to Naples, Genoa or Nice on the Rex or Conte di Savoia . . . or a leisurely itinerary embracing as many as ten fascinating ports on the popular Roma, Saturnia or Vulcania. And at the end of your Lido voyage, fast trains will speed you to European capitals!

The leading **TRAVEL AGENTS** *in your city are our representatives. Consult them freely—their services are gratis. Or apply to our nearest office: New York, Philadelphia, Boston, Cleveland, Chicago, San Francisco, New Orleans, Montreal, Toronto.*

Italian Line, 1937

The Italian Line was called "the Riviera afloat," and, for emphasis, swimming pools were surrounded by sand and decks were dotted with large beach umbrellas. Grandly classic interiors, as well as the sand, may have reminded passengers of the Lido, the Venice beach.

Die Italian Line wurde auch „schwimmende Riviera" genannt. Wie um dies zu betonen, verteilte man Sand rund um die Schwimmbecken und übersäte die Decks mit großen Strandschirmen. Stattliche klassische Interieurs und auch der Sand mögen den Gast an Venedigs Strand, den Lido, erinnert haben.

La Società di Navigazione était surnommée « la plage en pleine mer ». D'ailleurs, ses piscines étaient entourées de sable et ses ponts équipés de grands parasols. Les grandioses intérieurs classiques et le sable rappelaient peut-être le Lido – la plage de Venise – aux passagers.

► Alaska, 1935

THE GLACIERS ARE BIGGER

1935 "See Alaska" YEAR

The largest glaciers in the world are along the coast of Alaska. You can snowball upon them in summer—yet in June and July, wild flowers in profusion fringe their edges!

A most unusual country is Alaska. Imagine, if you will, a land where a baseball game can be played at midnight without artificial light! Where totem poles stand next to telephone poles in modern towns. Where vines grow three inches over night, in gardens near glacial fields of ice.

Travel by train across America. We have *air-conditioned* trains which are cool, clean, quiet and safe. Relax as you ride. Arrive at Seattle, refreshed and ready to sail. How much vacation time have you? Two weeks, three, or four? We can give you an Alaskan trip to exactly fit your time and pocketbook. And nowhere in the world can you find a vacation paradise to equal this enchanted land. May we figure costs from your home town?

in ALASKA

For free Alaska literature, write any of The All-American Services to Alaska:

NORTH WESTERN LINE
Dept. N-8, Chicago, Illinois

ALASKA RAILROAD
Dept. R-8, 333 North Michigan Avenue, Chicago, Illinois

THE MILWAUKEE ROAD
Dept. M-8, Chicago, Illinois

BURLINGTON ROUTE
Dept. B-8, Chicago, Illinois

GREAT NORTHERN RAILWAY
Dept. G-8, St. Paul, Minnesota

NORTHERN PACIFIC RAILWAY
Dept. P-8, St. Paul, Minnesota

UNION PACIFIC RAILROAD
Dept. U-8, Omaha, Nebraska

ALASKA STEAMSHIP COMPANY
Dept. A-8, Seattle, Washington

◂ Pan Am Clipper, 1938

Well-suited for the Clipper. These passengers, clearly too wealthy to be brought down by the Great Depression, are boarding a Clipper, the boat-plane that soared across the Pacific and Atlantic. Juan Trippe, the Pan Am chairman who developed the Clipper, was continually looking to keep his airline out ahead.

Genau richtig: Diese Passagiere, eindeutig zu reich, um von der Weltwirtschaftskrise in die Armut getrieben zu werden, steigen gerade in eine flinke Clipper ein – jenes Flugboot, das auf dem Pazifik wie Atlantik verkehrte. Juan Trippe, Chef von Pan Am und Entwickler der Clipper, war stets darauf bedacht, dass seine Fluglinie die Nase vorn hatte.

Bien habillés pour le Clipper : ces passagers, apparemment trop riches pour souffrir de la Grande Dépression, embarquent à bord d'un Clipper, le « bateau volant » qui traversait le Pacifique et l'Atlantique. Juan Trippe, le Président de la Pan Am qui développa le Clipper, cherchait constamment à préserver la longueur d'avance de sa compagnie aérienne.

United Air Lines, 1930

▸▸ Western Railroads, 1935

NEW WORLD'S RECORDS BY UNITED AIR LINES

☆ With a new fleet of 3-mile-a-minute, Wasp-powered Boeings, United Air Lines is giving the fastest service ever maintained with multi-motored planes. New York-Chicago is a morning, afternoon or evening flight. Chicago-Pacific Coast an overnight journey. And New York-California a trip of less than one day. These are world's records.

☆ The public's response to this service is to use it. During 1933 United Air Lines carried approximately 125,000 passengers. Another world's record.

☆ United's new Boeing planes make every provision for the passengers' comfort. Heated spacious cabins.

Stewardess service. Lunches served aloft included in economical fares.

60,000,000 MILES FLYING EXPERIENCE

CALIFORNIA TO NEW YORK . . . 20 HRS.
3 flights daily each way

CHICAGO TO NEW YORK . . . 4¾ HRS.
10 flights daily each way

CALIFORNIA TO CHICAGO . . . 14½ HRS.
3 flights daily each way

FT. WORTH-DALLAS TO CLEVELAND . . . 9 HRS.
2 flights daily each way

LOS ANGELES TO SEATTLE . . . 8 HRS.
2 flights daily each way

(West bound schedules slightly longer due to prevailing winds.)

Consult new United Air Lines' time table for schedule to intermediate and off-line points

UNITED AIR LINES

Subsidiary of United Aircraft & Transport Corporation

☆ Adjustable reclining chairs for relaxation or for sleeping during night flights.

☆ United Air Lines' year-round service utilizes every known aid to avigation. Multi-motored planes manned by two transport pilots. Two-way radio. Directive radio beam. Lighted airways. Frequent weather reports.

☆ Fly with United Air Lines — the fastest and most interesting way to travel. ☆ For schedules, tickets or reservations to 137 cities . . . call United Air Lines' ticket offices, Hotel Porters, Travel Bureaus, Postal or Western Union. ☆ Air Express — Phone Air Express Division, Railway Express Agency. Use Air Mail — it speeds business.

Two veteran pilots (averaging 4,000 hours of flying) on every multi-motored plane.

Now

REAL TRAVEL ECONOMY

Basic fares on Western Railroads are as low as 2c per mile round trip for sleeping car travel; correspondingly low for coaches and chair cars. Sleeping car accommodations one-third lower; no surcharge. Special bargains in Summer Excursion tickets on sale daily. All-Expense Tours available at railroad ticket offices and tour agencies. Ship your auto at reduced rates and travel in comfort by train. Your dollar goes farther on Western Railroads. See any railroad ticket agent.

TRAVEL BY TRAIN

to PACIFIC NORTHWEST • ALASKA • CALIFORNIA • SAN DIEGO EXPOSITION • AMERICAN ROCKIES • DUDE RANCHES • OZARKS • TEXAS GULF COAST • NORTH WOODS AND LAKES • SOUTHWEST • OLD MEXICO • NATIONAL PARKS • RESORTS OF EVERY CHARACTER

WESTERN TRAINS are *Air-Conditioned*

. . . FARES IN THE WEST ARE LOW . . .

● The Golden West is calling all Americans this year with a lavish list of wonderful attractions easily reached on air-conditioned trains. • Air-conditioning on wheels! The greatest contribution to travel comfort in 25 years! . . . Providing air so cool and clean that you look and feel "fresh as the breath of spring—*while* you travel and *when* you arrive." . . . Luxurious cars so quiet you relax at once into a delighted sense of well-being. . . . Air-conditioning makes the *finest* travel service in the world. And Western Railroads have made it the *most economical.* • All principal trains west of Chicago, St. Louis, Memphis and New Orleans have been air-conditioned. Western Railroads have spent millions of dollars in this improvement. But it costs you *not one penny extra.* These trains also offer incomparable dining car service at prices surprisingly modest. • So travel in the West this summer and really see America. Travel by train and enjoy ideal weather from the moment you leave regardless of climatic conditions en route. Save money. Save time. Travel at ease, in comfort and peace of mind. Train schedules are dependable. Train travel is safer. • Don't be satisfied with less modern transportation. For train travel in the West costs so little, offers so much.

On your Western Tour by train see at least one National Park

Consult any railroad representative for rates, routes, schedules or literature on places to visit

Visit Quaint Old Mexico

Keep Cool in the Rockies

Play on Pacific Beaches

See the National Parks

Walk Among the Big Trees

144

FOR A GLORIOUS TRIP TO

• Turn romantic pages of history in Germany. The time-mellowed ruins of ancient castles, the tomb of Charlemagne, the elaborate Guild Halls of medieval cities, the Romanesque and Gothic cathedrals of Cologne, Freiburg, Worms and Speyer, and Frederick the Great's palace of Sanssouci . . . these and many others . . . What glories of the past they echo! . . . What message of romance they bring you—as you tour through Germany . . . while operas and festivals, stage-craft and symphonies evidence in word and music the undying genius of Goethe, Wagner, Beethoven and Bach.

But the world marches on in Germany, also . . . Here you will find 20th Century progress. Or all modern sports and many that are uniquely German — piloting gliders on the Wasserkuppe or breasting the Rhine in a Faltboat. Then, too, there are great cities like Berlin, with their gay night life, splendid theatres, hotels and restaurants . . . And centers of culture, art and merrymaking like Munich, as famed for its museums as for its brew . . . Dresden, Nürnberg, Frankfurt, Stuttgart, Bayreuth, Weimar — all with a connotation of their own.

As for scenery: the Bavarian Alps, the Black Forest, Harz and Thuringia . . . the castles and vineyards of the Rhine and its gentle-flowing tributaries, the fruit trees and gardens of the Bergstrasse, the lovely sweep of sea and sky along the Baltic and North Sea. And the charm of Germany's famous health resorts.

All this you can enjoy, and more . . . in perfect comfort whether in hotel, train or steamer . . . good living at moderate prices, ***still further reduced by the use of registered Travel Marks.*** And the German Railroads grant you ***60% reduction of rail fares.*** Now is the time to see Germany. Begin planning your trip today.

CONSULT YOUR TRAVEL AGENT AND WRITE FOR BOOKLET 48

GERMAN RAILROADS INFORMATION OFFICE

665 Fifth Avenue at 53rd Street, New York, N. Y.

65

Hamburg-American Line, 1934

German Railroads Information Office, 1938

Workers' Club, Moscow

16 Days in 4 Great Cities of the SOVIET UNION $192*

TRAVEL IN THE

SOVIET UNION

XIth OLYMPIC GAMES
AUGUST 1·16th
BERLIN

GERMANY

● Olympic Year is the World's Festive Year in Germany. The XIth Olympic Games are centered in a grand programme of exciting attractions: The Bayreuth Wagner Festival Plays, the Munich Opera Festivals, International Olympic Art Exhibitions, brilliant theatricals, interesting expositions and conventions. German genius for organization has timed these events so that you can enjoy them during a glorious vacation in Germany. In addition: Scenic grandeur and natural beauty . . . famous health resorts . . . romantic castles . . . picturesque folk festivals . . . medieval towns . . . cosmopolitan cities . . . the Rhine. Modern travel comfort and the traditional hospitality of the land of Wanderlust and Gemütlichkeit. Railroad fares reduced 60% and Registered Travel Marks at low rates. Write for booklet 83.

GERMAN RAILROADS INFORMATION OFFICE

665 Fifth Avenue at 53rd Street, New York

Intourist, Inc., 1931

German Railroads Information Office, 1936

HARPER'S BAZAAR

SPECIAL REDUCED FARES ....TO THE ORIENT

Low Summer Rates

● Never before have such attractive rates to the Orient been offered to the American public. Round trip summer rates to Yokohama are now equivalent to approximately one-and-one-half minimum rates first, cabin, second, and tourist classes. ● De luxe first, second, and cabin classes from San Francisco and Los Angeles via Honolulu. Every comfort of the twentieth century on great new express motor liners. Magnificent dancing salons ...tiled swimming pools...gymnasiums...public rooms, the work of European stylists...and menus that would make any languid appetite laugh in eager anticipation. ● Also splendid new cabin and tourist cabin motor liners almost as luxurious... from Seattle and Vancouver direct to Japan.

JAPAN, CHINA and the PHILIPPINES

From Pacific Coast to Japan and Return

FIRST CLASS	CABIN CLASS	TOURIST CABIN
• $465	• $375	• $195 UP •

Now is the time to see the wonderful lands of the East. Full details as to rates and the exceptional service given on N. Y. K. ships are described in beautifully illustrated literature. Call or write to Department 19.

N·Y·K·LINE

(Japan Mail)

New York, 25 Broadway, 545 Fifth Avenue San Francisco, 551 Market Street • Seattle, 1404 Fourth Avenue • Chicago, 40 North Dearborn Street • Los Angeles, 605 South Grand Avenue • or any Cunard Line office. Consult your local tourist agent. He knows.

◂ *Harper's Bazaar* (Erté), 1933

N.Y.K. Line, 1932

New York World's Fair, 1939

► Chicago Century of Progress, 1934

Throughout the '30s, technology seemed to keep pace with the public's expectations. Innovations were regarded as destined to make life – and travel – more comfortable and enjoyable, despite the woes of the Great Depression. The 1933–34 Chicago World's Fair celebrated the wonders of modern technology with "A Century of Progress."

Während der gesamten 1930er-Jahre vermochte die Technologie offenbar mit den Erwartungen der Menschen Schritt zu halten. Von den Neuerungen erwartete man, dass sie das Leben wie das Reisen angenehmer und bequemer machten, ungeachtet aller durch die Weltwirtschaftskrise bedingten Sorgen. Die Chicagoer Weltausstellung 1933/34 zelebrierte die Wunderdinge der modernen Technik und den Fortschrittsglauben mit „A Century of Progress".

Tout au long des années 1930, la technologie sembla en phase avec les attentes du grand public, qui considérait que les innovations devaient rendre la vie – et le voyage – plus confortable et plus agréable, malgré la misère de la Grande Dépression. « Un Siècle de Progrès », l'Exposition Universelle de Chicago en 1933 et 1934, célébra les merveilles de la technologie moderne.

Your Keys to Chicago
MARSHALL FIELD AND COMPANY

THE POSTWAR ERA EMBRACED THE PREWAR INVENTION OF AIR CONDITIONING. WARM CLIMATES SUDDENLY FELT MORE CONGENIAL, AND PALM SPRINGS, FOR ONE, THRIVED.

ALS DIE WAFFEN WIEDER RUHTEN, GRIFF MAN GERN AUF DIE SCHON VOR DEM KRIEG ERFUNDENE KLIMAANLAGE ZURÜCK. PLÖTZLICH LIESS ES SICH IN WARMEN GEFILDEN BESSER AUSHALTEN, UND ORTE WIE PALM SPRINGS BOOMTEN.

L'APRÈS-GUERRE VIT L'ADOPTION D'UNE INVENTION D'AVANT-GUERRE : L'AIR CONDITIONNÉ. LES CLIMATS CHAUDS DEVINRENT SOUDAIN PLUS ATTIRANTS, ET PALM SPRINGS, ENTRE AUTRES, CONNUT UNE ÈRE DE PROSPÉRITÉ.

1940

WHEN THE WAR WAS WON
SIEGERMACHT USA
UN MONDE EN GUERRE

-1949

5505
000
PENNSYLVAN

◂ Pennsylvania Railroad, 1946

Association of American Railroads, 1944

AFTER THE INFAMOUS ATTACK ON PEARL HARBOR ON DECEMBER 7, 1941, PRESIDENT FRANKLIN D. ROOSEVELT DECLARED WAR ON GERMANY AND JAPAN. The United States immediately began to mobilize for World War II. Within weeks, gas and rubber rationing brought leisure travel to a near halt as American industry focused on the war effort.

Only one modern urban hotel was conceived and built between the start of the Great Depression and the end of World War II: the 1943 Washington Statler (now the Capitol Hilton). The Secret Service was consulted on its design, so the hotel could accommodate Roosevelt and his New Deal administration. The main entrance was in back, with a covered motorcar driveway, and a special elevator could bring the president's car directly to the ballroom level.

When the war ended in 1945, America rushed to make up for lost time. Greyhound Bus Lines, for one, could begin production on Raymond Loewy's designs for its Silversides motorcoach. Loewy also retooled the dog logo for a sleeker look.

The postwar era embraced the prewar invention of air conditioning. Warm climates suddenly felt more congenial. Palm Springs, for one, thrived. The desert city's image as elite playground was crystallized by Frank Sinatra. In 1946, the singer made his first million, and, to celebrate, commissioned an air-conditioned desert home. The E. Stewart Williams design—low-slung, glass-walled, and flat-roofed, with glass doors bringing the outside in—was the quintessence of the Palm Springs Modern movement.

That same year, the first air-conditioned hotel in America, Billy Wilkerson's Flamingo, opened in Las Vegas, with a casino, nightclub, and hotel suites under one roof. There were no clocks in the casino, encouraging gamblers to lose track of time. The city's gambling revenues increased 56% between 1941 and 1944, demonstrating to the Flamingo's financier, gangster Bugsy Siegel, and the mobsters who backed him, just how much money could be made in tourism—especially

gambling. (Lucky Luciano also put Cuba on the gambling map in '46, with a meeting of big mobsters at the Hotel Nacional in Havana.) By 1948, when McCarran Field airport opened in Las Vegas, the gambling capital had become an international tourist destination.

During this same time, well-established hotels received a postwar freshening up. The Beverly Hills Hotel brought in architect Paul R. Williams for renovations and additions in 1947. Society decorator Dorothy Draper oversaw a two-year overhaul of the Greenbrier Hotel, a 19th-century resort in West Virginia, culminating in a three-day reopening gala in 1948. Bing Crosby sang and the Duke of Windsor played drums.

Crosby was key to one of the decade's most effervescent products: Paramount's *Road* pictures. *Road to Singapore* (1940) was the start of a perfect relationship—between Crosby and Bob Hope. The travels of the two castaways continued in *Road to Morocco* (1942) and *Road to Rio* (1947), with slam-bang funny dialogue and insider jokes that the entire audience was in on. If these two fellas could make it on the high seas, anyone could. The democratization of travel was gaining speed.

1940

1940 First transcontinental flight of the Boeing 307 Stratoliner, which Howard Hughes helped design and pay for

Erster Transkontinentalflug der Boeing 307 Stratoliner, an deren Entwurf und Finanzierung Howard Hughes mitwirkte

Premier vol transcontinental du Boeing 307 Stratoliner, au design et au financement duquel Howard Hughes a participé

1942 Las Vegas becomes U.S. "wedding capital," as Clark County issues more than 20,000 licenses

Las Vegas wird zur „Hochzeitshauptstadt" der USA, als vom Clark County mehr als 20 000 Lizenzen ausgegeben werden

Las Vegas devient la « capitale du mariage » lorsque le Conté de Clark délivre plus de 20 000 autorisations

1942 Zany and clever *Road to Morocco* deemed best Bob Hope–Bing Crosby *Road* movie

Premiere der intelligenten Posse *Road to Morocco*, die als bester *Road-to*-Film des Duos Bob Hope/Bing Crosby gilt

Le film déjanté et plein d'esprit *En Route pour le Maroc* est considéré comme le meilleur road-movie du duo Bob Hope/ Bing Crosby

1944 Sonja Henie skating extravaganza, *Sun Valley Serenade*, set in Idaho skiing Mecca

Sun Valley Serenade, ein Film des Eislaufstars Sonja Henie; Schauplatz ist das gleichnamige Skifahrermekka in Idaho

Sortie du film *Tu seras mon mari* avec la patineuse Sonja Henie, tourné dans l'Idaho, la Mecque du ski

Budd, 1945

► American Airlines, 1942

IM ANSCHLUSS AN DEN NIEDERTRÄCHTIGEN ANGRIFF DER JAPANER AM 7. DEZEMBER 1941 AUF PEARL HARBOR ERKLÄRTE PRÄSIDENT FRANKLIN D. ROOSEVELT DEUTSCHLAND UND JAPAN DEN KRIEG. Die Vereinigten Staaten begannen unverzüglich mit den Vorbereitungen. Die Rationierung von Benzin und Kautschuk ließ die Urlaubsreisen binnen weniger Wochen fast auf Null zurückgehen, während die US-Industrie auf Rüstungsgüter umgestellt wurde.

Zwischen dem Beginn der Weltwirtschaftskrise und dem Ende des Zweiten Weltkriegs entstand lediglich ein modernes Stadthotel, nämlich das Washington Statler (das heutige Capital Hilton) von 1943. Der US-Geheimdienst wurde bereits in der Planungsphase hinzugezogen, damit Roosevelt und seine New-Deal-Administration dort sicher waren. Der Haupteingang lag nach hinten, es gab eine versteckte Zufahrt und einen speziellen Lastenaufzug, der die Karosse des Präsidenten direkt auf die Etage mit dem Tanzsaal beförderte.

Als der Krieg 1945 zu Ende war, beeilte sich Amerika, die verlorene Zeit aufzuholen. So konnten etwa die Greyhound Bus Lines nach Raymond Loewys Entwürfen für den Silversides-Bus mit der Produktion beginnen. Das verschlankte Hunde-Logo verdankt sich ebenfalls Loewy.

Auch griff man gern auf die schon vor dem Krieg erfundene Klimaanlage zurück. Nun ließ es sich in warmen Gegenden besser aushalten. Orte wie Palm Springs boomten. Das Image der Wüstenstadt als Spielwiese der Elite zeigt sich am Beispiel Frank Sinatras. Als der Sänger 1946 seine erste Million gemacht hatte, ließ er sich ein voll klimatisiertes Haus in der Wüste bauen. Der Entwurf von E. Stewart Williams – geduckt, mit Flachdach und viel Glas – war der Inbegriff des aufkeimenden Modernismus von Palm Springs.

Im gleichen Jahr wurde in Las Vegas Amerikas erstes klimatisiertes Hotel eröffnet: Billy Wilkersons Flamingo, mit Kasino, Nachtclub und Hotelsuiten unter einem Dach. Die städtischen Einnahmen aus dem Glücksspiel stiegen zwischen 1941 und 1944 um 56 %. Dies zeigte dem Gangster Bugsy Siegel (dem Finanzier des Flamingo), für wie viel Geld der Tourismus gut war – vor allem Glücksspiele. (Lucky Luciano stieg in dieser Sache 1946 auch auf Kuba ein, hierzu versammelten sich einige Gangsterbosse im Hotel Nacional in Havanna.) Als 1948 der McCarran Field Airport in Las Vegas eröffnet wurde, war aus der Spielerkapitale ein internationales Touristenziel geworden.

Unterdessen gönnte man den bereits etablierten Hotels eine Frischzellenkur. Das Beverly Hills Hotel beauftragte den Architekten Paul R. Williams 1947 mit Renovierungen und Erweiterungen. Die innovative Raumausstatterin Dorothy Draper dirigierte eine zweijährige Generalüberholung des aus dem 19. Jahrhundert stammenden Greenbrier Hotel in West Virginia. Den krönenden Abschluss bildete 1948 eine dreitägige Wiedereröffnungsgala mit Bing Crosby als Sänger und dem Herzog von Windsor am Schlagzeug.

Außerdem war Crosby maßgeblich an einer der temperamentvollsten Kreationen des ganzen Jahrzehnts beteiligt: den *Road-to-*Filmen von Paramount. *Road to Singapore* (*Der Weg nach Singapur*, 1940) markiert den Beginn einer perfekten Beziehung – zwischen Crosby und Bob Hope. Die Reisen der beiden Schiffbrüchigen setzten sich fort mit *Road to Morocco* (*Der Weg nach Marokko*, 1942) und *Road to Rio* (*Der Weg nach Rio*, 1947). Wenn diese beiden Kerle durchkamen, dann konnte es jeder. Die Demokratisierung des Reisens nahm Fahrt auf.

1945

1945 End of World War II

Ende des Zweiten Weltkriegs

Fin de la Seconde Guerre mondiale

1946 First Cannes Film Festival

Erstes Filmfestival von Cannes

Premier Festival du Film de Cannes

1946 Hotel Bel-Air, luxury boutique hotel, opens in Los Angeles

Eröffnung des Hotel Bel-Air, eines luxuriösen Boutiquehotels, in Los Angeles

Ouverture de l'Hotel Bel-Air, luxueux « boutique hotel », à Los Angeles

1946 Flamingo, first air-conditioned hotel in U.S., opens in Las Vegas, with casino, nightclub, and hotel under one roof

Eröffnung des Flamingo in Las Vegas, des ersten klimatisierten Hotels der USA mit Kasino, Nachtclub und Hotel unter einem Dach

Le Flamingo, premier hôtel climatisé des Etats-Unis, ouvre à Las Vegas avec casino, night-club et hôtel sous le même toit

TWA
TWA
PORTUGAL

◄ TWA, 1946

Matson Line, 1949

APRÈS LA TRISTEMENT CÉLÈBRE ATTAQUE DE PEARL HARBOR LE 7 DÉCEMBRE 1941, LE PRÉSIDENT FRANKLIN D. ROOSEVELT DÉCLARA LA GUERRE À L'ALLEMAGNE ET AU JAPON. Les Etats-Unis se mobilisèrent immédiatement pour entrer dans la Seconde Guerre mondiale. En quelques semaines, le rationnement d'essence et de caoutchouc paralysa quasiment tout le marché des voyages de loisir alors que l'industrie américaine se concentrait sur l'effort de guerre.

Entre le début de la Grande Dépression et la fin de la Seconde Guerre mondiale, on ne construisit qu'un seul hôtel moderne: le Washington Statler (aujourd'hui le Capital Hilton), en 1943. Sa conception nécessita les conseils des services secrets afin que l'hôtel puisse accueillir Roosevelt et son administration du New Deal. L'entrée principale se trouvait derrière l'hôtel, avec une allée couverte pour les voitures et un ascenseur spécial qui emmenait directement la voiture présidentielle à l'étage de la salle de conférence.

Après la signature de l'Armistice en 1945, l'Amérique était impatiente de rattraper le temps perdu. Par exemple, la compagnie Greyhound put lancer la production des cars Silversides conçus par Raymond Loewy. Ce dernier réactualisa donna aussi un look plus moderne au logo de chien.

L'après-guerre vit l'adoption d'une invention d'avant-guerre: l'air conditionné. Les climats chauds devinrent soudain plus attirants, et Palm Springs, entre autres, connut une ère de prospérité. Son image de ville désertique transformée en terrain de jeu pour l'élite fut immortalisée par Frank Sinatra, qui s'y fit construire une maison climatisée en 1946 dans le désert après avoir gagné son premier million. Le design d'E. Stewart Williams – maison basse à toit plat avec portes en verre ouvrant l'espace sur l'extérieur – représentait la quintessence du mouvement moderniste de Palm Springs.

La même année, Billy Wilkerson ouvrit le Flamingo de Las Vegas, premier hôtel climatisé du pays qui abritait sous le même toit un casino, une boîte de nuit et des suites. Pour que les joueurs perdent la notion du temps, il n'y avait aucune horloge dans le casino. Entre 1941 et 1944, les revenus issus du jeu augmentèrent de 56 %. Le gangster Bugsy Siegel, également financier du Flamingo, prit alors conscience de

tout l'argent que pouvait rapporter le tourisme, en particulier le jeu (Lucky Luciano fit de même pour Cuba quand il accueillit une réunion de grands parrains à l'Hotel Nacional de La Havane en 1946). Lors de l'ouverture de l'aéroport McCarran Field de Las Vegas en 1948, la capitale mondiale du jeu était déjà une destination touristique internationale.

Pendant cette période, les hôtels bien établis bénéficièrent d'un rafraîchissement d'après-guerre. Le Beverly Hills Hotel fit appel à l'architecte Paul R. Williams pour des rénovations et des extensions en 1947. La décoratrice de la haute société Dorothy Draper supervisa au Greenbrier Hotel, établissement du XIXe siècle situé en Virginie Occidentale, un réaménagement de deux ans couronné en 1948 par un gala de réouverture de trois jours qui vit chanter Bing Crosby avec le Duc de Windsor à la batterie.

Crosby contribua très largement au succès de la saga des films *En Route*. *En Route vers Singapour* (1940) marqua le début du duo Crosby et Bob Hope. Les aventures de ces deux naufragés se poursuivirent dans *En Route pour le Maroc* (1942) et *En Route pour Rio* (1947). Si ces deux-là arrivaient à s'en sortir dans les pays exotiques, alors tout le monde le pouvait. La démocratisation du voyage s'accélérait.

1947 *Queen Mary* resumes peacetime passenger service

Wiederaufnahme der zivilen Passagierbeförderung durch die *Queen Mary*

Avec le retour de la paix, le *Queen Mary* reprend le transport de passagers

1947 Paul R. Williams revamps Beverly Hills Hotel; banana leaf wallpaper and pink-green-and-white color scheme soon iconic

Paul R. Williams verleiht dem Beverly Hills Hotel ein neues Gesicht; Bananenblatt-Tapeten setzen neue Maßstäbe

Paul R. Williams relooke le Beverly Hills Hotel; feuilles de bananier et tons de rose/vert/blanc deviennent ses emblèmes

1948 Air India granted international flying privileges when India gains independence

Air India erhält internationale Flugrechte, als Indien die Unabhängigkeit erlangt

Air India se voit octroyer des droits de vol international quand l'Inde gagne son indépendance

1948 Greenbrier Hotel's gala reopening party after two-year redecoration; Bing Crosby sings, Duke of Windsor plays drums

Wiedereröffnungsgala des Greenbrier Hotel nach zweijährigem Umbau mit Bing Crosby als Sänger und dem Herzog von Windsor am Schlagzeug

Gala de réouverture du Greenbrier Hotel avec Bing Crosby au micro et le Duc de Windsor à la la batterie

Hiawatha

ROAD

For the SWORDS of today...

and the PLOWSHARES of tomorrow...

LOCKHEED LODESTAR

The swords of 1941 are fast and deadly fighting airplanes. Their blades are the whirling, powerful propellers that rocket them through the air at unprecedented speeds in defense of nations.

In building these airplanes Lockheed is doing a patriotic duty. But hopefully, Lockheed looks to the day when these blades will cleave new paths to commerce, peace and expanded industry.

LOOK TO *Lockheed* FOR LEADERSHIP IN BOTH

LOCKHEED AIRCRAFT CORPORATION BURBANK, CALIF.

ALL FIRST CLASS MAIL
by AIR
IT'S COMING!

◂◂ The Milwaukee Road, 1947

◂ Lockheed, 1941

Even as Lockheed was gearing up for the war economy, producing the squadrons of planes needed to fight the Germans and Japanese, the aircraft manufacturer was already betting that there would be pent-up travel demand when World War II ended. Americans enjoyed travel for pleasure all too much.

Bereits während sich Lockheed auf den Krieg einstellte, um die Unmengen von Flugzeugen zu produzieren, die man im Kampf gegen Deutschland und Japan brauchte, setzte der Flugzeughersteller auf den zivilen Nachholbedarf nach Kriegsende. Dafür fanden die Amerikaner einfach zu viel Gefallen an Vergnügungsreisen.

Même quand Lockheed travaillait à l'effort de guerre en produisant les escadrons d'avions requis pour combattre les Allemands et les Japonais, le constructeur se doutait déjà que la demande en voyages aériens augmenterait considérablement après la fin de la Seconde Guerre mondiale. Les Américains aimaient trop voyager pour le plaisir.

Martin Aircraft, 1945

Hi, mommy... flying's fun!

Just look at that smile! Whether you're 6 or 60, on pleasure or business, it'll be fun to travel by Martin airliner! No crowds, no noise, no dirt . . . the big Martin transport will be air-conditioned, sound-proofed, clean as a whistle! And such a quick trip! No long, tiring hours wasted en route. With a young hostess to watch over her . . . a big, soft seat to curl up in . . . an individual reading light and full-view window . . . she'll be as snug and comfortable as in an armchair at home!

SO DEPENDABLE, TOO!

On new Martin airliners, radar "will see" through rain, snow, fog or darkness. Special heating units will melt ice before it can form on wings, tail or propeller. Two Pratt & Whitney engines deliver nearly the horsepower of all 4 engines of many former wartime bombers; on only one of these big power-plants, high-flying Martin airliners could soar a third of a mile above the nation's highest mountain. For speed, luxury and dependability, no plane of its type can surpass a Martin airliner!

THE GLENN L. MARTIN COMPANY, BALTIMORE 3, MARYLAND

FLY VIA MARTIN TRANSPORT ON THESE GREAT AIRLINES!

Capital (PCA) • Eastern • Chicago & Southern
Braniff • United • Northwest • Delta
Dodero (Argentina) • Panagra • Commander
Cruzeiro do Sul (Brazil)

Martin
AIRCRAFT
Builders of Dependable Aircraft Since 1909

Wings for Your Wishes

"Wish I were in New York . . . wish I were in California . . . wish I were at home . . . wish I could have a longer vacation."

SIR . . . or Madam, there's a genie who grants such wishes! He's the helpful individual who reserves space for you on TWA. To summon him, simply use the magic dial of your telephone. In about the time it takes to say TWA, you'll find yourself set to travel on wings.

And it's luxury travel that you'll like every mile and every minute.

Flying TWA, you find a new note of hospitality in the air. You enjoy a personal radio . . . tempting food. And from take-off to landing you are pleasantly aware of the precision and thoughtfulness that mark *the airline run by flyers*.

Long known as the shortest, fastest coast-to-coast airline, we now offer *four* timely transcontinental flights each way every day . . . three "through Skysleepers" and the famous scenic daylight flight over majestic Grand Canyon. And city-to-city "commuter schedules" have been increased to get you there and back the same day. For example . . . *eighteen* flights daily, New York-Pittsburgh! Use TWA to gain time in your business. Use it for pleasure. *And watch this airline for great new things to come.*

•

FAST FLIGHT FACTS

LOS ANGELES TO NEW YORK
Shortest time: 15 Hrs. 41 Min. Fare . . $149.95

LOS ANGELES TO CHICAGO
Shortest time: 11 Hrs. 29 Min. Fare . . $105.00

CHICAGO TO PITTSBURGH
Shortest time: 2 Hrs. 27 Min. Fare . . $23.95

NEW YORK TO PITTSBURGH
Shortest time: 2 Hrs. 23 Min. Fare . . . $21.00

The **TRANSCONTINENTAL** *Line*
and Western Air, Inc.
10 RICHARDS ROAD, KANSAS CITY, MISSOURI

A New World in Travel

IT'S almost like traveling on the wings of a wish . . . this skimming through the air in the big, fast ships of TWA. You simply step aboard and before you can begin to believe it, *you're there.*

You travel so smoothly, surrounded by such luxury, that you thoroughly enjoy every minute aloft. That's because TWA has been doing things for you!

On Skyclub or Skysleeper, you'll find hospitality that is truly distinctive of TWA. Appetizing meals, restful appointments, a personal radio, alert attention to your every wish . . . nothing is omitted that could add to your pleasure. And you'll be glad to know, too, that TWA is *the airline run by flyers.* You'll sense this fact throughout the ship . . . and in every member of the crew.

For long distance travelers, TWA now offers *four* transcontinental flights daily. But you don't have to take a *long* trip to know the pleasure of flying TWA. For the shortest, fastest coast-to-coast airline has also stepped up "commuter" schedules from city-to-city. Make use of this service . . . for business, for pleasure. And watch this airline run by flyers *for great new things to come.*

FAST FLIGHT FACTS

NEW YORK TO PITTSBURGH
Shortest time: 2 Hrs. 23 Min. Fare . . . $21.00

PITTSBURGH TO CHICAGO
Shortest time: 2 Hrs. 56 Min. Fare . . $23.95

CHICAGO TO LOS ANGELES
Shortest time: 12 Hrs. 24 Min. Fare . . $105.00

DAYTON TO CHICAGO
Shortest time: 2 Hrs. 3 Min. Fare . . . $14.70

NEW YORK TO MINNEAPOLIS
Shortest time: 7 Hrs. 40 Min. Fare . . . $61.45

The **TRANSCONTINENTAL** *Line*
and Western Air, Inc.

TWA, 1940

TWA, 1941

▸ Bohn, 1945

Revolutionary Rockets!
Authorities predict that aircraft designs of tomorrow will be of the advanced rocket type. The new rocket models will permit much higher speeds at much higher altitudes. Thus new developments which require light alloys keep opening up avenues for improved products. The Bohn organization is one of the world's largest and leading specialists in the engineering and fabrication of aluminum, magnesium and brass products. When peace comes, Bohn metallurgists and engineers should be helpful to you in designing your products for tomorrow.
BOHN ALUMINUM AND BRASS CORPORATION
GENERAL OFFICES—LAFAYETTE BUILDING • DETROIT 26, MICHIGAN
Designers and Fabricators
ALUMINUM • MAGNESIUM • BRASS • AIRCRAFT-TYPE BEARINGS
BUY
WAR
BONDS
BOHN

163

Broader Wings

TO SPAN THE NATION...And the graceful sweep of their arrival marks an epochal advance in air travel. TWA's new Boeing Stratoliners are here! And with them come spaciousness, smoothness, luxury and speeds never before known along any commercial airway in the nation. By presenting Stratoliners today, TWA again, as in the past, is first to put the proved into practice, once more demonstrating that Progress goes hand in hand with Precision on the airline run by flyers.

TRANSCONTINENTAL & WESTERN AIR, Inc.

The TRANSCONTINENTAL *Line*

TWA *Stratoliner*

TWA

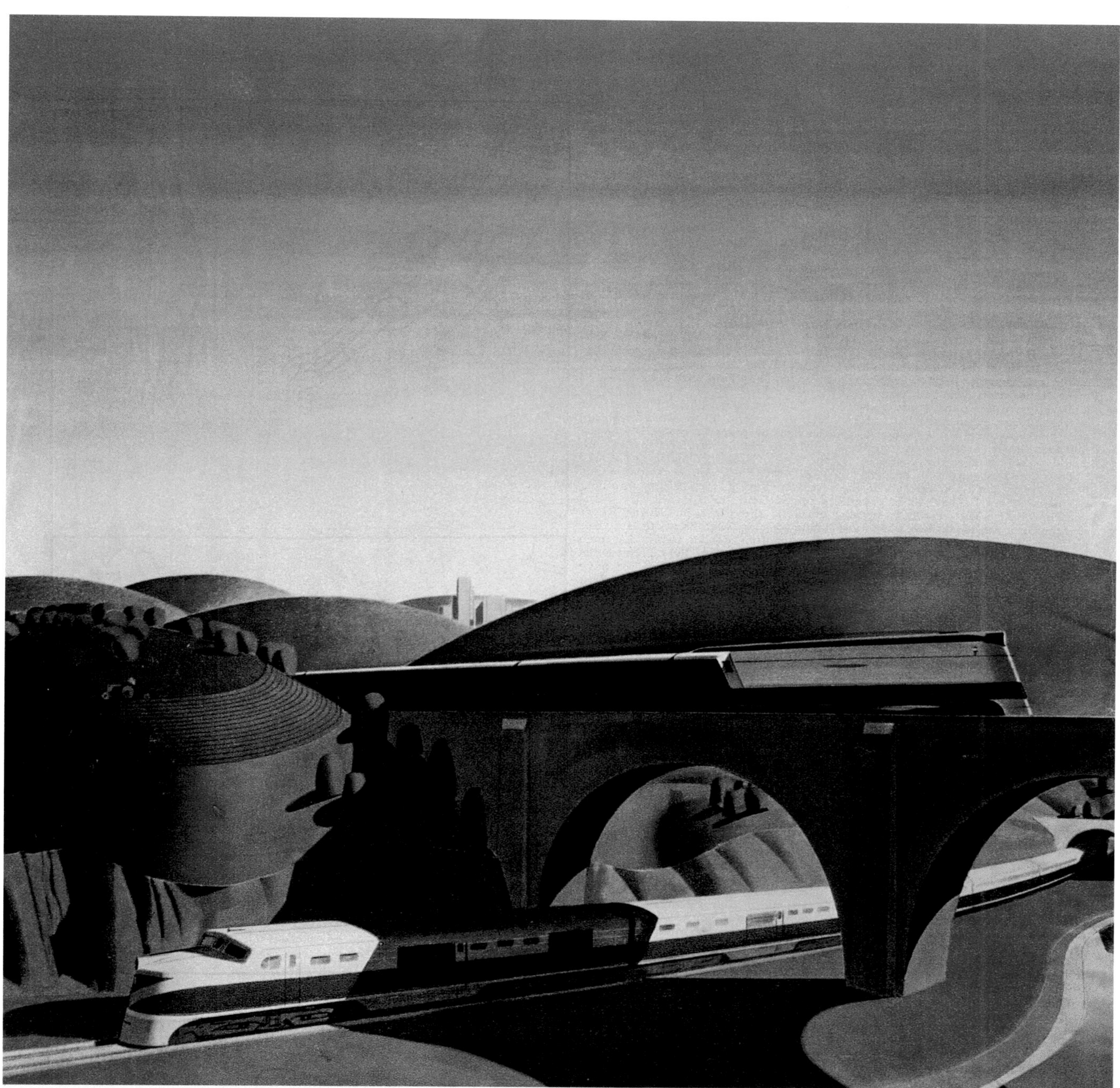

Two Trains of Thought

Sometimes we think Diesel-Liners are better for a certain purpose. Sometimes we think Steam-Liners are better. We play no favorites. We have no preferences. We make no snap judgments. We study each problem separately, and come up with our answer. Sometimes it's a Diesel-Liner. Sometimes it's a Steam-Liner. Whichever it is, we build it. It will do the job it was intended to do. And it will be one of the world's finest, most modern locomotives.

AMERICAN LOCOMOTIVE

DIESEL · STEAM · ELECTRIC

◂ TWA, 1940

American Locomotive Company, 1941

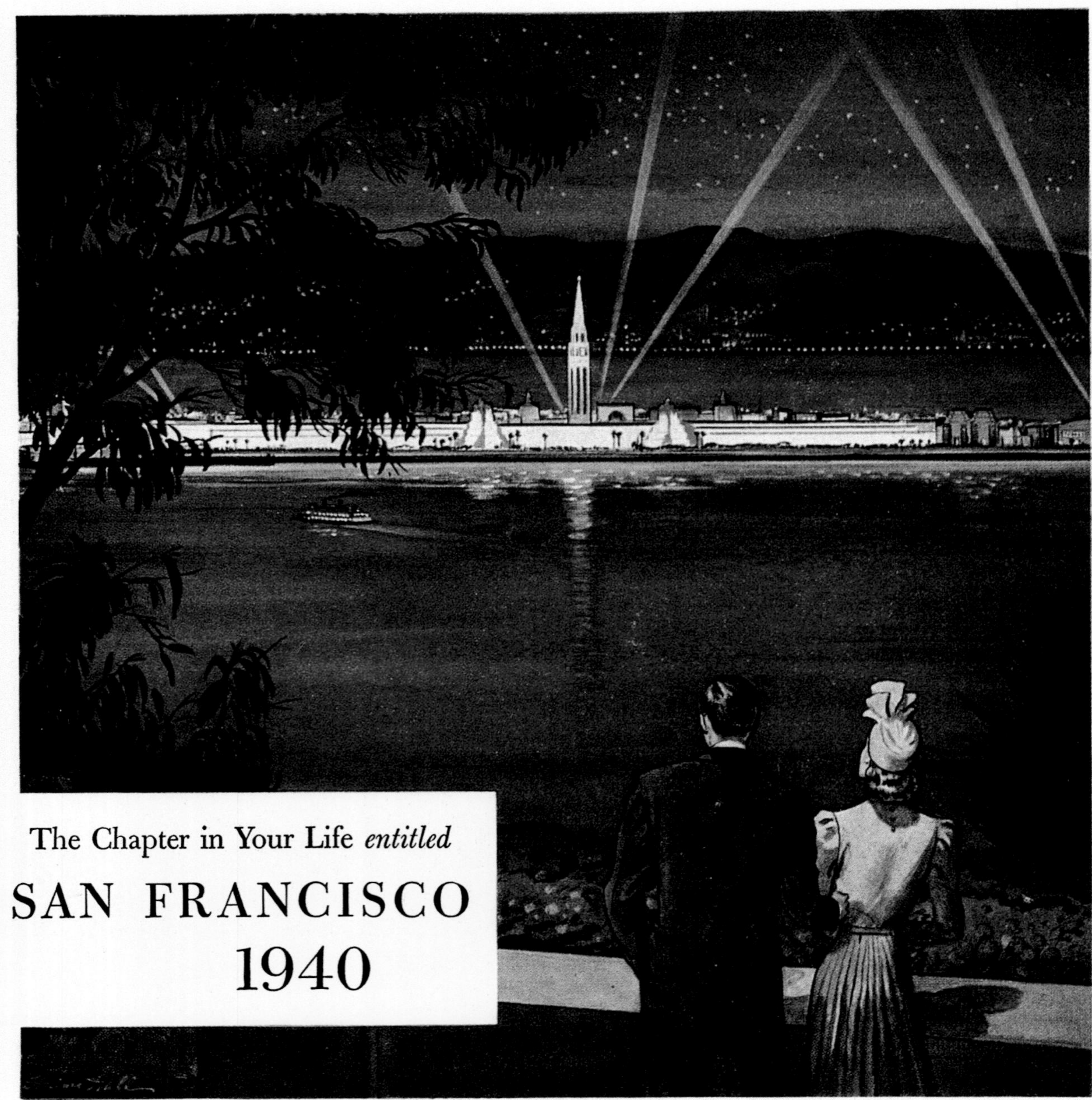
The Chapter in Your Life *entitled*
SAN FRANCISCO
1940

NEW GOLDEN GATE INTERNATIONAL EXPOSITION OPENS MAY 25 TO SEPTEMBER 29

One night this summer we'd like to take you up on Telegraph Hill to show you San Francisco's million lights, and Treasure Island framed by the world's two largest bridges.

Here, all that you ever dreamed about this City suddenly comes true. About you is the high-piled, storied metropolis that sprang from a Spanish pueblo overnight. There, the Golden Gate through which the 'Forty-Niners came from all the countries of the earth, bringing their customs and their tastes to linger on in the Latin Quarter, Chinatown and in a dozen other foreign colonies. These are the hills, so steep that cable cars were invented to climb them. And there, in the middle of the Bay... the world's most beautiful World's Fair.

This magic night you will remember always, as you will remember all your other nights and days in San Francisco... and on Treasure Island, with its lovely courts and gardens, exciting Gayway, fine new art exhibit, the Aquacade and the deeply moving pageant, *America! The Cavalcade of a Nation.*

In San Francisco you will dine around the world, dance where modern music was born, explore Golden Gate Park... Fishermen's Wharf... the long Embarcadero...

We've just prepared a new illustrated book that tells the whole exciting story of this City, its Exposition and the wonderland so close to San Francisco: the groves of giant Redwoods, Yosemite National Park, Lake Tahoe and the Land of Gold; hospitable Del Monte and sunny Santa Cruz, on Monterey Bay.

Send the coupon today for your free copy of this book. Find out how low all costs are here. See how easily and quickly you can come over smooth highways, or by train or plane or boat.

★ CALIFORNIANS INC.

Dept. 105, 703 Market Street, San Francisco, California. Please send me your new, free 1940 vacation book.

*Name*____________________

*Street*____________________

*City*____________________

*State*____________________

New Golden Gate International Exposition, 1940

The Chapter in Your Life *entitled*

SAN FRANCISCO 1940

Court of Pacifica on Treasure Island

NEW GOLDEN GATE INTERNATIONAL EXPOSITION OPENS MAY 25

The people of San Francisco... of all California, cordially invite you to the new Golden Gate International Exposition on Treasure Island, May 25 to Sept. 29, 1940.

We promise you that this new World's Fair will be more beautiful, even, than the one that thrilled so many million visitors last year. We promise you more entertainment, and more rare treasures from far Pacific lands. We promise you days and nights you'll cherish all your life. Days in the lovely courts of Treasure Island, gay with flowers and fountains. Days exploring San Francisco's hilly streets; shopping in Chinatown; strolling the romantic Embarcadero. The never-to-be-forgotten day you walk, or ride, across the Golden Gate on the longest span in the world.

You'll ride merry cable cars

Nights of fun in famous restaurants and cocktail lounges high above the City's million lights. Enchanted nights in the glowing fairyland of Treasure Island. The breathless night you stand on Telegraph Hill to watch the battle fleet weave their searchlights against the stars.

Send this coupon for our new illustrated guide book, "The Chapter in Your Life entitled San Francisco." It includes chapters about the thrilling vacationlands near San Francisco: Del Monte on the Monterey Peninsula and Santa Cruz, Yosemite National Park, the Redwood Empire, Lake Tahoe and the Land of Gold, the Shasta-Cascade Wonderland and all the rest. Find out how quickly you can come by highway, train or plane; how little this grand vacation really costs.

You'll play by Monterey Bay

★ CALIFORNIANS INC.

Dept. 104, 703 Market St., San Francisco, Calif.
Please send your new, free 1940 vacation book.

*Name*__________

*Street*__________

*City*__________

*State*__________

New Golden Gate International Exposition, 1940

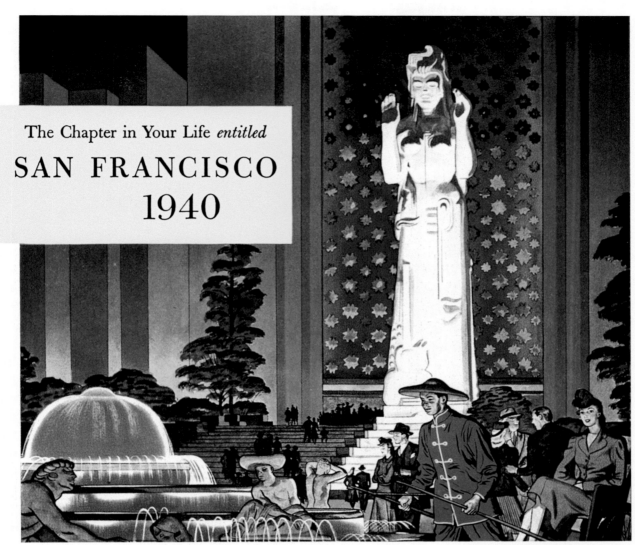

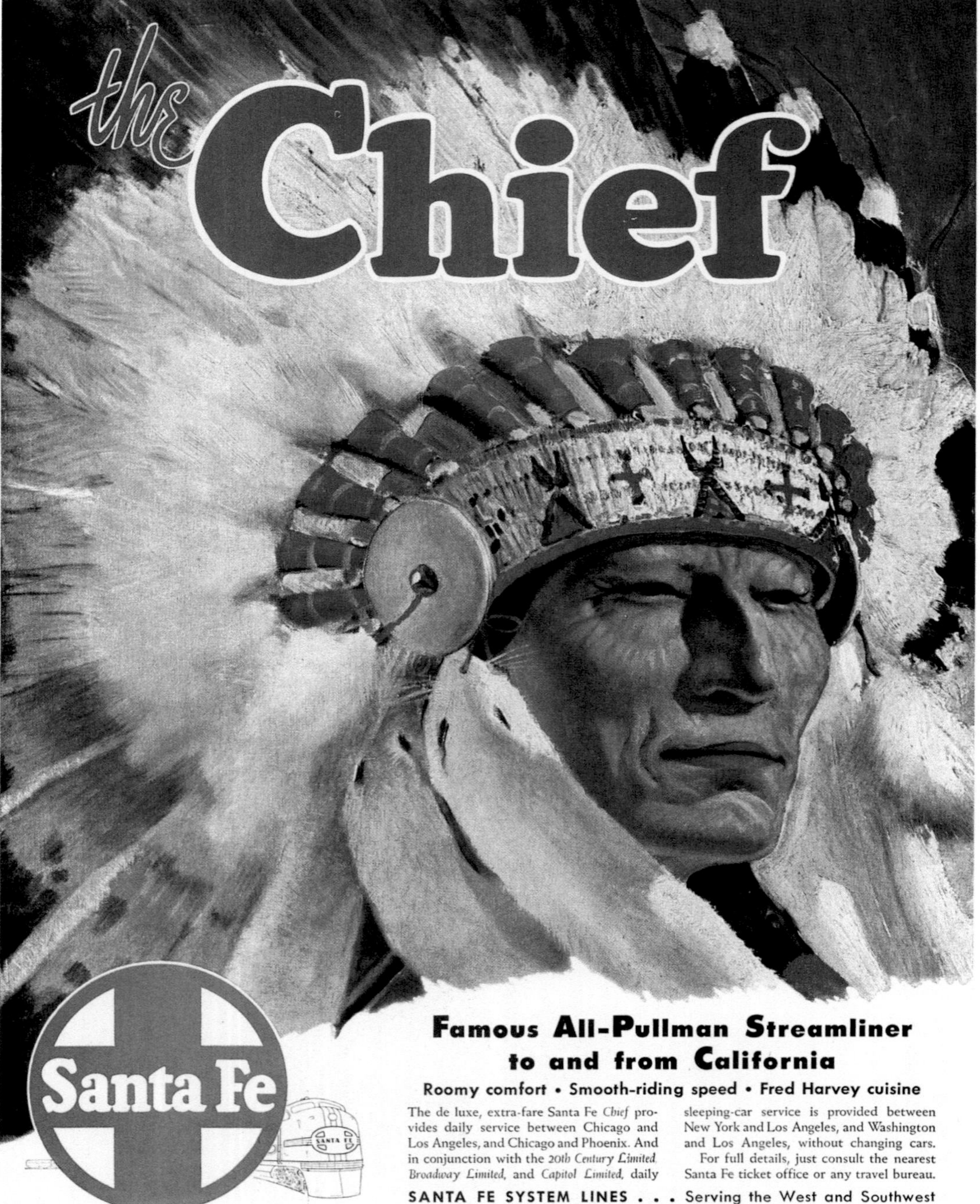

the Chief
Santa Fe
Famous All-Pullman Streamliner
to and from California
Roomy comfort • Smooth-riding speed • Fred Harvey cuisine
The de luxe, extra-fare Santa Fe Chief provides daily service between Chicago and Los Angeles, and Chicago and Phoenix. And in conjunction with the 20th Century Limited, Broadway Limited, and Capitol Limited, daily sleeping-car service is provided between New York and Los Angeles, and Washington and Los Angeles, without changing cars.
For full details, just consult the nearest Santa Fe ticket office or any travel bureau.
SANTA FE SYSTEM LINES . . . Serving the West and Southwest
T. B. Gallaher, General Passenger Traffic Manager, Chicago 4

Santa Fe Railway, 1947

U.S. railroads raked in big profits during the war, and expected this passenger surge to continue when fighting stopped. The Sante Fe Chief express service to California roared again. But with competition from cars and planes, Americans had many forms of travel to choose from. Train ridership never fully recovered.

Die Bahngesellschaften strichen während des Kriegs satte Profite ein und erwarteten auch nach Ende der Kampfhandlungen einen Fortbestand der Passagierflut. So verkehrte die Expresslinie Santa Fe Chief wieder nach Kalifornien. Angesichts der Konkurrenz durch Auto und Flugzeug hatten die Amerikaner die Qual der Wahl, sodass sich die Zahl der zivilen Bahnpassagiere nie wieder ganz erholte.

Les compagnies ferroviaires américaines amassèrent de gros bénéfices pendant la guerre, et s'attendaient à ce que cette hausse du trafic se poursuive après la fin du conflit. La ligne express Chief de la compagnie Sante Fe reprit du service vers la Californie. Avec la concurrence de la voiture et de l'avion, le train ne retrouva jamais vraiment ses anciens niveaux de fréquentation.

► Santa Fe Railway, 1949

The Chiefs

BETWEEN CHICAGO AND THE WEST AND SOUTHWEST

Santa Fe

Headed by the *Super Chief* and *The Chief*, the Santa Fe great fleet of trains between Chicago and California offers a choice of fine accommodations to satisfy every taste and fit every pocketbook. And between Chicago and Texas, it's the *Texas Chief*.

For smooth-riding comfort . . . friendly hospitality . . . delicious Fred Harvey meals . . . fascinating scenery . . . travel Santa Fe—*the Chief Way!*

R. T. Anderson, General Passenger Traffic Manager, Santa Fe System Lines, Chicago 4, Illinois

Step into the New World

Air travelers have said that in stepping into the modern airliner—for almost any kind of trip—they step into a new world.

It is a compact world, easy to get about in. You are picked up in one city—or on one continent—and set down in another with the smooth, effortless magic we used to associate only with fairy tales.

It is a world of quiet efficiency, where a man can get his work done in a hurry . . . without breathless haste . . . a kind of executive efficiency that will be much needed in days to come. And the Airlines will be superbly equipped to provide it, with still larger and faster planes, newer standards of service and at *radically reduced fares.*

For many months, war has been the Airlines' business because most of their passengers and cargoes have been *in that business.* But air transportation will speed them back to the cherished ways of peace just as readily as it has helped speed the nation to victory.

When you travel by Air *make reservations early; please cancel early if plans change.* When you use Air Express *speed delivery by dispatching shipments as soon as they're ready* by calling Air Express Division of Railway Express Agency. AIR TRANSPORT ASSOCIATION, 1515 Massachusetts Avenue, N. W., Washington 5, D. C.

This advertisement is sponsored by the nation's airlines and leading manufacturers in the aviation industry

THE AIRLINES OF THE UNITED STATES

LEADING THE WORLD IN AIR TRANSPORT

◂ The Airlines of the United States, 1945

American Airlines, 1946

With the end of World War II, civilian air travel was on the rise. Flights were now far more comfortable. American Airlines was an early adopter when it came to stewardesses—they had been on American flights since 1933.

Mit Ende des Zweiten Weltkriegs bekamen zivile Flugreisen Aufwind. Und die Flüge waren nun auch viel komfortabler. American Airlines entschied sich schon früh für Stewardessen, die es auf amerikanischen Flügen bereits seit 1933 gab.

Après la fin de la Seconde Guerre mondiale, le transport de passagers civils augmenta. Les vols en avion étaient désormais beaucoup plus confortables. American Airlines fut l'une des premières compagnies à embaucher des hôtesses de l'air – elles égayaient les vols américains depuis 1933.

THE SATURDAY EVENING POST March 9, 1946

Timesaving transportation and Flagship Hospitality for only 4½¢ a mile

AMERICAN AIRLINES System

THE NATIONAL AND INTERNATIONAL ROUTE OF THE FLAGSHIPS

ARIZONA: DOUGLAS • PHOENIX • TUCSON • **ARKANSAS:** LITTLE ROCK • TEXARKANA • **CALIFORNIA:** LOS ANGELES • SAN DIEGO • **CANADA:** TORONTO • WINDSOR • **CONNECTICUT:** BRIDGEPORT • HARTFORD • NEW HAVEN **DIST. OF COLUMBIA:** WASHINGTON • **ILLINOIS:** CHICAGO • PEORIA • SPRINGFIELD • **INDIANA:** INDIANAPOLIS • SOUTH BEND • **KENTUCKY:** LOUISVILLE • **MARYLAND:** BALTIMORE • **MASSACHUSETTS:** BOSTON HOLYOKE • SPRINGFIELD • WESTFIELD • **MEXICO:** MEXICO CITY • MONTERREY • **MICHIGAN:** ANN ARBOR • BATTLE CREEK • DETROIT • JACKSON • KALAMAZOO • **MISSOURI:** JOPLIN • ST. LOUIS • SPRINGFIELD **NEW JERSEY:** NEWARK • **NEW YORK:** ALBANY • BUFFALO • NEW YORK • NIAGARA FALLS • ROCHESTER • SYRACUSE • UTICA • **OHIO:** AKRON • CINCINNATI • CLEVELAND • COLUMBUS • DAYTON • **OKLAHOMA:** OKLAHOMA CITY • TULSA • **PENNSYLVANIA:** ERIE • PHILADELPHIA • SCRANTON • WILKES-BARRE • **RHODE ISLAND:** PROVIDENCE • **TENNESSEE:** JOHNSON CITY • KINGSPORT • KNOXVILLE • MEMPHIS • NASHVILLE • **TEXAS:** ABILENE • BIG SPRING • DALLAS • EL PASO • FORT WORTH • SAN ANTONIO • **VIRGINIA:** BRISTOL • LYNCHBURG • ROANOKE • **WEST VIRGINIA:** CHARLESTON • CLARKSBURG • DUNBAR • ELKINS • HUNTINGTON • PARKERSBURG

172

Fifty Millions for New Wings!

United's famous Main Line Airway is handling the greatest volume of traffic in history. To meet this demand and to bring air travel to still more people, United operates a growing and versatile fleet of modern transports—twin-engined Mainliner 180's for intercity frequency and convenience—four-engined Mainliner 230's for medium and long range flights. To these will be added the great new 300-mile-an-hour, four-engined Mainliner 300's and 340's, and the fast twin-engined Mainliner 303's. United Air Lines is spending $50,000,000 for the latest and finest flying equipment—planes that will set new standards of speed, comfort and luxury in coast-to-coast air travel.

United Air Lines holds the Award of Honor, presented by the National Safety Council, for having flown more than a billion and a half passenger miles without a fatal accident.

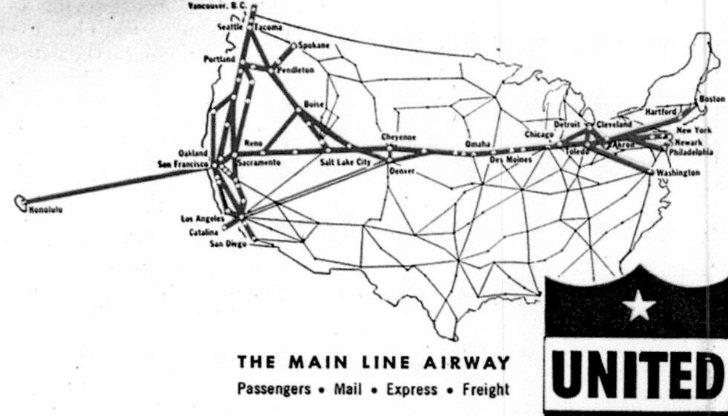

THE MAIN LINE AIRWAY

Passengers • Mail • Express • Freight

UNITED AIR LINES

AIR MAIL NOW 5c

◂ United Air Lines, 1946

The Airlines of the United States, 1945

The war was not quite over when this ad ran. But U.S. airlines were already positioning themselves as key to winning the peace—just they were vital to winning the war.

Der Krieg war noch nicht ganz vorüber, als diese Anzeige erschien. Und schon positionierten sich die US-Fluglinien als Schlüssel zum Gewinn des Friedens – so wie sie entscheidend zum Gewinn des Kriegs beigetragen hatten.

La guerre n'était pas encore tout à fait terminée quand cette publicité fut diffusée, mais les compagnies aériennes américaines se positionnaient déjà comme indispensables pour gagner la paix, tout comme elles l'étaient pour gagner la guerre.

"SEND THESE, THE HOMELESS, TEMPEST-TOST TO ME,
I LIFT MY LAMP BESIDE THE GOLDEN DOOR!"
—*Inscription on the Statue of Liberty*

Welcome Home!

AND now her lifted beacon hand bids welcome to her own. She gazes out to sea upon a mighty fleet of transports of the air, filled with her valiant sons returning from a work well done.

She bestows her benediction alike upon those who are home to stay and those who still must fight—but whose task will be done more quickly because their paths to Tokyo are the highways of the sky.

With compassionate eyes she looks upon the dawn of brighter days when all men everywhere will once more turn to paths of peace and these same transports of the air will span the far-flung continents in friendly trade between the nations of the world.

On foreign battlefields our boys have found their wings and henceforth they will fly. They will want this means of travel in their daily lives—in fields of commerce—in leisure hours with days to spend in distant places hitherto beyond the reach of modest means.

Yes, air transportation which has so ably met the needs of war will play no little part in building a finer and a better land in which these men will find that peace and freedom for which they fought. Welcome home!

When you travel by Air *make reservations early; please cancel early if plans change*. When you use Air Express *speed delivery by dispatching shipments as soon as they're ready*. Air Transport Association, 1515 Massachusetts Avenue, N.W., Washington 5, D. C.

This advertisement is sponsored by the nation's airlines and leading manufacturers in the aviation industry

THE AIRLINES OF THE UNITED STATES

LEADING THE WORLD IN AIR TRANSPORT

THE NEXT TIME YOU SEE PARIS

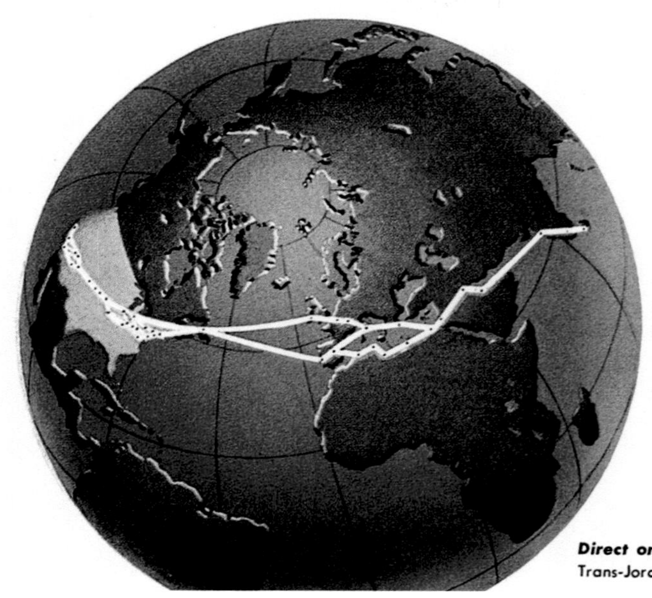

Like a great eagle soaring, your Sky Chief glides across the Seine. Below is the graceful needle of the Eiffel Tower. Behind you—only 17 hours of easy, restful travel since you left the Statue of Liberty.

You've followed the trails of TWA crews who were first to operate year-round schedules across the North Atlantic. They fly you with the deft skill born of more than 9,000 ocean flights, and with the same consideration for your safety and comfort that marks your TWA travels here at home.

The next time you see Paris it can be by TWA. Just ask your travel agent—or at the nearest TWA ticket office.

Direct one-carrier service to Newfoundland • Ireland • France • Switzerland • Italy • Greece • Egypt • Palestine Trans-Jordan • Iraq • Saudi Arabia • Yemen • Oman • India • Ceylon • Portugal • Spain • Algeria • Tunisia • Liby

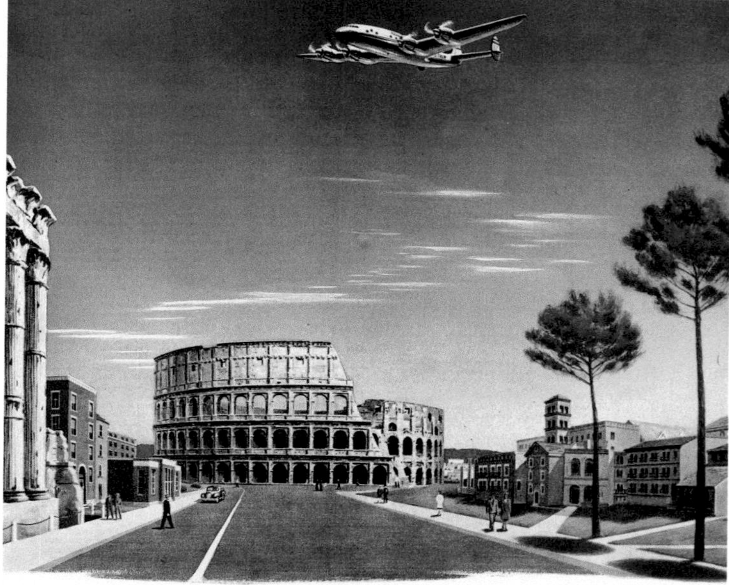

HIGH ROAD TO ROME

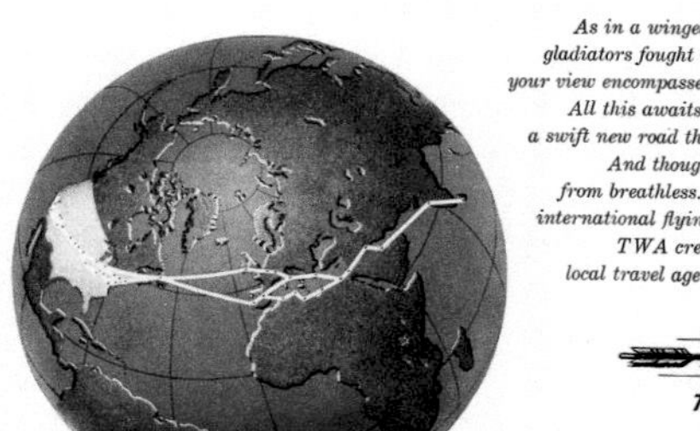

As in a winged chariot, you sweep across the Coliseum, where gladiators fought it out more than 1800 years ago. In a single glance, your view encompasses St. Peter's glistening dome and the majestic Vatican. All this awaits you at the end of today's high road to Rome, a swift new road that TWA has shortened to less than a day and a half.

And though you marvel at such speedy travel, you find it far from breathless. You find, instead, that 40,000,000 miles of international flying, with 9,000 overocean flights included, have taught TWA crews how to make it mighty easy going. See your local travel agent or TWA ticket office for information.

Direct one-carrier service to Newfoundland • Ireland • France • Switzerland • Italy • Greece • Egypt • Palestine Trans-Jordan • Iraq • Saudi Arabia • Yemen • Oman • India • Ceylon • Portugal • Spain • Algeria • Tunisia • Libya

OLD FAMILIAR FRIENDS

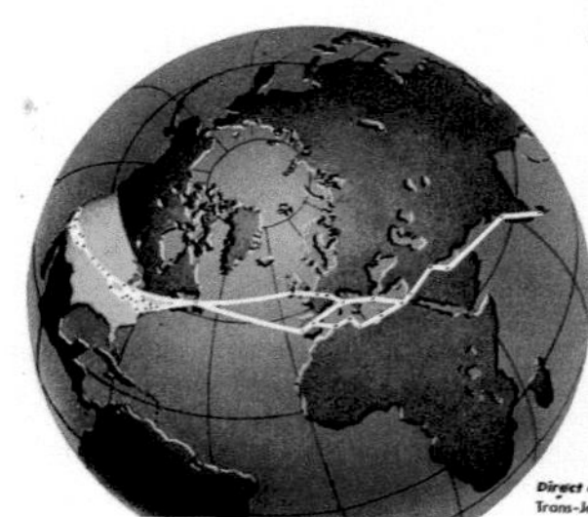

Rommel was knocking at the gates of Alexandria when TWA crews first landed their war-cargoed planes on Egyptian airfields. Now, in the air wake of such historic armadas, great Sky Chiefs wing there from America's shores in the stretch of a day and a half.

The peace of mind you feel as you travel springs from a huge backlog of such world-spanning experience. Twenty years of flying—more than 9,000 overocean flights—40,000,000 miles of international travel—all recommend TWA as today's most satisfying way to see the world. From California to Cairo, for first-class travel call on the nearest TWA ticket office—or your travel agent.

Direct one-carrier service to Newfoundland • Ireland • France • Switzerland • Italy • Greece • Egypt • Palestine Trans-Jordan • Iraq • Saudi Arabia • Yemen • Oman • India • Ceylon • Portugal • Spain • Algeria • Tunisia • Libya

TWA, 1946 ◂

TWA was known as "The Airline Run by Flyers," when Howard Hughes gained controlling interest in 1941. Hughes pushed for the elegant, cutting-edge Lockheed Constellation. In 1946, after Pan Am's legal designation as sole U.S. international carrier was broken, TWA began transatlantic flights and was renamed Trans World Airlines.

TWA war als die „Fluglinie der Flieger" bekannt, als Howard Hughes 1941 die Aktienmehrheit erwarb. Hughes forcierte die elegante, neuartige Lockheed Constellation. Nachdem Pan Ams Rechtsstatus als einzige internationale US-Fluglinie aufgehoben worden war, begann TWA 1946 mit Transatlantikflügen und wurde in Trans World Airlines umbenannt.

La TWA fut réputée comme « la compagnie gérée par ses passagers » dès que Howard Hughes en prit le contrôle en 1941. Il insista pour que la TWA acquière l'élégant et avant-gardiste Lockheed Constellation. En 1946, après la fin du monopole de la Pan Am en tant qu'unique transporteur international américain, la compagnie se lança dans les vols transatlantiques et fut rebaptisée Trans World Airlines.

TWA, 1946 (both)

▸▸ Pan Am, 1941

PAN AMERICA

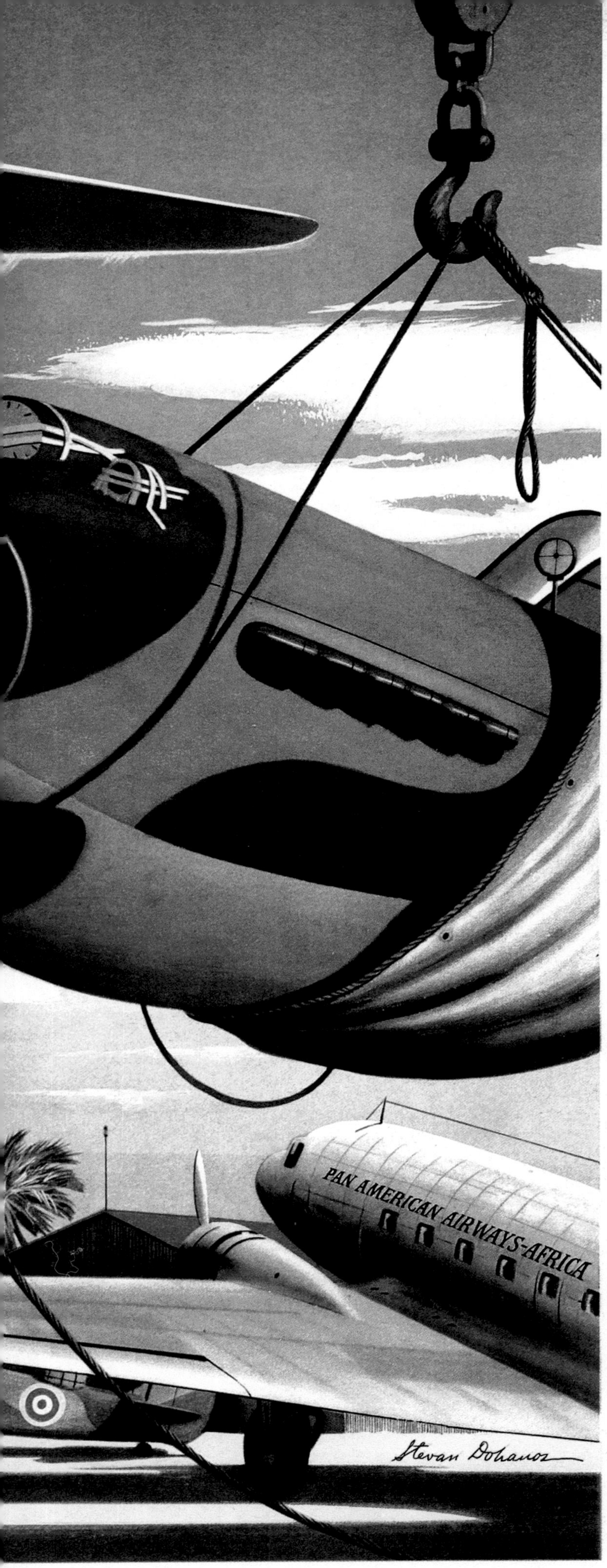

AMERICA'S NEW LIFELINE TO AFRICA

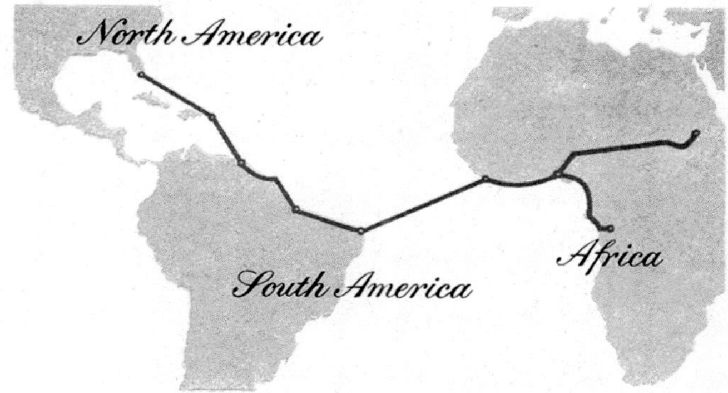

ON AUGUST 18 President Roosevelt announced plans for the world's most ambitious airways project.

It called for two things: First, a new air transport service from the U. S. to Africa and on across the Dark Continent to Egypt. Second, a new aerial "ferry service" linked with that system, delivering military planes to the Middle East.

This gigantic task was entrusted to Pan American Airways. The new airline spans 11,898 miles of ocean, jungle and desert. Normally its building would have taken years. Actually, Pan American got operations going in 60 days!

The White House statement on this undertaking reads in part: *"The ferry system and the transport service provide direct and speedy delivery of aircraft from the 'arsenal of democracy' to a critical point in the front against aggression. The importance of this direct line of communications between our country and strategic outposts in Africa cannot be overestimated."*

Pioneering is an old story to Pan American. A story made familiar through building 75,000 miles of aerial routes throughout Latin America, over the Pacific to China and New Zealand, up to Alaska and across the North Atlantic.

Cooperating with Uncle Sam and with our friendly neighbor nations is also nothing new. For example, in recent months Pan American took over thousands of miles of Nazi-controlled airlines in South America. Urgent defense needs were also met in linking Singapore and Manila by Clipper; in building and enlarging scores of airports.

One thing is sure. America's need of an efficient strongly-welded international air transport service will be even greater tomorrow than it is today—for both commerce and defense. And you can be certain that "America's Merchant Marine of the Air" will continue to anticipate the future and be ready with the necessary personnel, facilities, and experience.

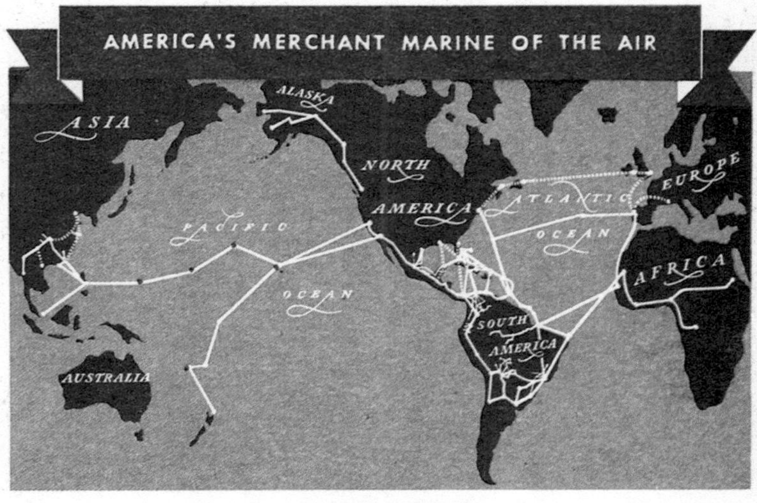

IRWAYS SYSTEM

"There's something really good about this morning!"

She feels as rested and relaxed this morning as she would had she slept in her own bed at home.

There are two reasons:

Modern trains follow modern locomotives. Since General Motors Diesel locomotives were introduced thirteen years ago, modernization of passenger equipment has made dramatic strides. But the locomotive itself deserves part of the credit. The flow of power in a GM Diesel locomotive is so smooth that you ride through the night without jerks at starting and stopping. You glide to a stop—start so smoothly that you would need to watch the landscape to know when your train starts to roll.

That is one of the many reasons why experienced travelers choose the trains with GM power up ahead.

And you can ride through the night—on a transcontinental journey—without a single change of locomotives.

And the savings in operating costs have enabled the railroads to provide extra comforts for passengers.

Fact is, the entire economy of the nation benefits as the railroads approach closer and closer to complete dieselization—the traveling public, shippers, investors and the railroads themselves.

ELECTRO-MOTIVE DIVISION
LA GRANGE, ILL.
GENERAL MOTORS
GM GENERAL MOTORS DIESEL POWER

Quiet Sunday dinner—100 miles an hour

WHEN a train powered by a General Motors Diesel locomotive glides into — or out of — a station, there's not even a ripple in the glass of water at your elbow.

You travel with a new smoothness — and a new speed, too. Often, on the straightaways, your train may make 100 miles an hour.

General Motors locomotives have also brought a new cleanliness to travel — no soot and cinders to mar your appearance; no clouds of smoke and steam to mar your view.

They have held, for several years, the records for on-time arrivals.

That's why it is easy to see why 200 of America's finest, fastest name trains are headed by General Motors power.

Easy to understand why better trains follow General Motors locomotives.

See the Electro-Motive Exhibit at the Chicago Railroad Fair.

ELECTRO-MOTIVE DIVISION
GENERAL MOTORS · LA GRANGE, ILL.
Home of the Diesel Locomotive
GM GENERAL MOTORS LOCOMOTIVES

178

General Motors Locomotives, 1947

General Motors Locomotives, 1948

► Pennsylvania Railroad, 1944

Advertising for vacation train travel virtually stopped during World War II, as in World War I. But here the Pennsylvania Railroad uses the immense U.S. mobilization effort to talk about the quality of its service. During World War II, U.S. railways moved 43 million armed service members in 114,000 special troop trains.

Die Werbung für Ferienreisen mit dem Zug kam nach dem Ersten nun auch im Zweiten Weltkrieg praktisch zum Erliegen. Hier indes bedient sich Pennsylvania Railroad der intensiven landesweiten Kriegsvorbereitungen, um die Qualität ihres Service herauszustellen. Im Zweiten Weltkrieg wurden insgesamt 43 Millionen Soldaten in 114 000 speziellen Truppenzügen befördert.

Pendant la Seconde Guerre mondiale comme au cours du précédent conflit international, les publicités pour les voyages en train disparurent pratiquement de la circulation. Ici, la compagnie Pennsylvania Railroad tire néanmoins parti de l'immense effort de mobilisation américain pour communiquer sur la qualité de ses services. Durant la Seconde Guerre mondiale, les trains américains accueillirent 43 millions de soldats dans 114 000 convois affectés au transport de troupes.

Luxurious comfort at money-saving fares in new VISTA-DOME chair coaches.

Feminine as a boudoir is the women's lounge. Men's lounges equally complete.

Enjoy Delicious Meals and personalized se
in the California Zephyr's beautiful dining

SCENIC WAY TO CALIFORNIA
TAKE THE VISTA-DOME *California Zeph*

◂ California Zephyr, 1949

Matson Line, 1941

Before the war, American popular culture had presented the pleasures awaiting tourists in Hawaii. Bing Crosby introduced the hit "Blue Hawaii" in his movie *Waikiki Wedding* (1937) and MGM's tap sensation Eleanor Powell danced across the Lido deck of an ocean liner in *Honolulu* (1939). So the Japanese attack on Pearl Harbor on December 7, 1941, had been viewed as an even more devastating blow. Here, Matson wants travelers to focus on comfortable future trips to the tropical paradise.

Vor dem Krieg hatte die amerikanische Populärkultur den Touristen die Annehmlichkeiten Hawaiis schmackhaft gemacht. Bing Crosby landete einen Hit mit „Blue Hawaii" in seinem Film *Waikiki Wedding* (1937), und MGMs Steppsensation Eleanor Powell tanzte über das Lido-Deck eines Ozeandampfers in *Honolulu* (1939). So wurde der japanische Angriff auf Pearl Harbor am 7. Dezember 1941 zu einem umso vernichtenderen Schlag. Hier möchte Matson die Aufmerksamkeit der Urlauber auf das tropische Paradies lenken.

Avant la guerre, la culture populaire américaine reflétait les plaisirs attendant les touristes à Hawaï. Bing Crosby chanta le tube « Blue Hawaii » dans le film *L'Amour à Waïkiki* (1937) et Eleanor Powell, la reine des claquettes de la MGM, dansa sur le pont d'un paquebot transaltantique dans *Honolulu* (1939). L'attaque de Pearl Harbor par les Japonais le 7 décembre 1941 n'en fut donc que d'autant plus dévastatrice. Ici, la Matson cherche à focaliser l'attention des voyageurs sur le confort de leurs futurs voyages vers ce paradis tropical.

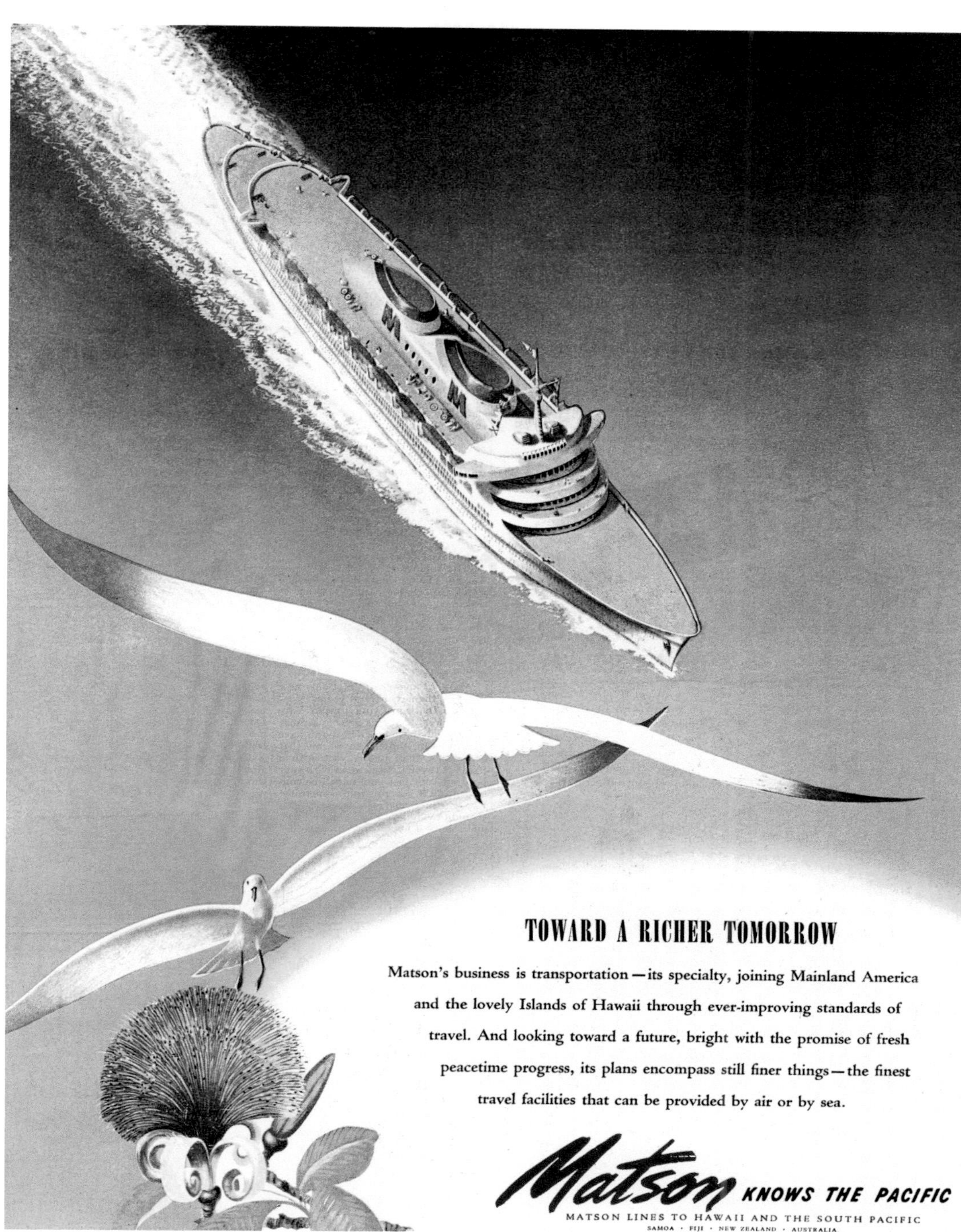

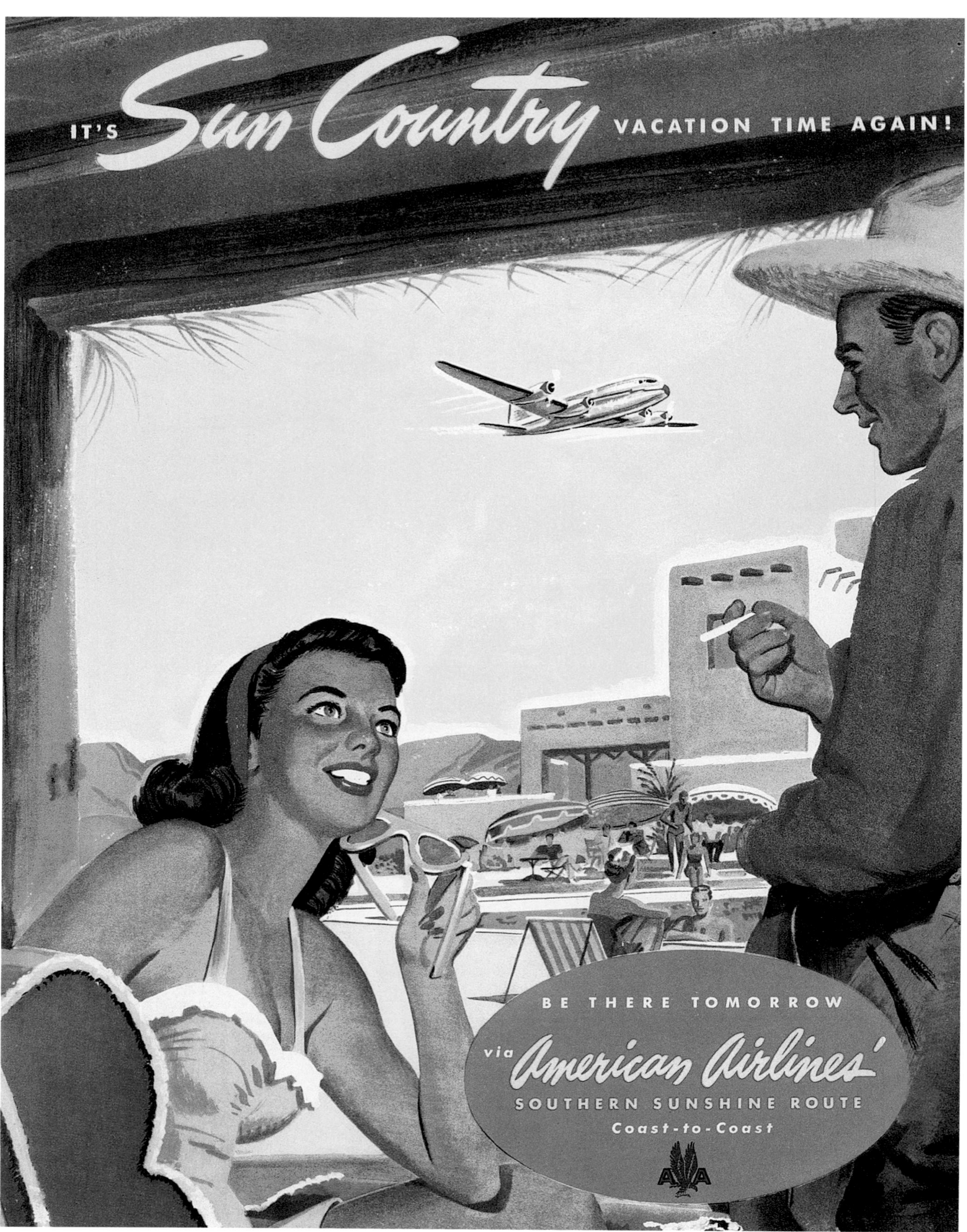

American Airlines, 1946

► American Airlines, 1947

►► American Locomotive Company, 1946

THE SOUTHERN SUNSHINE ROUTE
of AMERICAN AIRLINES
To and Through the SUN COUNTRY
of ARIZONA, TEXAS, NEW MEXICO
and SOUTHERN CALIFORNIA
DETROIT
CLEVELAND
AKRON
CHICAGO
INDIAN
-APOLIS
CINCINNATI
CHARLESTON
LOUISVILLE
ST. LOUIS
NASHVILLE
TULSA
OKLAHOMA CITY
LOS ANGELES
PHOENIX
FT. WORTH
DALLAS
SAN DIEGO
TUCSON
EL PASO
DOUGLAS
SAN ANTONIO
MONTERREY
MEXICO
CITY

LOOK WHAT'S COMING IN AMERICA'S

THE THEATRE THAT TRAVELS 90 MILES AN HOUR

Among the new wonders promised the rail traveler in the very near future is a club car that converts into a rolling movie theatre.

By day, you'll relax in a luxurious lounge. In the evening, you'll sit back and watch a latest Hollywood release as you speed on your journey.

This is no dream, but one of the many new features of trains which are in production right now. Conveniences and comforts like special playrooms for children. Telephone service for passengers en route. Roomier, more comfortable sleeping quarters than you ever dreamed of.

Such developments are part of a modernization program estimated at $1,600,000,000, the greatest ever undertaken by America's railroads. And you'll enjoy them not on some distant tomorrow, but as soon as the modern postwar trains hit the rails.

American Locomotive

NEW TRAINS!

LOCOMOTIVES AS REVOLUTIONARY AS THE TRAINS THEY PULL

To power your great new postwar trains, American Locomotive is building a line of Diesel-Electrics as revolutionary in design as the trains themselves.

These locomotives are the result of important wartime research. They will be *years* ahead in speed, power, smoothness, and economy of operation—super locomotives to handle every hauling job a railroad has.

For over the years, American Locomotive has been responsible for a large share of the basic new improvements in locomotives. Alco built America's *first* Diesel-Electric back in 1925. Alco built the record-breaking locomotives that are pulling so many crack trains today.

And soon, when you board the new postwar trains powered by American Locomotive, you'll be behind the finest locomotives ever built!

Company ***Sets the Pace for America's New Trains***

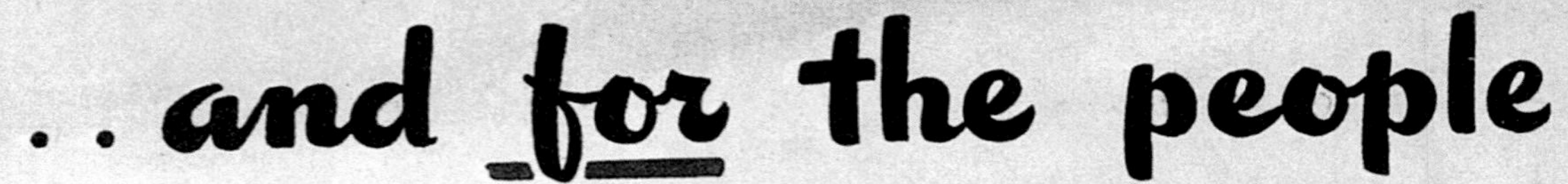

FINER BUS TRAVEL OVER AMERICA'S BROAD HIGHWA

In this nation, more than anywhere else in the world, highways are the heritage of all the people—a most vital part of their livelihood and their happiness.

And intercity buses—which have carried nearly three billion wartime passengers since Pearl Harbor—seek constantly to bring to the people of America the full benefits of their priceless highway heritage. Through the years, intercity buses have extended the convenience and economy of highway travel to the people of every State. They take millions to and from their daily employment. They bring trade and prosperity to small towns and giant cities alike. They lead the way to all the scenic grandeur of America.

All who depend upon bus transportation may count on the bus lines to keep pace with the continuing development of America's highways, which are growing steadily longer, and smoother and broader. Bus operators already have completed plans for spacious new terminals, and inviting new wayside inns.

And in the buses themselves, the greatest advances in travel comfort yet known can be achieved through important changes in bus size and design. Plans call for wider, roomier seats for greater riding ease . . . increased leg room . . . wider aisles . . . thicker wall insulation for better control of inside temperatures. Engineering progress would, at the same time, enhance the traditional safety of bus travel with larger brakes, wider tires and increased road stability.

These and a host of other improvements are just around the "bend in the road" for the millions of people whose social and economic welfare is daily enriched by bus transportation.

To assure that better day of travel, highway authorities all over America are now considering progressive steps to modernize regulations enacted in the days of narrow highways. Their revision of outmoded limitations on bus size and design will permit the finest and safest public travel ever known on the highways.

Write for the new and interesting booklet, "Modern Highways and How They Can Serve You Better."

THIS TIME.... HOME!

Another Great Job for the Bus Lines... the One We Like the Best!

With an honorable discharge tucked in his pocket, he's making the most thrilling trip of his life. Even his wounds are almost forgotten, for this is that long-dreamed-of bus trip home! He is one of a growing number of veterans now returning to civilian life... a vanguard of the millions who will be back later on.

Intercity buses carried the majority of these men to their induction centers... served them on leave and furlough trips. Now it is our privilege to carry them home again. Among all the wartime jobs we have, this is the one we like the best.

Because it gives flexible, convenient service to every city and town along 390,000 miles of highways, bus transportation is the returning veteran's natural choice. Usually, he can step right aboard a bus at his Army Separation Center and, shortly after, step out near his home.

And just as intercity buses serve our men in uniform from induction to homecoming so, too, do they serve millions of war workers and essential travelers of every type. This movement of manpower by intercity bus is all-important in relieving other public transportation of an overwhelming wartime load... in helping to keep the home front strong. More than two billion passengers have been carried since the war began!

In order to accomplish this, some travel conveniences have had to be sacrificed for a while. But when war jobs are finished, the public can look forward to the finest bus transportation that has ever been known along the highways. A better day is coming tomorrow!

MOTOR BUS LINES OF AMERICA

NATIONAL ASSOCIATION OF MOTOR BUS OPERATORS, WASHINGTON, D. C.

◄ Motor Bus Lines of America, 1946

Motor Bus Lines of America, 1945

Winter under the warm Cuban sun

Hotel Nacional de Cuba HAVANA

The Nacional, supreme luxury hotel of the tropics, is the winter center of cosmopolitans from all over the world. By day, the gay Cabana Sun Club, two swimming pools, tennis, shuffleboard and other recreation in the Nacional's 13 flowering acres. By night, dance and be entertained in the Nacional's new L'Arboleda night club and restaurant. There's no end to the things to do in the glamorous life of Havana, fun-capital of Latin America.

All the colour and romance of a foreign land, yet only minutes by air from the mainland!

A Kirkeby Hotel

See your travel agent, or make reservations at any Kirkeby Hotel

New York THE GOTHAM • HAMPSHIRE HOUSE • SHERRY-NETHERLAND • THE WARWICK • *Philadelphia* THE WARWICK • *Upper Saranac Lake, N.Y.* SARANAC INN
Chicago THE BLACKSTONE • *Atlantic City* THE AMBASSADOR • *Beverly Hills* BEVERLY WILSHIRE • *Hollywood* SUNSET TOWER • *Havana* HOTEL NACIONAL DE CUBA

◂ Hotel Nacional de Cuba, 1948

This stunning Spanish-Moorish hotel with a nightclub and casino was considered one of the best in the Caribbean—and cited as a center of mob control in Cuba. In 1946, the gangster Lucky Luciano called a meeting of powerful mobsters there to decide how to divvy up gambling money on this voluptuous island.

Dieses famose spanisch-maurische Hotel mit Nachtclub und Kasino galt als eines der besten in der gesamten Karibik – und als kubanischer Treffpunkt der Gangsterbosse. Lucky Luciano traf sich hier 1946 mit einigen Größen, um das auf der verlockenden Insel mit illegalem Glücksspiel eingesackte Geld aufzuteilen.

Ce surprenant hôtel hispano-mauresque avec nightclub et casino était considéré comme l'un des meilleurs des Caraïbes, ainsi que comme une plaque tournante de la mafia à Cuba. En 1946, le gangster Lucky Luciano y organisa une réunion de grands parrains pour débattre des moyens de détourner l'argent du jeu sur cette île de volupté.

Statler Hotel, 1943

The Washington Statler (now the Capital Hilton) was the only big, urban hotel developed and built between the start of the Depression and the end of World War II. But the D.C. housing crunch, and President Roosevelt's need for a secure meeting location, propelled the construction of this austere, sleekly neoclassical building.

Das Washington Statler (und heutige Capital Hilton) war das einzige große Stadthotel, das zwischen dem Beginn der Wirtschaftskrise und Kriegsende geplant und errichtet wurde. Beschleunigt wurde der Bau dieses schmucklos-glatten neoklassizistischen Gebäudes durch das knappe Immobilienangebot und die Notwendigkeit eines sicheren Versammlungsorts für die Roosevelt-Administration.

Le Washington Statler (aujourd'hui Capital Hilton) fut le seul grand hôtel urbain conçu et construit entre le début de la Dépression et la fin de la Seconde Guerre mondiale. La crise du logement dans la capitale américaine et la nécessité pour le Président Roosevelt de disposer d'un lieu de réunion sécurisé précipitèrent néanmoins la construction de cet édifice austère et purement néoclassique.

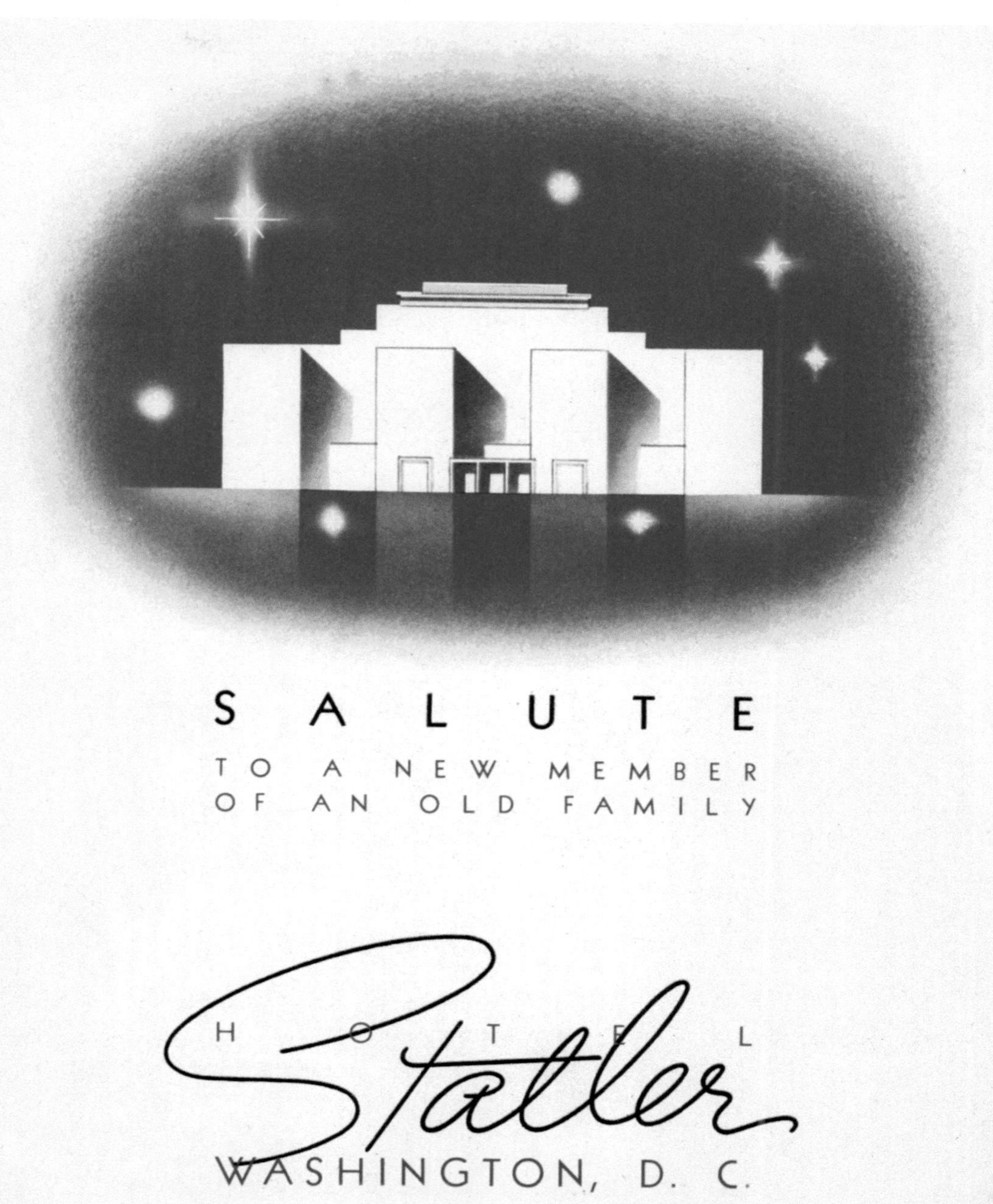

SALUTE
TO A NEW MEMBER
OF AN OLD FAMILY
HOTEL
Statler
WASHINGTON, D. C.

This is NEW MEXICO
THE LAND OF ENCHANTMENT

Mail This Coupon Today AND WE'LL SEND YOU OUR FREE BOOKLET AND MAPS, PRONTO

The Texas Special, crack train operated jointly by the Frisco and the Katy lines, runs between St. Louis, Dallas and San Antonio. The mecca of liberty-loving Americans who visit San Antonio is the Alamo, cradle of Texan independence where, in 1836, originated the inspiring battle-cry, "Remember the Alamo!"

191

SEE AMERICA FIRST CLASS

THERE'S one sure way to see America first class — pick out trains with a General Motors Diesel locomotive up ahead.

For these General Motors locomotives give a smoother ride. Trains start and stop without annoying jerks or jolts. You'll make your time count for more, too, because of faster, "on-time" schedules. And you'll see more because no smoke or steam will mar your view.

That's why General Motors locomotives are heading 197 of the nation's fastest, finest trains — and that's a majority of the Diesel-powered crack trains in the United States.

You'll find, as so many other smart travelers find, that *"Better trains follow General Motors locomotives."*

◂ New Mexico State Tourist Bureau, 1949

General Motors Locomotives, 1949

ONLY BY HIGHWAY
you'll meet these 'Amazing Americans' at home!
ALONG U. S. HIGHWAY 66, one of several Greyhound routes through the heart of the Southwest, Indians still weave their beautiful rugs and blankets, hammer out unique silver jewelry, and offer bright-colored pottery made with their own hands.
Put yourself in this picture, this Fall!
The setting is in the vast and colorful Southwest . . . an Indian rug weaver plies her skilled fingers as her ancestors have done for uncounted centuries . . . the girl from the waiting bus tries on one of the rainbow-tinted blankets, and gives her own big-city version of an Apache war whoop!
Such friendly scenes are typical of travel by highway, in the sun-drenched land of the first Americans. It's an interesting fact that many Indian tribes, with their fascinating customs and costumes, can still be seen along the highways, not only in the Southwest, but in the evergreen Northwest, among the Great Lakes, in the Midwest, in Florida, and even in New England! Greyhound trips and "Amazing America" Tours introduce you pleasantly to just such interesting people and places in all the 48 states, and in Canada. Whatever your reason for traveling—pleasure, business, or personal—we invite you to go the way that will help you to meet the real America . . . and real Americans!
TIMELY TIP: Early Fall, after the mid-summer rush, is the best time for travel of any kind. Transportation is less crowded, weather is milder, there is more room in hotels and resorts.
and remember... By Highway means By Greyhound!
GREYHOUND

WHEN THEY
Re-discover
AMERICA...
they'll find fun, friendship, beauty–by Highway
Just as American men and women have worked side-by-side in the shock of battle—as they have toiled together in the din of war plants—so they will one day re-discover the magnificent land for which they have fought . . . still side-by-side!
They will make their re-discovery trips by highway—because only the highways intimately reveal the lovely hidden places, the jewelled lakes and singing trout streams, the National Parks that are the heritage of every American.
Millions will go by Greyhound—because Greyhound will, in coming days, offer a finer type of highway travel than this old world has ever known. That will include luxurious new-type coaches, better terminal and post-house facilities, new expense-paid tours that will make travel more carefree than ever before.
NEW SUPER-COACHES LIKE THIS are more than a dream . . . they are shaping up right now in practical models that will be even further refined and improved for post-war travel.
GREYHOUND

Greyhound, 1945

Greyhound, 1946

► Greyhound, 1947

After the war, Greyhound was able to institute the design changes that Raymond Loewy had devised before World War II. Production finally started on the sleek new Silversides motorcoach design. The company also began using Loewy's streamlined image of its running dog logo.

Nach dem Krieg konnte Greyhound das von Raymond Loewy noch in Friedenszeiten erdachte neue Design umsetzen. Endlich konnte man mit der Fertigung des neuen, schnittigen Silversides-Busses beginnen. Und man begann, Loewys verschlanktes Windhund-Logo zu verwenden.

Après la guerre, Greyhound réussit à intégrer les modifications conçues par le designer Raymond Loewy avant 1939. La compagnie lança enfin la production de son nouveau modèle de car Silversides aux lignes épurées. Elle commença aussi à utiliser le logo de chien qui court remanié par Loewy.

►► Alcoa Steamship Company, 1949

YOUR VACATION WILL BE
Easy to Take
—when you take it by GREYHOUND
EASY TO TAKE! These three little words seem to sum up vacation trips by Greyhound—and here are the reasons why . . .
It's *Easy to Find* the right schedules—Greyhound buses leave so frequently, at such convenient hours. • It's *Easy to Reach* the choicest vacation places, since Greyhound serves all 48 States, Canada, Mexican border cities. • It's *Easy to Relax* in deeply-cushioned, recliner-type chairs.
Easy on the Eyes are the highway beauty spots, seen best by Greyhound . . . and *Easy to Like* are the congenial, cosmopolitan people who travel by bus. • *Easy to Buy* are Greyhound tickets, offering great big savings on almost any trip . . . *Easy to Plan* is your outing, with the help of a friendly Greyhound agent. Phone or call on him—and soon!
GAY SHORE RESORTS
GREAT SOUTHWEST
ATLANTIC COAST
NATIONAL PARKS
NORTHERN LAKES
Only by
GREYHOUND
YOU MEET THE *REAL* AMERICA

IN ISTANBUL, CAIRO, BERLIN, AND ATHENS, HILTONS WERE OPEN, AIRY, AND ACCESSIBLE–THE ESSENCE OF AMERICAN MODERNISM THRUST INTO THE CENTER OF AN ALIEN CITY.

DIE HILTONS WAREN OFFEN, LUFTIG UND LEICHT ERREICHBAR, SEI ES IN ISTANBUL, KAIRO, BERLIN ODER ATHEN – DIE ESSENZ DES AMERIKANISCHEN MODERNISMUS, MITTEN IN EINE FREMDE STADT HINEINGE-WORFEN.

A ISTANBUL, AU CAIRE, À BERLIN ET À ATHÈNES, LES STRUCTURES DES HÔTELS HILTON ÉTAIENT OUVERTES, LÉGÈRES ET ACCESSIBLES – L'EMBLÈME PAR EXCELLENCE DE LA POUSSÉE DU MODERNISME AMÉRICAIN AU CŒUR D'UNE VILLE ÉTRANGÈRE.

1950

PAX AMERICANA AND THE COLD WAR
PAX AMERICANA UND DER KALTE KRIEG
LA PAX AMERICANA ET LA GUERRE FROIDE

-1959

United
UNITED
D AIR LINES

◂ United Air Lines, 1952

Insurance by North America, 1957

AT THE HEIGHT OF THE COLD WAR, IN THE 1950S, CONRAD HILTON SAW HIS HOTELS AS THE VANGUARD OF AMERICAN VALUES—and the U.S. government did, too. A federal agency, the Economic Cooperation Administration, used Hilton hotels as a major selling point for U.S. soft power and influence. With this help from Washington, and foreign governments, Hilton hotels were built in major Cold War capitals—where the West faced off against the Soviet Bloc.

Hilton wanted his hotels to epitomize America, to "show the countries most exposed to Communism the other side of the coin—the fruits of the free world." In Istanbul, Cairo, Berlin, and Athens, his hotels were open, airy, and accessible—the essence of American modernism thrust into the center of an alien city, as Annabel Jane Wharton writes in her smart book, *Building the Cold War.* But Hilton was not only building hotels, he was buying them. In 1954, he acquired the entire Statler hotel chain for $111 million, the largest price paid for a real-estate venture since the Louisiana Purchase.

While standardized American values rubbed up against the "other" in Hiltons around the globe, the architect Morris Lapidus was shaking up Miami Beach. His modern baroque design for the 1954 Fontainebleau Hotel was loved by celebrities and the public but loathed by critics, who deemed the $13 million hotel and its "Staircase to Nowhere" far too gaudy.

Flashiness was the exception, not the rule, as a desire for standardization took hold across the nation. In 1952, the first Holiday Inn, offering inexpensive, reliable, family accommodations, opened in Memphis, Tennessee. In five years, Kemmons Wilson's franchises formed a chain of clean, family-friendly motels. By 1959, there were 100, all essentially replicas of the original. Meanwhile, the first Howard Johnson's Motor Lodge opened in Savannah, Georgia, in 1954. This chain was built around the popular restaurants, featuring an appealing—and standardized—menu. These and other motels thrived as America's roadways developed in the postwar era. In 1956, President Dwight Eisenhower signed the Interstate Highway Act, the largest public works project yet known to mankind.

Air travel also hit new heights when the first commercial jet liner took off on May 2, 1952. The Jet Set era began with BOAC's service from London to Johannesburg, flying 480 miles per hour, compared to 180 mph on the DC-3.

But travel did not have to be peripatetic. Golfing vacations were in vogue. In 1951, former pro golfer Johnny Dawson and other investors bought the Thunderbird Dude Ranch in Rancho Mirage, California. They turned it into Palm Springs's first 18-hole golf course and development. Bing Crosby, Jimmy Van Heusen, and Phil Harris were charter members.

On screen, the incomparable Marilyn Monroe assured travel's allure in films that virtually bookended the decade. First, as Lorelei Lee, a gold-digging showgirl bound for Europe on a liner in *Gentlemen Prefer Blondes* (1953), Monroe stole the picture singing "Diamonds Are a Girl's Best Friend." Then, in Billy Wilder's classic *Some Like It Hot* (1959)—set in "Florida" at San Diego's Hotel del Coronado—Monroe's version of "I'm Through With Love" stole America's heart.

1952

1952 First Holiday Inn, offering inexpensive, standardized family accommodations, opens in Memphis, Tennessee

Eröffnung des ersten Holiday Inn als preiswerte, solide Familienherberge in Memphis, Tennessee

Ouverture du premier Holiday Inn offrant un hébergement familial bon marché à Memphis, Tennessee

1952 *From Here to Eternity*, set on military base in Hawaii, features starry cast – Montgomery Clift, Deborah Kerr, Burt Lancaster

Der in Hawaii spielende Film *Verdammt in alle Ewigkeit* zeigt Montgomery Clift, Deborah Kerr und Burt Lancaster

Tant Qu'il Y Aura des Hommes est tourné sur une base militaire de Hawaï avec des stars (Montgomery Clift, Deborah Kerr, Burt Lancaster)

1953 Air Canada first airline to use computer reservation system with remote terminals

Air Canada als erste Fluglinie mit computerisiertem Reservierungssystem und Fernterminals

Air Canada devient la première compagnie aérienne à utiliser un système de réservation informatique avec terminaux distants

1953 Kiwi Sir Edmund Hillary and Nepali Tenzing Norgay first to reach summit of Mt. Everest, Earth's tallest mountain

Erstbesteigung des Mount Everest, des höchsten Bergs der Welt, durch den Neuseeländer Sir Edmund Hillary und den Sherpa Tenzing Norgay

L'alpiniste kiwi Sir Edmund Hillary et le Népalais Tenzing Norgay sont les premiers à atteindre le sommet du Mont Everest

AUF DEM HÖHEPUNKT DES KALTEN KRIEGS SAH CONRAD HILTON IN SEINEN HOTELS DIE SPEERSPITZE DER AMERIKANISCHEN WERTE – und die US-Regierung ebenfalls. Eine Bundesagentur, die Economic Cooperation Administration, bediente sich der Hilton-Hotels, um anderen den sanften Einfluss der USA schmackhaft zu machen. Mit Unterstützung durch Washington und ausländische Regierungen entstanden Hilton-Hotels in den wichtigen Kapitalen des Kalten Krieges – dort, wo der Westen dem Sowjetblock gegenüberstand.

Für Hilton sollten seine Hotels ein Symbol Amerikas sein, um „den Ländern, die dem Kommunismus am stärksten ausgesetzt sind, die andere Seite der Medaille zu zeigen – die Früchte der freien Welt". Seine Hotels waren offen und luftig, sei es in Istanbul, Kairo, Berlin oder Athen – die Essenz des amerikanischen Modernismus, mitten in eine fremde Stadt hineingeworfen, wie Annabel Jane Wharton in ihrem Buch *Building the Cold War* schreibt. Doch Hilton baute nicht nur Hotels, er kaufte sie auch. Für 111 Mio. $ erwarb er 1954 sämtliche Statler-Hotels – auf diesem Sektor die höchste je gezahlte Summe seit dem Kauf von Louisiana im Jahr 1803.

Währenddessen räumte der Architekt Morris Lapidus in Miami Beach auf. Sein moderner Barockentwurf von 1954 für das Fontainebleau Hotel wurde von Prominenten wie auch der Öffentlichkeit gut aufgenommen, doch von Kritikern verabscheut, die das 13 Mio. $ teure Hotel und seine „Treppe ins Nichts" als viel zu schrill empfanden.

Doch eine solche Aufdringlichkeit war nicht die Regel, denn man begann, landesweit verbindliche Standards anzustreben. In Memphis, Tennessee, eröffnete 1952 das erste Holiday Inn als preiswerte Familienherberge. Innerhalb von fünf Jahren führte Kemmons Wilsons Franchiseprojekt zu einer Kette von sauberen Motels. 1959 waren es bereits 100, im Wesentlichen schlichte Nachbildungen des Originals. Die erste Howard Johnson's Motor Lodge wurde 1954 in Savannah, Georgia, eröffnet. Hieraus sollte eine ganze Kette rund um die populären Restaurants mit ihrer attraktiven – und standardisierten – Speisekarte entstehen. Während man das Fernstraßennetz in der Nachkriegsära auszubauen begann, folgten noch viele weitere Motels. Präsident Dwight

Eisenhower unterzeichnete 1956 mit dem Interstate Highway Act das weiträumigste öffentliche Bauvorhaben aller Zeiten.

Auch mit den Flugreisen ging es steil nach oben, als sich am 2. Mai 1952 der erste kommerzielle Linienjet in die Lüfte schwang. Die Jetsetära begann mit dem Linienflug der BOAC von London nach Johannesburg – mit 770 km/h, verglichen mit den 290 km/h der DC-3.

Reisen musste nun aber nicht unbedingt Rastlosigkeit bedeuten. Auch Golfreisen waren gefragt. Zusammen mit anderen Investoren erwarb der frühere Profigolfer Johnny Dawson 1951 die Thunderbird Dude Ranch in Rancho Mirage, Kalifornien. So entstand Palm Springs' erster Golfplatz mit 18 Löchern.

Auf der Leinwand unterstrich Marilyn Monroe den Reiz des Reisens mit Filmen, die das Jahrzehnt praktisch einrahmten. Zunächst in *Gentlemen Prefer Blondes* (*Blondinen bevorzugt*, 1953) als Lorelei Lee, ein aufs Geld versessenes Showgirl auf einem Schiff nach Europa. Und in Billy Wilders Klassiker *Some Like It Hot* (*Manche mögen's heiß*, 1959), dessen Florida-Szenen im Hotel del Coronado unweit von San Diego (Kalifornien) gedreht wurden, gewann Monroes Version von „I'm Through With Love" die Herzen der Amerikaner.

1954

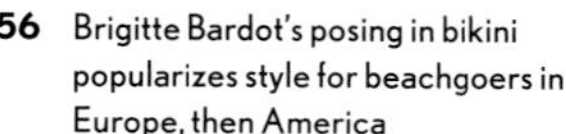

1954 First Howard Johnson's motor lodge opens in Savannah, Georgia

Eröffnung der ersten Howard Johnson's Motor Lodge in Savannah, Georgia

Ouverture du premier motel Howard Johnson à Savannah, Géorgie

1956 Brigitte Bardot's posing in bikini popularizes style for beachgoers in Europe, then America

Brigitte Bardot macht den Bikini als Strandoutfit zunächst in Europa und dann auch in den USA salonfähig

L'apparition de Brigitte Bardot en bikini lance cette mode auprès des amateurs de plage en Europe, puis en Amérique

1956 Airline travel in America hits 55 million passengers that year

Neuer Rekord mit 55 Millionen Flugreisenden in den USA

Le voyage aérien aux Etats-Unis atteint le pic des 55 millions de passagers

1956 Architect Morris Lapidus's glamorous Fontainebleau hotel sparks renaissance in Miami Beach, Florida

Das glamouröse Fontainebleau Hotel des Architekten Morris Lapidus verhilft Miami Beach, Florida, zu einer Renaissance

Rayonnant de glamour, l'hôtel Fontainebleau de l'architecte Morris Lapidus annonce la renaissance de Miami Beach, Floride

TWA
TWA
TWA
TWA

WESTERN AIR LINES

◄ Western Air Lines, ca. 1950

New Mexico, 1955

EN PLEINE GUERRE FROIDE, DANS LES ANNÉES 1950, CONRAD HILTON CONSIDÉRAIT SES HÔTELS COMME L'AVANT-GARDE DES VALEURS AMÉRICAINES – et le gouvernement américain vit dans les hôtels Hilton un argument commercial majeur pour le « soft power » des Etats-Unis. Avec l'aide de Washington et des gouvernements étrangers, les hôtels Hilton s'installèrent dans les grandes capitales de la Guerre Froide, là où l'Occident affrontait le Bloc soviétique.

Hilton voulait que ses hôtels symbolisent l'Amérique pour « montrer aux pays les plus exposés au communisme l'autre face de la médaille, les fruits du monde libre ». A Istanbul, au Caire, à Berlin et à Athènes, les structures de ses hôtels étaient ouvertes, légères et accessibles – l'emblème par excellence de la poussée du modernisme américain au cœur d'une ville étrangère, comme l'explique Annabel Jane Wharton dans son remarquable livre *Building the Cold War*. Hilton ne se contentait pas de construire des hôtels, il en achetait aussi. En 1954, il racheta toute la chaîne hôtelière Statler pour 111 millions de dollars, le prix le plus élevé jamais payé pour un projet immobilier depuis la Vente de la Louisiane par Napoléon en 1803.

Pendant que les valeurs standardisées de l'Amérique se frottaient à celles des « autres » dans les hôtels Hilton du monde entier, l'architecte Morris Lapidus révolutionnait Miami Beach. En 1954, son design baroque moderne pour le Fontainebleau Hotel enchanta les célébrités et le public, mais fut méprisé par les critiques qui trouvaient cet hôtel de 13 millions de dollars et son « escalier pour nulle part » de très mauvais goût.

Cette extravagance était l'exception et non la règle car un désir de standardisation s'emparait de tout le pays. En 1952, le premier Holiday Inn proposa des options d'hébergement bon marché et solides aux familles à Memphis dans le Tennessee. Cinq ans plus tard, les franchises de Kemmons Wilson formaient une chaîne de motels bien tenus et à l'ambiance familiale. En 1959, on en comptait déjà 100, autant de répliques quasi identiques à l'original. De même, le premier Howard Johnson's Motor Lodge ouvrit à Savannah, Géorgie, en 1954. Cette chaîne fut développée comme une extension des restaurants éponymes à succès qui proposaient un menu alléchant – et standardisé. De tels motels poussèrent comme

des champignons au fur et à mesure du développement du réseau routier américain. En 1956, le Président Eisenhower signa l'Interstate Highway Act, le plus grand projet de travaux publics de tous les temps.

Le voyage aérien atteignit aussi de nouveaux sommets quand le premier avion de ligne commerciale prit son envol le 2 mai 1952. L'ère de la jet-set s'ouvrit grâce à la liaison assurée par la compagnie BOAC entre Londres et Johannesburg, avec un appareil lancé à 770 kilomètres à l'heure, contre seulement 290 pour le DC-3.

On pouvait aussi voyager sur un mode sédentaire. Les séjours de golf étaient en vogue. En 1951, l'ancien golfeur professionnel Johnny Dawson et d'autres investisseurs achetèrent le Thunderbird Dude Ranch à Rancho Mirage, Californie. Ils en firent le premier parcours 18 trous et country club de Palm Springs. Bing Crosby, Jimmy Van Heusen et Phil Harris comptaient parmi ses membres fondateurs.

Au cinéma, Marilyn Monroe fit la promotion du voyage dans les films qu'elle tourna dans les années 1950 : dans *Les Hommes préfèrent les blondes* (1953), dans lequel elle incarne Lorelei Lee, danseuse qui voyage à bord d'un paquebot, ainsi que dans *Certains l'aiment chaud* (1959), qui se déroule en « Floride », à l'hôtel del Coronado de San Diego.

1957

1957 "Just say the words, and we'll beat the birds down to Acapulco Bay," Frank Sinatra sings in "Come Fly With Me"

In „Come Fly With Me" meint Frank Sinatra, es bedürfe nur der richtigen Worte, und schon sei man schneller als die Vögel in Acapulco

« Just say the words, and we'll beat the birds down to Acapulco Bay », chante Frank Sinatra dans « Come Fly With Me »

1958 Oscar Niemeyer's Brasilia Palace Hotel one of first structures to open in the stunningly modern Brazilian capital

Oscar Niemeyers Brasilia Palace Hotel als eines der ersten Gebäude in der neuen hypermodernen Hauptstadt Brasiliens eingeweiht

Le Brasilia Palace Hotel d'Oscar Niemeyer est l'un des premiers établissements ouverts dans la nouvelle capitale brésilienne

1959 Cairo Hilton opens with gala attended by President Gamal Abdel Nasser; site of all important local events for two decades

Eröffnungsgala des Kairoer Hilton in Anwesenheit von Präsident Gamal Abdel Nasser, das für zwei Jahrzehnte Schauplatz aller wichtigen lokalen Events sein wird

L'hôtel Hilton du Caire, qui ouvrit en présence de Président Nasser, fut un site majeur pendant vingt ans

1959 Cary Grant pursued in white-knuckle chase down Mt. Rushmore, in Alfred Hitchcock's *North by Northwest*

Cary Grant sucht im packenden Finale von Alfred Hitchcocks *Der unsichtbare Dritte* Zuflucht auf dem Mount Rushmore

Dans *La Mort aux trousses* d'Alfred Hitchcock, Cary Grant est victime d'une course-poursuite haletante devant le Mont Rushmore

204

Your fastest way to tropic sun—fly DC-7

Whatever your reason for getting there faster...

Nothing beats the DC-7—world's fastest airliner

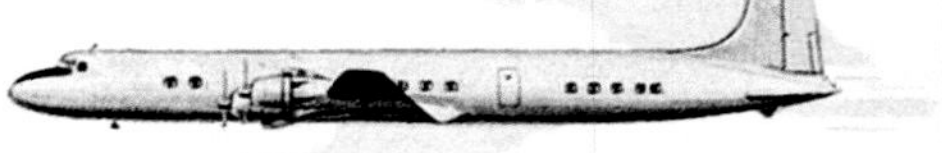

You go up to *50 mph faster* in the new DC-7 than in any other airliner—its top speed is 410! You fly in luxury, too, with scores of new comforts, new conveniences.

Next time, be sure to go by DC-7. See why twice as many people fly Douglas as all other airplanes *combined*.

◄ Douglas, 1956

The Douglas DC-7, first flown in 1953, was the last word in piston engines before the jet arrived. But its speed was heralded, since it allowed passengers to fly nonstop across the country in eight hours. Flying was indeed for pleasure.

Bevor die Jets aufkamen, verkörperte die ab 1953 verkehrende Douglas DC-7 die letzte Maschine mit Kolbenmotor. Doch ihre Geschwindigkeit kündete bereits von einer neuen Ära, denn nun konnte man in nur acht Stunden nonstop von einer Küste zur anderen gelangen. Und Fliegen machte wirklich Spaß.

Quand le Douglas DC-7 prit son envol en 1953, il représentait le nec plus ultra des appareils à moteurs à pistons, avant l'arrivée de l'avion à réaction. Il présageait toutefois sa vitesse, puisqu'il permettait aux passagers de traverser le pays sans escale en huit heures. Le voyage en avion devenait enfin un plaisir.

Northwest Airlines, 1955

Sunny Hawaii . . . exotic foods . . . lazy days . . . silver surf

HAWAII—where it's always springtime—is as near as tomorrow when you fly Northwest. And what a way to go to Hawaii! Before you know it you're wrapped in golden sunshine lazing on a breeze-kissed beach. You fly in Royal Aloha Service luxury aboard fast DC-6B's with two-abreast seating and exclusive Twin-Screen Radar. You're treated to complimentary champagne . . . delicious hot meals . . . beverage service is available. All at low, low tourist fares. And you can take advantage of Northwest's lowest-cost Fly Now—Pay Later plan. Only 10% down. So stop dreaming, start planning today! See your travel agent or call

NORTHWEST *Orient* AIRLINES

32 years of superior Airmanship

Fly NWA's Royal Aloha Service with complimentary champagne. For more information mail the coupon today.

HAWAII INFORMATION SERVICE
NORTHWEST ORIENT AIRLINES
St. Paul 1, Minnesota

Send me your illustrated Hawaii Guide Book describing where to go and what to see in *all* the islands of Hawaii. Enclosed is 25¢.

Name __________

Street __________

City ______ *Zone* ___ *State* ______

Hilton and Statler Hotels select **Avis** Rent-a-Car for their guests

These 28 distinguished hotels will deliver you a fine, new car from Avis . . . or reserve one for you when you reserve your room.

For they know the discriminating traveler wants the freedom and comfort of a personal car wherever he stays . . . on business or pleasure. And they know that Avis provides cars you are proud to drive . . . new models, sparkling clean, fully insured and serviced.

It's easy to reserve an Avis car. Call any Avis Office or Hilton-Statler—or ask your plane or train ticket agent. You can reserve a car almost anywhere in the world at Avis' 800 offices. They honor credit cards from Avis, Hilton-Statler, and many others.

Next time you travel have a new Avis car available wherever you go . . . for as long as you need it. And ask about the convenient "Rent it here—leave it there" service.

RENT-a-CAR

AWAY OR AT HOME...
A CAR OF YOUR OWN

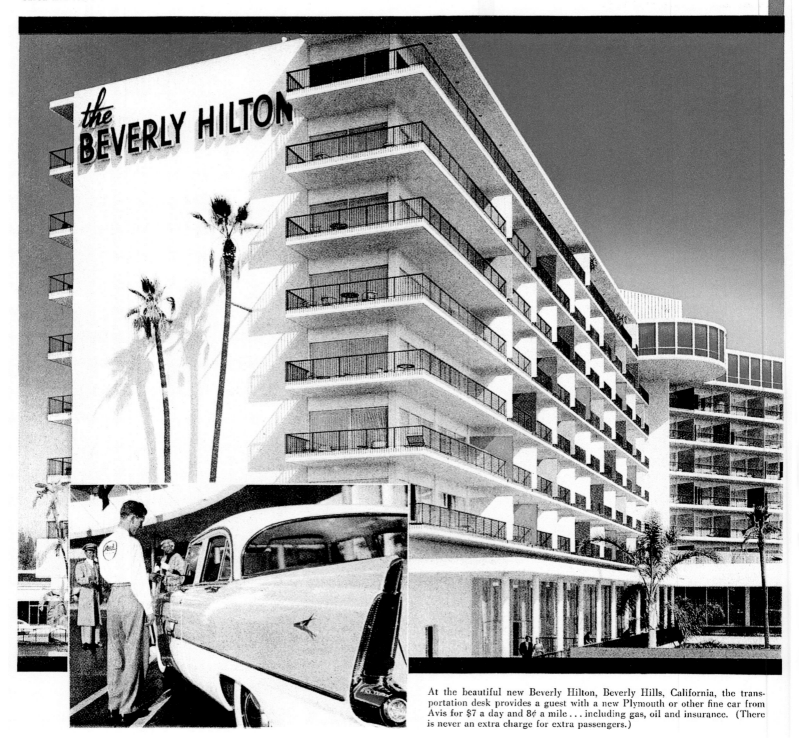

At the beautiful new Beverly Hilton, Beverly Hills, California, the transportation desk provides a guest with a new Plymouth or other fine car from Avis for $7 a day and 8¢ a mile . . . including gas, oil and insurance. (There is never an extra charge for extra passengers.)

◄ Avis, 1956

When the Beverly Hilton Hotel opened in 1955, it was labeled "The Motel in Cinemascope" by *Architectural Forum*. In a city based on the car, the Beverly Hilton was in the best possible location, where Wilshire and Santa Monica boulevards meet. In 1954, Conrad Hilton had bought the entire Statler Hotel chain.

Die Zeitschrift *Architectural Forum* bezeichnete das 1955 eröffnete Beverly Hilton Hotel als „Das Motel in Cinemascope". Das am Schnittpunkt des Wilshire und des Santa Monica Boulevard platzierte Beverly Hilton war wie geschaffen für eine Stadt, in der das Auto unverzichtbar war. Conrad Hilton hatte 1954 sämtliche Statler-Hotels erworben.

La revue *Architectural Forum* qualifia le Beverly Hilton Hotel de « motel en cinémascope » lors de son ouverture en 1955. Dans une ville dépendante de l'automobile, le Beverly Hilton se trouvait au meilleur endroit possible, au croisement de Wilshire et Santa Monica Boulevard. En 1954 Conrad Hilton, avait racheté toute la chaîne hôtelière Statler.

Hertz, 1957

►► TWA, 1950

Airlines gave travelers the ability to journey almost anywhere on the globe—even if they only had as little as two weeks to do it in. Travel was deluxe and exciting, and offered endless possibilities to so many who might never have considered a big trip during an earlier era.

Nun konnte man mit dem Flugzeug nahezu jedes Ziel auf dem Globus ansteuern – selbst wenn dafür nur zwei Wochen zur Verfügung standen. Das Reisen gestaltete sich luxuriös und zugleich aufregend und bot vielen Menschen, die früher nie an eine große Reise gedacht hätten, endlose Möglichkeiten.

Les compagnies aériennes permettaient à leurs passagers de se rendre presque partout sur la planète, même s'ils n'avaient que deux semaines de vacances. Le voyage était luxueux, excitant, et offrait des possibilités illimitées à beaucoup de personnes qui n'auraient auparavant jamais envisagé de faire un long périple.

Hertz rents the kind of cars you like to drive!

What's your pleasure? A Cadillac, maybe? Hertz rents Cadillacs. Hertz rents big Buicks and Oldsmobiles, too. Thousands of new Chevrolets and other fine cars. Station wagons, convertibles, sports cars. Take your pick at most Hertz offices.

They're all in A-1 condition, expertly maintained, more dependable, cleaner cars. More with power steering. That's The Hertz Idea. You'll get the kind of car you like to drive at over 1,350 Hertz offices in more than 900 cities—world-wide. That's *more* offices by far where you can *rent* a car. *More* cities by far where you can *leave* a car. *More* locations where you can make a *reservation* for a car!

Just show your driver's license and proper identification. The national average rate for a new Powerglide Chevrolet Bel Air is only $7.85 a day plus 8 cents a mile. And that includes the cost of *all* the gasoline and oil you use en route... and proper insurance. In addition to the Hertz charge card, we honor all air, rail, Diners' Club and hotel credit cards.

To be sure of a car at your destination—anywhere—use Hertz' more efficient reservation service. Call your local Hertz office for fast, courteous service. We're listed under "Hertz" in *alphabetical* phone books everywhere! Hertz Rent A Car, 218 South Wabash Avenue, Chicago 4, Illinois.

More people by far... use
HERTZ
Rent a car

"Rent it here... Leave it there" Now, nation-wide at no extra charge! (on rentals of $25.00 or more).

Explore colorful, cosmopolitan San Francisco and Hollywood. Or simply loaf in the sun along beautiful Pacific shores, enjoying the extra time TWA gives you.

Your camera lens captures unbelievable colors in the glorious Southwest, where outdoor fun reigns in the wide-open spaces of dude ranches and resorts.

For wonderful fishing, fly TWA to Chicago and head North to the pine-forested lake country. There's camping, resort life, golfing, swimming and sailing.

Look for the new, the old, the smart and unique in New York—served by more than 25 TWA flights daily. It's a vacation full of memorable sights and experiences.

New England holds a treas Americana, cool salt breezes Cod sand dunes and sparkling lakes nestled in the mountai

Where in the world <u>can</u> you go on just 2 weeks' vacation?

Here's an easy way to measure your own new horizons along the HIGH ways of TWA.

You pick the places you'd *like* to go, then check the TWA time-map below.* Possibilities are TWA can save you so much travel time you actually *can* go . . . even with limited vacation time off! And TWA fares are surprisingly easy on your budget.

So forget the old, usual vacation haunts. This year, follow the TWA highway to the Great Southwest, to the east or west coast; to the mountains; to the seashores; to the Golden Gate or the Grand Canyon or the canyons of New York. You pick it—you measure it—you can make it, easily, probably in mere hours from where you are right now!

But perhaps your eyes are on the Old World . . . way, way overseas. How far is it by TWA? Look at the map again and see what a vast distance one single day's flight can cover. Yes, you *can* go to Paris on a two weeks' vacation. You can go to Switzerland; to Rome; to Cairo; to Lisbon; to Madrid. You can take your pick of these and many other famed holiday centers and resort lands along TWA's direct world routes and *still keep well within the practical time limits of a short vacation!*

If *you* have been dreaming about a certain trip, don't put it off this year due to a short vacation. Plan to use the speed of Skyliner travel to bridge the distance and make that dream come true. Your travel agent will be glad to help with all the answers to your trip questions. Or call TWA.

**All flying times shown are approximate. Check your travel agent or TWA for exact schedules.*

Ireland is a season of color-
nd fun-filled events . . . from
and fine racing to the famous
se Show in August.

For leisurely sight-seeing, try the quiet lanes of provincial France. For gaiety and sidewalk cafes—there's nothing like Paris! 16 TWA flights weekly from the U. S.

Like luxurious living? Then take a 300-mph TWA Skyliner to the Mediterranean area. You'll find the finest hotels and smart casinos on the world-famous Riviera.

Motoring offers rich rewards in the Swiss Alps, where breath-taking new scenes await you at every turn. And car rentals are reasonable in Europe.

Magnificent monuments and ancient art masterpieces are everywhere in Rome, scene of the Holy Year observances. Less than a day from the U. S. by TWA.

of the pleasure on your vacation will be the few pleasant hours
ute, when you travel by world-proved 300-mph TWA Skyliner.
on as you board, the thoughtful TWA hostess sees that you're
ortably settled in a deep, reclining seat. She'll bring you maga-
, playing cards, writing material . . . serve you delicious hot meals
it's time to eat. As you relax and rest, your dependable Sky-
speeds you to your destination in *hours* instead of days.

Across the U.S. and overseas . . .
you can depend on

TWA

TRANS WORLD AIRLINE

U.S.A. · EUROPE · AFRICA · ASIA

Ship almost anything anywhere by TWA Air Cargo—fast, dependable, low-cost! For mail and small packages, use air mail and air parcel post.

TWA
TRANS WORLD AIRLINE
3/4 hrs
3 hrs
5½ hrs
12 hrs
PARIS
ZURICH
GENEVA
MILAN
MADRID
LISBON
ROME
ATHENS
ALGIERS
TUNIS
BENGASI
TRIPOLI
TEL-AVIV
CAIRO
BASRA
DHAHRAN
BOMBAY

NOW IN HAWAII

SHERATON

HOTELS

ON THE BEACH AT WAIKIKI

you'll find the fabled things that Polynesian dreams are made of — sun, surf, majestic Diamond Head and that impossibly blue Pacific.

PRINCESS KAIULANI

THE SURF RIDER

THE MOANA

ROYAL HAWAIIAN

Sheraton Hotels, 1959

► Hotel Nacional de Cuba, 1953

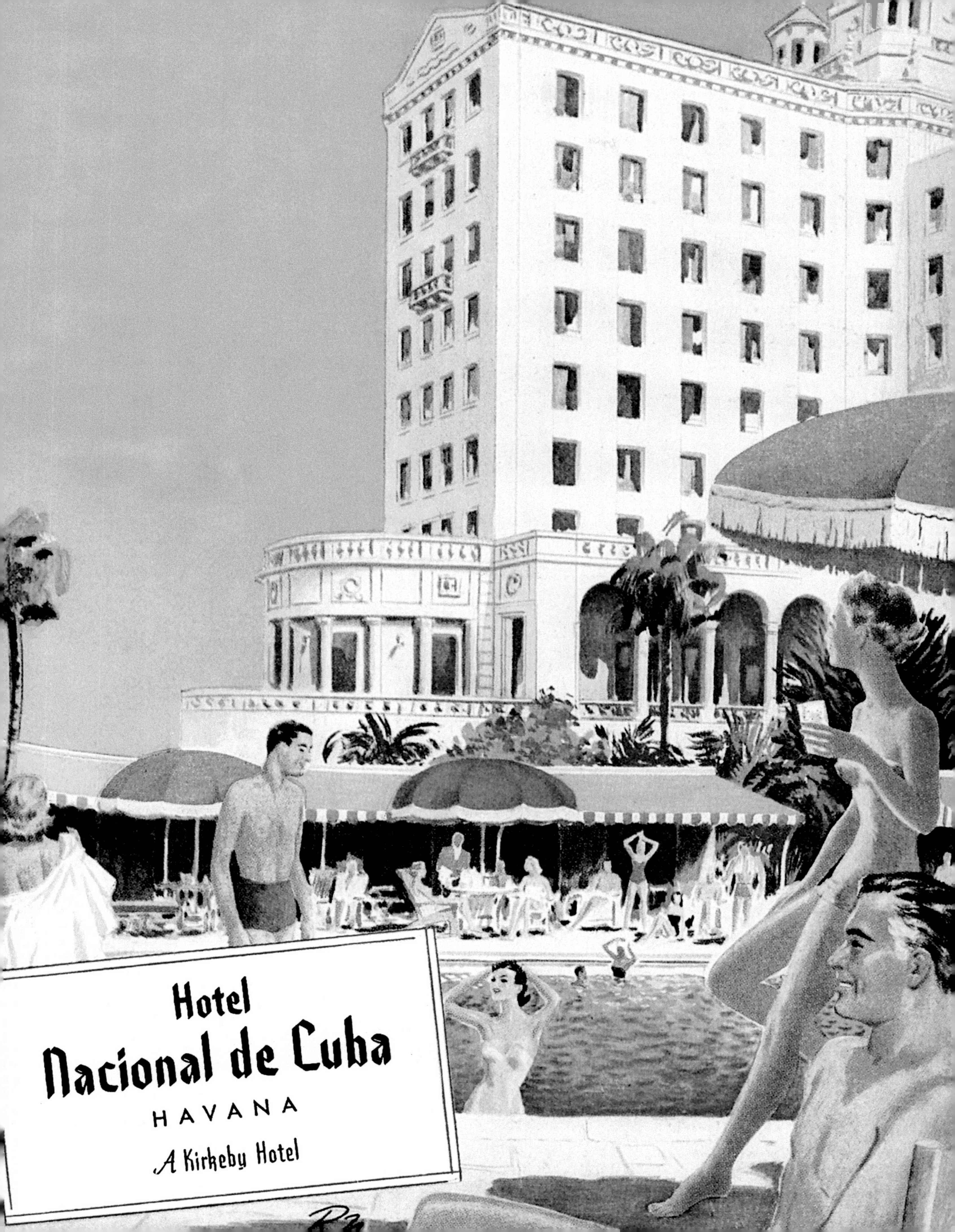
Hotel
Nacional de Cuba
HAVANA
A Kirkeby Hotel

*JETSTREAM IS A SERVICE MARK OWNED EXCLUSIVELY BY TWA

CAIRO—Another Hilton Hotel! New and beautiful as the mighty TWA JETSTREAM, longest-range airliner in the world today. The magnificent, 400-room Nile Hilton, on the banks of the majestic Nile, overlooks the Pyramids, the old Citadel and the city of Cairo with its mosques, museums and historic monuments. Completely air-conditioned, it is an ideal year-round meeting place for world travelers. Surrounded by symbols of ancient civilization and Pharaonic splendor, guests will enjoy every modern comfort, convenience and famous Hilton hospitality. And, TWA will fly you direct to Cairo.

RESERVATIONS: *See your Travel Agent or call New York, LOngacre 3-6900 • Chicago, FInancial 6-2772 • San Francisco, YUkon 3-0576 • Miami, FRanklin 9-3427 • Pittsburgh, COurt 1-5600 • Toronto, EMpire 2-3771 • London, Whitehall 3061 or any Hilton Hotel.* **CARTE BLANCHE**—*The Hilton All-Purpose Credit Card — Your Finest Credit Credential.*

EXECUTIVE OFFICES
THE CONRAD HILTON
CHICAGO 5, ILLINOIS

Hilton Hotels
AROUND THE WORLD
Conrad N. Hilton, President

Hilton Hotels, 1959

NOW OPEN... LATIN AMERICA'S TALLEST, LARGEST HOTEL
habana hilton
habana hilton

HAVANA, the glamorous, gay capital of Cuba, provides a sophisticated setting for the new 30-story high Habana Hilton. Overlooking Havana, historic Morro Castle and the harbor, this spectacular, completely air-conditioned hotel offers 630 lavishly appointed rooms and suites, each with a large private balcony, plus all the facilities of a magnificent resort. A swimming pool, colorful cabanas, an exciting Trader Vic's restaurant and a roof top cocktail lounge, the Sugar Bar, are just a few of the many outstanding features at Latin America's largest hotel, the fabulous new Habana Hilton.

Reservations: See Travel Agent or call New York, LOngacre 3-6900 • Chicago, FInancial 6-2772 • San Francisco, YUkon 6-0576 • Miami, FRanklin 9-3427 • Pittsburgh, COurt 1-5600 • Toronto, EMpire 8-2921 • Montreal, UNiversity 1-3301 • Havana, F-3296 or any Hilton Hotel.

EXECUTIVE OFFICES
THE CONRAD HILTON
CHICAGO 5, ILL.

Hilton Hotels
AROUND THE WORLD
Conrad N. Hilton, President

Hilton Hotels, 1959

IN CHICAGO IT'S THE
SHERATON
HOTEL

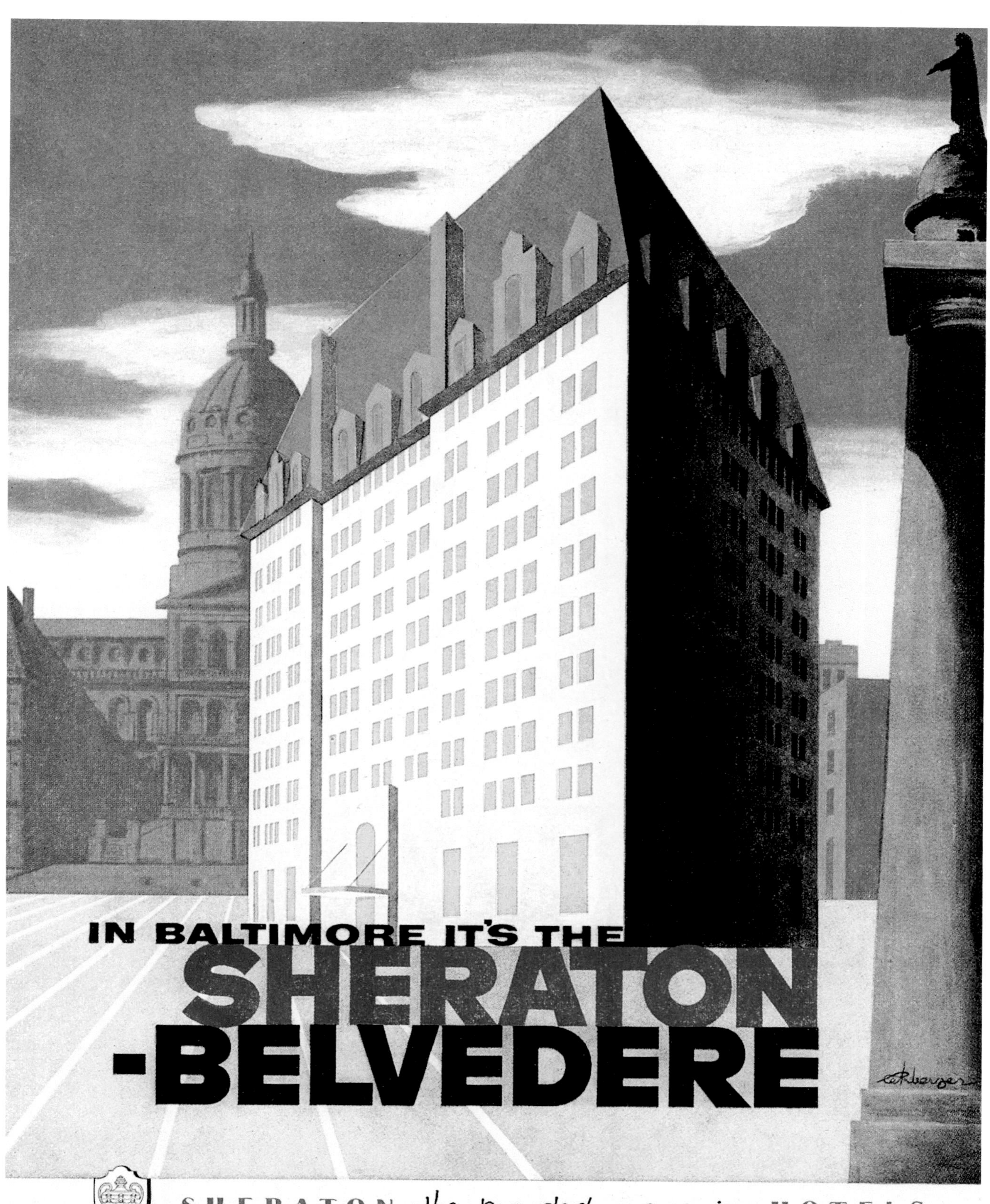

IN BALTIMORE IT'S THE
SHERATON
-BELVEDERE
SHERATON the proudest name in HOTELS

◂ Sheraton Hotels, 1954

Sheraton-Belvedere, 1954

▸▸ Santa Fe Railway, 1951

Be carefree, be comfortable and enjoy a

New World

Standard in Travel

The new Santa Fe

Super Chief

Advanced ideas for your travel luxury... new cradled smoothness in the ride... daily between Chicago and Los Angeles

From the flanges on the wheels to the tip of the Pleasure Dome, the Super Chief is new—entirely new.

To give you the smoothest ride of your life on rails, this new Super Chief glides on cushioned springs . . . revises any ideas you ever had about any train.

The keynote is comfort.

You find it in the distinctive Turquoise Room in the lounge car—a delightful place to relax, enjoy a cocktail or entertain your friends at dinner—the first time such a room has been provided on any train.

You find it in the Pleasure Dome—"top of the Super, next to the stars"—that brings you an unobstructed view of wonderful southwestern scenery.

You find it in the new dining cars where Fred Harvey chefs present new and exciting menus.

Accommodations in this beautiful all-room train are designed to pamper you every mile of the way. "Push-button" radio or music in your room when you *want* it . . . beds you just can't help sleeping in . . . charming apartments by day.

From the engineers who glide you across this great country to the porter who answers your bell, this is the train of thoughtful service.

For your next trip between Chicago and Los Angeles say "Super Chief." Now, more than ever, it is America's train of trains. Just consult your local ticket agent.

SANTA FE SYSTEM LINES
Serving the West and Southwest
Santa Fe

BURR TILLSTROM, KUKLA AND OLLIE, *whimsical, lovable stars of NBC television trade their five nights a week spotlight for days of sunlight on their recent Mediterranean holiday aboard the great new Sun-Liner Independence.*

Every voyage a Gay Cruise...

When you sail the Sun-Lane to Europe, it's not just a trip from one port to another but an exciting voyage that touches upon the loveliest lands of the Mediterranean. And liberal stop-over privileges make all of these garden spots yours to sample if you're in a hurry, or to linger in if you wish.

On the great new Sun-Liners of American Export Lines, you enjoy "Modern American Living at Sea"...a gay, friendly, carefree informality amid every comfort and service that American ingenuity can provide.

Even the weather on the Sun-Lane conspires to lift your spirits. Fall, winter and spring average 87 per cent rain-free days, and through the summer the gentle trade winds cool your smooth path to a perfect 71 degrees average. When you enter the Continent from the sunny, southern side you'll find much of the best of Europe all around you . . . the rest of Europe just hours away.

SEE YOUR TRAVEL AGENT OR **AMERICAN EXPORT LINES** 39 BROADWAY, N. Y. 6, N. Y.

INDEPENDENCE • CONSTITUTION
GIBRALTAR, CANNES, GENOA, NAPLES

EXETER • EXCALIBUR • EXOCHORDA • EXCAMBION
FRANCE, ITALY, EGYPT, LEBANON, SYRIA, TURKEY, GREECE, SPAIN

American Export Lines, 1952

Getting there is half the *fun!*

Autumn is ideal for your visit to Europe . . . when Britain and the Continent are at their sparkling, uncrowded best . . . and ideal, too, for a gay, relaxing ocean voyage! When you go Cunard, each day at sea and each brilliant, enchanted evening is a glorious new adventure shared with interesting companions amid all the comforts of a great seaside resort. You'll delight in the bright conviviality, the thoughtful, attentive service for which Cunard is famous . . . and the marvelous food, prepared for your sea-sharpened appetite by internationally trained chefs. See your travel agent about Cunard's lower "Thrift Season" rates.

Write for Cunard's attractive new brochure "Gracious Living at its Best."

Swimming Pool in the Queen Mary

No wonder more people prefer CUNARD

From New York: QUEEN ELIZABETH • QUEEN MARY • MAURETANIA • CARONIA • BRITANNIC • MEDIA • PARTHIA
From Canada: FRANCONIA • SCYTHIA • SAMARIA • ASCANIA

Cunard, 1953

THE CHARMING SETTING for your luxury flight overseas is the smart interior of your Air France Constellation. Limited number of "sky-lounger" chairs provide the most spacious accommodations in air travel for your individual comfort. You are served in the inimitable French manner by friendly English-speaking stewards and hostess.

Fly in Luxury UNEXCELLED IN AIR TRAVEL —AT NO EXTRA COST! *Fly Air France!*

VETERAN PILOTS—many of whom have logged more than a million miles in the air—fly the new-type AIR FRANCE Constellations. Seasoned world-travelers know and respect the world-famed AIR FRANCE reputation for regularity and dependability. They know, too, that AIR FRANCE offers the ultimate in gracious living aloft—luxury *unequalled* in air travel. Gourmet cuisine, prepared by masters of the art of French cooking. Champagne, too, or a vintage wine...a liqueur after dinner, of course. Your entire trip by AIR FRANCE is an adventure in living as *only* the French know how!

"THE PARISIAN"—Luxury trans-Atlantic air travel—an experience in gracious living. Departures from New York, Boston, and Montreal to Paris, Frankfurt, Berlin, Rome.

"THE PARISIAN SPECIAL"—The world-famous ultra-de-luxe AIR FRANCE flight—non-stop overnight from New York to Paris. Ten dollars additional fare.

NEW TOURIST SERVICE. New York-Paris round-trip $522 April 1-October 31. $453 November 1-March 31. New Type constellations. Meals obtained at moderate prices.

THE WORLD'S LARGEST NETWORK of AIR ROUTES Serving 76 Countries on 6 Continents

FRANCE

SPAIN

INDIA

SEE YOUR TRAVEL AGENT

AIR FRANCE

THE **LUXURY** WORLD-WIDE AIRLINE

AIR FRANCE, 683 Fifth Avenue, New York 22, PLaza 9-7000
Offices in Boston, Chicago, Cleveland, Dallas, Los Angeles, San Francisco, Washington, D. C., Bogota, Caracas, Havana, Mexico, Montreal.

What airline gives you Red Carpet* Service? United Air Lines

It's "Red Carpet" luxury all the way...

aboard United's special nonstop DC-7s!

Inviting lounge, superlative service...

de luxe meals and refreshments!

Games, kits, scores of travel items...

many other "extras" at no extra cost!

On United's "Red Carpet" flights you enjoy brilliant new service on DC-7s, the world's fastest airliners. Everything is special—from the red carpet itself, air travel's warmest welcome mat, to the extra-fast way your luggage is delivered to you on arrival. Choose "Red Carpet" Service—coast-to-coast and on other special nonstop flights. And for extra savings, fly half-fare Family Plan—now Monday noon through Thursday noon. Call or write United or your Authorized Travel Agent.

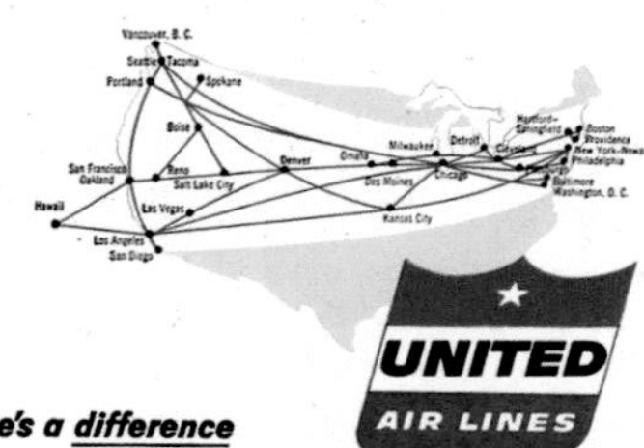

There's a difference when you travel in the Mainliner® Manner

◄ Air France, 1952

United Air Lines, 1956

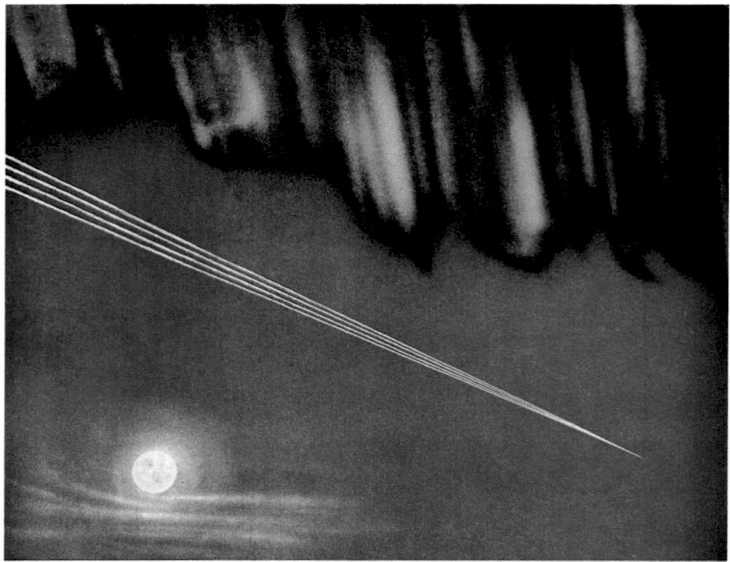

The Douglas DC-8 in flight, newest bearer of the most respected name in aviation

Look up to the DC-8 . . . world's newest jetliner!

Into the skies—from the Northern Lights to the Southern Cross—flies the Douglas DC-8. And with this flight, travel by air reaches a new high level of performance and comfort.

In the still, blue stratosphere, the miles tick away on the wings of this most modern of passenger planes. The earth's masses of land and water, awesome as they are, yield to the murmuring power of the DC-8 jet engines. Cradled in peace and luxury, you now can reach the world's farthest corners in less time than it takes the sun to go full circle.

But speed alone is not what distinguishes Douglas from all other names in aviation. The DC-8—like each of its world-famous predecessors—takes to the skies a family tradition of experience, dependability and comfort unrivalled in the annals of flight. It is this—*and more*—which makes passengers and pilots look up to Douglas . . . reveals, in part, why more people and more airlines fly Douglas than all other airplanes combined.

Your own personal introduction to the jet age is not far off. Like so many others, you will experience it in the nonpareil of the upper air, the fabulous . . .

DOUGLAS DC-8 JETLINER

Built by the most respected name in aviation

These famous airlines already have purchased the DC-8: ALITALIA-Linee Aeree Italiane • DELTA AIR LINES • EASTERN AIR LINES • JAPAN AIR LINES • KLM ROYAL DUTCH AIR LINES
NATIONAL AIRLINES • OLYMPIC AIRWAYS • PANAGRA • PANAIR DO BRASIL • PAN AMERICAN WORLD AIRWAYS • SCANDINAVIAN AIRLINES SYSTEM • SWISSAIR
TRANS-CANADA AIR LINES • TRANS CARIBBEAN AIRWAYS • TRANSPORTS AERIENS INTERCONTINENTAUX • UNION AEROMARITIME DE TRANSPORT • UNITED AIR LINES

LOOK UP TO THE DC-8!

The DC-8, now in flight, will soon carry you to new heights of luxurious air travel.

DC-8 introduces you to Her Serene Highness–the Stratosphere

Beneath the outstretched wings of the DC-8, the world falls swiftly below. The sky you climb into turns from blue to purple, and as you reach new heights, there comes over you a sense of serenity you've never known before.

Cradled in your pressurized cabin in the Douglas Jetliner eight miles high, with the sun and moon your neighbors, you gaze down on the toylike towns and peaks and waters of the world. Tranquilly suspended in the clear quiet of the stratosphere, you experience no sense of speed, no vibration, no engine's roar . . . nothing but a beautiful peace of mind and body.

But the DC-8 offers you more than speed and serenity. It brings you a family history of experience, dependability and comfort unmatched in the annals of flight. It is this—*and more*—which makes passengers and pilots look up to Douglas. You'll sense it all when you take your first flight in the fabulous . . .

DOUGLAS DC-8 JETLINER

Built by the most respected name in aviation

These famous air lines already have purchased the DC-8: ALITALIA-Linee Aeree Italiane • DELTA AIR LINES • EASTERN AIR LINES • JAPAN AIR LINES • KLM ROYAL DUTCH AIR LINES NATIONAL AIRLINES • OLYMPIC AIRWAYS • PANAGRA • PANAIR DO BRASIL • PAN AMERICAN WORLD AIRWAYS • SCANDINAVIAN AIRLINES SYSTEM • SWISSAIR TRANS-CANADA AIR LINES • TRANS CARIBBEAN AIRWAYS • TRANSPORTS AERIENS INTERCONTINENTAUX • UNION AEROMARITIME DE TRANSPORT • UNITED AIR LINES

Douglas, 1958

It is hard to have a Jet Set without a jet. The Douglas DC-8 jetliner took off in 1958, in direct competition with the Boeing 707. Passengers "getting away from it all" considered jet flight an enthralling experience.

Ein Jetset ohne Jet wäre ein Unding. Der Linienjet Douglas DC-8 schwang sich 1958 in die Lüfte, in direkter Konkurrenz zur Boeing 707. Fluggäste, die einfach mal alles hinter sich lassen wollten, zeigten sich überaus angetan.

Sans jet, pas de jet-set. L'avion à réaction Douglas DC-8 décolla en 1958, en concurrence directe avec le Boeing 707. Les passagers en quête d'évasion trouvaient qu'il n'y avait rien de plus excitant que de voyager en jet.

Douglas, 1958

► United Air Lines, 1951

United Air Lines is the

only airline linking the East,

the Middle West, all major

Pacific Coast cities and Hawaii.

Wherever you travel,

fly United's Main Line Airway—

truly the Nation's

No. 1 Coast-to-Coast Airline.

S·A·S inaugurates
FIRST NEW ROUTE
TO EUROPE
in a thousand years!
Since Viking days, both ships and planes have followed ocean lanes to Europe.
Now, S·A·S opens a *true direct route, north over the short polar path,* from Los Angeles to Copenhagen and all Europe, to Africa and Asia.
Royal Viking passengers cruise in regal comfort over Canada and Greenland, dine on continental cuisine with vintage wines, sleep in air-foam berths. No change of planes now, from California to the Continent, with first class luxury all the way.
Royal Viking flights, too, from New York to Europe, Africa, Near and Far East.
SAS
S·A·S POLAR ROUTE
LOS ANGELES
NEW YORK
all EUROPE
S·A·S
SCANDINAVIAN
AIRLINES SYSTEM
30 Rockefeller Plaza, New York

Service is an art from the heart. Your *SAS* cabin crew, skilled by training and tradition, welcomes you aboard . . . surrounds you with gracious attentions.

Cocktail hour in the sky is a bright occasion in the Global Express lounge. What would delight you most? Aperitif —sherry—whisky? The choice is yours.

Dinner is a triumph on *SAS.* Delicacies from the garden spots of the world are prepared with the famed mastery of *SAS* chefs, then served luxuriously.

To all the world, SAS speeds the hours with splendor

In all the geography of travel, splendor is a three-letter word spelled *SAS.* And it is yours to enjoy aboard the world fleet of *SAS* Global Express planes. To DC-7C speed, *SAS* adds radar magic that smooths the sky. Continental cuisine. Spacious berths. And hospitality around the clock! Next trip, ask your travel agent for *SAS,* First Class or Economy Class to Europe, transatlantic from New York or transpolar from California . . . to Africa . . . to the Near East and the Far East.

FIRST OVER THE POLE
SAS
SCANDINAVIAN
AIRLINES SYSTEM
THE GLOBAL AIRLINE

Soon . . . the Golden Age of Travel . . . SAS DC-8s and Caravelle Jets

638 Fifth Avenue, New York 20, N. Y.

◂ Scandinavian Airlines System, 1954

Scandinavian Airlines System, 1958

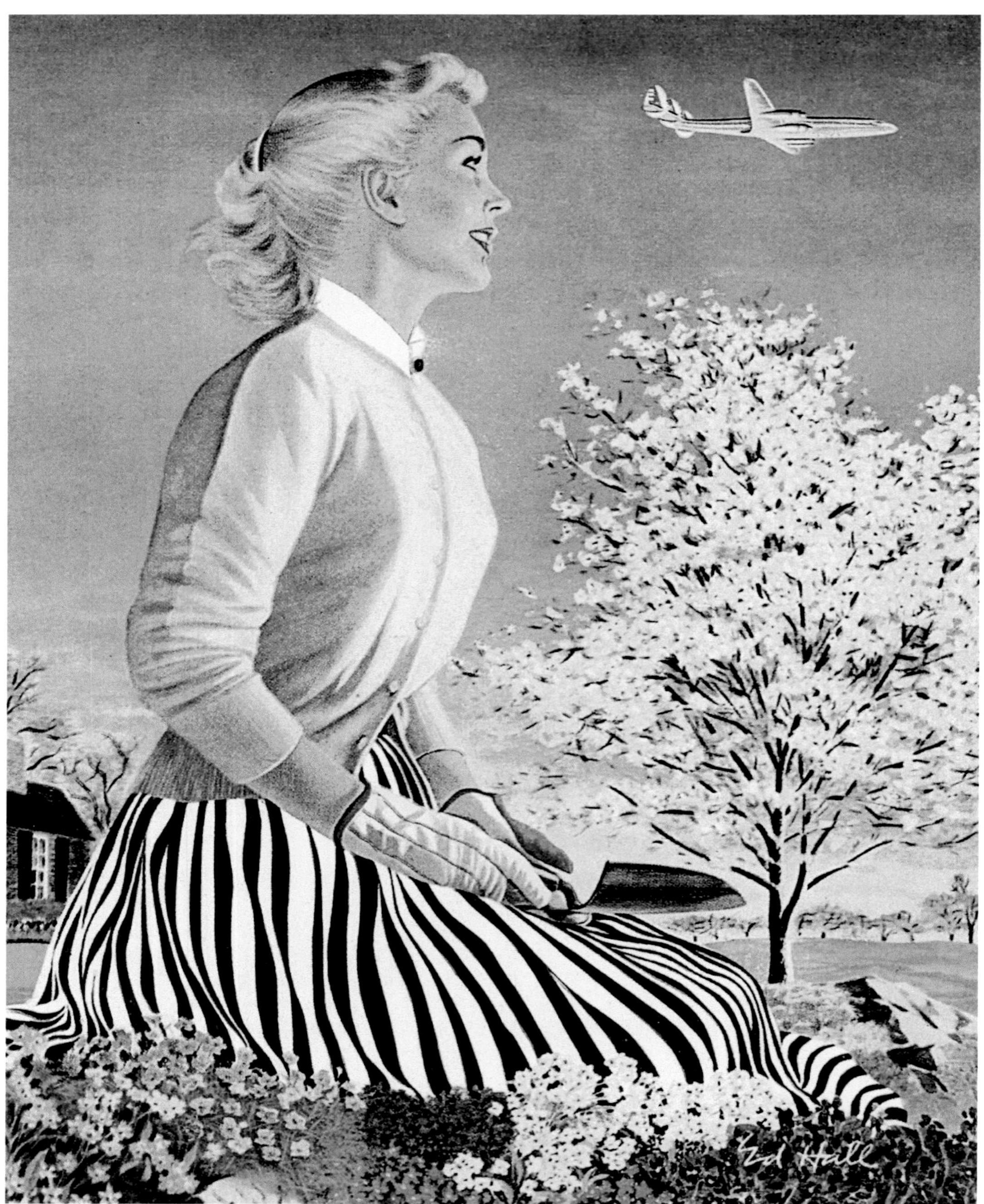

Capital Airlines, 1953

► American Airlines, 1956

Acapulco was a key Jet Set hub during the 1950s. Hollywood mingled with European aristocrats and American plutocrats in the hills above Acapulco Bay. The sybaritic Las Brisas Hotel, where each casita has its own private swimming pool, became the place to be when it opened in 1957.

Acapulco war in den 1950er-Jahren ein beliebter Treffpunkt des Jetset. Auf den Hügeln über der Bucht von Acapulco gaben sich Hollywoodstars, europäische Aristokraten und amerikanische Plutokraten ein Stelldichein. Das verschwenderische, 1957 eröffnete Las Brisas Hotel, wo jede Casita einen privaten Pool besaß, wurde zum absoluten Muss.

Pendant les années 1950, Acapulco était un rendez-vous incontournable pour la jet-set. Hollywood frayait avec l'aristocratie européenne et les plutocrates américains sur les collines de la Baie d'Acapulco. L'ultra luxueux Las Brisas Hotel, où chaque bungalow possédait sa propre piscine privée, devint le must dès son ouverture en 1957.

►► Convair, 1958

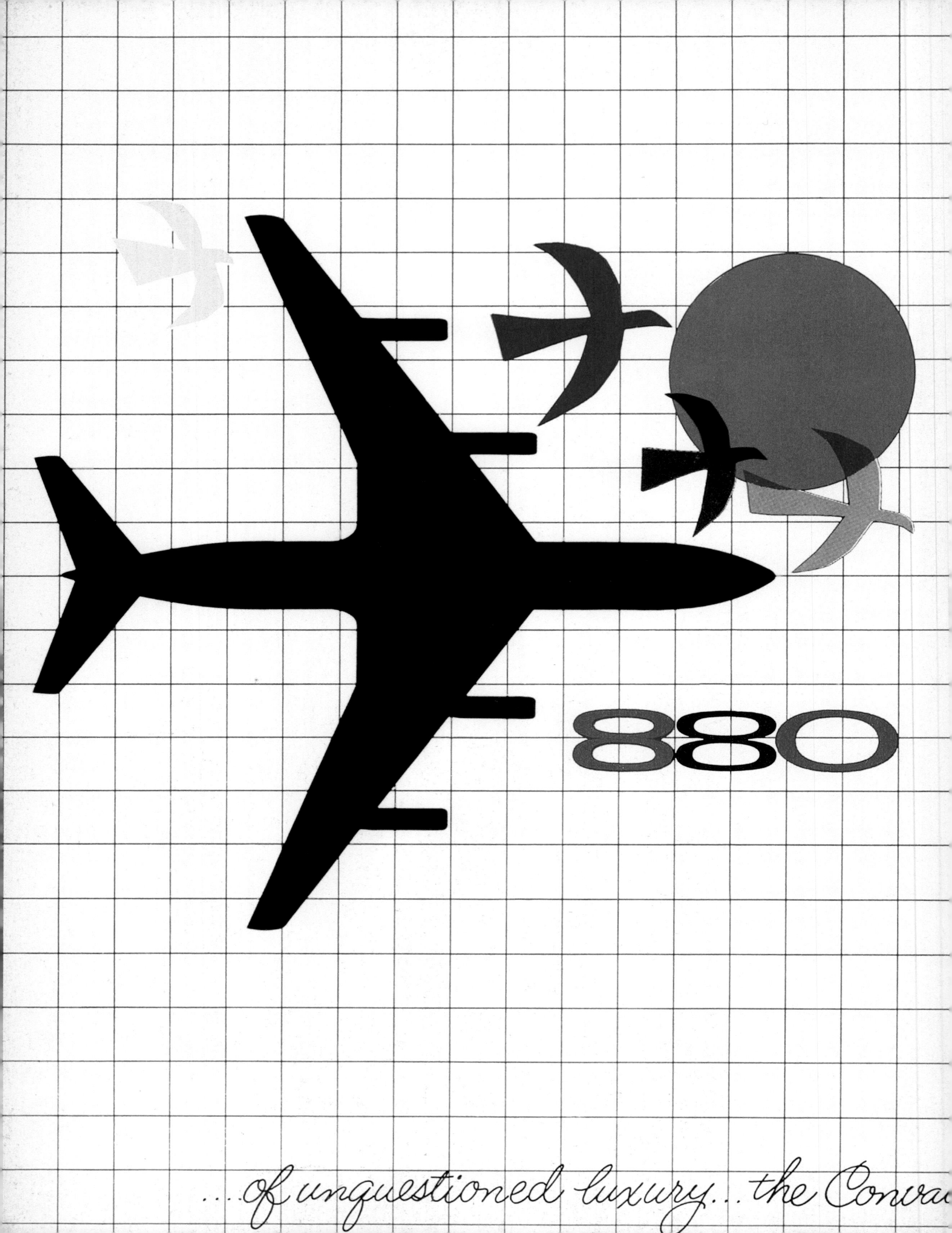
880
...of unquestioned luxury...the Convai

ght-eighty

The other 50 weeks are richer if you spend 2 abroad—so start planning your foreign vacation by Clipper *now.*

Live a lot...go abroad on even a 2-week vacation

Ever stop to think that your vacation lasts *you* a whole year? You look forward to it. You take it. You look back on it. So no matter when your vacation comes around, it should provide the lift that carries you through the year. That's why Pan American—the first choice of experienced travelers—will *never* let you down!

No place on earth is over 40 hours from your home on the wings of Pan Am's Flying Clippers*. As a matter of fact, many of the most glamorous places to which Pan American flies are only overnight. Indeed, in less time than it takes to drive 200 miles you can fly by Clipper to a foreign land from many parts of the U.S.A.

If your budget's tight, there are many ways to loosen it: Pan Am's Family Fare savings, thrifty tourist-fare *Rainbow* service, excursion fares, cost-inclusive *Pan Am Holidays* . . . all available on Pan Am's World-Wide Plan, Go Now—Pay Later: only 10% down.

Next year follow your heart, not the crowds. You're off to a flying start with a copy of *New Horizons*—the book that's put wings on the dreams of half a million world travelers. Call your Travel Agent or one of Pan Am's 53 offices in the U.S. and Canada. *TRADE-MARKS, REG. U. S. PAT. OFF.

YOUR VACATION PLANNER
Send for your copy of New Horizons*—Pan Am's 576-page, best selling world-wide travel guide. Mail $1 to Pan American, Dept. 170, Box 1111, New York 17, N.Y.
PAA PAA
Paris
Fiestas
Mexico
NASSAU
NEW HORIZONS WORLD GUIDE
PAN AM

WORLD'S MOST EXPERIENCED AIRLINE

Pan Am, 1957

► Rand McNally, 1956

CROSSING*

By Philip Booth

Stop, look, listen
as gate stripes
swing down,
count the cars
hauling distance
upgrade through town:
warning whistle,
bell clang,
engine eating steam,
engineer waving,
a fast-freight dream;
B. & M. boxcar,
boxcar again,
Frisco gondola,
eight-nine-ten,
Erie and Wabash,
Seaboard, U.P.,
Pennsy tank car,
twenty-two, three,
Phoebe Snow, B.&O.,
thirty-four, five,
Santa Fe cattle
shipped alive,
red cars, yellow cars,
orange cars, black,
Youngstown steel
down to Mobile
on Rock Island track,
fifty-nine, sixty,
hoppers of coke,
Anaconda copper,
hotbox smoke,
eighty-eight,
red-ball freight,
Rio Grande,
Nickel Plate,
Hiawatha,
Lackawanna,
rolling fast
and loose.
ninety-seven,
coal car,
boxcar,
CABOOSE!

There's poetry at every whistle stop. Rand McNally is proud of its 100 year history of printing maps, tickets, and timetables for buslines, airlines, railroads, and highway travel—the lifelines of America.

1856 *1956*
RAND McNALLY
100th Anniversary

PUBLISHERS • PRINTERS • MAP MAKERS • CHICAGO • NEW YORK • NASHVILLE • SAN FRANCISCO • WASHINGTON

how to work up an appetite for what's cooking in Caracas

Pirates had to eat, too, but they never had it so good as modern-day guests of the Hotel Tamanaco in Caracas, Venezuela, on the Ancient Spanish Main.

Whether you're licking your chops at the "groaning board" or "loafing it up" beside the sun-drenched swimming pool, you'll find yourself heir to the best of two worlds: the adventure of foreign travel, the comfort of American care.

From the food to the accommodations and entertainment, American attention to detail tempers Latin imagination. For that is what an Intercontinental vacation holds for you: service and efficiency blended with traditions of hospitality that are centuries old.

So if you've been looking for a vacation spot that's tailor-made for good times and good eating, the Hotel Tamanaco is your kind of place. Even without pirates, it's the most exciting place in Caracas.

Phone your travel agent or write Intercontinental Hotels, Chrysler Bldg., New York 17, N.Y. (If you prefer, call STillwell 6-5858 in New York.)

Elegant service — that's just one specialty of the house at the fabulous Hotel Tamanaco in Caracas, Venezuela

The World's Largest Group of International Hotels

So close...
So enticing!

A vacation costs so little
in these magical tropic isles!

■ The colorful fun of famous Waikiki . . . the music and dancing and feasts of old Polynesia . . . the romance of ancient life on dreamy island shores . . . these are the fabric of your adventure in Hawaii. Air and steamship lines link Hawaii with San Francisco, Los Angeles, Portland, Seattle, Vancouver. Short flights take you from Honolulu on **OAHU** to the grandeur of Haleakala on **MAUI** . . . to the acres of orchids of **HAWAII** . . . the unspoiled loveliness of **KAUAI.** Let your Travel Agent help you arrange to see all their scenic splendor.

HAWAII VISITORS BUREAU A non-profit organization maintained for your service by **THE PEOPLE OF HAWAII**

◂ Intercontinental Hotels, 1959

Hawaii Visitors Bureau, 1950

Karachi

Sunshine U.S.A.

This is Florida—Sunshine, U.S.A.—where everything you do and every place you go are filled with glorious adventure.

This year take it *all* in—the brilliance of Florida's palm-fringed beaches and sun-warmed surf; the tingling excitement of landing that first, or *hundred*-and-first, big-game fish; the thrill of driving one down the middle of velvet-green fairway. This year discover for yourself the splendor of Florida's scenic landmarks; the glamour of its renowned spectator events; the romance of its nights under the stars. And this year see with your own eyes why so many millions agree, there's no place like Florida for sunny pleasure, healthful relaxation, and sheer good living.

Plan it today—your sparkling Winter with Sunshine in Florida—the vacation adventure you'll remember a lifetime.

RACKOW

Florida

MAIL THIS COUPON TODAY

STATE OF FLORIDA,
2201 COMMISSION BUILDING, TALLAHASSEE.

Please send at once new, free 48-page booklet in full color: "Florida, the Sunshine State."

Name____________________

Street and No.____________________

City__________ Zone____ State______

◂ American President Lines, 1951

State of Florida, 1950

A chapter in your life you'll never forget
ALL too few are the occasions in life so gloriously, immeasurably perfect in every way that one cherishes their memory for a lifetime. Yet, the moment you step aboard your luxurious Italian Line flagship you'll know in your heart that *this* trip will be one of them.
You sail away from worry and care into another world of leisurely living . . . gracious service . . . superb cuisine . . . exciting visits to fascinating lands. You return rested, refreshed . . . rich in experiences you will treasure always, as you relive them in memory again and again.
COMING SOON! The new 25,000-ton luxury liner s.s. ANDREA DORIA. Completely air conditioned. Fine, spacious accommodations.
Italian Line
"ITALIA" SOCIETA di NAVIGAZIONE, GENOVA
See your Travel Agent or AMERICAN EXPORT LINES, General Agents, 39 Broadway, N. Y. 6, N. Y.
SATURNIA • VULCANIA • CONTE BIANCAMANO • The "Sunny Southern Route" to LISBON • GIBRALTAR • BARCELONA • PALERMO • NAPLES • CANNES • GENOA

Italian Line, 1952

► Italian Line, 1952

The Italian Line brought in the influential Gio Ponti to redesign the interiors of its ships, SS *Conte Biancamano* and *Conte Grande*, as well as the *Giulio Cesare*, *Africa* and *Oceana*. He reenvisioned this fleet as a sleekly modern "manifestation of the arts" of Italy. Ponti favored anodized-gold aluminum, which he seemed to use wherever possible. He talked about it as the best possible material—extremely light and aesthetically pleasing. Ponti also designed the interiors of the ill-fated SS *Andrea Doria*, the Italian Line's biggest and swiftest ship. In 1956, it collided with another vessel and sank the next day.

Die Italian Line engagierte den einflussreichen Architekten Gio Ponti für den Neuentwurf der Interieurs ihrer Schiffe, SS *Conte Biancamano* und *Conte Grande* ebenso wie *Giulio Cesare*, *Africa* und *Oceana*. Ponti verwendete Goldeloxal, wo immer möglich, für ihn war es das bestmögliche Material – extrem leicht und zugleich gefällig. Ebenso entwarf er das Interieur der unglückseligen *Andrea Doria*, des wohl flottesten und größten Schiffs der Italian Line. Es kollidierte 1956 mit einem anderen Schiff und sank am Tag darauf.

La Società di Navigazione italienne demanda à l'influent Gio Ponti de réaménager les intérieurs de ses navires, le *Conte Biancamano* et le *Conte Grande*, ainsi que le *Giulio Cesare*, *l'Africa* et *l'Oceana*. Il reconçut la flotte avec une modernité épurée, à l'image d'une « manifestation des arts » de l'Italie. Ponti privilégiait l'aluminium anodisé doré dès qu'il le pouvait. Il en parlait comme du meilleur des matériaux, à la fois extrêmement léger et esthétique. Il conçut aussi les intérieurs de l'infortuné *Andrea Doria*, considéré comme le paquebot le plus grand et le plus rapide de la compagnie italienne. En 1956, il heurta un autre bateau et coula le lendemain.

The lovely new *Andrea Doria*

These men have built a ship...

What gives a ship that thing called personality? From where come those qualities of warmth and friendliness? How do you take the coldness out of steel? How do you breathe life into glass and tile? You won't find the answer in blueprints. You can't do it with money or calloused hands. You build such a ship with your heart.

Into every detail of this lovely vessel have gone the skill and pride of the greatest artisans of Italy. Every mural, every tapestry, every rug and chair... each exquisite bit of glassware and every glowing tile is the work of craftsmen. Yes, a ship is built of many hearts. This is the tradition of Italy. This is the *Andrea Doria*.

The completely air conditioned *Andrea Doria* enters transatlantic service to New York in January. *Special West Indies Cruise January 30 . . . 17 glorious days.*

"ITALIA"—Societa di Navigazione—Genova

See your Travel Agent or

AMERICAN EXPORT LINES (General Agents)

39 Broadway, New York 6, N. Y.

ANDREA DORIA express service on the "Sunny Southern Route" • 6 days to GIBRALTAR • 8 days to NAPLES • 9 days to CANNES and GENOA

SATURNIA · VULCANIA to LISBON • GIBRALTAR • BARCELONA • PALERMO • NAPLES • CANNES • GENOA

Vacation Corner

of the

Delta-C&S Golden Triangle

Golden Crown DC-7's - Fastest to

Miami Beach

and the Caribbean

Royal Biscayne .. **CHICAGO-MIAMI** .. 3⅓ hrs. Non-Stop
Royal Hibiscus . **CINCINNATI-MIAMI** .. 3 hrs. Non-Stop
Royal Poinciana .. **ATLANTA-MIAMI** ... 2 hrs. Non-Stop

Also the Royal Ranger, ***Chicago-St. Louis-Houston***
Coming in April, DC-7 service, ***Atlanta-Birmingham-Dallas-West Coast***
and ***Chicago-New Orleans-Havana-Montego Bay-Caracas***

Fly Now—Pay Later
No Down Payment

Delta C&S

AIR LINES

General Offices:
Atlanta, Georgia

Delta-C&S Flies on Seth Thomas Time

◂ Delta-C&S Air Lines, 1955

Delta-C&S Air Lines, 1954

Morris Lapidus's Fontainebleau Hotel, a medley of fabulous French baroque, breathed new life into the tired Miami Beach scene when it opened in 1954. The next year, Lapidus designed the flamboyant Eden Roc Hotel, an Italian fantasy and business rival, right beside it. The sands sizzled.

Morris Lapidus' 1954 eröffnetes Fontainebleau Hotel, ein Mix aus französischen Barockfantasien, hauchte der ermatteten Szene von Miami Beach neues Leben ein. Im Jahr darauf entwarf Lapidus das extravagante Eden Roc Hotel, eine italienische Fantasie und Konkurrentin in unmittelbarer Nachbarschaft. Der Sand brodelte.

A son ouverture en 1954, le Fontainebleau Hotel de Morris Lapidus, pot-poussi fabuleux de baroque français insuffla une vie nouvelle à un Miami Beach fatigué. L'année suivante, Lapidus conçut son concurrent juste à côté, le flamboyant Eden Roc Hotel au style italien fantaisiste. Leurs plages ne désemplissaient pas.

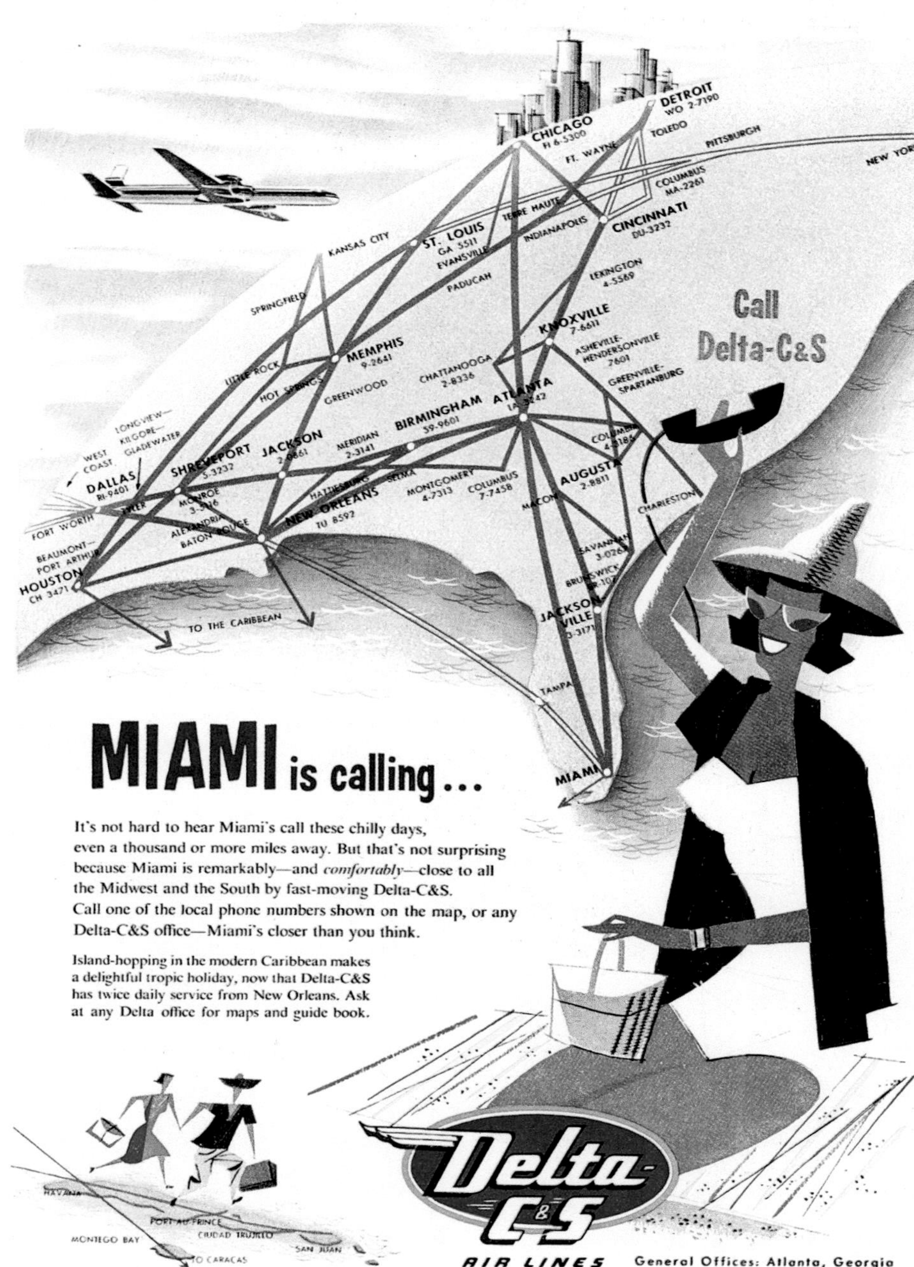

Call
Delta-C&S
CHICAGO
DETROIT
ST. LOUIS
CINCINNATI
KNOXVILLE
MEMPHIS
BIRMINGHAM
ATLANTA
JACKSON
SHREVEPORT
DALLAS
HOUSTON
NEW ORLEANS
AUGUSTA
JACKSONVILLE
MIAMI
TO THE CARIBBEAN
MIAMI is calling...
It's not hard to hear Miami's call these chilly days, even a thousand or more miles away. But that's not surprising because Miami is remarkably—and *comfortably*—close to all the Midwest and the South by fast-moving Delta-C&S. Call one of the local phone numbers shown on the map, or any Delta-C&S office—Miami's closer than you think.
Island-hopping in the modern Caribbean makes a delightful tropic holiday, now that Delta-C&S has twice daily service from New Orleans. Ask at any Delta office for maps and guide book.
Delta-C&S
AIR LINES
General Offices: Atlanta, Georgia

Getting there is half the fun!

For more than a century the name Cunard has been the hallmark of transatlantic travel luxury . . . relaxation . . . gaiety. Your first day aboard will show you why more travelers choose Cunard than any other li
See your local travel agent.

QUEEN ELIZABETH · QUEEN MARY · MAURETANIA · CARONIA · BRITANNIC · MEDIA
PARTHIA · CARINTHIA · IVERNIA · SAXONIA · FRANCONIA · SCYTHIA · ASCANIA

◂ Cunard, 1956

Las Vegas, 1952

Las Vegas emerged as a sophisticated, and decadent, getaway. In 1950, the Desert Inn opened on the Strip. Its celebrated "crystal showroom" nightclub featured a slew of big names, including a memorable series of shows with Frank Sinatra and the entire Rat Pack when they were shooting *Ocean's Eleven* there at decade's end.

Las Vegas entwickelte sich zu einem durchgeplanten – und dekadenten – Zufluchtsort. In dem als „kristallener Schauraum" gefeierten Nachtclub des 1950 am Strip eröffneten Desert Inn ließen sich einige große Namen blicken, und es gab eine Reihe denkwürdiger Auftritte von Frank Sinatra und seinem Rat Pack während der Dreharbeiten von *Ocean's Eleven* (*Frankie und seine Spießgesellen*) gegen Ende des Jahrzehnts.

Las Vegas apparut d'abord comme une destination sophistiquée et décadente. En 1950, le Desert Inn ouvrit sur le Strip. Sa célèbre salle de spectacles, le « crystal showroom », accueillit une cohorte de grands noms, notamment une série de représentations mémorables avec Frank Sinatra et tout le Rat Pack pendant le tournage de *L'Inconnu de Las Vegas* à la fin de la décennie.

▸▸ American Airlines, 1954

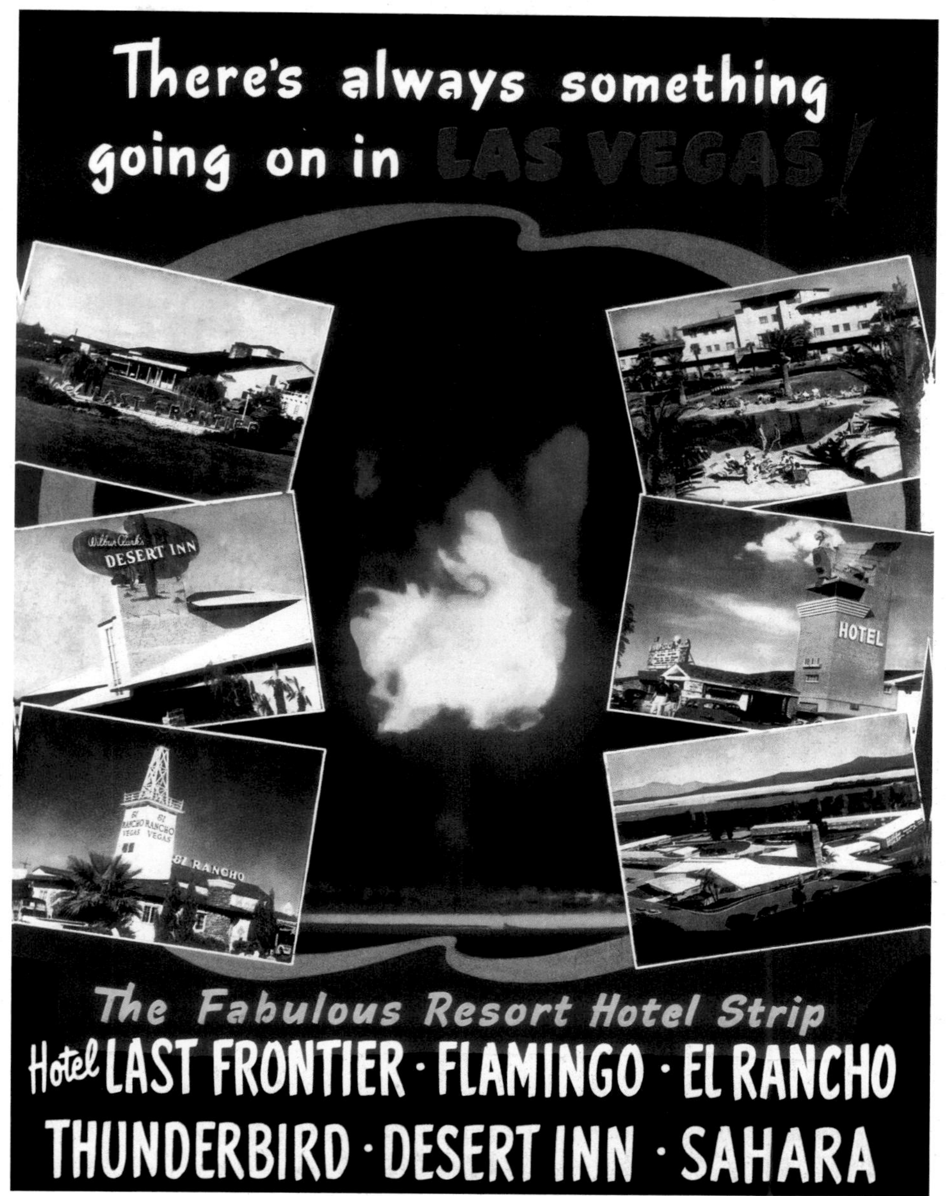

American's New DC-7 Lea

In 1954 YOU'LL FLY THE MOST MODERN FLEET OF TRANSPORT AIRCRAFT IN THE WORLD ON THE ROUTE OF THE FLAGSHIPS

In 1954 American's new DC-7 is leading the finest Flagship Fleet in history. It includes such outstanding passenger carriers as the popular inter-city Convair and the famous long range DC-6 and DC-6B Flagships as well as the DC-6A, the biggest, fastest cargo plane in operation today.

American's magnificent new Turbo Compound DC-7 Flagship is the *first* plane especially designed for NONSTOP transcontinental travel and the *only* aircraft capable of nonstop coast-to-coast service under 8 hours.

This means that American now offers the fastest service between New York and Los Angeles and New York and San Francisco. The addition of the DC-7 also enables American to greatly expand its nonstop service between major cities on its 10,800 miles of routes.

So welcome aboard the Flagship Fleet for '54. Welcome *to* the most modern fleet of transport aircraft in the world. And welcome *from* American's 17,000 trained personnel whose friendly attentive service has long set the standard for air transportation.

AMERICAN AIRLINES INC.

America's Leading Airline

he Finest Flagship Fleet Ever

244

MAUREEN O'SULLIVAN and her 7 attractive children leaving for Ireland on the World's Most Experienced Airline.

Q. Which airline carries the most passengers to Europe?

A. PAN AMERICAN, the only airline that has completed over 48,000 Atlantic crossings . . . and the only airline that can fly you direct to so many European cities.

"El Presidente"
Step aboard at New York and step out at Rio de Janeiro in 20⅔ hours . . . fly on to Buenos Aires in 6⅓ hours. This is a deluxe all-sleeper service with double-decked "Strato" Clippers.
The
BLUE RIBBON
AIR SERVICE
PAA
Clipper Friendship
The Sleeperette* is Pan American's exclusive, foam-soft easy chair which reclines to almost horizontal so you can sleep *lying down. No extra charge is made for Sleeperettes.*
This is the way to travel! "El Presidente" leaves New York, Mondays, Thursdays and Saturdays, at 11:00 A.M. Your first stop is Port-of-Spain early the same evening. 9:40 the next morning you step out, fresh as a daisy, at Rio de Janeiro—or continue on to Buenos Aires, arriving there at 5 in the afternoon.
NEW YORK
LOS ANGELES
NEW ORLEANS
HOUSTON
MIAMI
SAN JUAN
MEXICO CITY
PORT OF SPAIN
BALBOA
CARACAS
BELEM
LIMA
ANTOFAGASTA
RIO DE JANEIRO
MONTEVIDEO
SANTIAGO
BUENOS AIRES
PAN AMERICAN
WORLD'S MOST EXPERIENCED AIRLINE
On "El Presidente" nobody sits up at night! You have your choice of a Sleeperette seat (above) at no extra charge, or of fifteen upper berths at $10 and two lower berths at $20. Berths are big, wide and comfortable.
—And there are many, many other luxuries aboard "El Presidente." This is, without question, the Blue Ribbon service of the Western Hemisphere! . . . You are served a 7-course Continental dinner with vintage wines . . . You are waited on by extra cabin attendants—and there's even Lanvins' *Arpège* perfume for the ladies!
No wonder a blue carpet is rolled out for every departure of "El Presidente"! It climaxes 23 years of Pan American service between the U.S.A. and Latin America. Yet the surcharge all the way from New York to Rio is only $10; to Buenos Aires, only $20. For reservations call your Travel Agent or Pan American's nearest office.
*Trade Mark, Reg. U.S. Pat. Off.

◂ Pan Am, 1955

Pan Am, 1950

In this ad, Pan American boasts about 23 years of service to Latin American. Many mistakenly believed that Juan Trippe, the debonair yet ruthless head of Pan Am, was Cuban. This scion of an old American family and graduate of Yale was glad to have people believe he had special ties to Latin America.

In dieser Anzeige spricht Pan Am stolz davon, seit bereits 23 Jahren Ziele in Lateinamerika anzusteuern. Viele hielten Juan Trippe, den stets heiteren, doch rücksichtslosen Chef von Pan Am, fälschlich für einen Kubaner. Dem Spross einer alteingesessenen Familie und Yale-Absolventen kam die Annahme, er sei mit Lateinamerika besonders verbunden, nur gelegen.

Dans cette publicité, la Pan American revendique 23 ans de service vers l'Amérique Latine. Beaucoup de gens croyaient à tort que Juan Trippe, le directeur raffiné mais impitoyable de la compagnie, était cubain. Héritier d'une vieille famille américaine et diplômé de Yale, il était ravi qu'on lui prête des liens particuliers avec l'Amérique Latine.

June Allyson starring in "YOU CAN'T RUN AWAY FROM IT" produced and directed by Dick Powell. A Columbia Picture in CinemaScope. Color Print by Technicolor.

The best vacations begin with Samsonite Luggage

It's the most popular luggage in the world! As the Dick Powells will be the first to tell you, one brand of luggage stands head and shoulders above the rest... Samsonite Streamlite.

They ought to know, too. Going on vacation, heading out on location, Dick and June have found Samsonite is a born traveller. It's strongest... strong enough to stand on. Its "better-than-leather" finish resists scuffing and wipes clean with a damp cloth. Its special tongue-in-groove closures keep out dust and dampness. Sleek, non-tarnishing drawbolts can't pop open accidentally.

June, who knows how important fashion is to a screen star, loves the high-fashion Samsonite finishes: Bermuda Green, Colorado Brown, Rawhide Finish, Saddle Tan, Admiral Blue, London Grey and Alligator Finish. The whole Powell family agrees: "Samsonite is *strongest* and *smartest!*"

CASES FEATURED IN SADDLE TAN: LADIES' WARDROBE, $25, TRAIN CASE, $17.50, O'NITE CASE, $19.50, PULLMAN CASE, $27.50

Samsonite *Streamlite* Luggage

Take a tip from the Dick Powells! Vacation by *Air-Conditioned* Scenicruiser

Just as lovely June Allyson (Mrs. Dick Powell) rides a Greyhound *Scenicruiser* in the exciting new production, "You Can't Run Away From It", so *you* can travel to Vacationland almost anywhere in North America aboard this remarkable coach – along time-saving Express routes. On the *Scenicruiser* (or its smart companion, the *Highway Traveler*) you'll find velvet-smooth Air Suspension Ride...perfected air conditioning...the World's finest, safest drivers...and sensational panoramic sightseeing along beauty-bright highways. The raised-level *Scenicruiser* even has complete washroom facilities, with running water and toilet. Yet it costs you not a penny more than Greyhound's usual low fares to travel in Low-Cost Luxury!

GREYHOUND®

Greyhound, 1956

► Santa Fe Railway, 1957

SANTA F
708

ONE MILLION

passengers have now flown the Boeing 707 jetliner!

These airlines have ordered 707 or shorter-range 720 jetliners: AIR FRANCE • AIR-INDIA INTERNATIONAL • AMERICAN AIRLINES • BRANIFF INTERNATIONAL AIRWAYS • BRITISH OVERSEAS AIRWAYS CORPORATION • CONTINENTAL AIR LINES • CUBANA DE AVIACION • IRISH AIR LINES • LUFTHANSA GERMAN AIRLINES • PAN AMERICAN WORLD AIRWAYS • QANTAS EMPIRE AIRWAYS • SABENA BELGIAN WORLD AIRLINES • SOUTH AFRICAN AIRWAYS • TRANS WORLD AIRLINES • UNITED AIR LINES • VARIG AIRLINES OF BRAZIL • *Also the* MILITARY AIR TRANSPORT SERVICE

BOEING 707 and 720

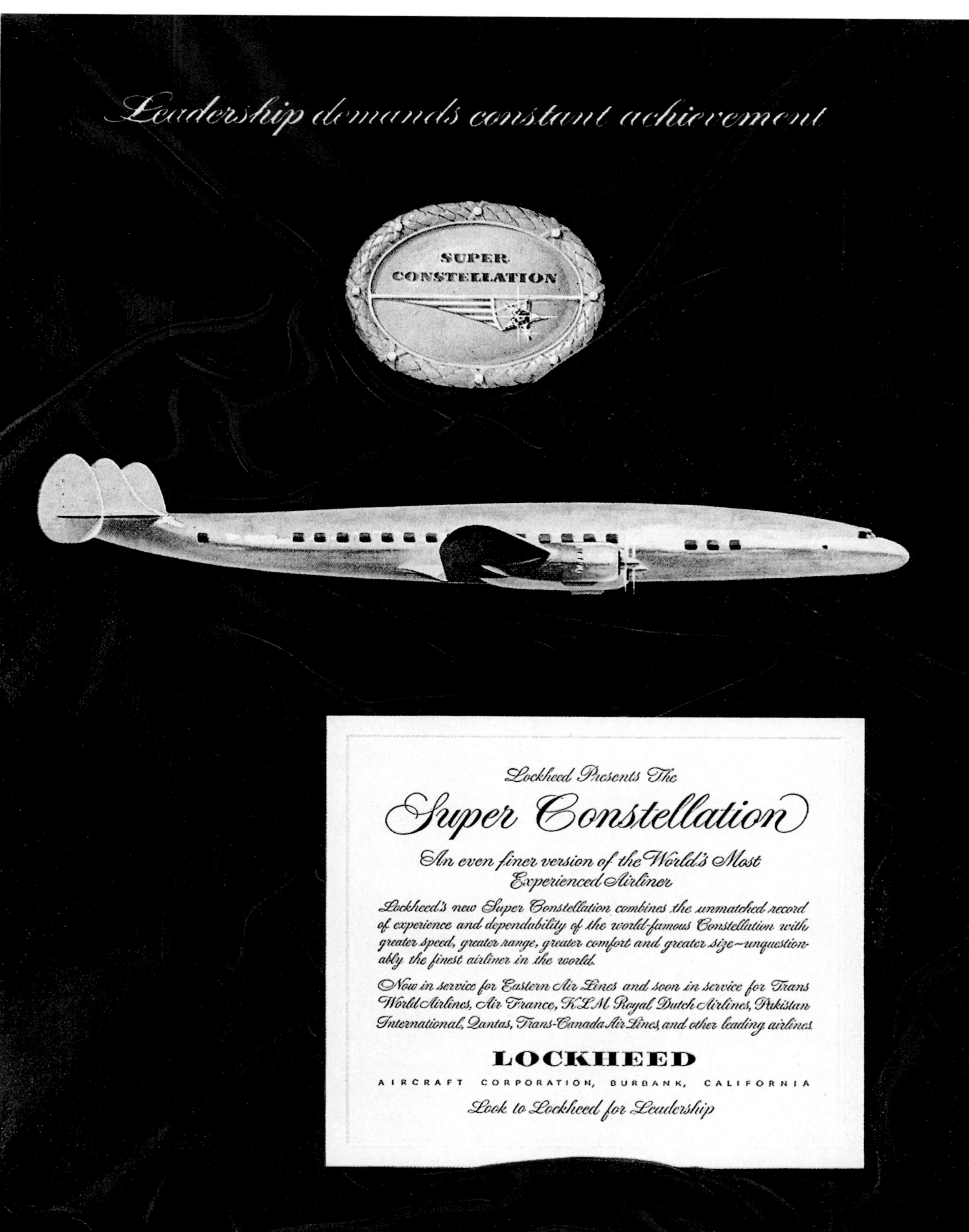

◂ Boeing, 1959

Lockheed, 1951

Don made the Trip

—TOO LATE AGAIN

John made the Sale

—HE TOOK THE PLANE

America's Leading Airline AMERICAN AIRLINES INC.

American Airlines, 1952

▸ TWA, 1958

▸▸ Douglas, 1959

TWA Captain Thomas Lynch brings in Flight 4

We're proud of our clock-watchers at TWA!

It takes *team* work to send the mighty Jetstreams* winging to their destinations all over the world, departing *on schedule*, arriving *on time!* And it takes a *big* team of clock-watchers to do it—maintenance men, weather analysts, flight dispatchers, operating crews. TWA is proud of them. You'll understand why . . . when, after the smoothest, most luxurious flight you've ever had . . . *your* TWA plane taxis in *on time!* For reservations, telephone your travel agent or nearest TWA office today.

FLY THE FINEST... FLY TWA TRANS WORLD AIRLINES

**Jetstream is a service mark owned exclusively by TWA.*

MODERN TRAVEL WAS GOING TO BRING EVERYONE CLOSER TOGETHER, AND AIRPLANES WOULD BE THE VEHICLE OF CHOICE.

MODERNE VERKEHRSMITTEL SOLLTEN DIE MENSCHEN NÄHER ZUEINANDERBRINGEN, UND DAS FLUGZEUG WAR DAS GEFÄHRT DER WAHL.

LE VOYAGE MODERNE ALLAIT RAPPROCHER LE MONDE ENTIER, AVEC L'AVION COMME VÉHICULE DE PRÉDILECTION.

1960

JET SET AT FULL THROTTLE
DER JETSET GIBT VOLLGAS
LA JET-SET À PLEINS GAZ

-1969

B. Peak

◄ Italian Line, 1960

Ken-L-Products, 1960

MAY 25, 1961, PRESIDENT JOHN F. KENNEDY DECLARED TO THE NATION, AND THE WORLD: "WE CHOOSE TO GO TO THE MOON." The charismatic president vowed that Americans would stand on the moon by decade's end. Technology was viewed as a powerful and positive force. Anything was possible. The 1964 New York World's Fair joyously proclaimed "It's a Small World After All," and its 51 million visitors agreed. Modern travel was going to bring everyone closer together—and jets were the vehicle of choice.

This heady optimism was epitomized in Eero Saarinen's swooping TWA Terminal at Idlewild—later John F. Kennedy—Airport. Air travel never looked as alluring and glamorous as in that 1963 structure. Movie audiences savored the élan of the first James Bond movie, *Dr. No* (1962), which hopscotched across the globe—a sexy travelogue disguised as a spy thriller. And Federico Fellini's acclaimed *La Dolce Vita* (1960) was punctuated by the celebrity arrivals at the Rome airport.

Braniff International Airways hired advertising whiz Mary Wells, whose remarkable "End of the Plain Plane" campaign in 1965 enlisted the Jet Set's favorite fashion designer, Emilio Pucci, to create futuristic stewardess uniforms with layers, bold patterns, and plastic "space" helmets. She brought in Alexander Girard to revamp the planes, waiting areas, check-in counters, and ticket offices. He saturated every surface with strong colors, inside and out.

But air travel was no longer just for the wealthy. It was increasingly essential to business executives. Eastern Airlines, seeing this, introduced its Air Shuttle service between New York and Washington, D.C., in 1961. Passengers needed no reservations, had no hard ticketing, and had guaranteed seating on hourly flights. In 1967, United Air Lines launched a sparkling TV campaign featuring a chorus line of wives singing to their businessmen husbands, "Take Me Along."

By 1965, with the introduction of the Boeing 707 jet, air travel upshifted into mass ridership: The annual U.S. air passenger count hit 100 million, doubled from 1958. Boeing's 737 became the most ordered and most produced jet in history—ultimately more than 1,250 of them were airborne at any time, with one departing or landing somewhere every five seconds on average.

As airlines further democratized travel, once-exclusive locales welcomed a panoply of guests. In Hawaii, tourism revenue reached $161 million in 1960, for the first time bringing in more money than the island's leading staples, pineapples and sugar. Elvis Presley compounded the tropical allure with his 1961 hit movie *Blue Hawaii*. The appeal of sun and surf also made a cult hit of *The Endless Summer* (1966), in which two surfers travel the globe in search of the perfect wave. Yet even as travelers sought a sultry tropical paradise, they expected to get there quickly. Ocean liners had lost their mystique. In 1967, Cunard Lines announced that the *Queen Mary* and *Queen Elizabeth* had each lost $1.8 million that year and the company wanted to send them to the scrap heap.

1960

1960 Adventures and misadventures of college students on spring break in Florida come to screen in *Where the Boys Are*

Der Streifen *Dazu gehören zwei* handelt von den Abenteuern und Missgeschicken einiger Collegestudenten während der Frühjahrsferien in Florida

Where the boys are conte les aventures et mésaventures des étudiants passant leurs vacances de Pâques en Floride

1961 Paul Williams–designed futuristic Theme Building opens as restaurant at Los Angeles International Airport

Eröffnung des von Paul Williams entworfenen futuristischen Themengebäudes als Restaurant auf dem internationalen Flughafen von Los Angeles

Le « Theme Building » futuriste de Paul Williams ouvre en tant que restaurant à l'aéroport international de Los Angeles

1961 Work begins on Albert Frey's Palm Springs Aerial Tramway, largest double reversible passenger tramway in world

Baubeginn von Albert Freys Palm Springs Aerial Tramway, der längsten Luftseilbahn der Welt

Début des travaux du Palm Springs Aerial Tramway, le plus grand téléphérique à double sens du monde

1962 American Airlines and IBM partner to release Sabre, first airline electronic booking system

American Airlines und IBM präsentieren mit Sabre das erste elektronische Flugbuchungssystem

Partenariat entre American Airlines et IBM pour le lancement de Sabre, premier système de réservation électronique pour compagnies aériennes

American Airlines, 1961

▶ Pan Am, 1964

AM 25. MAI 1961 ERKLÄRTE PRÄSIDENT JOHN F. KENNEDY DER GANZEN WELT: „WIR WOLLEN ZUM MOND." Er versprach, dass Amerikaner am Ende der Dekade auf dem Mond stehen würden. Technologie galt als ein starkes, positiv besetztes Instrument. Nichts war unmöglich. Die New Yorker Weltausstellung 1964 verkündete freudig: „Eigentlich ist die Welt doch klein", und die 51 Millionen Besucher stimmten zu. Moderne Verkehrsmittel sollten die Menschen näher zueinanderbringen – und der Jet war das Gefährt der Wahl.

Sinnbild dieses berauschenden Optimismus war Eero Saarinens flügelartiger TWA-Terminal des Idlewild (später John F. Kennedy) Airport. Flugreisen besaßen nirgendwo sonst einen derartigen Reiz und Glamour wie in diesem Gebäude aus dem Jahr 1963. Das Kinopublikum ließ sich vom ersten Bond-Film *Dr. No* (*James Bond jagt Dr. No*, 1962) mit seinen zahlreichen Schauplätzen mitreißen, ein Reisebericht mit Sex-Appeal im Gewand eines Spionagethrillers. Und in Fellinis gefeiertem *La Dolce Vita* (*Das süße Leben*, 1960), einem Blick auf die Hautevolee der Via Veneto, trudelten die Berühmtheiten auf dem Flughafen von Rom nur so ein.

Braniff International Airways wandte sich an die Top-Werberin Mary Wells, bei deren bemerkenswerter Kampagne „End of the Plain Plane" Emilio Pucci, der vom Jetset bevorzugte Modeschöpfer, für die Stewardessen futuristische Uniformen kreierte – mit kühnen Mustern und „Astronautenhelmen" aus Plastik. Alexander Girard fiel die Aufgabe zu, die Maschinen, Wartezonen, Empfangsschalter und Ticketbüros aufzumöbeln. Hierzu tauchte er sämtliche Flächen in kräftige Farben, innen wie außen.

Doch Flugreisen waren nun nicht länger nur den Reichen vorbehalten. Für Geschäftsleute wurden sie zunehmend unverzichtbar. So startete Eastern Airlines 1961 einen Shuttleservice zwischen New York und Washington, D. C. – eine echte Revolution. Nun brauchte man nicht mehr zu reservieren und hatte auf den stündlichen Flügen garantiert einen Sitzplatz. Während die Geschäftsreisen rapide zunahmen, lancierte United Air Lines 1967 einen TV-Spot mit Hausfrauen als Revuegirls, die ihre geschäftlich verreisenden Männer singend baten, sie doch mitzunehmen („Take Me Along").

Dank Einführung der Boeing 707 waren die Flugreisen 1965 zum Massenmarkt geworden: Die Vereinigten Staaten zählten nun jedes Jahr 100 Millionen Flugpassagiere, doppelt so viele wie 1958. Die Boeing 737 wurde zum meistproduzierten Jet aller Zeiten – heute befinden sich jederzeit mehr als 1250 Maschinen in der Luft, und durchschnittlich alle fünf Sekunden startet oder landet eine irgendwo auf der Welt.

Während Flugreisen für immer mehr Menschen erschwinglich wurden, fanden sich die unterschiedlichsten Gäste an den einstmals exklusiven Ferienorten ein. In Hawaii erzielte man 1960 mit dem Tourismus erstaunliche 161 Mio. $, erstmals mehr als mit den beiden Haupterzeugnissen Ananas und Rohrzucker. Mit *Blue Hawaii* (*Blaues Hawaii, 1961*) leistete Elvis Presley einen nicht unbedeutenden Beitrag. Die Verlockungen von Sonne und Wellen machten *The Endless Summer* (1966), in dem zwei Surfer auf der Suche nach der perfekten Welle um die Welt reisen, zum Kultfilm. Aber auch jene, die ein sinnliches Tropenparadies ansteuerten, wollten schnell hinkommen. Die Linienschiffe hatten ihren einstigen Nimbus eingebüßt. Cunard Lines gab bekannt, dass die *Queen Mary* und die *Queen Elizabeth* 1967 Verluste von je 1,8 Mio. $ eingefahren hatten. Die Ozeanriesen drohten auf dem Schrotthaufen zu landen.

1963 Opening of Mandarin Hotel's flagship in Hong Kong

Eröffnung des Mandarin Oriental, des Flaggschiffs der gleichnamigen Hotelkette, in Hongkong

Ouverture du fleuron des hôtels Mandarin à Hong Kong

1963 Pan Am flight bags reach iconic status

Pan-Am-Taschen werden zum Statussymbol

Les sacs de voyage Pan Am deviennent de vrais objets culte

1964 Gio Ponti designs Parco dei Principi Hotel, in shades of green and white, in Rome

Gio Ponti entwirft das ganz in Grün und Weiß gehaltene römische Hotel Parco dei Principi

A Rome, Gio Ponti conçoit le Parco dei Principi Hotel dans des tons de vert et de blanc

1967 United Air Lines ad campaign features wives singing to businessmen husbands, "Take Me Along"

Werbekampagne von United Air Lines mit Frauen, die ihre viel fliegenden Männer singend bitten, sie doch mitzunehmen

La campagne publicitaire de United Air Lines présente des femmes chantant « Emmène-moi avec toi » à leurs maris hommes d'affaires

PAN AM

◂ TWA, 1963

United Air Lines, ca. 1966

LE 25 MAI 1961, LE PRÉSIDENT JOHN F. KENNEDY DÉCLARA À LA NATION ET AU MONDE ENTIER : « NOUS CHOISISSONS D'ALLER SUR LA LUNE ». Le charismatique chef d'Etat promit que les Américains iraient sur la Lune avant la fin de la décennie. On considérait la technologie comme une grande force très positive. Tout devenait possible. En 1964, la Foire Internationale de New York proclama joyeusement « Le Monde est petit ». Le voyage moderne allait rapprocher le monde entier, avec l'avion comme véhicule de prédilection.

Cet optimisme enivrant fut symbolisé par le terminal en forme d'oiseau stylisé conçu par Eero Saarinen pour la TWA à l'aéroport d'Idlewild, rebaptisé plus tard Kennedy Airport. Dans cette structure de 1963, voyager en avion n'avait jamais semblé plus glamour. Le public des cinémas se délecta de l'impétuosité d'un nouveau personnage globe-trotter dans *James Bond 007 contre Dr. No* (1962), véritable catalogue touristique sexy déguisé en film d'espionnage. Les spectateurs adorèrent aussi *La Dolce Vita* (1960) de Federico Fellini, un film sur l'élite sophistiquée de la Via Veneto, dont l'histoire était ponctuée par l'arrivée de célébrités à l'aéroport de Rome.

Braniff International Airways fit appel au génie publicitaire de Mary Wells Lawrence. En 1965, sa campagne « End of the Plain Plane » bénéficia des talents d'Emilio Pucci, le couturier favori de la jet-set, qui créa des uniformes futuristes pour les hôtesses, assortis de superpositions, de motifs audacieux et de casques « spatiaux » en plastique. Mary Wells collabora avec Alexander Girard pour relooker les avions, les salles d'embarquement, les comptoirs d'enregistrement et de vente de billets. Il satura de couleurs vives toutes les surfaces, à l'intérieur comme à l'extérieur.

Le voyage aérien n'était cependant plus réservé aux plus riches ou aux plus ambitieux. Les hommes d'affaires ne pouvaient désormais quasiment plus s'en passer. Eastern Airlines flaira le bon filon et lança en 1961 une ligne effectuant la navette entre New York et Washington qui révolutionna le voyage aérien. Les passagers n'avaient pas besoin de réservations ni de billets, et se voyaient garantir un siège sur les vols horaires. Face à la croissance rapide des voyages d'affaires, United Air Lines diffusa en 1967 une brillante campagne

télévisée présentant une troupe de femmes en train de chanter « Emmène-moi avec toi » à leurs businessmen d'époux.

Avec l'arrivée du Boeing 707 en 1965, le nombre annuel de passagers aux Etats-Unis atteignit les 100 millions, soit le double du chiffre de 1958. Le Boeing 737 devint l'avion le plus produit de l'histoire aéronautique, à tel point qu'on en comptait plus de 1250 en vol simultané, avec un décollage ou un atterrissage toutes les cinq secondes dans le monde.

Des destinations autrefois exclusives accueillaient désormais toutes sortes de touristes. En 1960, les revenus du tourisme à Hawaï atteignirent les 161 millions de dollars, rapportant pour la première fois plus que les ananas et le sucre, principales ressources de l'île. Elvis Presley imposa le style tropical en 1961 dans *Sous le ciel bleu de Hawaï*. L'attrait du soleil et du surf transforma aussi en film culte le documentaire *The Endless Summer* (1966), qui suit deux surfeurs parcourant le monde en quête de la vague parfaite. Les voyageurs tenaient à se rendre rapidement dans les paradis tropicaux. Les paquebots avaient perdu de leur mystique. En 1967, la Cunard Line annonça que le *Queen Mary* et le *Queen Elizabeth* avaient chacun perdu 1,8 million de dollars cette année-là. Les majestueux navires s'apprêtaient à finir au rebut.

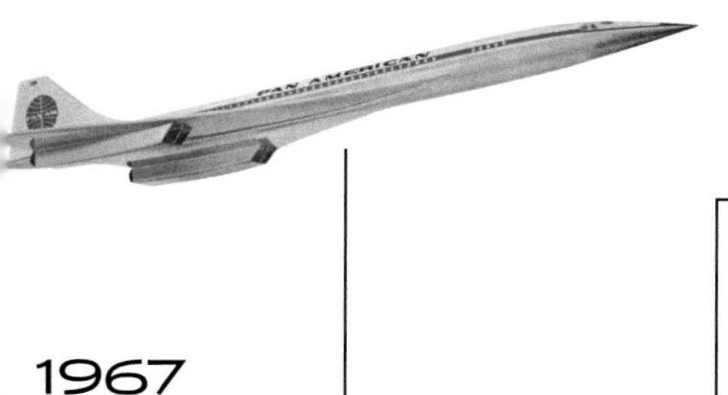

1967

1967 U.S. air carriers begin announcing future Concorde flights to the general public; most will not materialize

US-Fluggesellschaften versprechen künftige Concorde-Flüge für alle – was weitgehend unerfüllt bleibt

Les compagnies aériennes américaines annoncent de prochains vols en Concorde pour le grand public ; la plupart de ces projets n'aboutiront jamais

1967 Opening of Hyatt Regency Atlanta, John Portman's influential hotel design based on multistory atrium

Eröffnung des Hyatt Regency Atlanta mit mehrstöckigem Atrium, ein revolutionäres Hoteldesign von John Portman

Ouverture du Hyatt Regency d'Atlanta, avec un design hôtelier révolutionnaire de John Portman reposant sur un atrium de plusieurs étages

1969 In *If It's Tuesday, This Must Be Belgium*, an American tour group visits seven countries in 18 days

In *If It's Tuesday, This Must Be Belgium* absolviert eine Reisegruppe aus den USA sieben Länder in 18 Tagen

« Si on est mardi, c'est qu'on est en Belgique » : les touristes américains peuvent visiter sept pays en 18 jours

1969 In *Easy Rider*, a pair of bikers (Peter Fonda and Dennis Hopper) travel across country in seach of America

In *Easy Rider* machen sich zwei Biker (Peter Fonda und Dennis Hopper) auf die Suche nach Amerika

Dans *Easy Rider*, deux motards (Peter Fonda et Dennis Hopper) traversent le pays en quête de l'Amérique

TWA

TWA
N754TW
StarStream 707
TWA
TWA

Our weekend special
Lower fares in effect to May 31st
The long weekend seafari on ss United States is one of the most luxurious specials going. It goes to Europe about every two weeks. And from now to May 31st the fares are lower but fun runs high. When you sail with us you'll relax through 4½ days of gracious living. Once aboard you'll choose wines from the largest wine cellar afloat. Enjoy memorable dinners. Dance all night. Our Meyer Davis tempos have a way of coaxing the most reluctant. Take in a pre-release movie. Perhaps you'd like to play bridge, an excellent way to meet the kind of people you enjoy. Set your own pace—be as lazy or as lively as you like.
SAFETY INFORMATION. The ss United States, world's fastest ship, meets International Safety Standards for new ships developed in 1960.
s.s. UNITED STATES!
Top Resort between New York and Europe
For information and reservations call your Travel Agent or United States Lines, One Broadway, New York, N.Y. 10004.

264

◂◂ TWA, 1967

SS *United States*, 1968

The SS *United States* took the Blue Riband for fastest transatlantic crossing in 1952 and remained one of the most desirable ships that decade. But by the '60s, ocean liners struggled in a Jet Set world—where speed mattered most. Here, low fares are promised. Grand liners, like Cunard's *Queen Mary*, lost money every year.

Die SS *United States* eroberte 1952 das Blaue Band für die schnellste Atlantiküberquerung und blieb in der gesamten Dekade eines der gefragtesten Schiffe. Inzwischen aber hatten die Linienschiffe zu kämpfen – in einer vom Jetset bestimmten Welt, der es vor allem ums Tempo ging. Diese Anzeige lockt mit niedrigen Preisen. Ozeanriesen wie die *Queen Mary* von Cunard schrieben indes Jahr für Jahr rote Zahlen.

Le paquebot *United States* remporta le Ruban Bleu en 1952 pour la traversée la plus rapide de l'Atlantique et demeura l'un des navires les plus demandés au cours de la décennie. Dans les années 1960, la jet-set délaissa pourtant les paquebots car elle recherchait avant tout la vitesse. Cette publicité promet des tarifs bas. Même les plus beaux bateaux, comme le *Queen Mary* de la compagnie Cunard, perdaient de l'argent chaque année.

▸ American Airlines, 1960

r American Airlines:
I average 50,000 miles per year on commercial
rlines-so I recognize good service when I
e it. My flight was made unusually
easant–thanks to your Miss Clare Vize and
s Valerie Franks. I'd like to have them
my public relations department!
W. E. Uzzell

ited in-flight letter from Mr. W. E. Uzzell, Vice-President of Royal Crown Cola Co., Columbus, Georgia

Our Stewardesses, Mr. Uzzell, are another reason why American Airlines is first choice of experienced travelers. We choose just 1 in 23 from over 15,000 annual applicants for an intensive 77-subject course at our Stewardess College, the only one of its kind. The young ladies graduate with honors in the gracious art of making people happy.

AMERICAN AIRLINES
America's Leading Airline

SAN FRANCISCO
LOS ANGELES
NEW ORLEANS
NEW YORK
HOUSTON
MEXICO CITY
MIAMI
GUATEMALA CITY
PANAMA
CARACAS
PORT OF SPAIN
QUITO
GUAYAQUIL
LIMA
LA PAZ
BRASILIA
RIO DE JANEIRO
SAO PAULO
SANTIAGO
BUENOS AIRES
MONTEVIDEO

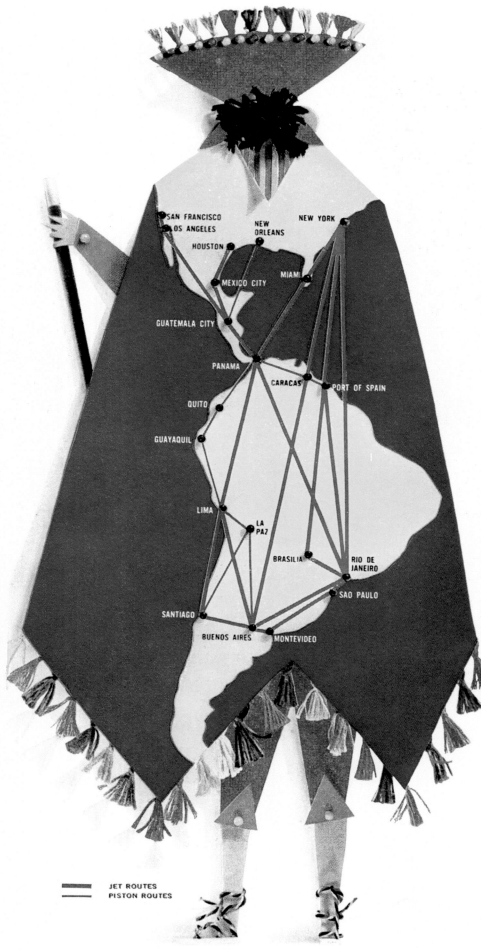

JET ROUTES
PISTON ROUTES

THE ONLY JET SERVICE 'ROUND SOUTH AMERICA

Only with Pan American and Panagra can you enjoy speedy Jet service down both coasts of South America. Go one way, return the other with the U.S. airline system that has 33 years of experience in Latin America.

No other airline system offers such a variety of Jet routes in South America from so many gateways in the U.S.A.

Choose first-class or low-fare service. From New York, down the West Coast of South America fly daily Jet without change of plane over the routes of National, Pan American and Panagra. On the East Coast, fly Pan Am Jet all the way.

Many preplanned *Pan Am Holidays* give you full benefit of favorable exchange rates in South American republics. They include Jet flights, fine hotels, sightseeing! Rates are surprisingly low. Free folder gives you full details. You will also enjoy the 128-page book, "How to Get the Most out of Your Trip to South America." For either or both write to Pan American, Dept. 152, Box 1111, New York 17. (Enclose 25¢ for the book.) See your Travel Agent or your nearest Pan American office.

Saludos Amigos! Here's the biggest foreign travel bargain ever! Western's Amigo Flights on swift Jet/Powered Electra II's put you in Mexico City and return for just $144.50. That's right. It's round-trip —and it's tax-free. You'll like the bright Mexican atmosphere you'll find aboard, and the festive Mexican snacks. We think you'll like our night-flight schedule, too—because it saves you a night's hotel bill in the bargain, puts more pesos in your fun-purse.

Want even more fun on a budget? Take Western's "Magic Week in Mexico." 8 full days in Mexico City, Taxco, and Acapulco, for just $199.00, including round-trip air fare, hotels, sightseeing.

If you want to see Mexico in really high style, fly Western's 720B Fan/Jet Fiesta Flight. Nothing faster or finer. Just ask your Travel Agent. Get all the details on Western's wonderful vacations to Mexico now, and let yourself go—Mexico!

Fares shown above are from Los Angeles or San Diego. From San Francisco, round-trip excursion fare is $167.36; "Magic Week in Mexico" is $221.86.

WESTERN AIRLINES

Why do well-traveled people travel Sabena? "Flight-seeing" via helicopter is only part of it. People who know Europe know Sabena shows it off best: with the world's only 3-speed fleet of Boeing "Intercontinental" jets, *Caravelle "Continental" jets and Sikorsky helicopters; with a special savoir-faire that extends to and through Europe, Africa and the Middle East. Next trip . . . fly Sabena. Le service Belgique–c'est magnifique!

*(soon)

Ask your Travel Agent to book you Sabena all the way . . . or simply call Sabena Belgian World Airlines. More than 200 offices in the principal cities of the world

◂ Panagra, 1961

Western Airlines, 1963

Sabena, 1961

▸▸ Hilton Hotels, 1964

Conrad Hilton expanded his empire by offering a standardized level of accommodations. He saw his international hotels as islands of America in exotic foreign lands. Hilton described them as emissaries for American values—transparent, welcoming, and modern. U.S. travelers liked them because they felt familiar.

Conrad Hilton baute sein Imperium aus, indem er einen genau festgelegten Hotelstandard anbot. Er betrachtete seine internationalen Hotels als amerikanische Inseln in exotischen fremden Ländern, als Botschafter der amerikanischen Werte – transparent, einladend und modern. Auf Amerikaner wirkten sie sehr vertraut und dadurch angenehm.

Conrad Hilton étendit son empire en proposant un niveau d'hôtellerie standardisé. Il considérait ses hôtels internationaux – transparents, accueillants, modernes – comme des ambassadeurs des valeurs américaines, des îlots d'Amérique au milieu de pays étrangers et exotiques. Les voyageurs américains les appréciaient car ils s'y sentaient comme chez eux.

The new Hilton Hotels: in San Francisco, Washington, D

San Francisco. Next trip to the Golden Gate, take in the breathtaking new 18-floor San Francisco Hilton. If you're driving you'll be delighted to find you can drive your car *upstairs*, along a unique interior ramp which leads to the first seven guest floors. And on the upper floors: swimming pool, tropical gardens, four floors of cabaña rooms overlooking the p the delights of resorting right in San Francisco's business, shoppi entertainment district. Next to Airport Bus Terminal and just two from Union Square. Free parking for registered guests. Opening M

nolulu, Mayaguez, Guadalajara, Tel Aviv.

gton, D.C. The 1240-room Washington Hilton will esort living to the city's convenient downtown em- rea. For your relaxation: tennis courts, Olympic- vimming pool, gardens, children's wading pool, four restaurants. For business and diplomatic functions: gton's finest ballroom seating 4300, plus 36 other meeting and dining rooms. Opens early 1965.

Honolulu. With Diamond Head to the west and ead to the east, facing a white, coral-free beach, in ded area, is the magnificent new Kahala Hilton, just It offers sailing, surfing, golf, tennis or just plain in the sun. Dine in the Maile Lanai beside a lagoon, mally on the Hala Terrace near the swimming pool. looners invited? Encouraged is the word.

Mayaguez, Puerto Rico. Overlooking Puerto Rico's third largest city from a beautifully-landscaped 25-acre hilltop site is the new Mayaguez Hilton. Here you can swim in the fresh water pool, play tennis, romp on nearby beaches. The deep sea fishing is some of the best in the world, too. Ample facilities here for meetings and conventions—for those of a mind to mix business with pleasure. Opening spring, 1964.

Guadalajara, Mexico. Amid the centuries-old fiestas and colorful bullfights of Mexico's second city—just one hour by air from Mexico City—stands the new Guadalajara Hilton. You'll enjoy air-conditioned comfort in all of the hotel's 250 rooms, superb Mexican and international cuisine, exciting local color, year-round swimming in the hotel pool and 12-month springtime climate. Opening spring, 1964.

Tel Aviv. Right on the edge of the Mediterranean, close to Tel Aviv's business and shopping center, near its theatres and night life, is the dramatic new 403-room Tel Aviv Hilton. Every Hilton comfort is being planned for this new hotel, opening in the spring of 1965—from individually air-conditioned rooms and suites with balconies to a salt water swimming pool.

Rome.
And you thought Irish only flew to Ireland.

You didn't know that Rome is an Irish city! So are twenty-four other European cities outside the Emerald Isle. On your way, going or coming, we can arrange a splendid vacation bargain... Ireland itself, for no extra air fare! Ask your Travel Agent.

OFFICES IN: New York, Boston, Chicago, Cleveland, Dallas, Detroit, Washington, D.C., Los Angeles, Philadelphia, San Francisco, Montreal, Toronto, Vancouver.

◄ Irish Aer Lingus, 1969

The Plaza, 1967

The Plaza, celebrated as one of world's best hotels since opening in 1907, was perhaps most famous in the mid-1960s. Truman Capote gave his famous masked Black and White Ball there in 1966, and everyone who was anyone went. This ad demonstrates the Plaza's chic panache in that era.

The Plaza, seit seiner Eröffnung im Jahr 1907 als eines der weltbesten Hotels gefeiert, stand vielleicht Mitte der 1960er-Jahre auf dem Gipfel seines Ansehens. Truman Capote gab hier 1966 seinen berühmten Maskenball „Black and White", und jeder, der etwas darstellte, ging hin. Diese Anzeige zeugt vom Chic des Plaza in jener Ära.

Le Plaza, encensé comme l'un des meilleurs hôtels du monde depuis son ouverture en 1907, atteignit sans doute l'apogée de sa gloire au milieu des années 1960. En 1966, Truman Capote y donna son fameux Bal masqué en Noir et Blanc qui vit danser tout le bottin mondain. Cette publicité démontre le grand chic et le panache du Plaza à cette époque.

When you come to New York this summer, catch a great show. The Plaza.

Stay where it's liveliest on the eve of your crossing. Till the children arrive from camp. While you take in the Broadway hits that you missed.

Midnight ambience afterglows the Oak Room. The tom-tom throbs in Trader Vic's. Cupid mit schlag sweetens the Palm Court evenings. And the Persian Room stars come out between dances.

That's the great thing about The Plaza. It turns on in the summer. Like the air-conditioning.

THE PLAZA

HOTEL CORPORATION OF AMERICA

Best Western, 1968

► Air New Zealand, 1967

►► TWA, 1964

Aren't vacations all about escaping routine? And monotony? Shouldn't each day be filled with excitement? And surprise? And anticipation? And happiness and fun?

Well, your vacation fun can follow you right into a Best Western Motel. Because the only monotonous feature about us is **excellence** . . . hard-earned, rigidly enforced excellence that's your assurance of superb accommodations in 800 cities coast to coast.

From then on, Best Western is a world of 1043 different surprises. Maybe tonight it's a Mediterranean setting that starts you dreaming . . . tomorrow night you go Western Style, pardner . . . the next night you luxuriate in a French Provincial atmosphere.

Whatever the mood, it's fun. Whether it's fine food, or swimming, or recreational facilities, or children's play areas, your Best Western host serves it in a way that makes every Best Western night a happy and memorable experience.

Join the 27 million Individualists who'll go Best Western this year. Contact any Best Western Motel and make a **free advance reservation** for your first night on the road. Or send coupon for our new 1968 Travel Guide.

Be an Individualist! Go where new experiences await you every night.

2

FREE! 1968 TRAVEL GUIDE . . . complete information on 1043 individually-owned motels that make Best Western the world's largest network of fine motels.
Best Western, 2910 Sky Harbor Blvd., Phoenix, Arizona 85034

Name__________
Address__________
City/State/Zip__________

Fly the Flight Fantastic

AIR NEW ZEALAND's 27 years' experience brings to perfection a blend of South Seas decor and service called the Flight Fantastic. The Flight Fantastic features exquisite cabin decor, Polynesian dishes and fabulous drinks prepared by Don the Beachcomber. The Flight Fantastic's wide choice of destinations includes both gateways to the South Pacific — Hawaii and Tahiti.* Stop over in both. Go one way, return the other. See magnificent New Zealand and make it home base for all your Down Under tours that will make this the trip of a lifetime. AIR NEW ZEALAND's DC-8 Five Star Jets leave from Los Angeles twice a week for New Zealand and Australia via Honolulu; once a week via Tahiti. All are evening departures. For full details see your travel agent, AIR NEW ZEALAND, or our General Sales Agents, BOAC. For free colorful literature, write AIR NEW ZEALAND, Dept. H6, 510 West Sixth Street, Los Angeles, California 90014.

AIR NEW ZEALAND

THE AIRLINE THAT KNOWS THE SOUTH PACIFIC BEST.

WITH QANTAS AND BOAC OFFERS 16 FLIGHTS WEEKLY DIRECT FROM THE UNITED STATES TO THE SOUTH PACIFIC.

Los Angeles, Honolulu, Auckland, Wellington, Christchurch, Sydney, Melbourne, Brisbane, Fiji, New Caledonia, Norfolk Island, Samoa, Singapore, Hong Kong.* Tahiti service begins late 1967.

TWA
Star Stream

PSA AISLE SEATS $13.50*
WHILE THEY LAST
On other airlines everybody wants the window seats. On PSA they prefer the aisle view. Guess why? More new jets and 900 flights a week connecting Northern and Southern California. Call PSA or your travel agent for something very interesting on the aisle.
*L.A.-San Francisco 727 Super Jets
PSA gives you a lift

GO

where the action is!

You'll find more action... more of everything at the Stardust. Spend an hour and forty five minutes at our lavish and spectacular Lido Revue. Then, catch entertainers like the Kim Sisters, Esquivel and other great acts in the Stardust Lounge. They're on from dusk 'til dawn! Have a gourmet's delight in AKU AKU, our world-famous Polynesian restaurant. Swim. Sun. Tan. Play golf at our championship course. Yes, GO... to your travel agent. Make a reservation for excitement! Or, write Reservations Director, Suite 203. Economy minded? See our "Heavenly Holidays" brochure.

Stardust

HOTEL & GOLF CLUB, LAS VEGAS, NEVADA

1,000 LUXURY ROOMS AT $8 - $10. PLUS 500 DELUXE ROOMS AND SUITES

PSA Airlines, 1968

The job of airline stewardess was considered exciting in the '60s. The travel possibilities seemed boundless and social restrictions were easing. Freedom was the rule—after all, mini-skirts were the fashion. But this ad's promise of inexpensive tickets and many flights weekly suggests that exclusive air travel was soon to be a thing of the past.

In den 1960er-Jahren war der Job der Stewardess noch mit Faszination verbunden. Die Reisemöglichkeiten schienen grenzenlos, und die sozialen Schranken begannen zu fallen. „Freiheit" lautete die Devise – schließlich war ja der Minirock in Mode. Das in dieser Anzeige gegebene Versprechen preiswerter Tickets und zahlreicher wöchentlicher Flüge lässt ahnen, dass exklusive Flugreisen bald der Vergangenheit angehören würden.

Dans les années 1960, le métier d'hôtesse de l'air était considéré comme fascinant. Les possibilités de voyage semblaient illimitées et les contraintes sociales moins fortes. La liberté dictait sa loi : après tout, la mode était aux minijupes. Cette promesse publicitaire de billets bon marché et de nombreux vols hebdomadaires annonçait toutefois que le voyage aérien de luxe ne serait bientôt plus qu'un souvenir.

Stardust Hotel & Golf Club, 1967

ALITALIA'S ITALY

Sophia Loren, one of the wonders of Italy today. Soon to be seen with Omar Sharif in M-G-M's romantic comedy "More Than A Miracle." A Carlo Ponti production in Metrocolor.

Alitalia, 1968

“Take me along”

Or how to turn your husband’s next business trip into a swinging time for both of you.

How long has it been since you danced together?
Explored a city together?
Or been alone together?
United will show you the way.
With our “Take Me Along” fare, that saves you up to ⅓ of a wife’s fare.
With our credit card, that lets you charge it.
We’ll even give you side-by-side seating. Naturally.
What’s more, you can get reduced hotel and car rental rates on the weekend in most cities. So you can stay over and stretch your trip.
Sound good?
Say “Take Me Along” tonight.
Then dust off your suitcase, and call United or your Travel Agent.

"But, Don, we can't dance on the plane!"

fly the friendly skies of United.

Try the lyrics below on your husband.
They're from the Broadway Musical "Take Me Along."

“Take me a-long, if you love-a-me. Take me a-long, if you love-a-me. Take me a-long with you.

My heart will ride, sweet and glo-ri-ous, high a-bove the throng, if you will take me a-long with you.”

◄ United Air Lines, 1967

As more businessmen traveled, United Air Lines produced a sparkling campaign about wives traveling along. The effervescent TV ad featured a chorus line of wives, in Pop Art–colored chorine costumes, imploring their husbands to "Take Me Along." Michael Cimino, who later won an Oscar for the Vietnam War movie *The Deer Hunter*, was the unlikely director.

Im Zuge zunehmender Geschäftsreisen brachte United Air Lines einen prickelnden Fernsehspot über mitreisende Ehefrauen, die – in poppige Revuekostüme gekleidet – ihre Männer im Chor anflehen, sie doch mitzunehmen („Take Me Along"). Regie führte niemand anderes als Michael Cimino, der später für den Spielfilm *The Deer Hunter* (*Die durch die Hölle gehen*) den Oscar gewann.

Comme les hommes d'affaires voyageaient toujours plus, United Air Lines diffusa une brillante campagne mettant en scène les épouses qui les accompagnaient. Un spot TV pétillant présentait une troupe de femmes vêtues de costumes aux couleurs Pop Art en train de chanter « Emmène-moi avec toi ». Michael Cimino, plus tard oscarisé pour son film sur la guerre du Vietnam *Voyage au bout de l'Enfer*, en était le réalisateur.

United Air Lines, 1967

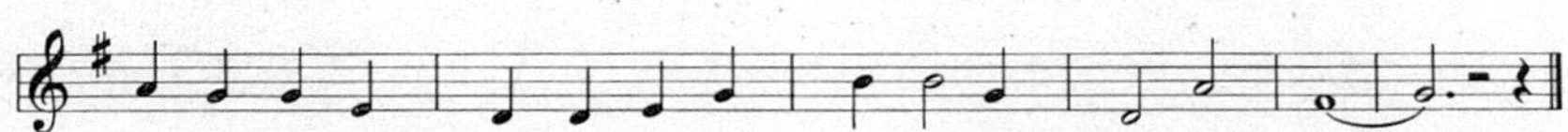

And this'll sound like music to his ears, too!
United's "Take Me Along" fare will save up to one-third of a wife's fare both ways.
We'll let you charge it with our credit card.
We'll give you side-by-side seating.
And what's more, you can even get reduced hotel and car rental rates on the weekend in most cities.
So you can stay over and stretch your trip.
Why not try our song?
It's really a pretty sound idea.
First Step: Call United or your Travel Agent.

fly the friendly skies of United.

"Dave, they're playing our song."

The former Miss Butterfingers.

Two months ago Sheri Woodruff couldn't even balance a cup of coffee.

But she was friendly, intelligent, and attractive. And wanted more than anything else to be a great stewardess.

So we put her to the test. (We take only one out of thirty applicants.) Five and a half weeks at United's Stewardess School.

We taught Sheri how to serve a gourmet dinner, how to soothe a first-flyer, how to apply everything from make-up to first-aid. Along with courses like aviation principles and geography.

Today she can warm a baby's formula with one hand and pour four cups of coffee with the other.

But more than that.

She's still the same Sheri Woodruff. Friendly, intelligent, attractive. And wants more than anything else to be a great stewardess.

She is.

"This is what I call a balanced meal."
fly the friendly skies of United.

United Air Lines, 1967

► Israel Government Tourist Office, 1963

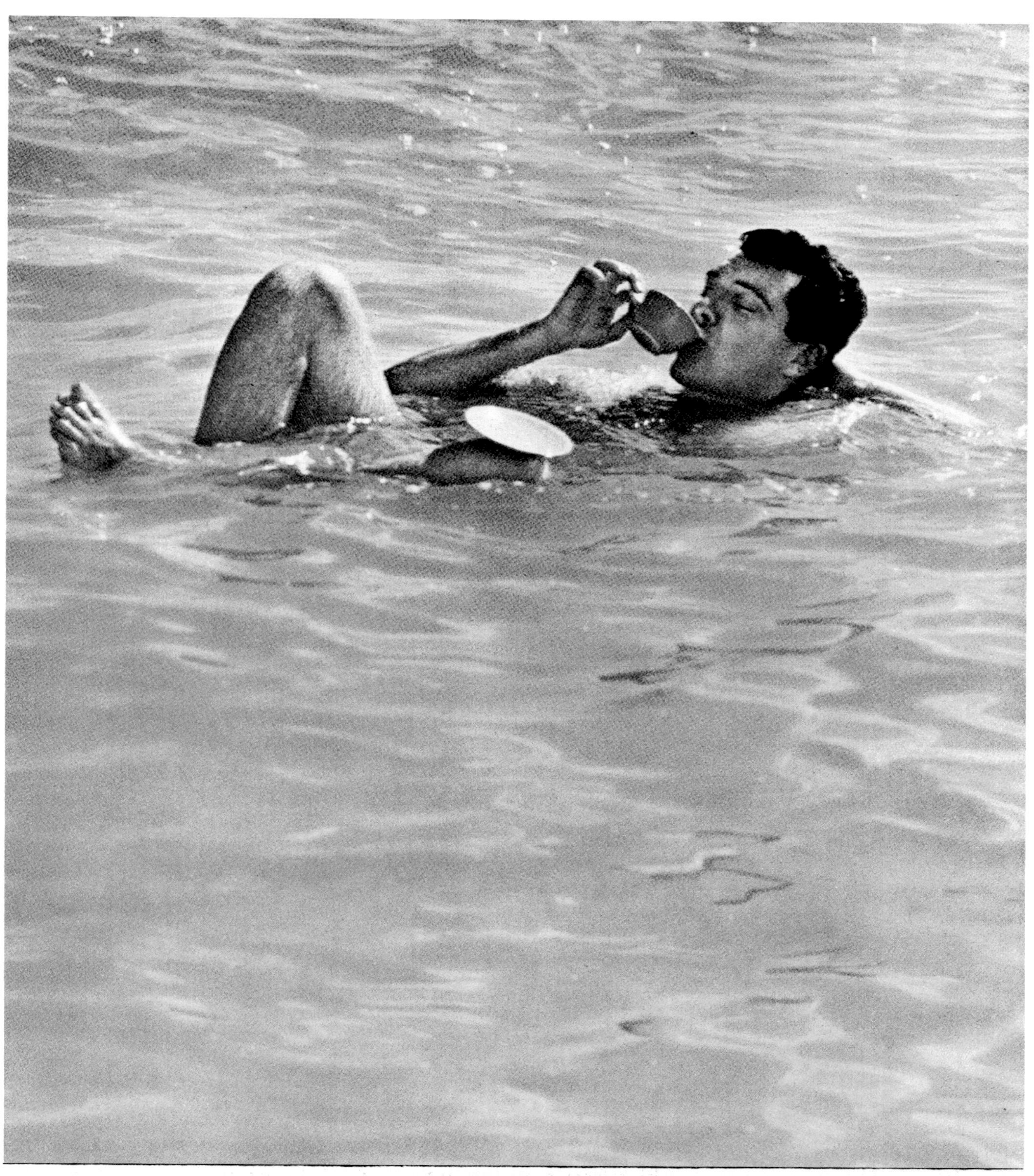

High tea on the Dead Sea.

Israel's Dead Sea is the lowest spot on earth.

You go down 1,292 feet through a moonscape to get there. Cups and saucers float on it. So do bridge tables. And so do you: You pop right to the top.

You can float clear to Sodom, if you like.

Nearby, in Beersheba, there's a newer source of water: a swimming pool in the land of Abraham.

Everywhere in Israel, the Bible is part of the scenery.

You can skin dive at Ashkelon, at the beach where Samson met Delilah. At the Sea of Galilee, you can watch fishermen toss nets for St. Peter's fish as they did 2,000 years ago.

Afterwards, you can visit a kibbutz with a concert hall and a banana plantation, enjoy St. Peter's fish for dinner and pay the bill with your Diners' Club card.

Where else in the world?

For more details, contact your travel agent or **ISRAEL GOVERNMENT TOURIST OFFICE** New York, Chicago, Beverly Hills or Montreal.

Funny. You don't look like
a French restaurant.

Ah, but don't let our disguise fool you.

Any time you're on a Pan Am® Jet Clipper,® you're dining out with *Maxim's of Paris*. The same *Maxim's* you'll find along Rue Royale in Paris.

The same *Maxim's* that dreams up the finest international menu that ever got off the ground.

Plan to fly First-Class President Special. Or Rainbow Economy. Either way, you can go just about anywhere in the world.

And you'll know you're flying the very best there is: the world's most experienced airline.

Ask a Pan Am Travel Agent to make your reservations. And make it dinner for two.

World's most experienced airline.

Pan Am makes the going great.

◂ Pan Am, 1968

Convair, 1960

This jet with exclusively first-class seating seems to be taking a page from the early deluxe "flyer" service on trains in the early part of the century. It was increasingly common for businessmen to bring their wives along on a work trip—and extend stays a few extra days for a quick getaway.

Dieser exklusive Business-Class-Jet macht offenbar Anleihen bei den luxuriösen „Flyer"-Schnellzügen aus der Frühzeit des Jahrhunderts. Immer mehr Geschäftsleute nahmen ihre Ehefrauen mit auf die Dienstreise – um für eine kurze Auszeit ein paar Tage anzuhängen.

Cet appareil configuré entièrement en classe affaires semble s'inspirer des premiers voyages de luxe proposés par les compagnies ferroviaires au début du siècle. Il était de plus en plus courant que les hommes d'affaires emmènent leurs femmes avec eux lors de leurs déplacements professionnels, et qu'ils prolongent leur séjour par une petite escapade à deux.

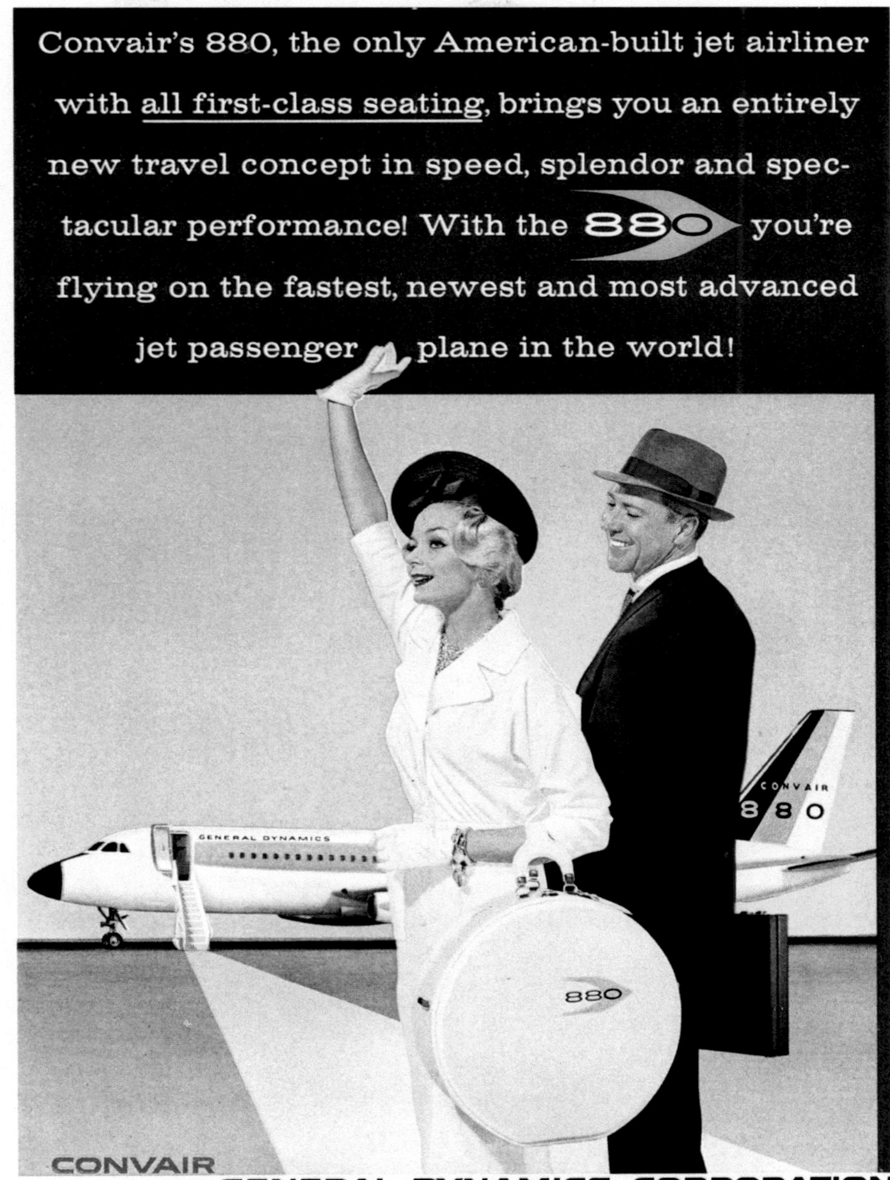

"TO EXPRESS THE EXCITEMENT OF TRAVEL"

... EERO SAARINEN

This is the new Trans World Flight Center in New York. Architect Saarinen designed it to express the special excitement of jet travel. Its soaring roof and sweep of glass enclose a hundred new ideas to speed your departure and arrival—like TWA's fast new jet check-in and boarding, and automatic baggage delivery. International shops are here. Comfortable lounges. Glamorous restaurants. One other fact makes the Trans World Flight Center entirely unique: it's the only airline terminal where routes from 70 cities in the U. S. are linked to routes in Europe, Africa, and Asia. One world under one roof.

TWA, 1962

Eero Saarinen designed the Trans World Airlines Terminal at Idlewild (later John F. Kennedy) Airport as one of his last works. The famed architect produced a swooping, dazzling building epitomized the élan and brio of flying. It looked like it was about to take off.

Eines der letzten Werke von Eero Saarinen ist der Terminal von Trans World Airlines auf dem Idlewild (und späteren John F. Kennedy) Airport. Der berühmte Architekt schuf ein dynamisch geschwungenes Gebäude, beseelt mit all dem Schwung und Elan des Fliegens, das so aussieht, als würde es gleich abheben.

Eero Saarinen conçut le terminal de Trans World Airlines à l'aéroport Idlewild (rebaptisé plus tard John F. Kennedy). Pour ce projet qui fut l'un de ses derniers, le célèbre architecte imagina un édifice éblouissant en forme d'oiseau stylisé prenant son envol avec élan et brio. Il donnait l'impression d'être prêt à décoller.

► McDonnell Douglas, 1969

Happy landings. DC-9.

Whether you're commuting only 100 miles, or traveling 1,000 miles away, you'll enjoy the happy landings that come at the end of a perfect flight aboard a DC-9 jetliner. Our advanced wing design makes landings easier, makes takeoffs quicker. We also placed its twin fanjets at the rear, to give you smoother, quieter flights. Our Douglas Aircraft Company has been making comfort a way of flight for 36 years. And in 1971 we'll introduce still another high in luxury with our new-generation jet, the DC-10. Anything that has to do with flight—for air travelers or astronauts—is only one of the things McDonnell Douglas does best.

MCDONNELL DOUGLAS

VACATIONS ARE ALWAYS IN SEASON when you go by Boeing jetliner. In incredibly few hours, Boeing jets can take you to *any* part of the world... whisk you from winter into summer, or to the climate and vacation activities you enjoy most. This year, spend more vacation time *there*—fly Boeing!

BOEING Jetliners

LONG-RANGE 707 · MEDIUM-RANGE 720 · SHORT-RANGE 727

These airlines offer Boeing jetliner service: AIR FRANCE · AIR-INDIA · AMERICAN · AVIANCA · B.O.A.C. · BRANIFF · CONTINENTAL · EASTERN · EL AL · IRISH · LUFTHANSA · NORTHWEST · PAKISTAN PAN AMERICAN · QANTAS · SABENA · SOUTH AFRICAN · TWA · UNITED · VARIG *and* WESTERN. *Boeing jets go into service later with:* CUNARD EAGLE · ETHIOPIAN · PACIFIC NORTHERN *and* SAUDI ARABIAN.

◂ Boeing, 1962

This Boeing ad looks remarkably like the logo of The Four Seasons, the sophisticated boîte in the legendary Seagram Building in New York. The restaurant served as an elite clubhouse for Jet Set plutocrats, including Madison Avenue panjandrums, who nursed old fashioneds in the Mies van der Rohe–Philip Johnson–designed bar.

Diese Anzeige von Boeing ähnelt auffallend dem Logo des Nobelrestaurants The Four Seasons im legendären Seagram Building in New York, einem elitären Clubhaus schwerreicher Jetsetter – wie der Bonzen der Madison Avenue –, die in der von Mies van der Rohe und Philip Johnson entworfenen Bar ihre Old-Fashioned-Cocktails schlürften.

Cette publicité Boeing rappelle vraiment le logo du restaurant The Four Seasons, rendez-vous chic installé dans le légendaire immeuble Seagram de New York. Ce restaurant faisait office de club pour les plutocrates de la jet-set, gros bonnets de Madison Avenue y compris, qui venaient biberonner leurs « old fashioneds » dans le bar conçu par Mies van der Rohe et Philip Johnson.

Lockheed JetStar, 1961

▸▸ Samsonite, 1963

All other corporate planes fly lower and slower. This is the Lockheed JetStar—the corporate-size jetliner: 500-550 mph cruise—up to 45,000 feet altitude, far above the weather. It will take you to a nearby city—or another hemisphere. Operates from more than 1,000 airports in the U.S. and Canada—hundreds more in South America and overseas. Four Pratt & Whitney pure jets provide power plus dependability. But you hear hardly more than a murmur, because the engines are located behind you, and so is the noise. Lockheed Aircraft Corporation, Marietta, Georgia.

LOCKHEED
JETSTAR
FLAGSHIP FOR YOUR CORPORATE FLEET

OLÉ

introducing Samsonite Sentry **the new Vivid Look** in Luggage starting at only $19.95

No luggage ever looked like this before... could ever make you look so vibrant and spirited. Samsonite Sentry is lavished with fashion-freshness—an impressive new shape, vivacious new colors, lively new linings, hidden locks. Plan to travel with Samsonite Sentry for eons. Its lightweight, dent-resistant body, strong magnesium frame, and scuff and stain-resistant covering are there to keep its vivid look constant. Expensive? Not at all. You can easily afford a matching set, and bring a new air of excitement to the longest or the shortest trip.

SAMSONITE SENTRY®

The luggage that comes to attention... smartly!

For women: Beauty Case, $19.95; Ladies' Tote, $19.95; 21" Ladies' O'Nite, $19.95; Ladies' Wardrobe, $32.95; 26" Pullman, $32.95. In Mist White, Cardinal Red, Marigold, Surf Blue, Fern Green. For men: 21" Companion Case, $19.95; Two-Suiter, $32.95; Three-Suiter, $34.95. In Rich Brown, Seal Black, Black Olive.

Shwayder Bros., Inc., Luggage Div., Denver, Colo. Makers of Samsonite Folding Furniture. Prices plus existing taxes. Available in Canada through Samsonite of Canada, Ltd., Stratford, Ont.

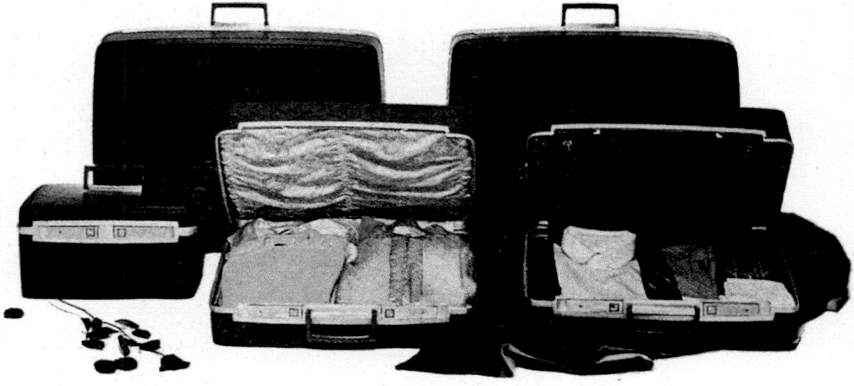

For Women: Beauty Case $19.95; 26" Pullman $32.95; Ladies' O'Nite (open) $19.95, in Cardinal Red.

For Men: Two-Suiter $32.95; Companion Case (open) $19.95, in Seal Black

SEATTLE WORLD'S FAIR 1962

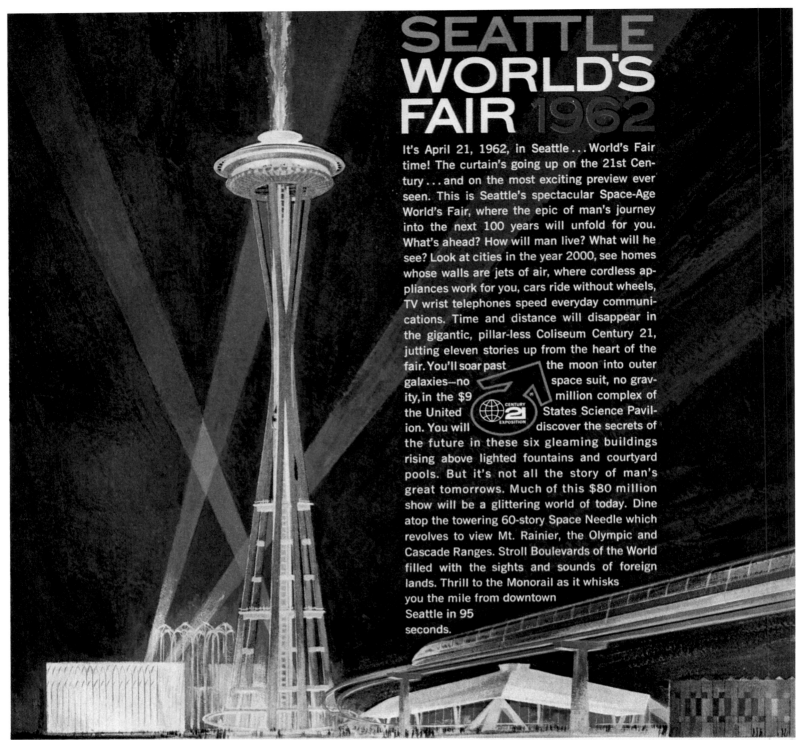

It's April 21, 1962, in Seattle . . . World's Fair time! The curtain's going up on the 21st Century . . . and on the most exciting preview ever seen. This is Seattle's spectacular Space-Age World's Fair, where the epic of man's journey into the next 100 years will unfold for you. What's ahead? How will man live? What will he see? Look at cities in the year 2000, see homes whose walls are jets of air, where cordless appliances work for you, cars ride without wheels, TV wrist telephones speed everyday communications. Time and distance will disappear in the gigantic, pillar-less Coliseum Century 21, jutting eleven stories up from the heart of the fair. You'll soar past the moon into outer galaxies—no space suit, no gravity, in the $9 million complex of the United States Science Pavilion. You will discover the secrets of the future in these six gleaming buildings rising above lighted fountains and courtyard pools. But it's not all the story of man's great tomorrows. Much of this $80 million show will be a glittering world of today. Dine atop the towering 60-story Space Needle which revolves to view Mt. Rainier, the Olympic and Cascade Ranges. Stroll Boulevards of the World filled with the sights and sounds of foreign lands. Thrill to the Monorail as it whisks you the mile from downtown Seattle in 95 seconds.

CENTURY 21 EXPOSITION

290

Rembrandt, Gauguin, and 65 world masters have been specially loaned for the Fair

Cultures of foreign lands in a potpourri of color and fun in the Boulevards of the World

Enjoy famed artists from all over the world performing in the opulent Opera House, intimate Playhouse, the Arena and Stadium. Relax in a rollicking Gayway where special rides hold fun-appeal to all ages. The Seattle World's Fair . . . the big family adventure of our times! See it all, April 21 to October 21, in Seattle!

Washington State Department of Commerce & Economic Development, Albert D. Rosellini, Governor.

WASHINGTON Is a Thrill-Filled State . . . See It All While You're Here!

SEATTLE WORLD'S FAIR, SEATTLE 9, WASH.

Please send me the following:

Further information about a Washington State vacation ☐

Further information about Seattle World's Fair ☐

Further information about housing accommodations ☐

NAME ....

ADDRESS ....

CITY .... STATE ....

(PLEASE PRINT CLEARLY) C-21 LN

◂ Seattle World's Fair, 1962

Expo 67, 1967

Expo 67 was the century's most successful world's fair, with more than 50 million visitors. "Man and His World" focused on housing. Popular exhibits included the U.S. pavilion, a geodesic dome by Buckminster Fuller, and Habitat 67, a landmark housing complex. But most popular was the Soviet Union pavilion, which drew 13 million visitors.

Mit über 50 Millionen Besuchern war die Expo 67 die erfolgreichste Weltausstellung des Jahrhunderts. Das Wohnen stand im Mittelpunkt von „Der Mensch und seine Welt". Besonderen Zulauf fanden der US-Pavillon in Form einer geodätischen Kuppel von Buckminster Fuller sowie Habitat 67, ein bahnbrechender Wohnhauskomplex. Absoluter Publikumsmagnet war jedoch der Pavillon der Sowjetunion mit 13 Millionen Besuchern.

Avec plus de 50 millions visiteurs, l'Expo 67 fut l'exposition internationale qui remporta le plus de succès au XXe siècle. Avec pour thème « Terre des Hommes », elle s'intéressait au logement. Parmi les pavillons plébiscités figuraient celui des Américains, un dôme géodésique de Buckminster Fuller, et Habitat 67, un complexe d'habitation révolutionnaire, mais le pavillon le plus visité fut celui de l'Union soviétique, qui attira 13 millions de personnes.

Look what the Russians are building, just 40 miles from the U.S.A.

As an American, you should look into it.

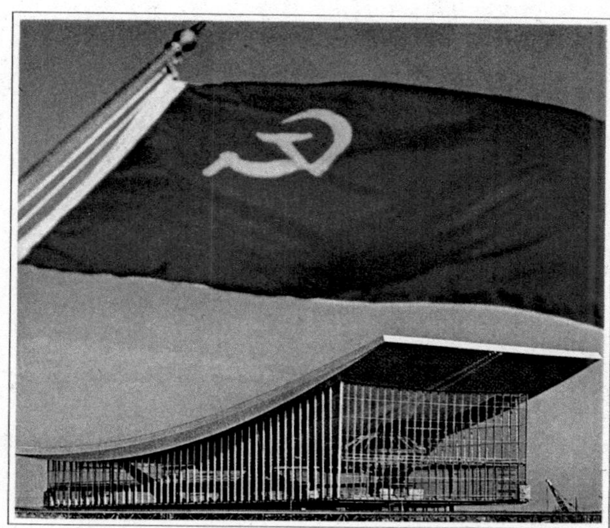

The U.S.S.R. hopes you will. You're invited to step in, and take a look at life in the Soviet Union. Meet the people, see what they do for a living in Vladivostok or Minsk, and how they have fun.

What kind of ideas do the Russians have, about education, medicine, housing, industrial development, space exploration? You'll find out here. In the great Lunar Hall, they'll treat you to an eerie expedition to the moon. On the way, you'll discover what the feeling of weightlessness is like (just *how* is their secret).

And on the lighter side of things, you can see what the Moscow miss is wearing, at a fashion parade. Browse through nearby stores that sell the identical items you'd find in shops in Leningrad or Kiev. Drop into the 600-seat cinema and watch a Russian movie. And wind up in one of the restaurants, where you can take your pick of specialties from every part of the country. (Incidentally, they've ordered 20 tons of sturgeon, eight tons of caviar and 28,000 litres of vodka, just for starters.)

The place to come for this fascinating experience is the U.S.S.R. Pavilion at Expo 67, Montreal, Canada. It's just across the way from the giant U.S.A. Pavilion — another world of wonders. And a few steps away, the French, British, Italians, Japanese, Canadians — more than two thirds of all the nations on earth — spread before you the best of their arts and culture. The latest in science and technology. Their past, present and future.

In all, some 70 governments have spent hundreds of millions of dollars to make Expo 67 the greatest world exhibition of them all, and the *first of its kind* on this continent. It opens on April 28th, for six wonderful months only. You'll find it the experience of a lifetime.

Start planning now. Expo 67 admission tickets *at reduced advance prices* save you up to 29%, are on sale at banks, department stores, American Express offices, and wherever you see the Expo 67 sign.

Accommodations in Montreal? No need to worry. LOGEXPO, the official accommodation bureau, guarantees you a place to stay, at government controlled prices. Reserve now — just write, mentioning dates, type of accommodations preferred, and the number in your party, to LOGEXPO, Expo 67, Harbor City, Montreal, Quebec, Canada. Or see your travel agent.

Or write for free Expo 67 vacation planning information to Expo 67 Information Services, 150 Kent St., Ottawa, Ont., Canada.

expo67

MONTRÉAL, CANADA

The Universal and International Exhibition of 1967
Montreal, Canada/APRIL 28-OCTOBER 27, 1967

HOLIDAY / MARCH

meet some of our first ladies

Most countries have only one first lady. Our country, the Continental States of America has many—our charming, helpful hostesses. You'll meet them on our Proud Birds and they'll make you feel like a visiting dignitary all during your trip.

It's not just their friendly greeting as you come aboard...or the way they serve your meal...or keep your children entertained. Much more important is how they do their jobs—with an almost patriotic pride.

You feel this pride in their thoroughness...their attention to detail. And as a result you feel good, comfortable, confident. That's the reason for choosing an airline—the way it does things, not because it just happens to go to a city you'd like to visit.

In the C.S.A., come travel with us, and feel the difference pride makes. Your travel agent or Continental will arrange it. Please call.

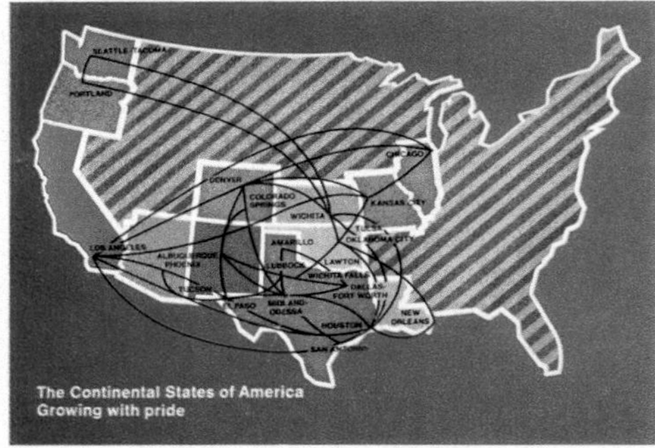
The Continental States of America
Growing with pride

Continental Airlines

the proud bird with the golden tail

Continental Airlines, 1967

► American Airlines, 1968

►► Braniff, 1966

The advertising whiz Mary Wells took on the Braniff International Airways account in 1965 and devised a seminal campaign. She brought in Jet Set favorite Emilio Pucci to revamp the stewardess uniforms. He created layers of clothing, in Pop Art colors. Air travel was always sexy; she made it overtly so.

Die Werbeikone Mary Wells, die ab 1965 für die Werbung von Braniff International Airways verantwortlich zeichnete, schuf eine bahnbrechende Kampagne. Sie zog Emilio Pucci, den Liebling des Jetset, hinzu, der den Uniformen der Stewardessen mehr Pfiff verlieh – mit mehrlagigen Kombinationen und poppigen Farben. Flugreisen waren schon immer sexy, und sie brachte es nun an den Tag.

En 1965, le génie de la publicité Mary Wells se vit confier la publicité de Braniff International Airways. Elle conçut une campagne qui resta dans les annales. Elle fit appel au chouchou de la jet-set Emilio Pucci pour relooker les hôtesses, qu'il enveloppa de superpositions de vêtements dans des couleurs Pop Art. Les voyages en avion avaient toujours été sexy, et Mary Wells le faisait savoir ouvertement.

Think of her
as your mother.
She only wants what's best for you.
A cool drink. A good dinner. A soft pillow and a warm blanket.
This is not just maternal instinct. It's the result of the longest
Stewardess training in the industry.
Training in service, not just a beauty course.
Service, after all, is what makes professional travellers prefer American.
And makes new travellers want to keep on flying with us.
So we see that every passenger gets the same professional treatment.
That's the American Way.
Fly the American Way
American Airlines

Introducing
the
Air Strip
We had a girl go through the
motions to show you just what's
coming off at Braniff International.
As in the picture below,
our hostess appears at the airport
wearing a reversible cold-weather
coat, matching gloves and
boots and, if it's raining, an
ingenious plastic helmet.
When she boards our
Zip
sheds these outer garments
greet you in a raspberry suit
color co-ordinated shoes.
This ensemble is too
to risk soiling during dinner
at the appropriate moment,
Zip
Snap
Zip

ıanges into a lovely serving dress
'hich we call a Puccino (named for its
:eator, Emilio Pucci, who
elieves that even an airline hostess
ıould look like a girl).
After dinner, our hostess
Zip
ips out of the Puccino, revealing
ıe way-out outfit on the right.
Each change is made in a flash,
which allows her to give you constant
attention, from the time you take
off to the time you land.
If the flight seems all too short,
that's the whole idea.
Braniff International
Flies United States Mexico South America

HONG KONG?

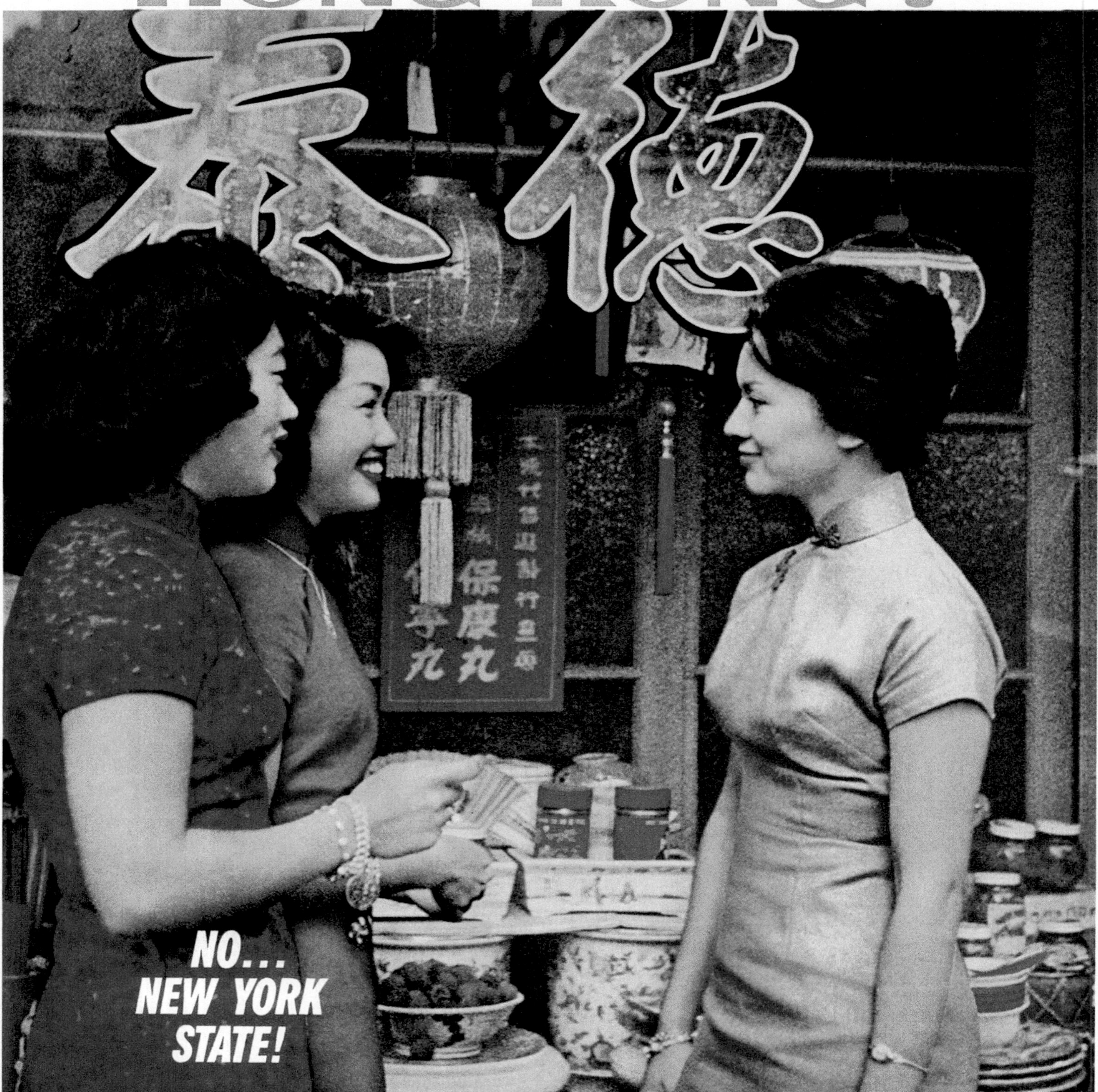

This curio shop could have a Hankow Road address in the Crown Colony of the Far East. And the first names of these chatting beauties could be as delightfully oriental as their smiling faces. Actually, this picture was snapped on Mott Street in the heart of Manhattan's Chinatown, with the help of Judy in red, Pat in blue, and Nina in the cool green. All three invite you to explore their exotic city within a city this summer. Wander through the quaint shops for Mandarin fashions, oriental jewelry and novelties. Stroll through the colorful markets for Chinese delicacies, and a fascinating museum for fun mixed with mystery. Then top off your stay with an unforgettable feast in one of Chinatown's many world-famed restaurants. Not far from "Hong Kong," you'll feel the breath of Paris blowing round corners in Greenwich Village; savor Old Spain in the Cloisters; and visit Little Italy, Little Germany, Little Syria, and Little...practically anywhere else in the mammoth metropolis of New York City.

On March 10, Tokyo's legendary hotel begins a new chapter.

In the heart of Tokyo, the Orient's biggest, most luxurious hotel. Fourteen hundred rooms, each with air-conditioning, color television and refrigerator. Ten superb Oriental or Western-cuisine restaurants, including the famous Theatre Restaurant Imperial. An experienced staff of 1,700 ready to assist you in every way. A unique blend of 21st century facilities and 19th century service—in the tradition of luxury begun 80 years ago. The new Imperial . . . and the legend continues. **IMPERIAL HOTEL, TOKYO**

T. Inumaru, President and General Manager

◂ Chinatown, New York City, 1961

Imperial Hotel, 1969

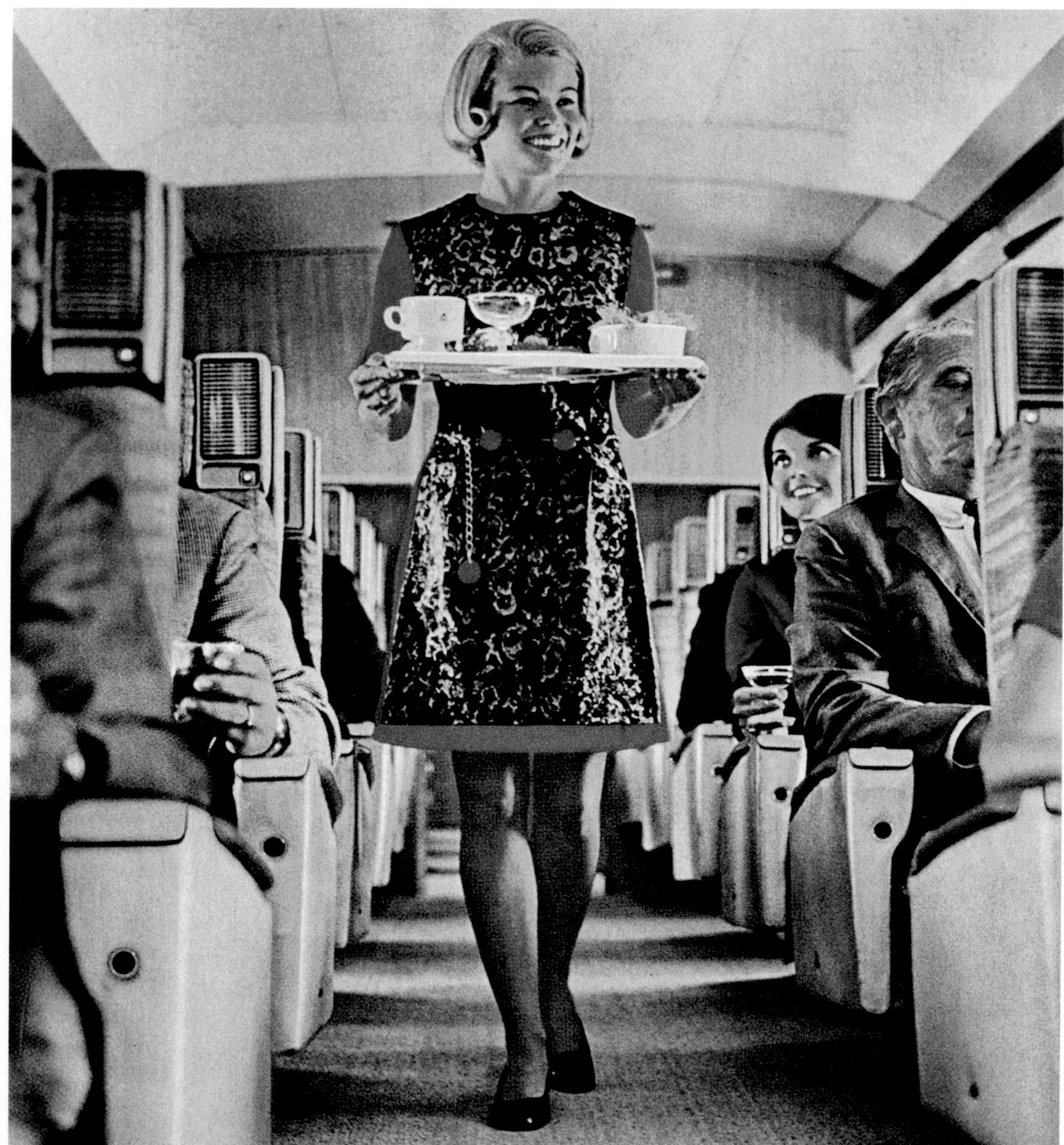

No floor show

just a working girl working

This is for real. No model. No put-on smiles. Her name is Carol Koberlein. But it could be Virginia White. Or Linda Epping. Or any one of the other 1724 stewardesses who work for Delta. In her new chic outfit, she looks like anything but a stewardess working. But work she does. Hard, too. And you hardly know it. Even when she spreads Delta's new eight-course, 1200-mile first-class meal before you. Or a Tourist meal that seems anything but economical. Next trip, come see our working girls work. It's no floor show. But it's funny how you get to feel like a leading man.

Delta Air Lines, Inc., General Offices, Atlanta Airport, Atlanta, Ga. 30320 DELTA

Delta is ready when you are!

The end of the plain plane, explained.

It's obvious that our airplanes look—well—different than other airplanes.

Not so obvious, perhaps, is why we made them look different.

You see, all airplanes look pretty much the same. And it was this monotonous *sameness* that we were trying to get away from.

(Oooooh, how those 3-hour plane rides can bore you. Especially if you're a guy who travels a lot for his living.)

Painting our airplanes different colors was a step in the other direction.

We also changed the fabrics on the seats, the uniforms our hostesses wear, our passenger lounges, our food service.

The list goes on and on.

In fact, we've made 17,543 changes in our airline so far. (This includes the small ones, like the rather satisfying change we made in the package that holds the sugar for your coffee.)

Since no other airline has ever gone to so much trouble before, you may still not understand why *we* did.

But even if you can't understand it, you can relax and enjoy it.

Braniff International

United States Mexico South America

◂ Delta Air Lines, 1966

Braniff, 1966

Mary Wells's campaign for Braniff International Airways aimed to show that travel on this airline was unlike any other—special even for jaded business travelers. She brought in the influential designer Alexander Girard, known for his chic, important restaurants, and he saturated the jets with strong colors—inside and out.

Mary Wells Kampagne für Braniff International wollte zeigen, dass diese Fluglinie etwas ganz Besonderes bot – sogar für übersättigte Vielflieger. Alexander Girard, der für seine schicken Restaurantausstattungen berühmte Designer, tunkte die Jets in kräftige Farben – innen wie außen.

La campagne conçue par Mary Wells pour Braniff International visait à prouver que cette compagnie aérienne n'avait rien à voir avec les autres, même pour les voyageurs d'affaires les plus blasés. Elle collabora avec l'influent designer Alexander Girard, réputé pour son travail de décoration dans les grands restaurants, qui satura les avions de couleurs vives à l'intérieur comme à l'extérieur.

TWA (Bob Peak), 1962

► Tropicana, 1963

The showgirls of Las Vegas were traditionally not dancers. They sashayed – usually wearing very little. But in 1959 the Tropicana brought in the Folies Bergère dancers, and they performed nightly through the end of the century.

Die Showgirls von Las Vegas waren traditionell keine Tänzerinnen. Nein, sie tänzelten – meist spärlichst bekleidet. Das Tropicana engagierte 1959 jedoch die Folies Bergère, die bis zum Ende des Jahrhunderts allabendlich auftraten.

Traditionnellement, les showgirls de Las Vegas n'étaient pas danseuses. En général, elles se contentaient de déambuler en très, très petite tenue. En 1959, le Tropicana fit venir des danseuses des Folies Bergère, qui y donnèrent des représentations tous les soirs jusqu'à la fin du siècle.

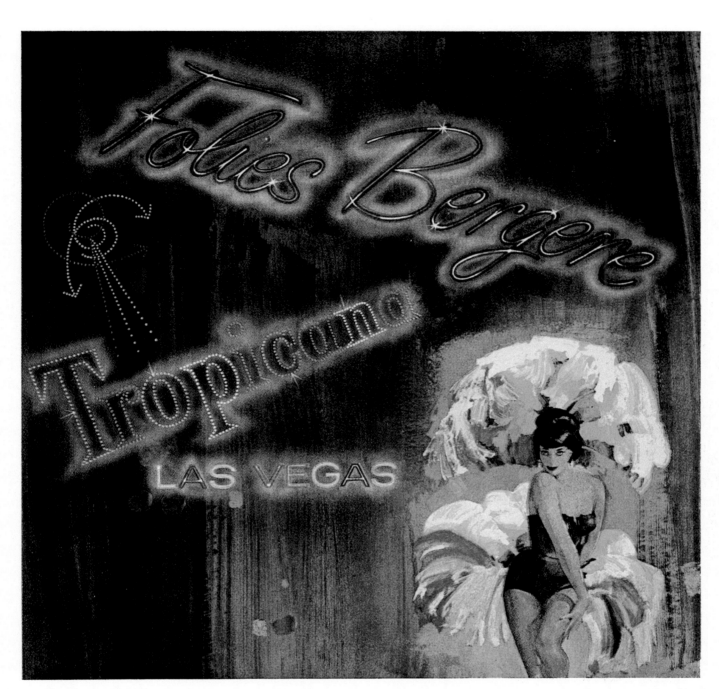

ESCAPE TO A WHOLE NEW WORLD OF PLEASURE! To the gay and glamorous resort-world of the Hotel Tropicana—bright and shining star of Las Vegas—America's luxurious answer to the excitement of Monte Carlo!

Discover the challenge of our magnificent golf course/enjoy to the hilt the superb pool, continental cuisine, unexcelled health club/and relax in a world of luxurious creature comforts designed to delight and pamper you.

All that plus the daring, the dazzling DIRECT-FROM-PARIS FOLIES BERGERE—all brilliantly and completely 1963 NEW! See the most ravishing showgirls in the world—the most spectacular stars of Europe. See the show that's like no other show on earth—the pride of Paris, the talk of Las Vegas!

For a memory-making holiday, fly straight and true to the Tropicana—we're experts in proving that nothing is too good for you! Room rates: $15 to $25 a day.

FREE! Illustrated Brochure.
Write Dept. F-T1, Hotel Tropicana
Las Vegas, Nevada.

—that's where all the life is!

FOR ROOM RESERVATIONS, CALL YOUR TRAVEL AGENT OR OUR NEAREST OFFICE: CHICAGO: FI 6-7237 / DALLAS: RI 1-6814 / DENVER: 534-1811 FORT WORTH: EN 3980 / HOUSTON: MO 5-5421 / LOS ANGELES: MA 6-7581 / NEW ORLEANS: WX 3980 / NEW YORK: CI 5-3238 / SAN FRANCISCO: YU 2-6905

The Sun of Miami.

It's not the same as the sun that rises over New York, Chicago or Boston. Miami is where the su spends the winter. Where it's just as warm in January as it is in June.

Where you can lie on the beach or beside one of a thousand different pools. And be pampere like a maharajah in one of a hundred different hotels as luxurious as the Taj Mahal.

Eastern can take you there more easily than any other airline because we have more flights t Miami from more cities than anybody else.

Come with Eastern to Miami. And feel just as warm and comfortable in the sky as you will fee when you arrive under the sun of Miami.

Call your travel agent or Eastern for reservations to Miami, or any of the seven suns of Easter

EASTERN The Wings of Man.

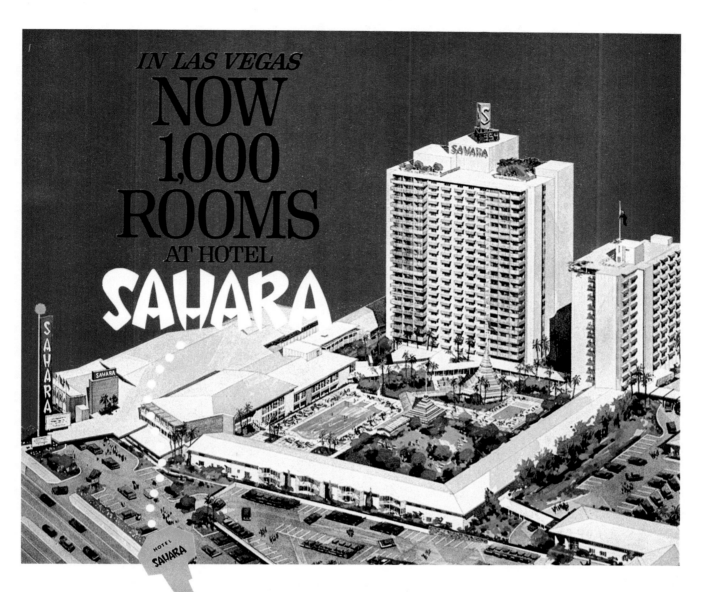

IN LAS VEGAS
NOW 1,000 ROOMS
AT HOTEL
SAHARA

Your Key to a TREASURE OF PLEASURE

Hotel Sahara . . . the new vacation wonder in the world's wonder city . . . now with 1,000 rooms and room for everbody! All the luxurious leisure, the fun and relaxation you expect in one of the world's finest resort hotels... at rates anyone can afford.

Sun-swimming in three spacious pools . . . dining in three famous restaurants... star entertainment in two great showrooms. Shops, buffets, health club, golfing, riding... a real "Treasure of Pleasure"—the vacation visit of a lifetime, Hotel Sahara!

ALSO—THE WEST'S MOST COMPLETE AND LUXURIOUS PRIVATE CONVENTION FACILITIES—FOR 10 TO 1600 PERSONS.

1,000 "YEARS-AHEAD" ROOMS all with radio and TV.

DON THE BEACHCOMBER dining-dancing.

HOUSE OF LORDS elegant dining.

THREE LUXURIOUS SWIMPOOLS temperature-controlled.

LIVELY CASBAR THEATRE dusk-'til-dawn shows.

STAR-STUDDED SHOWS in the great Congo Room, where famous names reign supreme. Colorful, captivating show productions!

HOTEL
SAHARA
LAS VEGAS • NEVADA

Enjoy a "GOLDEN WEB OF HOSPITALITY" at these other DEL E. WEBB hotels: MOUNTAIN SHADOWS • SCOTTSDALE, ARIZ. / OCEAN HOUSE • SAN DIEGO / TOWN HOUSE • SAN FRANCISCO

◂ Eastern Airlines, 1969

Sahara, 1963

SHERATON

AT THE HEART OF **WAIKIKI**

THE FOUR HOTELS THAT MADE WAIKIKI FAMOUS

ROYAL HAWAIIAN
Pleasure . . . 18-acres big beside the sparkling Pacific!

PRINCESS KAIULANI
Orchid swimming pool for Polynesian splash parties!

MOANA AND SURFRIDER
Glamorous twosome, side by side, to double your fun!

STAY AT ONE–PLAY AT ALL FOUR

Sheraton's where the fun is! Just 4½ jet-hours from the mainland. 70° surf-and-sun days, Fun Festivals to brighten every Diamond Head night, feasts every meal, service every moment. Family plan: children share adult's accommodations free. For easy reservations, just call your travel agent or your nearest Sheraton Hotel.

Open Dec. 1: Sheraton-Maui, dazzling resort hotel on magnificent Kaanapali Beach • Maui, Hawaii

Sheraton shares are listed on the New York Stock Exchange. *Diners' Club card honored for all hotel services.*

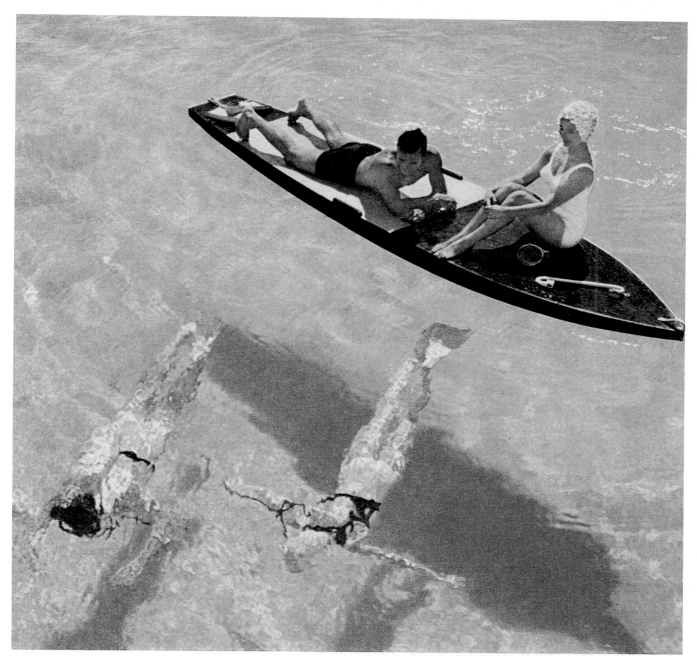

Swim party off Nassau. Photographed by Ozzie Sweet

Liquid sunshine...

There's just one place where the sea looks like this. The Bahamas. Search beneath the surface for coral gardens or pieces of eight . . . you'll find the show underwater is equal to the beauty above.

But, adventurous or not, you'll go overboard, too, for the life ashore that pampers vacationers the year around. These lush islands are British—with a tropic accent. Take High Tea, or cocktails and calypso. Go native and spice your evenings with a goombay beat.

You can reach these resort islands easily. A wide choice of clubs and hotels offers sharply reduced rates from now right through to December 15. Smartly informal or grandly luxurious, they're all easy to take and hard to leave.

Your Travel Agent will make all arrangements. Or should you wish further information, please write to Dept. NK, Bahamas Development Board, 620 Fifth Avenue, New York 20. Telephone PLaza 7-1611.

The Resort Islands of the **Bahamas**

BY SEA: From New York on the **M. S. ITALIA** every Saturday at 4 P.M. Seven-day cruises (two days and a night in Nassau) from $170. Home Lines, 42 Broadway, New York 4.
From Miami on the **S.S. BAHAMA STAR** every Monday and Friday at 5 P.M. Three-day, all-expense cruises (two days and a night in Nassau) from $54. Eastern Steamship Corp., Miami 1.
BY AIR: Direct, daily flights from New York (2½ hours); Miami (50 minutes) and other principal Florida cities. Direct service from Toronto and Montreal.

◂ Sheraton Hotels, 1962

Bahama Islands, 1962

▸▸ TWA, 1964

Enjoy fine films such as "Good Neighbor Sam," starring Jack Lemmon and Romy Schneider. A David Swift production. A Columbia re

Across the U.S., across the Atlantic: **Movies in flight are he**

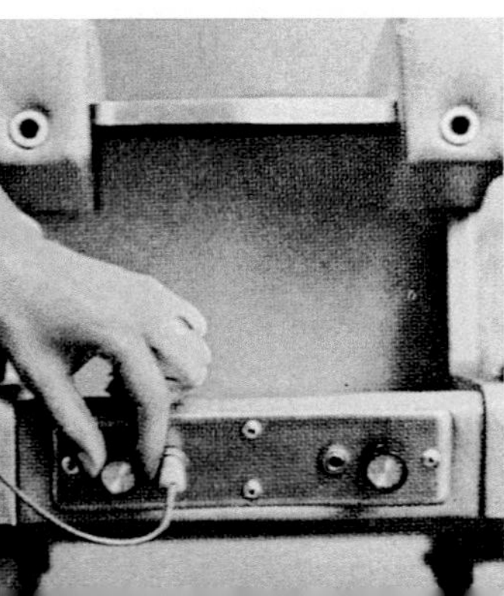

EARPHONES are so lightweight an fortable you'll forget they're on. An you're listening, no one else will be dis

VOLUME is adjusted by a single, control at your fingertips. Then jus and be entertained by the best from wood and Europe.

DINING is an experience on TWA. Firs meals are elegant feasts. In Jet Co Economy, they're not quite as elabor certainly as delicious.

*Optional at $1 in Coach and Economy Complimentary in First Class.

Films by Inflight Motion Pictures, Inc.

. only on TWA jets!

re yourself skimming along on a big TWA jet—nph or better, but so smooth and quiet you'd know it. You put on featherweight earphones, t a fingertip volume control, settle back . . . and a movie! Not the one you saw last year, but ne that just hit Broadway. Movies in flight—'s most talked-about airline service, and only World Airlines has it!

The films are shown on non-stop TWA transcontinental flights in First Class, *and now in the Coach* section too!* On transatlantic flights, in both First Class and Economy.* If you're planning a vacation trip to the World's Fair this year, or maybe a holiday in Europe—see how much more the right airline ticket buys. Call your nearest Trans World Airlines office, or see your travel agent and specify TWA.

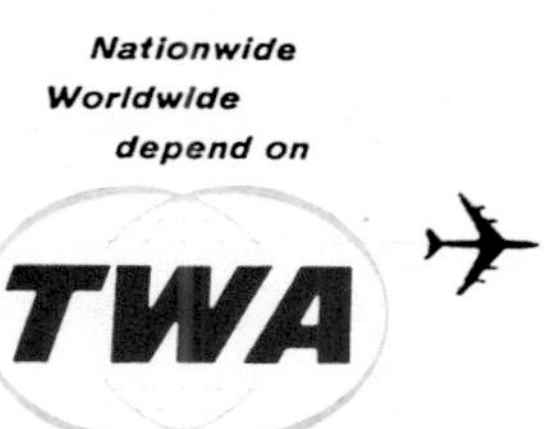
Nationwide
Worldwide
depend on
TWA

THIS DECADE WAS ULTIMATELY ABOUT THE POWER OF THE MASS MARKET. AS EVER-BIGGER JETS TOOK FLIGHT, TICKET PRICES FELL—AND MORE PEOPLE COULD, AND WOULD, BUY THEM.

LETZTLICH HANDELT DIESE DEKADE VON DER MACHT DES MASSENMARKTS. WÄHREND DIE JETS IMMER GRÖSSER WURDEN, SANKEN DIE PREISE FÜR EIN FLUGTICKET, UND IMMER MEHR MENSCHEN KONNTEN – UND WÜRDEN – SICH EINES KAUFEN.

CETTE DÉCENNIE RESTERA MARQUÉE PAR LA PUISSANCE DU TOURISME DE MASSE. ALORS QUE DES AVIONS TOUJOURS PLUS GROS PRENAIENT LEUR ENVOL, LE PRIX DES BILLETS NE CESSAIT DE CHUTER. UN NOMBRE CROISSANT DE PERSONNES POUVAIT – ET ALLAIT – EN ACHETER.

1970

ALL ABOARD!
ALLES EINSTEIGEN!
TOUS À BORD !

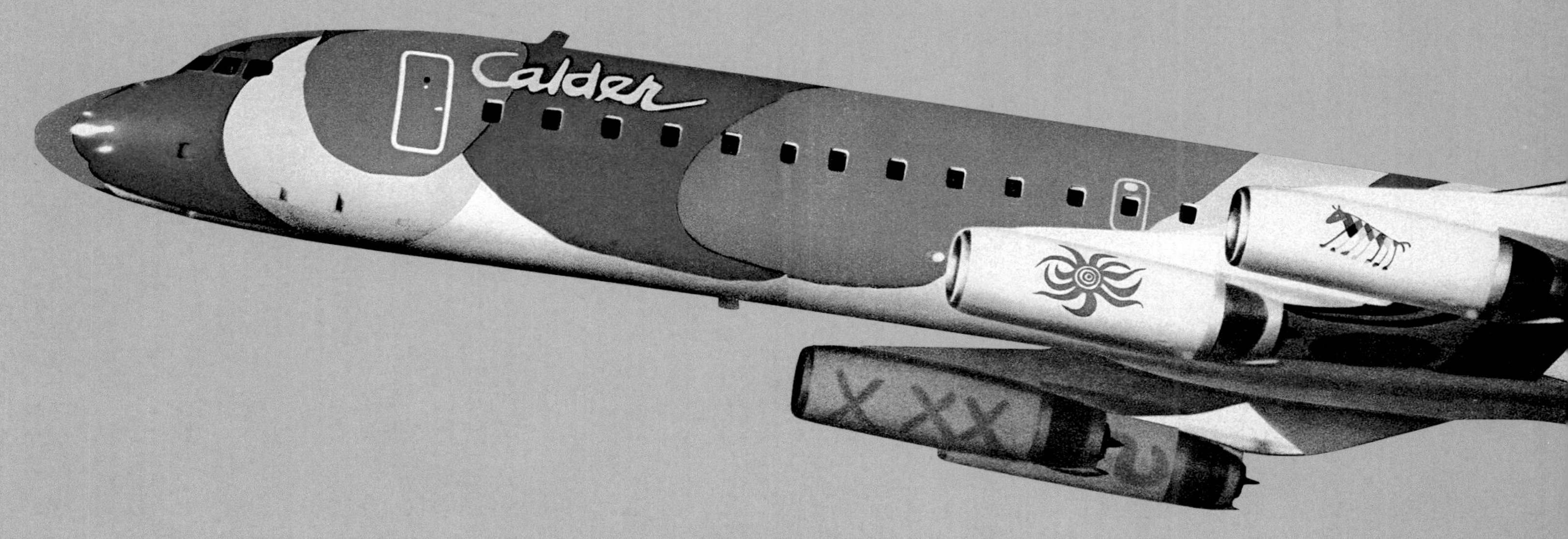

-1979

SARAO
ISUZU C-221
SARAO Super de Luxe

◄ Philippine Airlines, 1977

Western Air Lines, 1971

IN 1973, AIR FRANCE HIRED THE INFLUENTIAL DESIGNER RAYMOND LOEWY TO DO THE INTERIORS OF ITS NEW SUPERSONIC, SUPER-DELUXE CONCORDE. Passengers could fly New York to Paris in roughly three and one-half hours—for an astronomical fee. The glamour associated with air travel was still potent. Braniff International Airways remained a brand to watch. In 1973, Mary Wells, the advertising impresario who revamped the brand in the '60s, commissioned the artist Alexander Calder to paint a jet—a Douglas DC-8 that was christened "Flying Colors." For the stewardess uniforms and plane interiors, Wells brought on Halston, the darling of the chic set, to create his "Ultra Look."

But this decade was ultimately about the power of the mass market. As ever-bigger jets took flight, ticket prices fell—and more people could, and would, buy them. By 1970, airlines accounted for 73% of U.S. passenger travel. The Boeing 747 "jumbo jet," a two-level plane 2.5 times the size of the 707, accelerated this shift. It first lifted off in 1970, and held the passenger capacity record for the rest of the century. The growth in airline travel even seemed little affected by the 1973 energy shortage, though ticket prices skyrocketed. Road travel proved more vulnerable to the oil embargo. Profits at Howard Johnson's, for example, fell sharply, since motorists accounted for 85% of its revenues.

The ocean liner era was now largely a memory. By 1976, Matson ended passenger service between Hawaii and California. This stately mode of travel looked doomed, and popular culture reflected this. In *The Poseidon Adventure* (1972), an ocean liner flips over after being hit by a tidal wave, and a group of passengers—including Gene Hackman, Shelley Winters, and Ernest Borgnine—struggles to get to safety. Even a private yacht meant trouble. In *The Last of Sheila* (1973), a Mediterranean cruise by Hollywood elite ends in murder.

Yet short, all-inclusive cruises, the opposite of exclusive, began to take hold by the second half of the decade. Riding this wave, the crew on the TV series *The Love Boat* welcomed a full roster of passengers aboard the *Pacific Princess* in 1977. It ran for nine years. Club Med, an all-inclusive, if stationary, vacation, developed a big following.

The notion of high-end train travel also seemed outdated. The all-star cast of *Murder on the Orient Express* (1974)—Ingrid Bergman, Albert Finney, Lauren Bacall, Sir John Gielgud—looks as creaky as the train. True, the 1976 update of the classic '30s train thriller *Silver Streak* was a breakout hit, but largely due to the dynamic teaming of Gene Wilder and Richard Pryor. Railroad travel now accounted for only 7.2% of the domestic market. Most rail lines had filed for bankruptcy. Washington cobbled them together to create the publicly subsidized Amtrak in 1971. It was continually starved for funds.

The 1970s marked the last years of truly glamorous airline travel. In 1978, Congress passed the Airline Deregulation Act, ending all restrictions on routes and new services.

When it took effect, in 1982, air travel would never be the same.

1970

1970 Airlines account for 73% of all U.S. passenger travel; railroads only 7.2%

In den USA erfolgen 73 % der Personenbeförderung mit dem Flugzeug, per Bahn sind es nur 7,2 %

L'avion représente 73 % du transport de passagers aux Etats-Unis, et le train, seulement 7,2 %

1970 Sheraton first hotel chain to offer toll-free phone number for direct guest access

Sheraton als erste Hotelkette mit gebührenfreier Buchungshotline

Sheraton devient la première chaîne hôtelière à proposer un numéro d'appel gratuit à ses clients

1971 First-class airline lounges go disco

Discofeeling nun auch in der ersten Klasse

Dans les aéroports, les salons de première classe se mettent à la mode disco

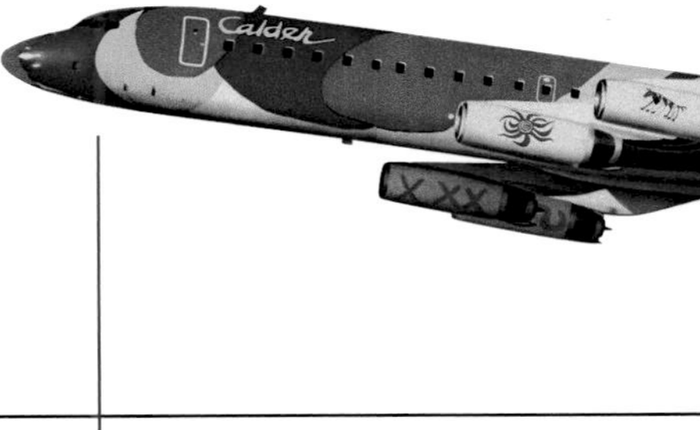

1973 Braniff hires artist Alexander Calder to paint Douglas DC-8 jet, dubbed "Flying Colors"

Alexander Calder taucht die Douglas DC-8 für Braniff in neue Farben („Flying Colors")

La compagnie Braniff demande à Alexander Calder de peindre son Douglas DC-8, surnommé « Flying Colors »

AIR FRANCE BEAUFTRAGTE 1973 DEN DESIGNER RAYMOND LOEWY MIT DER GESTALTUNG DES INTERIEURS IHRES NEUEN ÜBERSCHALLFLUGZEUGS, DER CONCORDE. Nun konnte man in rund dreieinhalb Stunden von New York nach Paris fliegen – zu einem astronomischen Preis. Der Glamour des Fliegens war noch nicht verflogen. Braniff International Airways war für eine weitere Überraschung gut: Mary Wells, jene Top-Kreative, die der Marke bereits in den 1960er-Jahren neuen Glanz verliehen hatte, beauftragte den Künstler Alexander Calder, eine Douglas DC-8 anzumalen – seine Kreation erhielt den Namen „Flying Colors". Für die Uniformen der Stewardessen und das Interieur erfand der Modeschöpfer Halston den „Ultra Look".

Doch im Grunde handelt diese Dekade von der Macht des Massenmarkts. Während die Jets immer größer wurden, sanken die Preise für ein Flugticket, und immer mehr Menschen konnten sich eines kaufen. 1970 kamen die Fluglinien für 73 % des Personenverkehrs auf. Beschleunigt wurde dieser Prozess durch den „Jumbojet", die Boeing 747, ein Großraumflugzeug, zweieinhalbmal so groß wie die 707. Der 1970 eingeführte Jumbojet vermochte sich bis zum Ende des Jahrhunderts als Flugzeug mit der größten Sitzplatzkapazität zu behaupten. Selbst die Energiekrise von 1973 konnte dem Wachstum der Flugreisen wenig anhaben, obwohl die Ticketpreise in die Höhe schnellten. Reisen mit dem Auto erwiesen sich als anfälliger für das Ölembargo. So etwa verzeichnete Howard Johnson's einen drastischen Gewinnrückgang, da Autofahrer 85 % des Umsatzes ausmachten.

Die Ära der Linienschiffe war nun weitgehend Geschichte. Die Reederei Matson stellte 1976 die Passagierbeförderung zwischen Hawaii und Kalifornien ganz ein. Diese würdevolle Art des Reisens schien dem Untergang geweiht. Auch die Populärkultur zeugt davon: In *The Poseidon Adventure* (*Die Höllenfahrt der Poseidon*, 1972) wird das Schiff von einer Monsterwelle erfasst und kentert. Einige Passagiere – darunter Gene Hackman – kämpfen ums Überleben. Doch auch auf einer Privatjacht war man nicht sicher. In *The Last of Sheila* (*Sheila*, 1973) endet eine Mittelmeerkreuzfahrt auf der Jacht eines Hollywoodproduzenten mit einem Mord.

In der zweiten Hälfte der Dekade gab es indes immer mehr All-inclusive-Kreuzfahrten (also das Gegenteil von exklusiv). So konnte die Crew der neun Jahre laufenden Fernsehserie *The Love Boat* (*Love Boat*, 1977) zahllose Passagiere an Bord der *Pacific Princess* begrüßen. Als ortsfestes All-inclusive-Pendant fand auch der Club Med zahlreiche Anhänger.

Anspruchsvolle Zugreisen waren nun auch altmodisch. Die Stars in *Murder on the Orient Express* (*Mord im Orient-Express*, 1974) – Ingrid Bergman, Lauren Bacall und Sir John Gielgud – waren, wie der Zug selbst, in die Jahre gekommen. Sicher, *Silver Streak*, die Neuauflage eines Zugthrillers aus den 1930er-Jahren, war ein Kassenschlager, doch er verdankt dies vor allem dem Zusammenspiel von Gene Wilder und Richard Pryor. Bahnreisen machten nun nur mehr 7,2 % des Binnenmarktes aus. Die meisten Eisenbahngesellschaften hatten Konkurs angemeldet. Washington bastelte 1971 daraus die staatlich subventionierte Amtrak, die unaufhörlich viel Geld verschlang.

Die 1970er sind die letzten Jahre der wirklich glamourösen Flugreisen. Mit dem 1978 verabschiedeten Airline Deregulation Act endeten sämtliche Restriktionen hinsichtlich der Ticketpreise, Routen und Flugpläne. Als das Gesetz 1982 in Kraft trat, sah sich der Flugverkehr nachhaltig verändert.

1973

1973 Air France asks Raymond Loewy to design interiors of its first Concorde

Air France beauftragt Raymond Loewy mit dem Entwurf des Interieurs seiner ersten Concorde

Air France demande à Raymond Loewy de concevoir l'intérieur de son premier Concorde

1974 In period thriller *Murder on the Orient Express* every passenger aboard the luxury train could be a murder suspect

In dem historischen Kriminalfilm *Mord im Orient-Express* sind alle Fahrgäste des Luxuszugs verdächtig

Dans le thriller historique *Le Crime de l'Orient-Express*, chaque passager du train de luxe est considéré comme suspect

1976 Elvis performs final Las Vegas shows at the Hilton

Elvis absolviert im Hilton seine letzten Auftritte in Las Vegas

Elvis donne ses dernières représentations au Hilton de Las Vegas

1976 *Queen Elizabeth 2*'s maiden voyage, an 80-day cruise around the world, tops out at $86,240 per passenger

Jungfernfahrt der RMS *Queen Elizabeth 2* als 80-tägige Kreuzfahrt rund um die Welt; ein Ticket kostet bis zu 86 240 $

Croisière inaugurale du *Queen Elizabeth 2*, un itinéraire de 80 jours autour du monde pour jusqu'à 86 240 dollars par personne

VENEZUELA
DOHN RUSSELL

◄ Cerromar Beach Hotel, 1978

Royal Viking Line, 1979

►► Desert Inn, 1978

EN 1973, AIR FRANCE RECRUTA L'INFLUENT DESIGNER RAYMOND LOEWY POUR CONCEVOIR L'INTÉRIEUR DE SON TOUT NOUVEAU CONCORDE SUPERSONIQUE GRAND LUXE. Les passagers pouvaient voler de New York à Paris en trois heures et demi environ, moyennant un prix astronomique. Le voyage aérien faisait encore rêver. Braniff International Airways était toujours une marque à suivre de près. En 1973, Mary Wells, la conceptrice publicitaire qui avait refaçonné la marque dans les années 1960, demanda à l'artiste Alexander Calder de peindre un avion, un Douglas DC-8 baptisé « Flying Colors ». Pour la tenue des hôtesses et la décoration intérieure, Mary Wells fit appel à Halston, le chouchou de la scène chic, qui créa ainsi son « Ultra Look ».

Cette décennie restera toutefois marquée par l'essor du tourisme de masse. Alors que des avions toujours plus gros prenaient leur envol, le prix des billets ne cessait de chuter. Un nombre croissant de personnes pouvait – et allait – en acheter. En 1970, l'avion représentait 73 % du trafic de voyageurs aux Etats-Unis. Le « jumbo jet » Boeing 747, un avion à deux niveaux d'une taille 2,5 fois supérieure à celle du 707, accéléra cette évolution. Après son premier décollage en 1970, il conserva le record de capacité d'accueil de passagers pendant 32 ans. La croissance du voyage aérien sembla à peine affectée par la crise énergétique de 1973, alors que le prix des billets s'envolait. Le voyage en voiture s'avéra plus vulnérable à l'embargo sur le pétrole, ce qui frappa de plein fouet la chaîne Howard Johnson dont les automobilistes représentaient 85 % des revenus.

L'ère des paquebots était désormais révolue. En 1976, Matson mit un terme au transport de passagers entre Hawaï et la Californie. Ce majestueux moyen de transport semblait condamné, comme le reflétait la culture populaire. Dans *L'Aventure du Poséidon* (1972), un paquebot est frappé par un raz-de-marée, et un groupe de passagers lutte pour sauver sa peau. Même un simple yacht privé était synonyme de malheur : dans *The Last of Sheila* (1973), une croisière accueillant l'élite d'Hollywood à son bord se conclut sur un meurtre.

Toutefois, les croisières « tout compris » de moindre durée et tout sauf luxueuses commencèrent à séduire les touristes

dès 1975. Surfant sur cette tendance, l'équipage du feuilleton télévisé *La Croisière s'amuse* accueillait toutes sortes de passagers à bord du *Pacific Princess* en 1977. La série dura neuf ans. Le Club Med, voyagiste spécialisé dans les séjours « tout compris » (hors excursions), rencontra également un grand succès.

Les voyages en trains de luxe semblaient également passés de mode. La distribution étoilée du *Crime de l'Orient-Express* (1974) – avec Ingrid Bergman, Albert Finney, Lauren Bacall et Sir John Gielgud – semble aussi fatiguée que le train. *Transamerica Express,* remake du classique des années 1930, dut son succès au duo dynamique formé par Gene Wilder et Richard Pryor. Le voyage en train ne représentait plus désormais que 7,2 % du marché américain. La plupart des compagnies ferroviaires s'étaient déclarées en faillite. En 1971, Washington sauva de justesse la compagnie partiellement publique Amtrak en lui réinjectant des fonds.

Les années 70 furent les dernières années vraiment glamour du voyage aérien. En 1978, le Congrès américain vota l'Airline Deregulation Act, une déréglementation des transports aériens mettant un terme à toutes restrictions en matière d'itinéraires et de nouveaux services. Quand la loi entra en vigueur en 1982, elle changea pour toujours le visage du voyage aérien.

1976

1976 Reforms in U.S. Congress pave way for Boston-to-Washington, D.C., route to become Amtrak's most profitable

Reformen des U.S. Congress machen Boston–Washington, D.C., zur profitabelsten Strecke von Amtrak

Des réformes du Congrès américain font de la ligne Boston-Washington, D.C. la plus rentable d'Amtrak

1977 Braniff hires Halston to design crew uniforms, replacing Pucci

Braniff Airlines beauftragen Halston (als Nachfolger von Pucci) mit der Kreation neuer Uniformen für das Personal

Après Pucci, Braniff Airlines recrute Halston pour créer les uniformes de ses membres d'équipage

1977 Detroit Marriott, designed by John Portman, is tallest all-hotel skyscraper in Western Hemisphere

Das von John Portman entworfene Detroit Mariott ist der höchste ausschließlich als Hotel genutzte Wolkenkratzer der westlichen Hemisphäre

L'hôtel Mariott de Detroit, conçu par John Portman, est le plus haut gratte-ciel/hôtel du hémisphère occidentale

1979 Texas-based Southwest Airlines begins interstate service

Texanische Southwest Airlines expandiert mit Flugverbindungen in andere Bundesstaaten

La compagnie texane Southwest Airlines commence à proposer des vols inter-Etats

Now shining in the Las Vegas sky, the newest, most brilliant star—a unique, self-contained resort in the middle of the glitter and glamor of the Strip. So fantastic that it out-dazzles Las Vegas itself.

This star they call
THE DESERT INN.
For reservations, call your travel agent or toll-free 800-634-6906

318

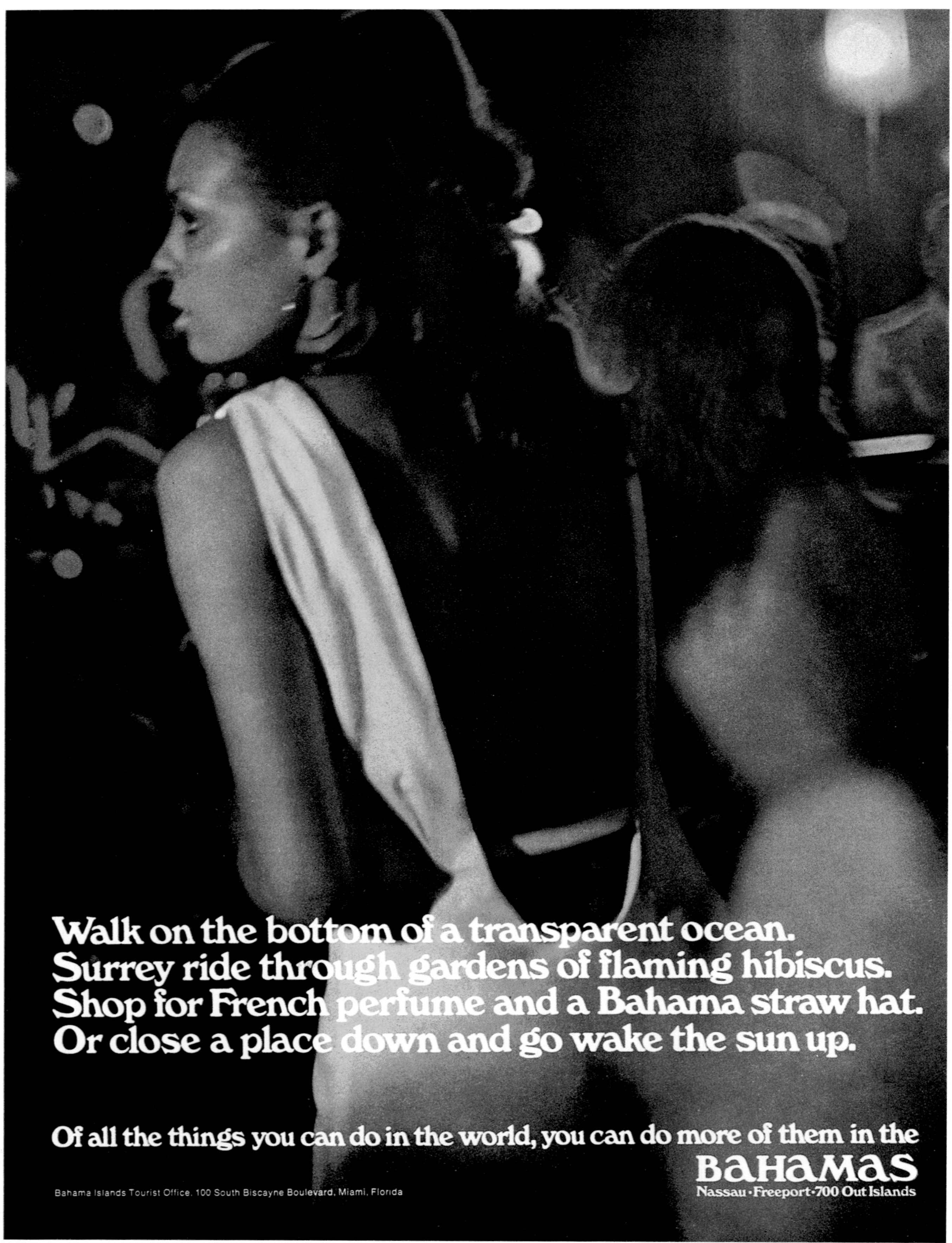

Walk on the bottom of a transparent ocean.
Surrey ride through gardens of flaming hibiscus.
Shop for French perfume and a Bahama straw hat.
Or close a place down and go wake the sun up.
Of all the things you can do in the world, you can do more of them in the
BAHAMAS
Nassau · Freeport · 700 Out Islands
Bahama Islands Tourist Office, 100 South Biscayne Boulevard, Miami, Florida

Bahamas Islands Tourist Office, 1970

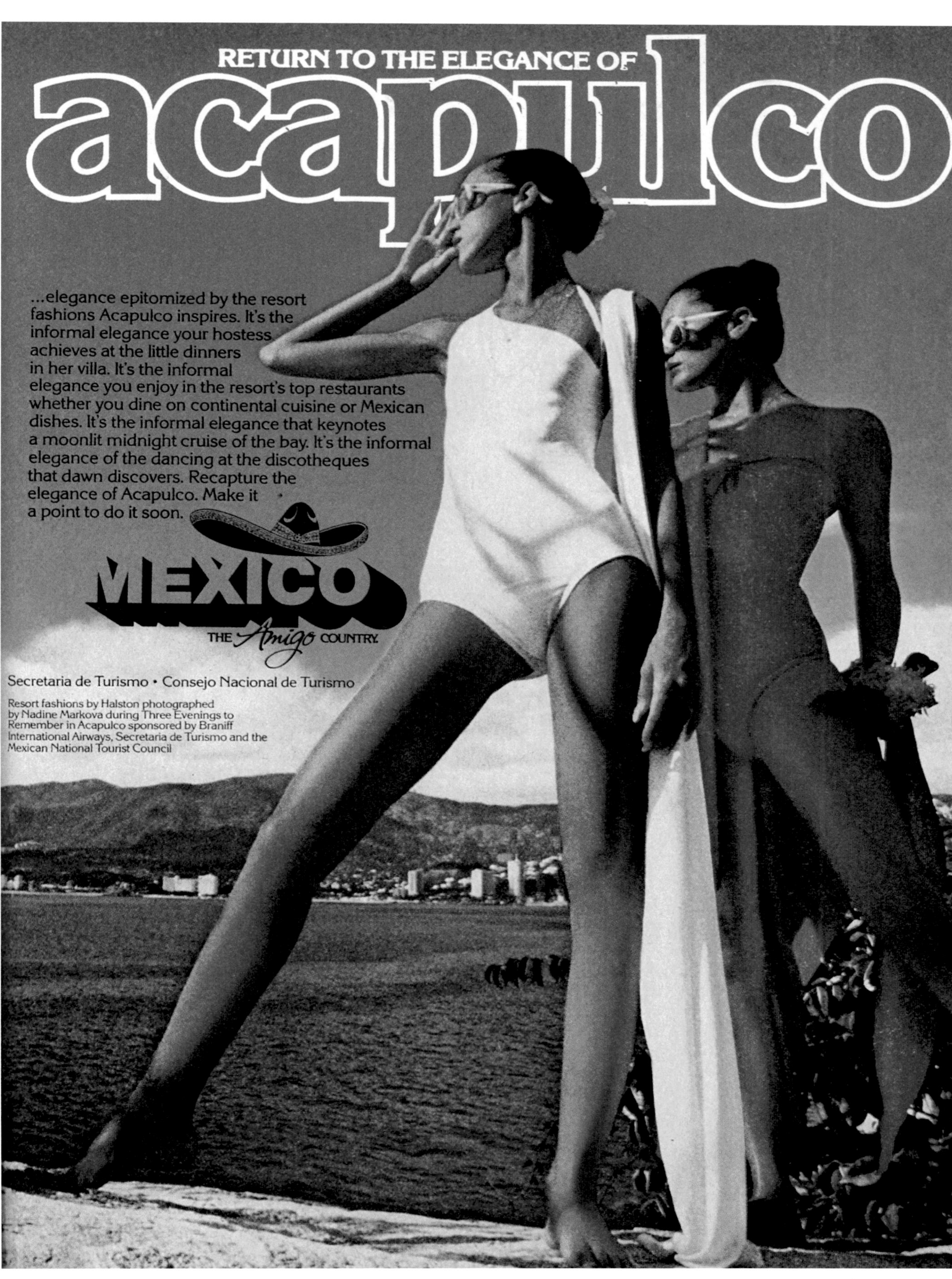

RETURN TO THE ELEGANCE OF
acapulco
...elegance epitomized by the resort fashions Acapulco inspires. It's the informal elegance your hostess achieves at the little dinners in her villa. It's the informal elegance you enjoy in the resort's top restaurants whether you dine on continental cuisine or Mexican dishes. It's the informal elegance that keynotes a moonlit midnight cruise of the bay. It's the informal elegance of the dancing at the discotheques that dawn discovers. Recapture the elegance of Acapulco. Make it a point to do it soon.
MEXICO
THE Amigo COUNTRY.
Secretaria de Turismo • Consejo Nacional de Turismo
Resort fashions by Halston photographed by Nadine Markova during Three Evenings to Remember in Acapulco sponsored by Braniff International Airways, Secretaria de Turismo and the Mexican National Tourist Council

Mexico Secretary of Tourism, 1977

No one else on Waikiki can rent you this kind of room.
With twenty tropical acres to play in, you could have t
vacation of your life and never leave our Village. You can samp
the fare of eight outstanding restaurants. Unwind in nine live
bars. Take in native shows and luau feasts. All on our grounds
Or take a sunset cruise and dine offshore on our Rainbow Catamarans.
Explore our fabulous Rainbow Bazaar. Shop in the tranquility of Imperial Japan, the bustle of Hong Kong, the history of Missionary Hawaii. And take some home with you.
Or get away from it all and try your hand at marlin fishing at the magnificent Kona Hilton on the Big Island of Hawaii.
Call the Hilton Reservation Service in your city or your travel agent for the details. Then come visit the Hiltons in Hawaii.
Hilton Hawaiian Village

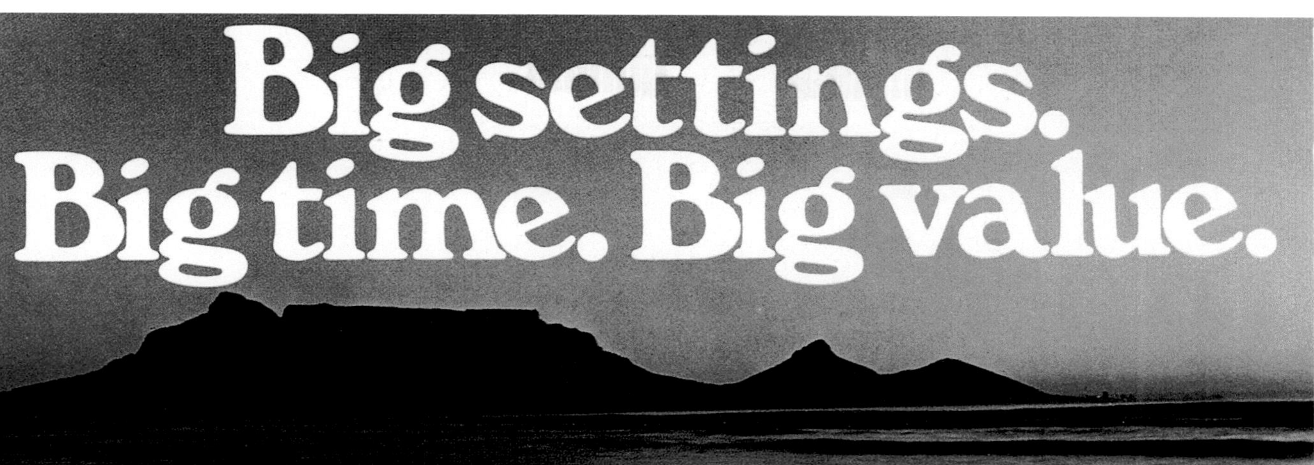
Big settings.
Big time. Big value.

Big Sunsets. Those typical glowing sunsets south of the equator are as big as the scenes they colour. For anyone who has visited South Africa there is the memory of evening after evening of glorious sunsets.
Big Variety. For every evening, great reddened settings of mountains, river valleys, umbrella-treed game reserves and surf-washed coastlines in contrast with modern city skylines. Every day brings its new, exciting attractions.
Big Value. With such an incredible variety of things to see and do, there is one other great attraction – the low cost. Exciting game touring from as little as $9,46 per night.
Hotels with all the comforts from $8,60 per night to $20,64 and upwards for 5-star status.
Discover that there is still a place on earth where a plate-sized grilling steak costs under $3,44, in fact, where even the cost of travel, entertainment or almost anything one can buy in a shop just hasn't caught up with the rest of the world.
Big Welcome. Yet one of the best things in South Africa is free – the traditional warm hospitality.
Ask the many who come.

satour

South African Tourist Corporation
New York: Rockefeller Center, 610 Fifth Avenue, New York 10020.
Los Angeles: Suite 721, 9465 Wilshire Boulevard, Beverly Hills, California 90212. **Toronto:** Suite 1001, 20 Eglinton Avenue West, Toronto M4R 1K8.
Also at: **Chicago, London, Frankfurt, Amsterdam, Paris, Milan, Zürich, Sydney, Salisbury, Tokyo, Buenos Aires and Pretoria.**
S/1

Please send me full colour literature to plan my South African tour.
Name________________
Address________________

South Africa.
A world tour in one country.

KMP 4132/e

321

◂ Hilton Hotels, 1978

South African Tourist Corporation, 1978

Million-miler Capt. Shin (2nd from the left) and airline personnel offer you a unique blend of American efficiency and Korean hospitality.

We fly with an American accent.

Sure, the crew looks Korean. But step aboard and the feeling is wonderfully American.

Because flying Korean Air Lines is a lot like flying an American airline. That's a Korean custom you'll truly appreciate.

It means that our planes are built in America. A luxurious fleet of wide-bodied 747's and DC-10's.

It means that Korean crews that fly them, fly them American. With a majority of the pilots and navigators licensed by the Federal Aviation Authority. And every wide-bodied jet captain a 15 year veteran. A skilled million-miler.

It means that our lovely stewardesses speak American. Pampering you in the style to which you'd love to be accustomed.

And it means no surprises. We want your flight with us to be as comfortable, secure and pleasant as we can make it.

So we give you superb American efficiency, combined with superb Korean service. A custom we take wherever we go, and wherever you go with us.

At Korean Air Lines, we do cherish the unique, the exciting, the exotic.

But only on the ground. Not in the air.

And that's an accent we know you'll understand.

FLY KAL KOREAN

Korean Air Lines, 1977

► Host International Restaurant, 1976

The only international restaurant in Los Angeles with its own airport.

You've seen it a hundred times.
The Theme Building at Los Angeles International Airport. You might know there's a restaurant inside. You might not know there's a superb restaurant inside. With convenient, complimentary valet parking outside.

Let us tempt you to try it:

Our dinner menu contains sumptuous appetizers, soups, salads, entrees and beverages from twenty-two countries. Prepared by continental chefs from carefully collected and tested international recipes. All served in the classic French manner by a captain and internationally-costumed waitresses.

To complement your meal, you will find a bountiful selection of fine imported and domestic wines.

Our rich Columbian coffee brews slowly at your table while you dine.

For an encore, our dessert menu offers a tempting array of world-renowned pastries, ice cream and flaming crepes.

The beautiful harp, piano and violin music you hear throughout the restaurant is live. And the unique view from your table is a continuous airshow provided by 36 airlines.

Next time you're looking for an unusually elegant dining experience at moderate prices, don't look in the usual places.

Look for our place right in the center of Los Angeles International Airport.

Open daily 10 am to 12 midnight. Lunch, Afternoon Sandwiches, Cocktails, Dinner and Weekend Brunch. Entertainment in the lounge from 4 pm. Reservations: (213) 646-5471.

Host International Restaurant

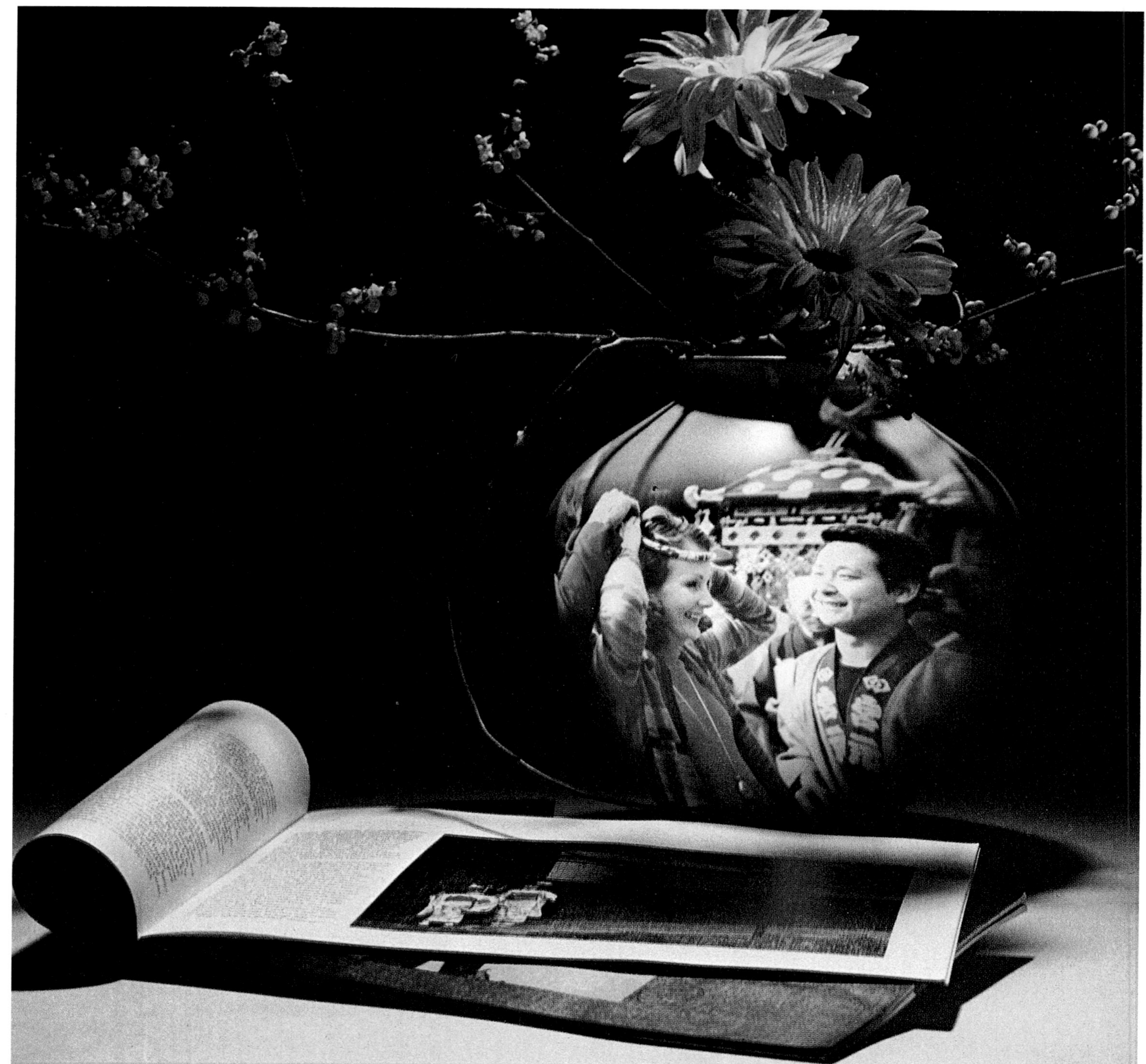

JAL made it to the top by helping tourists know the Orient instead of merely looking at it.

On JAL's Happi Holidays tours of the Orient, you see a world where the sights aren't merely variations of the sights back home. Where wonders are commonplace. Where splendor is taken for granted.

Even more important, JAL's Orient is a place where you gather memories of the people you've met as well as the sights you've seen.

These are the reasons why more people tour the Orient with JAL than with any other airline.

Come to JAL's Orient. See your travel agent or send us the coupon today. And come this year, not next year or the year after. As an old Japanese proverb says, "Time flies like an arrow." Another suggests, "The day you decide to do a thing is the best day to do it."

HAPPI JAL HOLIDAYS

We never forget how important you are.

JAPAN AIR LINES

Box 618, N.Y., N.Y. 10011

☐ Please send JAL's ORIENT booklet with complete tour listings and ORIENT TOUR BUYING GUIDE.

Name__________

Address__________ City__________

State_____ Zip_____ Tel._____

My Travel Agent__________ Key #

NS 052278

Now.
Japan's most beautiful gardens blossom aboard the world's most spacious jet.

Starting this summer, during EXPO '70, the first of eight JAL 747 jets will cross the Pacific. Outside it will be the biggest commercial airliner ever developed. Inside it will feature the most extraordinary decor ever created.

For each section of this spacious jet will have one of our country's most beautiful features: the Japanese Garden.

First Class will have the elegant Garden of Wisteria with an upstairs lounge called Teahouse of the Sky.

In Economy, you can choose from one of three unique sections: the Gardens of Wild Orange, Pine or Maple. Each has decor all its own and individualized service. More comfort, too. Thanks to wider seats and stand-up headroom everywhere.

There will be wide screen movies, stereo entertainment and the finest of international beverages and cuisine.

Best of all, there will be more of what legends are made of – our lovely hostesses in kimono who will pamper you throughout your flight. And introduce you to the subtle delights of Japanese comfort and hospitality.

Your travel agent is now accepting reservations for our maiden flight. Be one of the first to reserve a seat in the garden of your choice on our new 747 Garden Jet.

JAPAN AIR LINES 747 Garden Jet

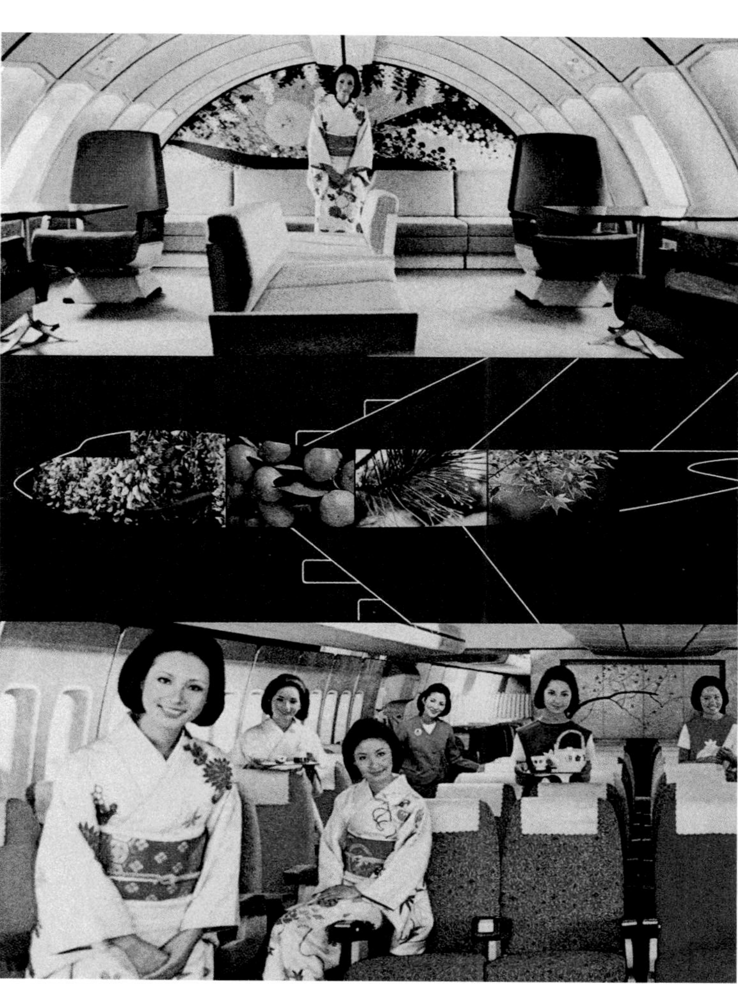

◂ Japan Air Lines, 1978

Japan Air Lines, 1970

In the 1970s, *mass* began to overwhelm class in air travel. Bigger planes, packed with more people, filled the skies. The exclusivity and glamour of flying was becoming a thing of the past. This ad focuses on Japan Air Lines' serene and courteous service, but that was growing harder to deliver.

In den 1970er-Jahren siegte bei den Flugreisen allmählich *Masse* über *Klasse*. Immer größere, mit immer mehr Menschen vollgestopfte Flugzeuge bevölkerten den Himmel. Exklusivität und Glamour des Fliegens waren bald dahin. Die Anzeige betont den entspannt heiteren Service von Japan Air Lines, doch der ließ sich zunehmend schwerer erbringen.

Dans les années 1970, la *masse* commença à surpasser la *classe* en matière de voyage aérien. De plus gros avions encore plus bondés emplissaient le ciel. Le luxe et le glamour du voyage en avion appartenaient désormais au passé. Cette publicité se concentre sur le service discret et courtois de Japan Air Lines, mais il était de plus en plus difficile d'assurer de telles prestations.

We enjoy flying from Los Angeles to visit our kissing cousins down under. So will you.

Every time one of our BOAC VC10s takes off from Los Angeles on its direct flight to Sydney or Melbourne, Australia, it's like visiting family.

Perhaps that's why so many passengers tell us they enjoy our service across the South Pacific so much. Enjoy the comfort of really being looked after. The courtesy of being waited on. Even the old-fashioned delight of having someone say please and thank you.

But we mustn't take all the credit for making a lengthy trip pass so pleasantly. Our VC10 jets are a joy to fly. With a roomier economy seat than any comparable jet. Overhead lockers to keep your hand luggage out of your lap. And a blissfully peaceful cabin, thanks to four powerful rear-mounted engines that leave all the noise behind.

So be our guest next time you visit our Australian family "out west." For reservations and details of our many and varied tours of the Pacific see our Travel Agents in and around Los Angeles. Or call us. British Overseas Airways Corporation, 1901 Ave. of the Stars, Los Angeles, California 90067. Tel: 272-8866.

BOAC takes good care of you.

British Overseas Airways Corporation

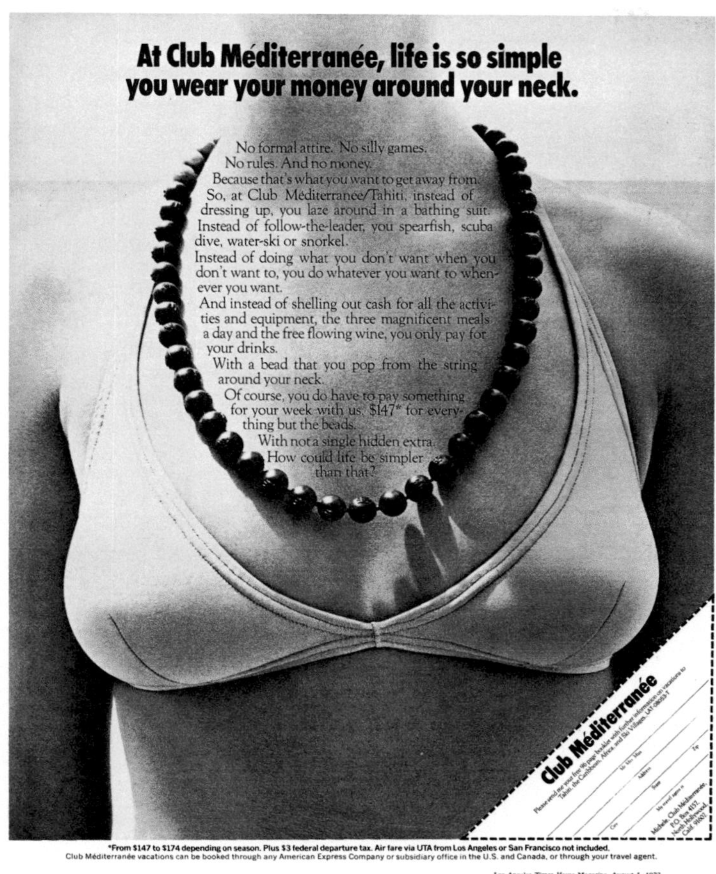

At Club Méditerranée, life is so simple
you wear your money around your neck.
No formal attire. No silly games.
No rules. And no money.
Because that's what you want to get away from.
So, at Club Méditerranée/Tahiti, instead of dressing up, you laze around in a bathing suit.
Instead of follow-the-leader, you spearfish, scuba dive, water-ski or snorkel.
Instead of doing what you don't want when you don't want to, you do whatever you want to whenever you want.
And instead of shelling out cash for all the activities and equipment, the three magnificent meals a day and the free flowing wine, you only pay for your drinks.
With a bead that you pop from the string around your neck.
Of course, you do have to pay something for your week with us. $147* for everything but the beads.
With not a single hidden extra.
How could life be simpler than that?
Club Méditerranée
*From $147 to $174 depending on season. Plus $3 federal departure tax. Air fare via UTA from Los Angeles or San Francisco not included.
Club Méditerranée vacations can be booked through any American Express Company or subsidiary office in the U.S. and Canada, or through your travel agent.
Los Angeles Times Home Magazine, August 5, 1973

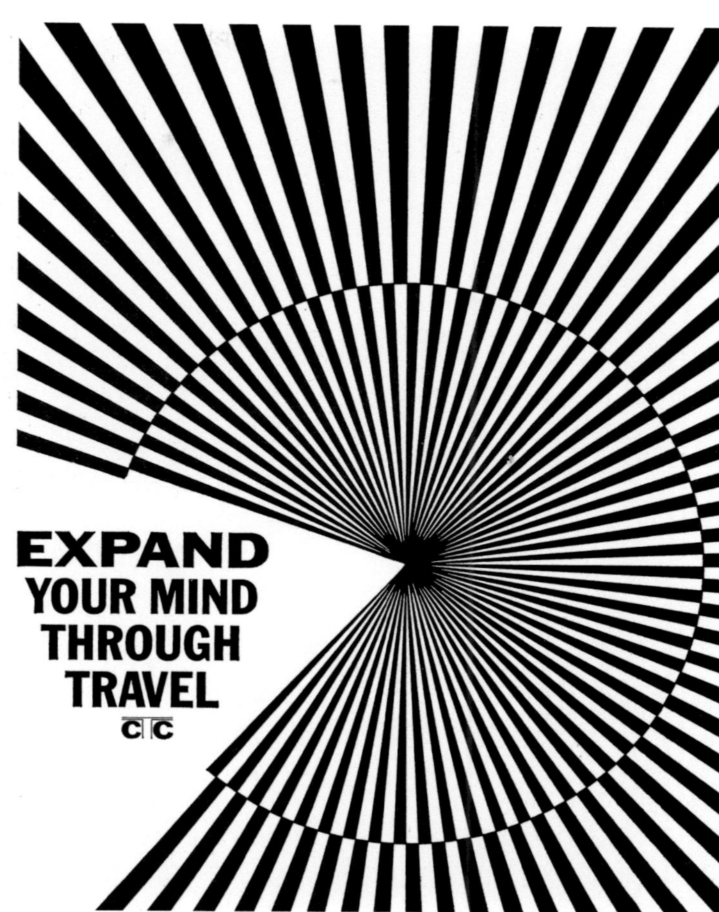

◄ British Overseas Airways Corporation, 1971

Club Méditerranée, 1973

The sybaritic enticements of a Club Med are clear. These resorts offered an all-inclusive stay, where everything was part of the package—a sort of stationary cruise. The clubs had been developed for a singles scene, but family-oriented resorts also flourished in the '70s. Parents could have a vacation while their children were occupied elsewhere.

Ein Club Med geizt nicht mit seinen Reizen. Sein All-inclusive-Angebot enthält praktisch alles und bietet so etwas wie eine ortsfeste Kreuzfahrt. Die Clubs waren eigentlich für Singles geschaffen worden, doch in den 1970er-Jahren florierten auch die familienorientierten Resorts. Hier konnten die Eltern Urlaub machen, während man sich anderswo um ihre Kinder kümmerte.

Les charmes sybaritiques du Club Med sont clairs. Ses clubs proposaient des séjours où tout était inclus dans le forfait, comme dans une sorte de croisière stationnaire. Les clubs avaient été conçus pour une clientèle de célibataires, mais les complexes destinés aux familles explosèrent aussi dans les années 1970. Les parents pouvaient profiter de leurs vacances sans avoir leurs enfants dans les pattes.

Cooks Travel Cheques, 1970

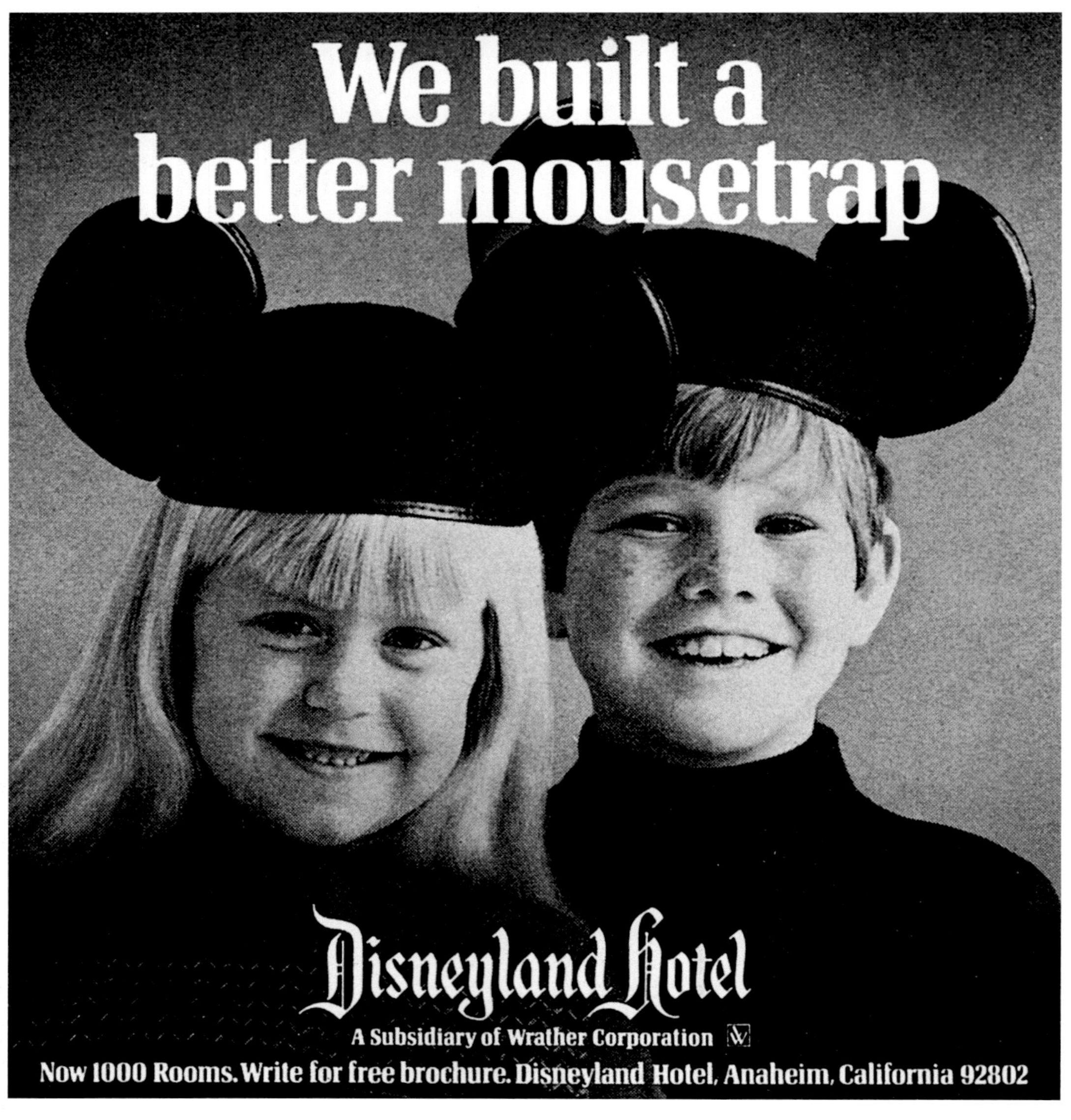

We built a
better mousetrap
Disneyland Hotel
A Subsidiary of Wrather Corporation
Now 1000 Rooms. Write for free brochure. Disneyland Hotel, Anaheim, California 92802

Disneyland Hotel, 1970

When Disneyland opened in 1955, construction had proven so costly that Walt Disney arranged for a developer to build the Disneyland Hotel. To finally gain control, the Walt Disney Company bought the developer's entire company in 1989. When Disney World opened, Disney owned and operated 23 of the 35 resorts and hotels there.

Als Disneyland 1955 eröffnet wurde, hatte man bereits so viel Geld ausgegeben, dass Walt Disney den Bau des Disneyland Hotel aus der Hand gab. Um die Kontrolle zu gewinnen, erwarb die Walt Disney Company 1989 gleich die gesamte Firma des Bauunternehmers. Als Disney World seine Pforten öffnete, besaß und betrieb Disney 23 der 35 dortigen Resorts und Hotels.

Quand Disneyland ouvrit en 1955, les travaux s'avérèrent si onéreux que Walt Disney demanda à un promoteur immobilier de construire le Disneyland Hotel. Pour en reprendre le contrôle, Walt Disney Company racheta l'entreprise du promoteur en 1989. A l'ouverture de Disney World, Disney possédait et gérait 23 de ses 35 hôtels et clubs de vacances.

▸ Brazilian Tourism Authority, 1979

"I'm a Brazil nut."
—Marlene Dietrich
Says Miss Dietrich: "Brazil isn't a country. It's a poem." In Brazil, you find the most beautiful baroque churches in the Western Hemisphere and the world's most startling modern architecture. You experience the pandemonium of a Rio soccer game and the perfect peace of jungle rivers where the only sounds are birds. Brazil is yesterday—colonial towns that have remained in the 17th century. And it's Brasilia, a surrealist's dream. But mostly it's people who move like dancers, talk like songs, and smile like friends. Travelers don't simply like Brazil, they go mad for the place.
You can spend seven nights in Rio for as little as $630,* including roundtrip airfare, first class hotel, full Brazilian breakfasts, transfer services and sightseeing tours. See your travel agent.
For this beautiful 112 page booklet on Brazil call 800-447-4700 (toll free).
In Illinois call 800-322-4400.
In Canada write: Brazilian Travel Offer, Box 3900, Peoria, Ill. 61614.
EMBRATUR/BRAZILIAN TOURISM AUTHORITY
BRAZIL
1976
TRAVEL DIGEST
*Based on Miami departure. Similar tours available for departure from New York ($674) and Los Angeles ($804). Rates are per person, double occupancy.

330

See your ASTA Travel Agent
ASTA
MEXICO
The Amigo Country
MEXICAN GOVERNMENT
TOURIST OFFICE
9701 Wilshire Boulevard — Suite 1201
Beverly Hills, CA. 90212
Tell me more. Please send your "Wonderful Mexico" brochure.
Name
Address
City
State
Zip
(Please print)
E-12/79
MEXICO
THE Amigo COUNTRY
Secretaria de Turismo · Consejo Nacional de Turismo

HIGHWAY TRAVEL

$ 0 0 0 VENTA TOTAL

$ 0 0 0 VENTA TOTAL

More Mileage for your dollar in MEXICO

MEXICAN GOVERNMENT DEPARTMENT OF TOURISM
National Tourism Council
625 North Michigan Ave. Chicago Ill., 60611
3106 Wilshire Blvd. Los Angeles, Cal.
630 Fifth Ave. New York, N. Y. 10020
Av. Juárez No. 92. México 1, D. F.

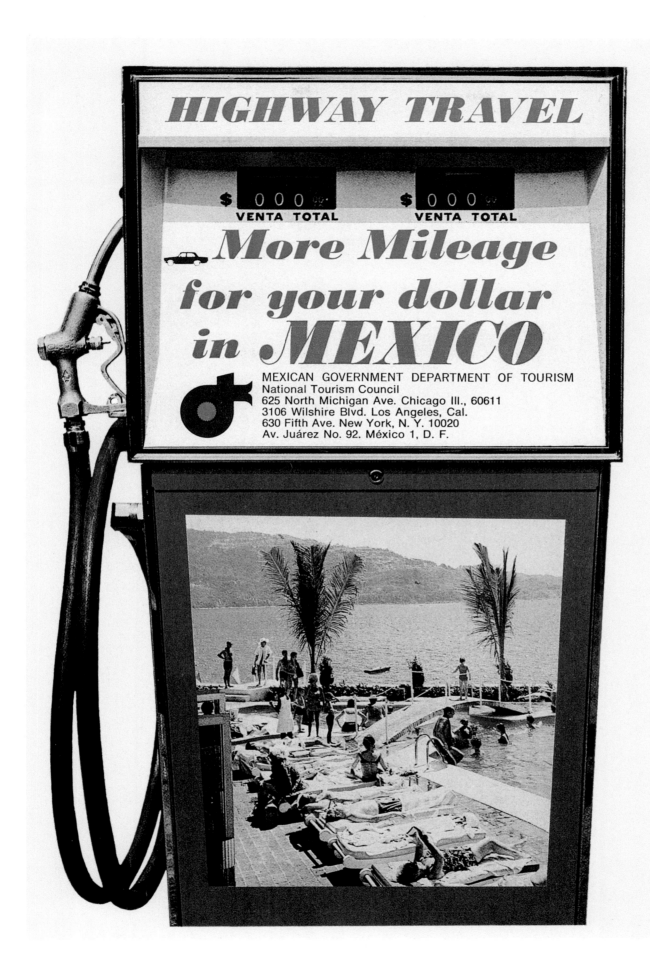

◂ Mexican Government Tourist Office, 1979

Mexican Government Department of Tourism, 1972

South America. Braniff gets you there with Flying Colors.

At reasonable prices – This spring and summer.

Braniff commissioned Alexander Calder to paint Flying Colors as the introduction to the color and excitement of a vacation in South America. It now leads Braniff's jet fleet that flies daily to South America. This was the start of a whole new idea in foreign travel – Flying Colors vacations – reasonable air fares and more for your dollar after you get to South America. Your travel agent has Flying Colors tour folders.

Chile $754 round trip air fare.

It's summer in December and January, winter in July and August. Start out in Santiago, see the port of Valparaiso and the beach resort of Vina del Mar. And try the different Chilean white wines wherever you are.

Paraguay $797 round trip air fare.

The old Spanish charm of Asuncion, the capital, Ride a ring-a-ding, 19th century trolley. Buy yourself hand-made Nanduti lace. Listen to an old Indian harp play a sweet ancient strain. Venture forth into the Chaco jungle. Or pick an orchid while you look down the Devil's Throat, the colossus of waterfalls called Iguassu.

Bolivia $754 round trip air fare.

Come down to earth in La Paz. Scoop up alpaca sweaters and llama rugs at some of the world's lowest prices. Tour the Colonial Museum and picturesque Indian market. Take the hydrofoil trip on Lake Titicaca where the famous reed boats are strangely like those in ancient Egypt.

Peru $538 round trip air fare.

See Peru, cradle of the Incas, and Lima, jewel of Pizarro, the great cathedral, the Mujica Gold Museum and the Torre Tagle Palace. See the changing of the guard at the Presidential Palace. Sip a Pisco Sour. Dine on Langosta, the big South American lobster. And, dance till dawn at the Unicorn discotheque.

Argentina $681 round trip air fare.

Includes Argentina, Brazil and Peru.

Argentina is Buenos Aires, the land of the gauchos, barbecued beef, red wine, cruises on El Tigre River – and a lot more. There's the 9 de Julio (widest avenue in the world), opera house, the pink Presidential Palace – and dinner in La Boca where some say it's New Year's Eve every night.

Brazil $681 round trip air fare.

Includes Brazil, Argentina and Peru.

Rio is the beat of the bossa nova, the beach of Copacabana, the 11-story statue of Christ the Redeemer, a cable car to Sugar Loaf, shopping for semi-precious stones. This is where your Brazil begins.

"How to Travel South America with Flying Colors." by Jim Woodman

Braniff sent veteran travel writer, Jim Woodman, on a tour of these nations and Colombia, Ecuador and Panama. The result is a vivid, personal guidebook about hotels, prices, shopping bargains, food and drink and points of interest – what you'll see and do on any of five Flying Colors vacations.

South America with Flying Colors

Braniff International
Flying Colors – Room 908
Exchange Park, P.O Box 35001
Dallas, Texas 75235

Name ______
Address ______
City ______ State ______ Zip ______
Phone ______ NLA617

☐ Please enclose $1 for this 62-page, colorfully illustrated booklet, to help you plan now for your trip to South America with Flying Colors.

I'd like to know more about Flying Colors tours to:

- ☐ Brazil – Peru – Argentina $322 for 16 days plus air fare
- ☐ Paraguay – 14 day to 28 day Excursion fare
- ☐ Bolivia – 10 day to 28 day Excursion fare
- ☐ Peru – $82 for 8 days plus air fare
- ☐ Chile – 14 to 28 day Excursion fare

Air fares listed are round trip economy class from Los Angeles for groups of at least 5 to 10 to Peru, Argentina and Brazil, staying a minimum of 7 nights and a maximum of 14 days depending on countries visited. To Paraguay, Bolivia and Chile fares are excursion rates for trips from 14 to 28 days. Tour prices shown meet the requirements for these fares and are based on double occupancy and include meals where indicated, baggage tips and airport transfers. Prices effective June 1 and subject to change.

Braniff, 1974

Advertising legend Mary Wells, as part of her continuing campaign to show Braniff International as unique, brought in the artist Alexander Calder. He used one of the company's jets as a canvas. "Flying Colors" became an international sensation. Calder's bright colors also connected strongly with Latin America, where Braniff flew regularly.

Für ihre Dauerkampagne, die Einzigartigkeit von Braniff International herauszustellen, konnte Mary Wells den Künstler Alexander Calder gewinnen. Er nutzte einen der Jets gleichsam als Leinwand, und seine „Flying Colors" wurden zur internationalen Sensation. Calders leuchtende Farben verweisen zudem deutlich auf Lateinamerika, das von Braniff regelmäßig angeflogen wurde.

Dans le cadre de sa campagne présentant Braniff International comme une compagnie unique en son genre, la légende de la publicité Mary Wells fit appel à l'artiste Alexander Calder. Il utilisa l'un des avions de la compagnie comme une toile. « Flying Colors » fit sensation dans le monde entier. Les couleurs vives de Calder créaient aussi un lien fort avec l'Amérique Latine, régulièrement desservie par Braniff.

► Mexicana, 1979

MEXICO& MEXICANA

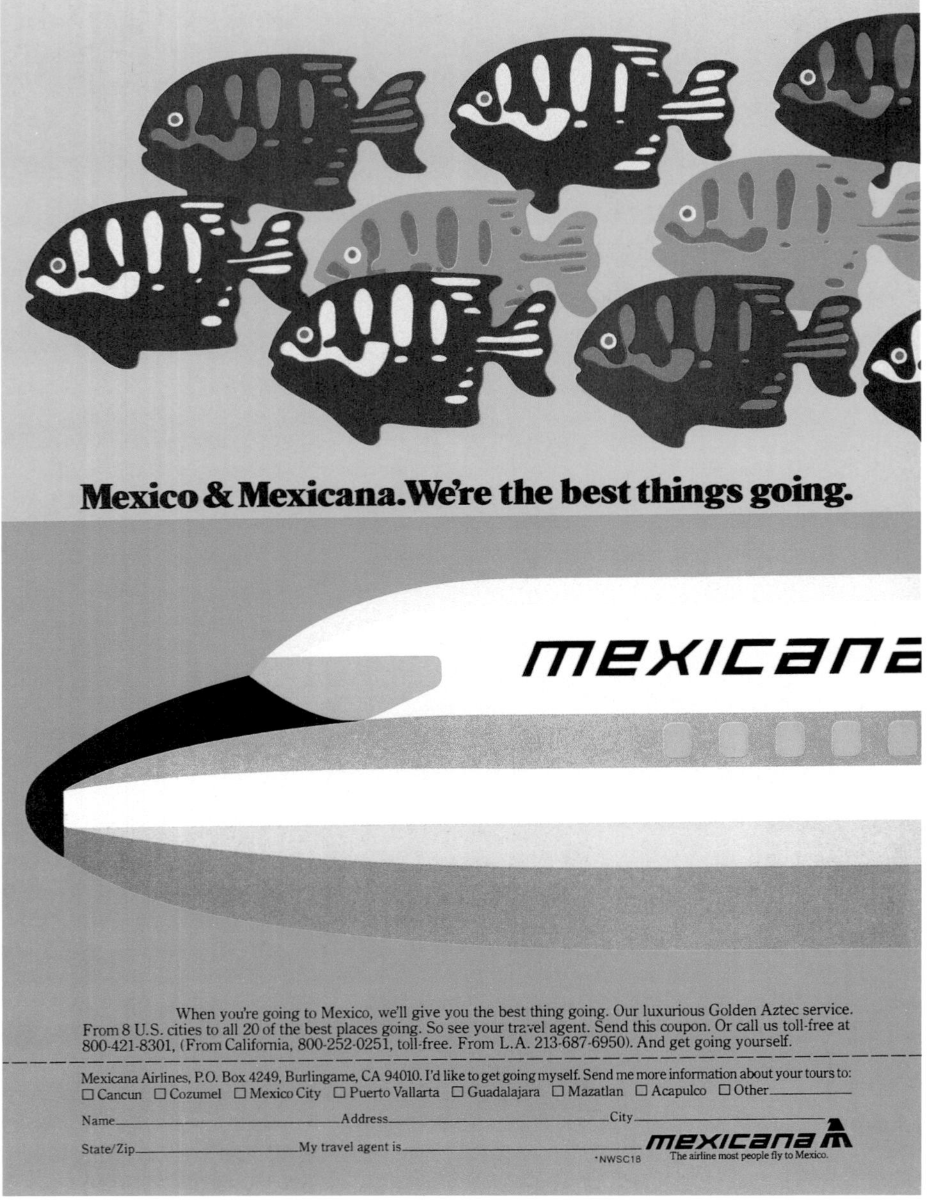

Mexico & Mexicana. We're the best things going.
mexicana
When you're going to Mexico, we'll give you the best thing going. Our luxurious Golden Aztec service. From 8 U.S. cities to all 20 of the best places going. So see your travel agent. Send this coupon. Or call us toll-free at 800-421-8301, (From California, 800-252-0251, toll-free. From L.A. 213-687-6950). And get going yourself.
Mexicana Airlines, P.O. Box 4249, Burlingame, CA 94010. I'd like to get going myself. Send me more information about your tours to:
☐ Cancun ☐ Cozumel ☐ Mexico City ☐ Puerto Vallarta ☐ Guadalajara ☐ Mazatlan ☐ Acapulco ☐ Other
Name Address City
State/Zip My travel agent is
*NWSC18
mexicana
The airline most people fly to Mexico.

Mexicana, 1972

This Mexicana Airline ad may talk of Aztec service, but the design is dramatically contemporary. The colors are acid-trippy, with the pop of Pop Art. This stylish design signals the sophistication of the multilayered Mexican culture that awaits travelers who go there.

Auch wenn in dieser Anzeige der Fluglinie Mexicana von aztekischem Service die Rede sein mag, ist sie doch überaus modern gestaltet. Ihre modernen Farben zeugen vom Schwung der Pop-Art. Das raffinierte Design gibt einen Vorgeschmack auf das Raffinement der vielschichtigen mexikanischen Kultur, die den Reisenden erwartet.

Cette publicité de Mexicana Airline évoque peut-être le passé aztèque du pays, mais son design est absolument contemporain. Les couleurs acidulées possèdent tout le pep du Pop Art. Ce design élégant annonce la complexité de la culture mexicaine attendant les voyageurs.

► Air New Zealand, 1970

Fly the Flight Fantastic to the South Pacific
Fancy food like New Zealand pheasant, Canterbury lamb or poh-loh-kai chicken; and fanciful drinks like frosted Mai Tais, Blue Hawaiis, and New Zealand wines; and pleasures from a fantastical crew, will make your DC-8 flight from Los Angeles to New Zealand, Australia and the South Pacific absolutely, fantastic. Stop over in Hawaii going and Tahiti returning—or vice versa. Either way—it's fantastic.
AIR NEW ZEALAND
510 West 6th Street
Los Angeles, California 90014
Dept. NG-5-69
Please send me your tour folder on:
☐ BEST OF THE SOUTH PACIFIC—New Zealand, French Polynesia, Samoa, Fiji, Australia.
☐ FRENCH POLYNESIA—Tahiti, Bora Bora, Moorea, Raiatea.
☐ CIRCLE PACIFIC—New Zealand, Australia, French Polynesia, Samoa, Fiji, Singapore, Bangkok, Hong Kong, Tokyo.
I prefer: ☐ escorted ☐ independent vacations.
Name
Address
City
State
Zip
AIR NEW ZEALAND
The Airline That Knows The South Pacific Best
With BOAC and Qantas, 17 flights weekly from The United States to the South Pacific.
Connecting Los Angeles with Tahiti, Honolulu, Auckland, Wellington, Christchurch, Sydney, Melbourne, Brisbane, New Caledonia, Norfolk Island, Fiji, Samoa, Singapore, Hong Kong, Rarotonga—Cook Islands.

Memphis is ready for take-off. Come soar with us. You'll like our style, because we're looking for the same thing you are: expansion. What's more, the very assets that make us look good are the ones that will mean profit and growth for your company in Memphis.
Memphis has big-city production capabilities: manpower, land, low utility rates, location, and fine transportation facilities. Big-city office space, too. And we offer all this without big-city problems. As Memphis grows bigger, it grows better —carefully maintaining a friendly, relaxed way of life.
If you'd like the best of two worlds for your people, write on your company letterhead to **Dan Dale,** Director of Industrial Development, Memphis Light, Gas and Water, Box 388C, or **Ralph U. Thomas,** Mgr., Economic Development Dept., Memphis Area Chamber of Commerce, Box 224R, Memphis, Tennessee 38101.
MEMPHIS
CITY OF MANAGEABLE SIZE

Memphis Chamber of Commerce, 1971

► Las Vegas Convention Authority (Bob Peack), 1973

LAS VEGAS

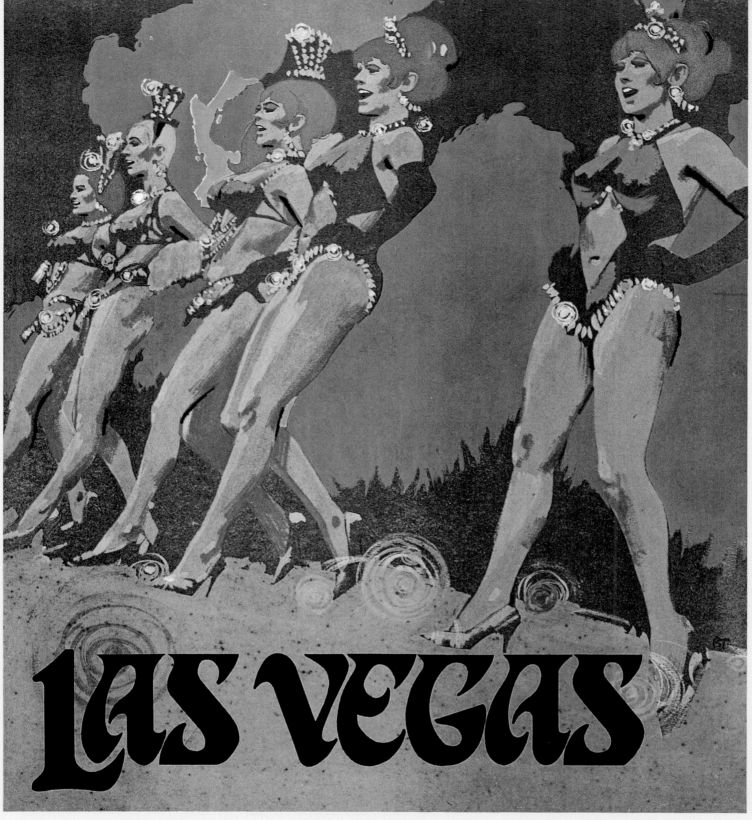

Waiting just over the horizon is a dream vacation of top entertainment, delicious dining, excellent hotel and motel accommodations, all at a moderate cost. Las Vegas is a 24 hour town of sophisticated indoor fun and offers 12 full months of outdoor recreation, ranging from frosty ski slopes at 12,000 foot Mt. Charleston to sunny shores on sparkling Lake Mead. Tennis, golf, fishing, water skiing, horseback riding and swimming complete the Las Vegas sports picture. Downtown Las Vegas, the most photographed street in the world, is a million volt valley of light, brightening the midnight sky, and the famous "Strip" sparkles like a silver ribbon through the moonlit Nevada desert. See Las Vegas, the entertainment capitol of the world... your travel agent can get you in the act. Call him today!

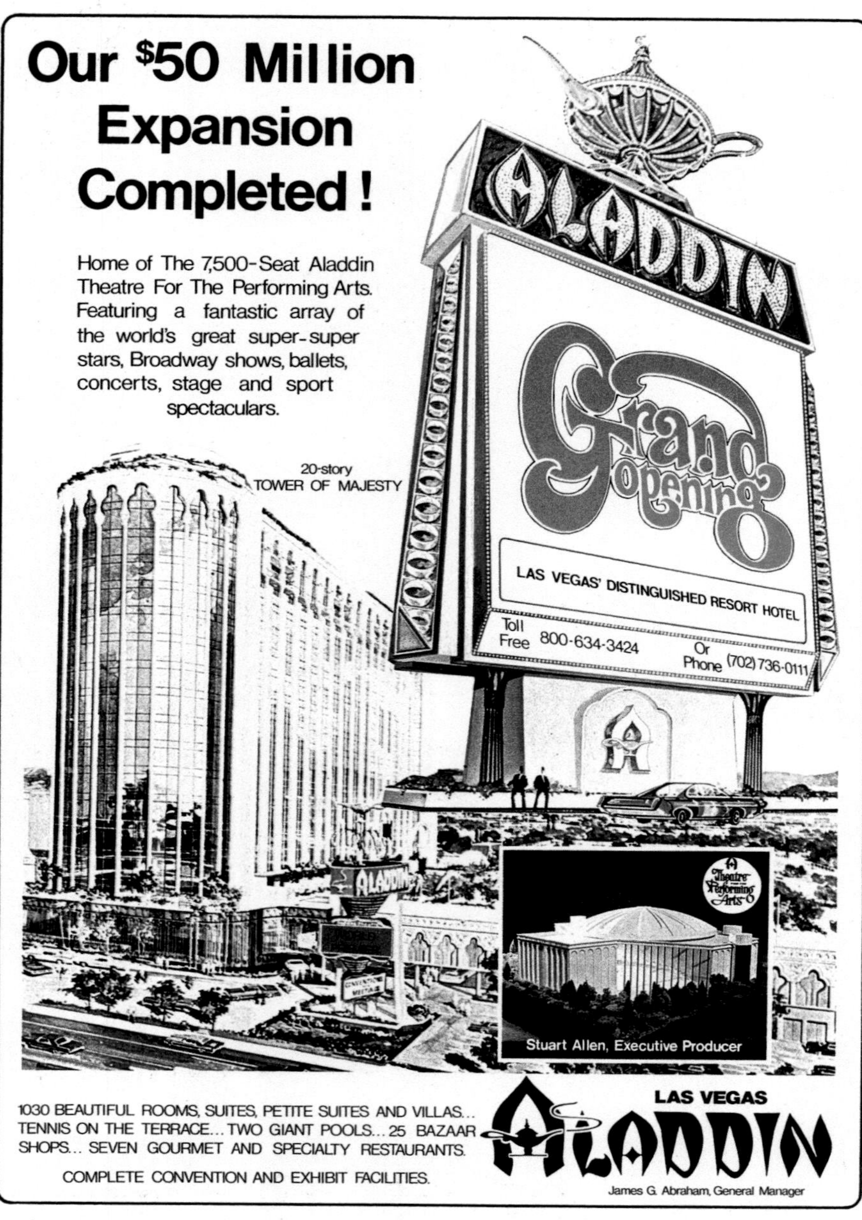

Aladdin Hotel, 1976

The Aladdin Hotel, one of the first big casinos on the Strip, had a string of owners, often later revealed as mob-related. The re-opening party this time featured Neil Diamond, reportedly paid $750,000 for two shows. By 1979, one of these new owners was indicted in a million-dollar kickback scam. The hotel was again up for sale.

Das Aladdin Hotel, eines der ersten großen Kasinos auf dem Strip, hatte mehrere, oft nicht ganz lupenreine Eigentümer. Star dieser Wiedereröffnungsparty war Neil Diamond, der für zwei Auftritte angeblich 750 000 $ kassierte. Einer der neuen Eigentümer wurde 1979 im Rahmen eines millionenschweren Provisionsbetrugs angeklagt. Und das Hotel stand erneut zum Verkauf.

L'hôtel Aladdin, l'un des premiers grands casinos du Strip, avait de nombreux propriétaires qui s'avéraient souvent liés à la Mafia. Cette fois, sa soirée de réouverture accueillit Neil Diamond : on dit qu'il aurait touché 750 000 dollars pour deux représentations. En 1979, l'un des nouveaux propriétaires fut inculpé dans une affaire de pots de vin de plusieurs millions de dollars. L'hôtel fut mis en vente une fois de plus.

► Hilton Hotels, 1979

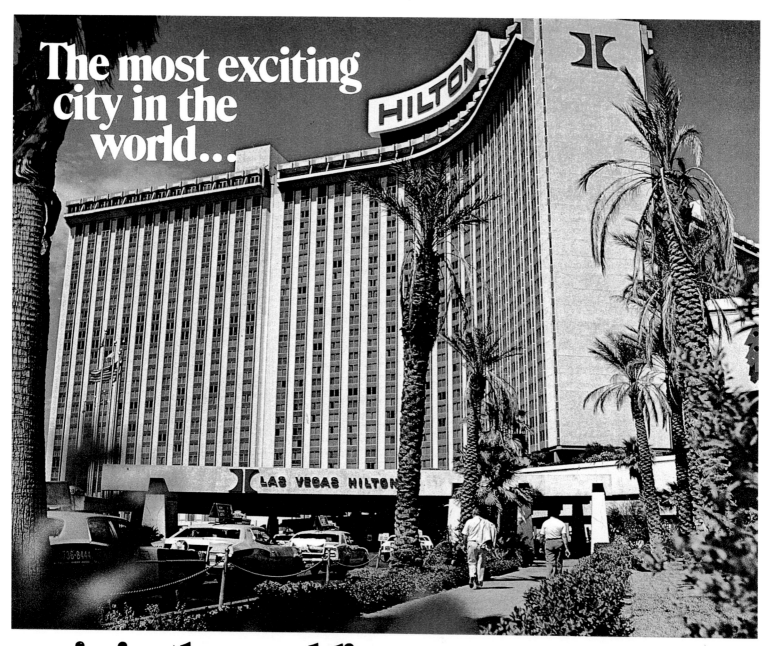

The most exciting city in the world...

...is in the world's most exciting city!!

Las Vegas! The name pulsates with excitement. And the magnificent Las Vegas Hilton has taken it one step beyond. With 2,783 exquisitely furnished rooms and suites, we make sure that you sleep and rest in splendor. Add that to the brightest stars in show business, 11 international restaurants including spectacular Benihana Village, 8 intimate cocktail lounges, our unique youth hotel just for the youngsters, a 10 acre rooftop recreation deck and our world-famous Hilton hospitality and you'll agree — the Las Vegas Hilton truly is the world's most exciting city!

Liberace, and a cast of 60, July 3 thru July 23 / Bill Cosby, Doug Henning, July 24 thru August 6 / Lou Rawls, Milton Berle, August 7 thru August 20 / Paul Anka, August 21 thru September 3 / John Davidson, September 4 thru September 24 / Osmonds, September 25 thru October 15

Las Vegas HILTON

The end of the rainbow.

For information and reservations (702) 732-5111 or call your nearest Hilton Reservations Service

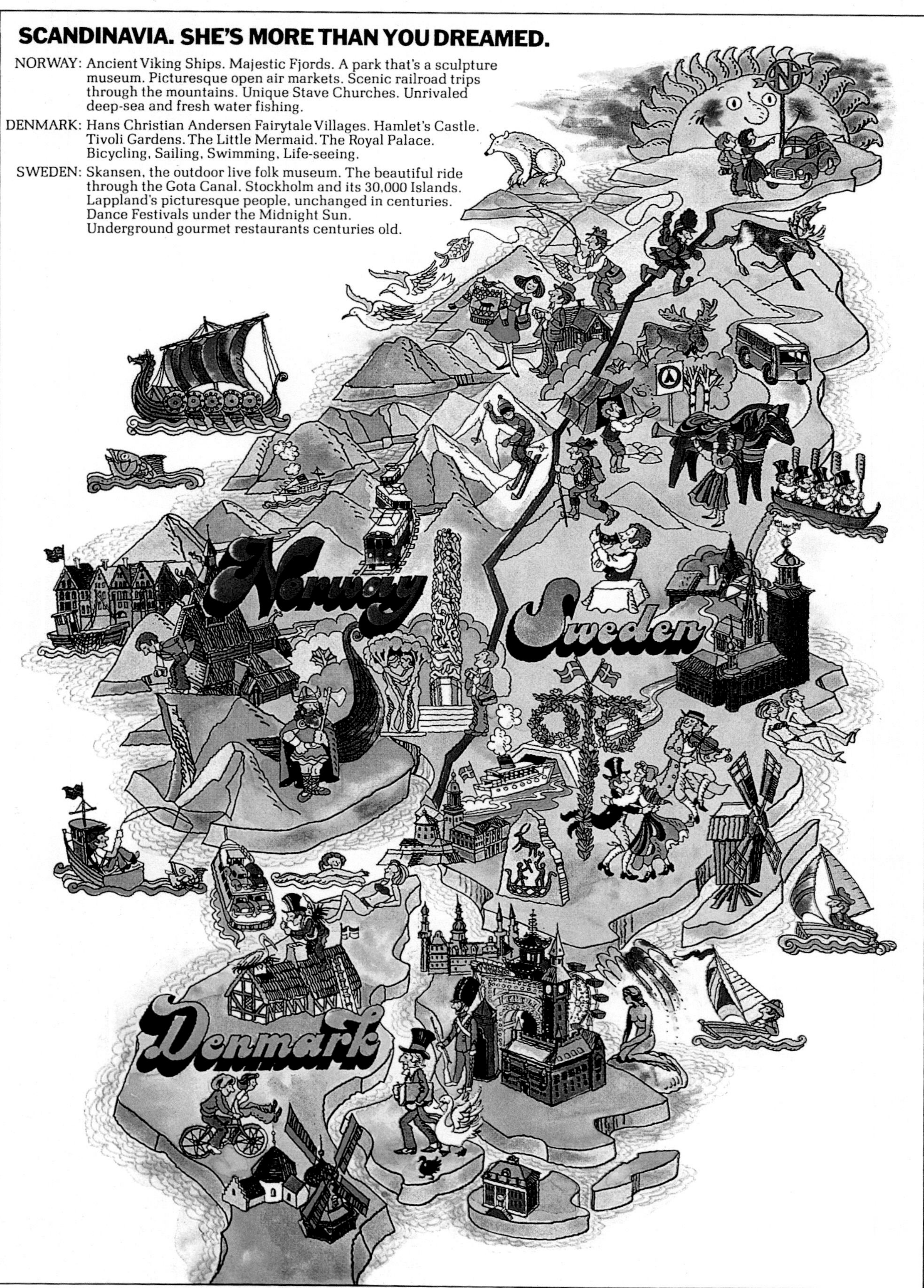

SCANDINAVIA. SHE'S MORE THAN YOU DREAMED.
NORWAY: Ancient Viking Ships. Majestic Fjords. A park that's a sculpture museum. Picturesque open air markets. Scenic railroad trips through the mountains. Unique Stave Churches. Unrivaled deep-sea and fresh water fishing.
DENMARK: Hans Christian Andersen Fairytale Villages. Hamlet's Castle. Tivoli Gardens. The Little Mermaid. The Royal Palace. Bicycling, Sailing, Swimming, Life-seeing.
SWEDEN: Skansen, the outdoor live folk museum. The beautiful ride through the Gota Canal. Stockholm and its 30,000 Islands. Lappland's picturesque people, unchanged in centuries. Dance Festivals under the Midnight Sun. Underground gourmet restaurants centuries old.
Norway
Sweden
Denmark

Scandinavian Tourist Board, 1974

▸ Las Vegas Convention Authority, 1973

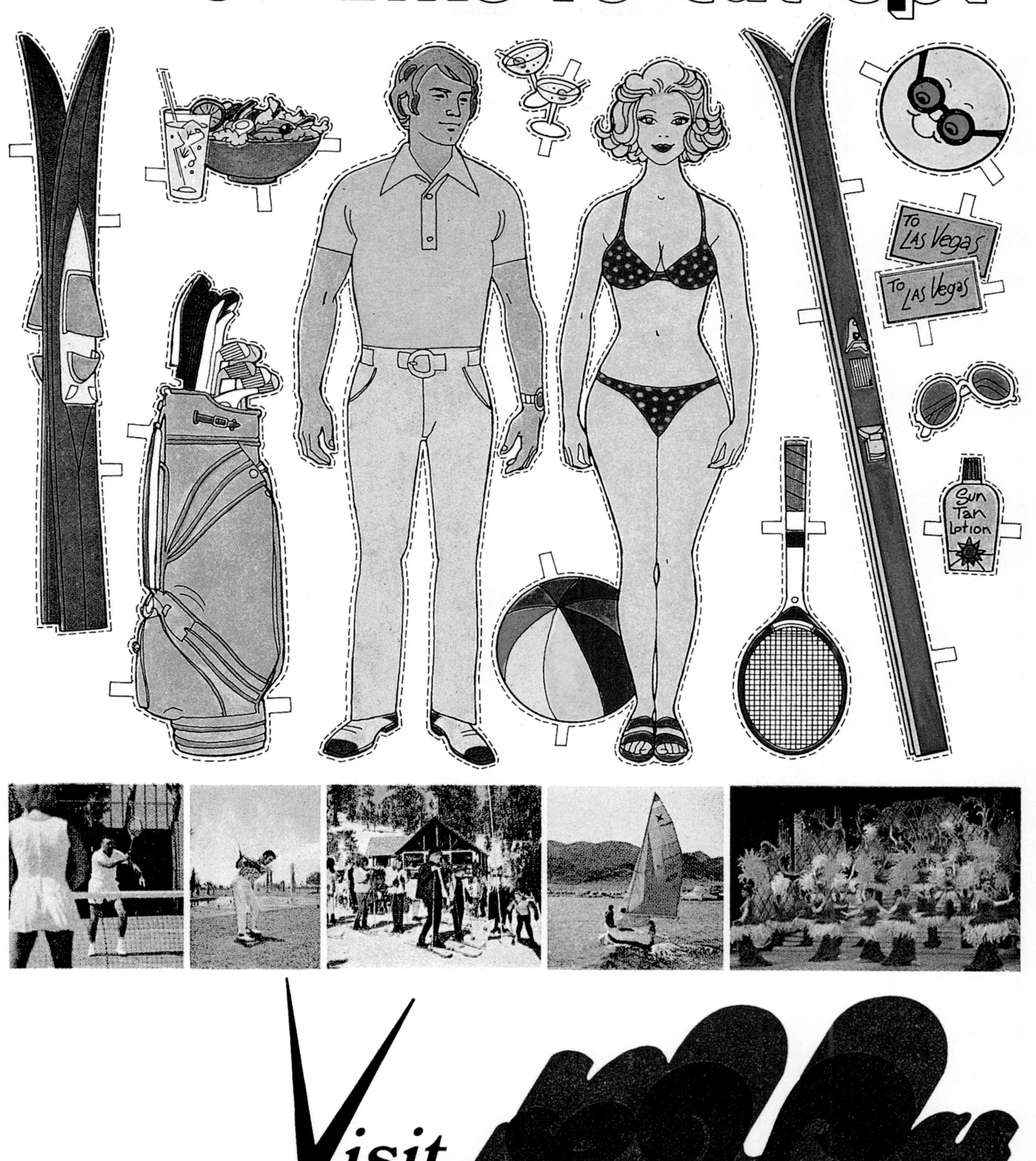
If You Like To Cut Up!
To Las Vegas
To Las Vegas
Sun Tan Lotion
Visit
call your travel agent!
A Las Vegas Convention Authority Advertisement.

We tackle 24 out of 26 N.F.L. teams.

"You Can't Win Them All."

◂ United Air Lines, 1972

United Air Lines, 1973

▸▸ American Airlines, 1971

The '70s opened with the first flight of the Boeing 747. This two-level jumbo jet is two times the size of a 707. The ad compared its first-class section to an ocean liner, but air travel time to Europe was a fraction of what it was on a ship. Mass-market travel had taken off – literally.

Die Siebziger starteten mit dem ersten Flug der Boeing 747 alias Jumbojet. Dieses Großraumflugzeug war zweimal so groß wie die 707. Auch wenn die Anzeige den Komfort der ersten Klasse mit dem eines Linienschiffs vergleicht, benötigte man für einen Flug nach Europa doch nur noch einen Bruchteil der Zeit. Und mit den Pauschalreisen ging es steil nach oben – wortwörtlich.

Les années 1970 s'ouvrirent sur le premier envol du Boeing 747. Ce « jumbo jet » à deux niveaux est deux fois plus gros que le 707. La publicité comparait sa première classe à celle d'un paquebot, même si on pouvait rejoindre l'Europe infiniment plus vite qu'en bateau. Le tourisme de masse avait littéralement décollé.

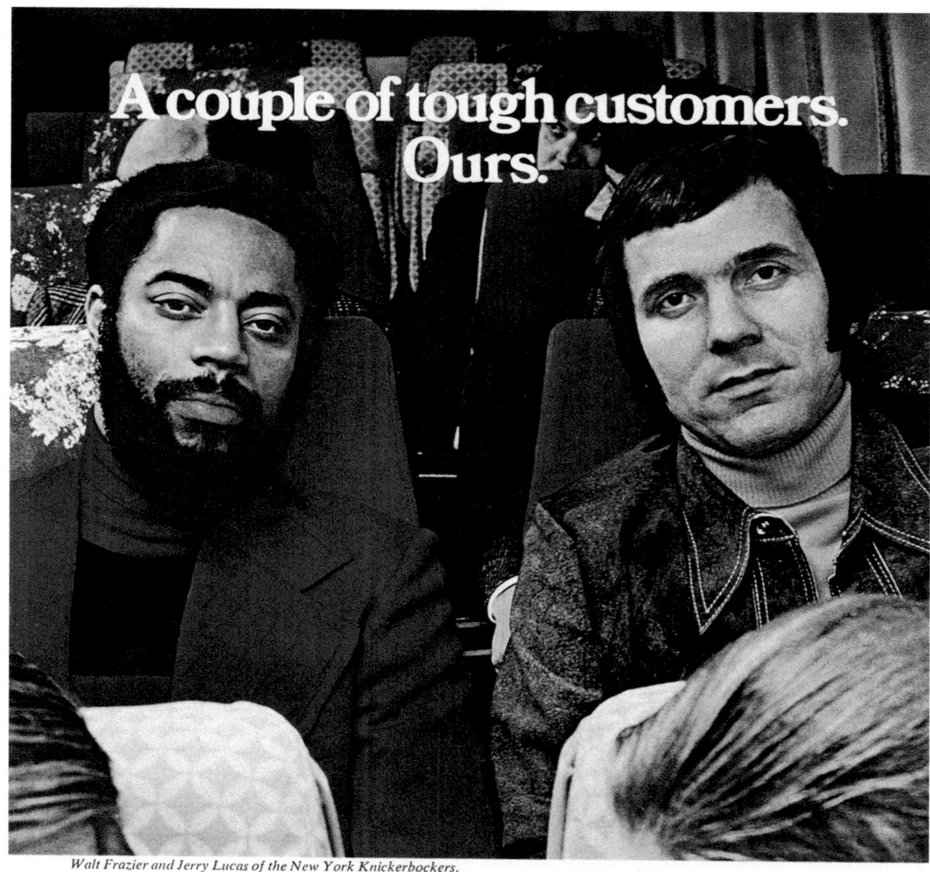
A couple of tough customers.
Ours.

Walt Frazier and Jerry Lucas of the New York Knickerbockers.

When the men of the National Basketball Association go out of town on business they expect to have a rough time.

But on the way to and from, they want things made easy.

United understands.

Maybe that's why all 17 NBA-teams fly United to away games. And, in fact, why we fly more pro and college sports teams than any other airline.

Because we don't play games with them.

These guys are travel pros, too. They want convenience, attention, service, without asking. And in the friendly skies, they've got it.

United knows that business people come in all shapes and styles. So we take them one at a time. And make things easy for all of them. Each in his own way.

The next time you're going out of town, call your Travel Agent, or United.

And say you're a tough customer. We'll take you on, too.

The friendly skies of your land

United Air Lines

Partners in Travel with Western International Hotels.

American Airlines
The plane with

Coach Lounge.

No matter where you've been in the world, you've never gone in comfort like this. From our spacious new Coach Lounge, with its stand-up bar, all through the plane and up the stairs, to our totally redesigned first class lounge.
It's a new standard in flying comfort.
The American Airlines 747 LuxuryLiner.
First of all, in coach, there's a lounge bigger than most living rooms.

It's a place where you can mingle, make new friends, have a snack, have some fun.
Enjoy being sociable, or just enjoy the space.
No other airline has anything like it.
And back down the aisle at your seat, we've rearranged the rows. So besides getting **more leg room and sitting room,** you'll have more getting up room whe you try out the lounge.
If you're flying first class, why not call ahead

New 747 LuxuryLiner.
no competition.

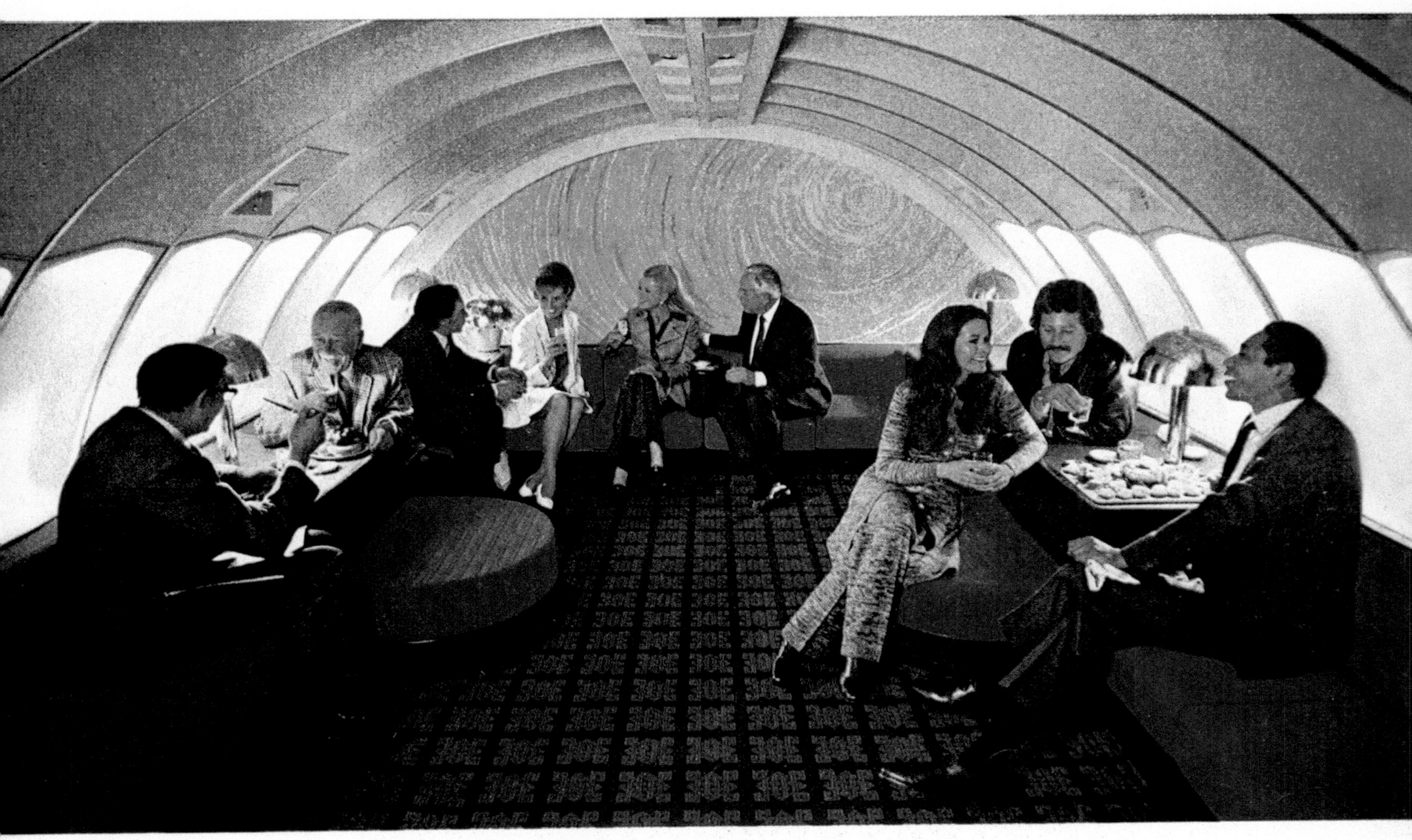

First Class Lounge.

and **reserve a table for four.** You can wine and dine with friends, do a little business, or maybe play some bridge.

And a floor above is our beautiful new first class lounge.

A plush, intimate spot where you can socialize over after-dinner liqueurs or champagne.

And for everybody on transcontinental flights, there's an added service. Flagship Service.

Featuring Polynesian food. Special warming wagons to keep your food piping hot. And pretty new outfits for our stewardesses.

So if you like going places to see things, this new airplane is something to see.

Every one of our 747s is now a LuxuryLiner.

And all of the extra comforts won't cost you an extra cent.

For reservations call us or your Travel Agent.

American Airlines 747 LuxuryLiner

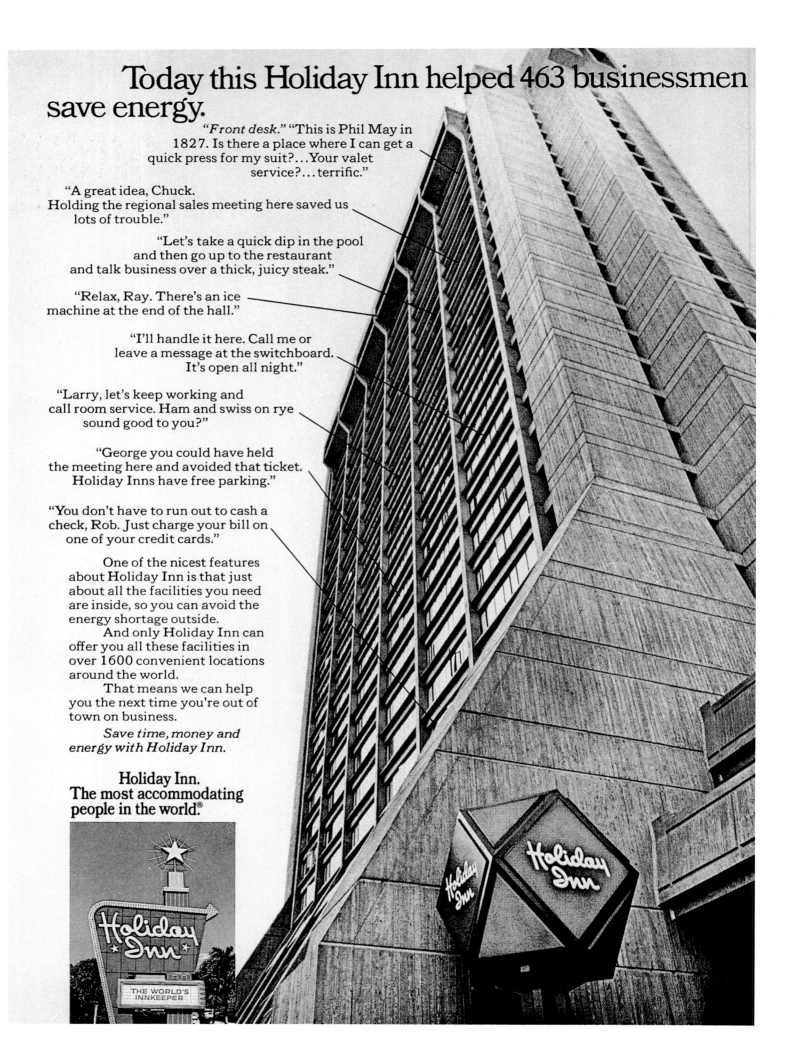

Today this Holiday Inn helped 463 businessmen save energy.

"Front desk." "This is Phil May in 1827. Is there a place where I can get a quick press for my suit?... Your valet service?... terrific."

"A great idea, Chuck. Holding the regional sales meeting here saved us lots of trouble."

"Let's take a quick dip in the pool and then go up to the restaurant and talk business over a thick, juicy steak."

"Relax, Ray. There's an ice machine at the end of the hall."

"I'll handle it here. Call me or leave a message at the switchboard. It's open all night."

"Larry, let's keep working and call room service. Ham and swiss on rye sound good to you?"

"George you could have held the meeting here and avoided that ticket. Holiday Inns have free parking."

"You don't have to run out to cash a check, Rob. Just charge your bill on one of your credit cards."

One of the nicest features about Holiday Inn is that just about all the facilities you need are inside, so you can avoid the energy shortage outside.

And only Holiday Inn can offer you all these facilities in over 1600 convenient locations around the world.

That means we can help you the next time you're out of town on business.

Save time, money and energy with Holiday Inn.

**Holiday Inn.
The most accommodating people in the world.®**

In Chicago, Hyatt's a 700-foot column of Oriental kites rising through spanning bridges and hanging gardens. In Atlanta, Hyatt's glass bubble elevators glide through a park 24 stories tall.
In Knoxville, Hyatt's an Aztec pyramid. In Toronto, a tower of shimmering glass.
Hyatt's got butler service in San Francisco. A lounge that orbits Houston. The largest swimming pool in Acapulco.
And the toll free number gets you information and reservations at any Hyatt Hotel. Call your Travel Agent. Or Hyatt. And get it all.
HYATT HOTELS
800-228-9000
Gets You
Hyatt

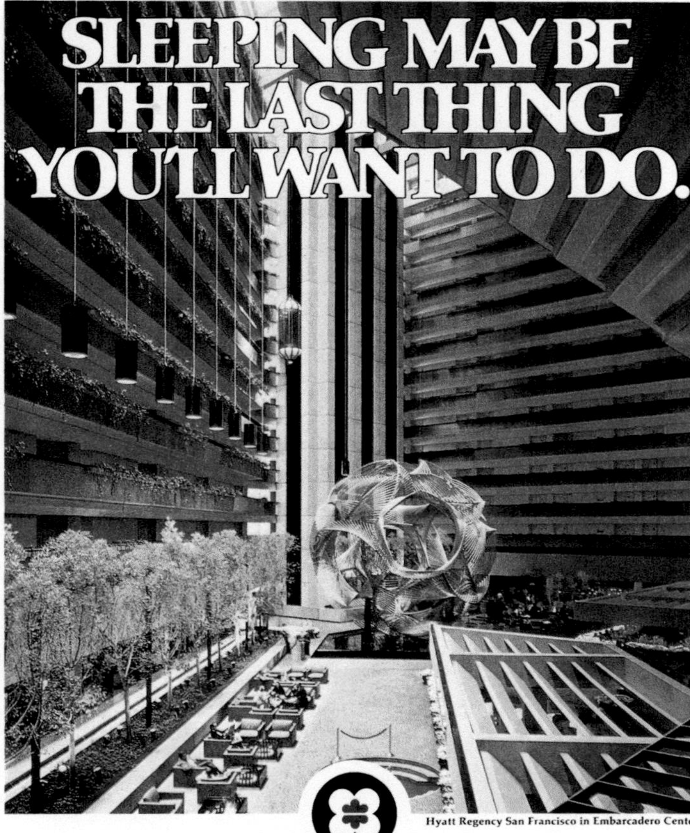

SLEEPING MAY BE
THE LAST THING
YOU'LL WANT TO DO.
Hyatt Regency San Francisco in Embarcadero Center
HYATT HOTELS
800-228-9000 gets you 57 Hyatt Hotels world wide.
Toll free.

◂ Holiday Inn, 1974

Hyatt Hotels, 1972

In 1967, Hyatt opened the world's first atrium hotel, changing the look of the hospitality industry. The architect John Portman structured the building around a dramatic multi-story atrium. The view down from the sleek glass elevators was jaw-dropping. The chain flourished throughout the '70s—nationally and internationally.

Als Hyatt 1967 das weltweit erste Atrium-Hotel eröffnete, war ein neuer Look geschaffen. Der Architekt John Portman machte ein imposantes, mehrgeschossiges Foyer zum Mittelpunkt des Gebäudes, und die eleganten gläsernen Aufzüge boten einen einfach phänomenalen Blick hinab. Die Hotelkette florierte während der gesamten 1970er-Jahre, national wie international.

En 1967, Hyatt ouvrit le premier « hôtel atrium » du monde et transforma le visage de l'industrie hôtelière. L'architecte John Portman structura l'édifice autour d'un atrium spectaculaire de plusieurs étages. La vue depuis les ascenseurs en verre était à couper le souffle. La chaîne prospéra tout au long des années 1970, aux Etats-Unis comme à l'étranger.

Hyatt Hotels, 1975

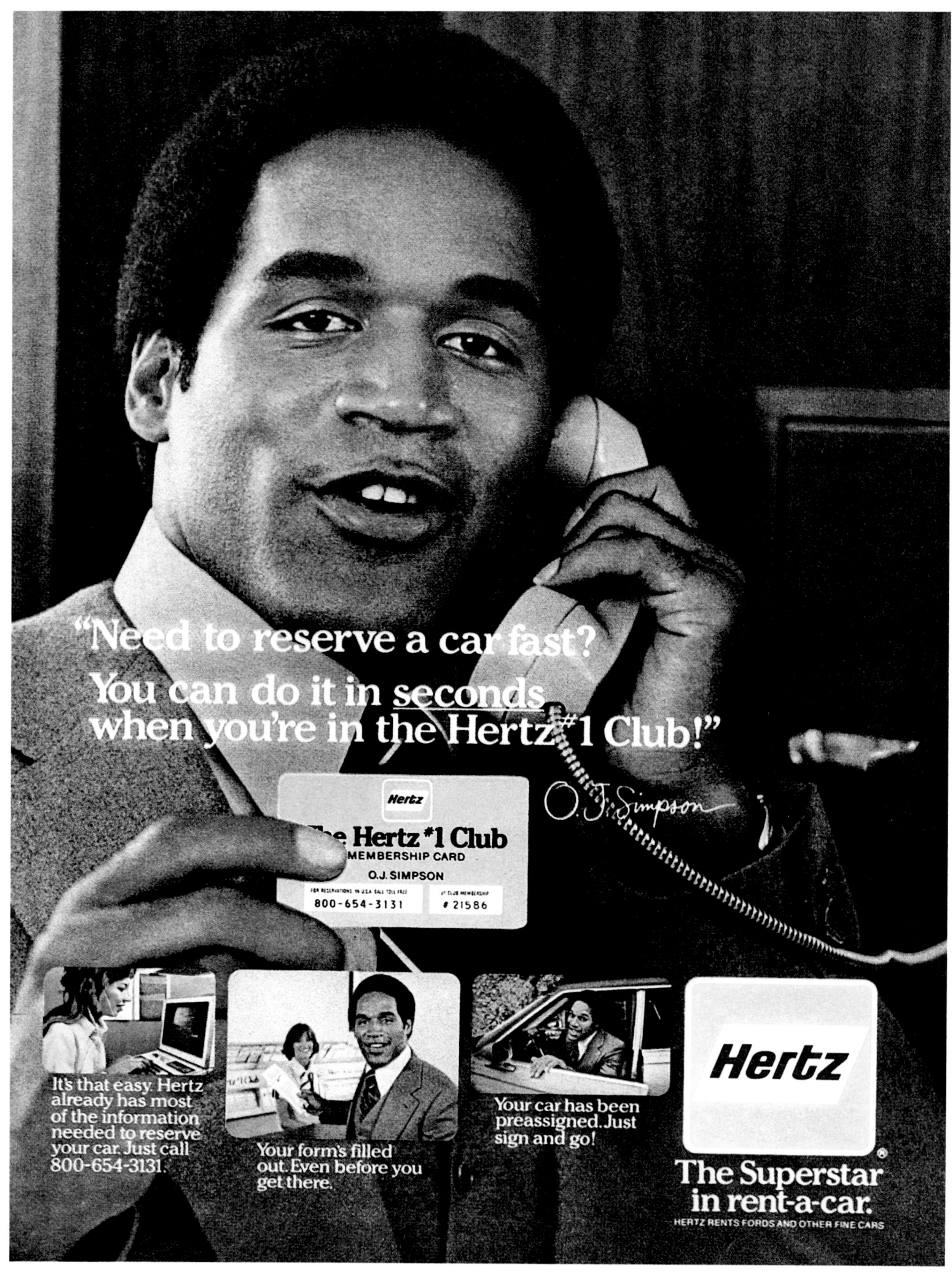

Hertz, 1976

▸ Holiday Inn, 1972

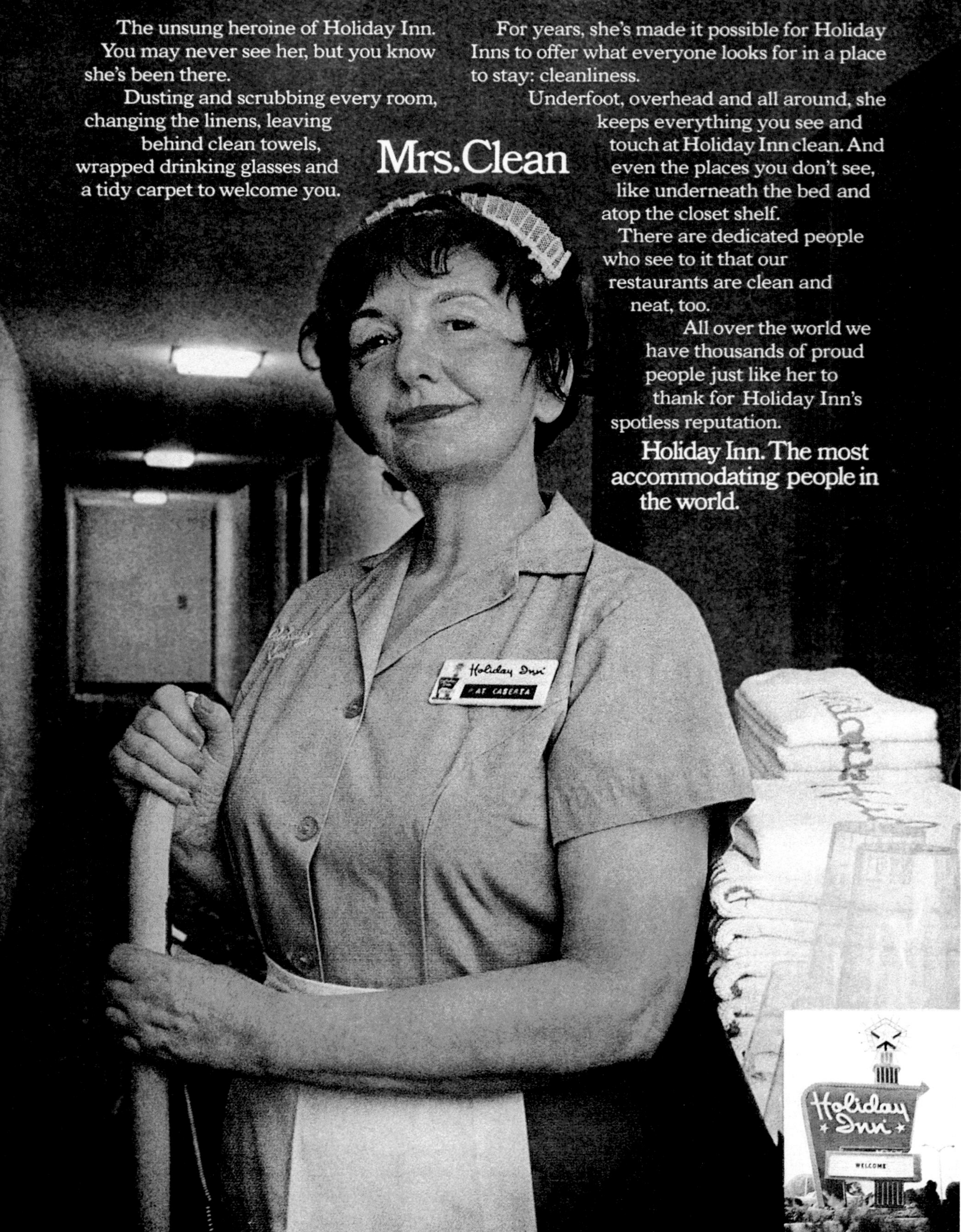
The unsung heroine of Holiday Inn. You may never see her, but you know she's been there.
Dusting and scrubbing every room, changing the linens, leaving behind clean towels, wrapped drinking glasses and a tidy carpet to welcome you.
Mrs. Clean
For years, she's made it possible for Holiday Inns to offer what everyone looks for in a place to stay: cleanliness.
Underfoot, overhead and all around, she keeps everything you see and touch at Holiday Inn clean. And even the places you don't see, like underneath the bed and atop the closet shelf.
There are dedicated people who see to it that our restaurants are clean and neat, too.
All over the world we have thousands of proud people just like her to thank for Holiday Inn's spotless reputation.
Holiday Inn. The most accommodating people in the world.
Holiday Inn
Holiday Inn
WELCOME

349

MASS TRAVEL ENCOURAGED EXCLUSIVITY AT THE HIGH END, AND BOUTIQUE HOTELS BECAME ALL THE RAGE.

PAUSCHALREISEN FÖRDERTEN DIE EXKLUSIVITÄT DES TOPSEGMENTS, UND BOUTIQUEHOTELS WAREN DER LETZTE SCHREI.

LE TOURISME DE MASSE ENCOURAGEA PLUS D'EXCLUSIVITÉ SUR LE SEGMENT HAUT DE GAMME DU MARCHÉ, ET LES « BOUTIQUE HOTELS » FIRENT D'AUTANT PLUS FUREUR.

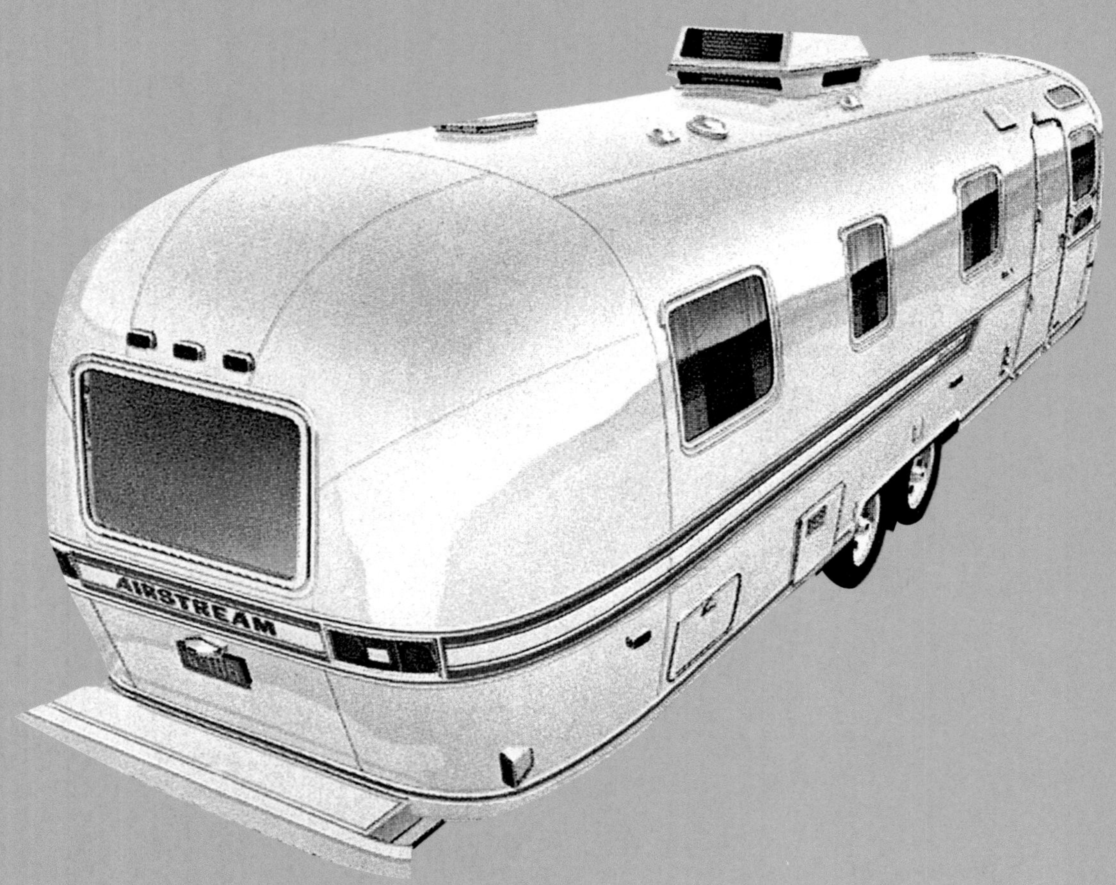

1980

JOINING THE CROWD

BAD IN DER MENGE

LE TOURISME DES MASSES

-1999

BUILDING
47
DC 10 DOCK 2
FOR AIRCRAFT
→USE ONLY←

◂ United Air Lines, 1985

Delta Air Lines, 1990

THE 1978 AIRLINE DEREGULATION ACT ENDED ALL RESTRICTIONS ON ROUTES ON JANUARY 1, 1982. That year, domestic airfare regulation ended. Long-established airlines faced strong competition from nimble new rivals with less-powerful unions. It was telling that the decade opened with *Airplane!*, a zany spoof of every airline disaster movie ever made. Meanwhile, a new sort of airline, People Express, no-frills and low-cost, began service out of Newark Airport. At the opposite end of the spectrum, Richard Branson's luxury-obsessed Virgin Atlantic Airways began flying between Newark and London's Gatwick in 1984, and was profitable that first year. It was the once-flourishing air carriers that had trouble. For example, Braniff International Airways closed up in 1982. Ultimately nine major airlines folded.

During this same period, a new kind of hotel emerged: the intimate yet stylish boutique hotel. Guests could choose their brand of bottled water, even the pillow they would sleep on. It began when Ian Schrager and Steve Rubell, the former owners of New York nightclub Studio 54, opened Morgans Hotel in New York in 1984. It was so chic, no apostrophe was needed. This Andrée Putman–designed hotel changed the rules of the hospitality industry. They followed up with a bigger success, the Royalton, in 1988. Every detail here was planned by Philippe Starck. The cool, dark lobby became the hottest cocktail lounge in New York.

But the wealthy were, as usual, on to the next thing. If grand hotels felt musty and boutique hotels chichi, then ultra-exclusive eco-conscious enclaves like the Aman Resorts appeared. These small, sumptuous hotels emphasized natural surroundings. Amanpuri, the flagship, opened in Phuket, Thailand, in 1988.

Las Vegas responded by becoming family friendly. More than 14.2 million visitors came to the gambling capital in the first 11 months of 1986 alone. Hotels there were now supersized. In 1989, the visionary gaming impresario Steve Wynn opened the Mirage, the largest private hotel in the world, with 3,303 guest rooms. The cost: a half-billion dollars. It was fully booked.

Tired Of Being Raised Like Cattle?

Las Vegas was, in a sense, offering all-inclusive vacations. Its hotels served a guest's every need, like a cruise ship. As people's daily lives grew busier, they clearly wanted every detail taken care of — so vacations really could be vacations. No wonder, then, that the number of cruise passengers to the Caribbean more than doubled between 1980 and 1990 — growing to 7.8 million from 3.8 million.

Aside from that, in the '80s speed mattered. While air travel boomed, it was not only about bargain airlines. The private jet was increasingly common, a kind of family car for the super-rich.

AT A CENTURY'S END, NOSTALGIA IS OFTEN THE FASHION. So filmmakers probably thought it was a good idea to remake *Sabrina*, the 1954 Audrey Hepburn confection about a charming chauffeur's daughter and two wealthy, if very different, brothers. In the 1995 version, it is bizarre that the brother who is a powerful businessman makes a big deal out of going to Paris. After all, he owns a private jet and lives in New York, where commercial jets take off for

1980

1980 *Airplane!* spoofs every airport disaster movie ever made

Airplane! nimmt jeden je gedrehten Flugkatastrophenfilm auf die Schippe

Y a-t-il un Pilote dans L'Avion ? parodie tous les films de catastrophe aérienne jamais tournés

1982 Enactment of 1978 Airline Deregulation Act sends industry into tailspin, more than 100 small carriers go out of business

Der Airline Deregulation Act von 1978 bringt die gesamte Branche ins Trudeln und kostet über 100 Fluglinien die Existenz

Avec l'entrée en vigueur de l'Airline Deregulation Act voté en 1978, plus de 100 compagnies aériennes déposent le bilan

1982 The Go-Go's release hit single "Vacation"

The Go-Go's präsentieren ihre Hitsingle „Vacation" (Urlaub)

Les Go-Go's sortent le tube « Vacation »

1984 With air travel now mainstream, airlines begin to design more subdued, business-like cabins

Flugreisen gehören inzwischen zum Alltag, und so greift man zu eher verhaltenen, geschäftsmäßigen Interieurs

Face à la démocratisation du voyage en avion, les compagnies aériennes conçoivent des cabines plus neutres

Eastern Airlines, 1985

▶ United States Virgin Islands, 1989

Paris from three local airports virtually every hour. It's odd that he *hasn't* been to Paris.

By the 1990s, getting on an airplane was like boarding a bus—if less enjoyable. Travel was quick and super-convenient. In 1994, after decades of planning, high-speed trains finally started running through the Channel Tunnel. The project cost doubled from its original estimate to £9.5 billion. But trains now took two hours 15 minutes between Paris and London.

Mass travel encouraged exclusivity at the high end, and boutique hotels became even more the rage. Ian Schrager opened the Paramount in New York in 1990; headed south for a $20-million makeover of the Delano, a 1947 Miami Beach streamline moderne hotel, in 1995; then out to Los Angeles to revamp the Mondrian on the Sunset Strip, in 1996. Boutique hotels even caught on in Paris, the city of the grandest hotels. In 1991, the Costes brothers opened Hôtel Costes, and it became one of the City of Light's brightest spots.

Still, mass-market travel kept growing. In 1999, less expensive versions of boutique hotels appeared. The Starwood chain, owner of St. Regis hotels, launched W, while Andre Balazs, who owned high-end hostelries like the Chateau Marmont on the Sunset Strip, opened the first Standard. JetBlue Airways, with its budget fares, was announced the same year.

And travel transformed Las Vegas, as the age demographics shifted downward. Las Vegas was the fastest-growing city in America, particularly for retirees. But the city's median age plummeted after Peter Morton opened the Hard Rock Hotel & Casino in 1995. Younger visitors used it as their beachhead.

Modern art and architecture also influenced travel patterns. Art cognoscenti turned San Sebastian, Spain, into a travel Mecca when Frank Gehry's stunning Guggenheim Museum opened in nearby Bilbao in 1997. In 1996, Thermal Baths opened in the sleepy Swiss hamlet of Vals. The design

by Peter Zumthor, who later won a Pritzker Prize, garnered attention—and a waiting list. Major art exhibitions, like those in Venice, Italy, and Kassel, Germany; as well as big art fairs in Basel, Switzerland, and Miami were Stations of the Cross for devoted art followers.

It seemed almost a metaphor when Pamela Harriman, the U.S. ambassador to France, died during her morning swim at the Ritz in Paris in 1997. Pamela Digby Churchill Hayward Harriman had traveled far. A former English debutante, she married multimillionaire diplomat W. Averell Harriman, who controlled the Union Pacific Railroad and had built Sun Valley, the first U.S. ski resort. The belle of many an Atlantic crossing, whose charm had attracted a string of wealthy and powerful beaus, Pamela Harriman had morphed into a Jet Set power player. Yet she died at the Ritz, the grande dame of grand hotels, which had opened before the 20th century, in 1898. In a way, this could be viewed as more than the death of one person. Harriman's death marked the passing of an entire way of life—and travel.

1984

1984 Virgin Atlantic Airways begins service between Newark and Gatwick and is profitable in first year

Virgin Atlantic Airways beginnt mit der Strecke Newark–Gatwick und macht bereits im ersten Jahr Gewinn

Virgin Atlantic Airways commence à assurer la liaison entre Newark et Gatwick et devient rentable dès la première année

1984 First Embassy Suites hotel opens, Overland Park, Kansas; chain targets businessmen by making every room a suite

Overland Park in Kansas, erstes Embassy Suites Hotel mit ausschließlich Suiten, soll Geschäftsleute ansprechen

Ouverture du premier hôtel Embassy Suites à Overland Park, Kansas : la chaîne attire les hommes d'affaires en ne proposant que des suites

1985 Washington officially replaces Route 66, dubbed "The Mother Road" by John Steinbeck, with the Interstate Highway System

Route 66 offiziell aus dem U.S. Highway System entfernt, das durch das Interstate Highway System ersetzt wird

La Route 66 est officiellement retirée du système autoroutier américain et remplacée par l'Interstate Highway System

1985 Eurailpass unofficial passport of young Americans traveling across Europe

Eurail-Pass als inoffizieller Reisepass für Europareisen junger US-Bürger

L'Eurail Pass devient le passeport officieux des jeunes Américains qui voyagent en Europe

◂ Hyatt Hotels, 1990

Stonehenge, 1985

MIT INKRAFTTRETEN DES AIRLINE DEREGULATION ACT VON 1978 AM 1. JANUAR 1982 FIELEN SÄMTLICHE EINSCHRÄNKUNGEN BEZÜGLICH DER FLUGPREISE, -ROUTEN UND -PLÄNE WEG. Neue flexible Fluglinien mit weniger gewerkschaftlichem Einfluss wurden den etablierten Airlines zur ernst zu nehmenden Konkurrenz. Eingeläutet wurde die Dekade bezeichnenderweise mit *Airplane!* (*Die unglaubliche Reise in einem verrückten Flugzeug*, 1980), einer irrwitzigen Persiflage auf sämtliche je gedrehten Flugzeugkatastrophenfilme. Auf dem Flughafen von Newark, New Jersey, nahm unterdessen mit People Express eine neuartige Fluglinie ohne Schnickschnack und mit niedrigen Preisen den Betrieb auf. Am anderen Ende des Spektrums begann die von Luxus angetriebene Virgin Atlantic Airways von Richard Branson 1984 mit Flügen von Newark nach London-Gatwick und war gleich im ersten Jahr profitabel. Probleme hatten indes die einstmals florierenden Fluglinien. So musste Braniff International Airways 1982 dichtmachen. Letztlich überlebten neun größere Fluglinien nicht.

Derweil entwickelte sich eine neue Art von Herberge: das intime und doch stilvolle Boutiquehotel. Als Gast konnte man die Tafelwassermarke und sogar die Art des Kopfkissens selbst auswählen. Alles begann 1984, als Ian Schrager und Steve Rubell, einstige Eigentümer des New Yorker Nachtclubs Studio 54, das Morgans Hotel in New York eröffneten. Es war so schick, dass man sogar auf den Apostroph im Namen verzichten konnte. Dieses von Andrée Putman designte Hotel sollte die Regeln der Beherbergungsindustrie verändern. Schrager und Rubell ließen 1988 mit dem Royalton einen noch größeren Hit folgen, der bis ins letzte Detail die Handschrift von Philippe Starck trug und dessen coole, dunkle Lobby zur heißesten Cocktaillounge von New York wurde.

Doch die Reichen waren wie gewöhnlich schon wieder auf der Suche nach Neuem. Grandhotels wirkten irgendwie angestaubt und Boutiquehotels gekünstelt. Nun aber gab es höchst exklusive, ökobewusste Enklaven wie die Aman Resorts – kleine, luxuriöse Hotels, die sich gut in die natürliche Umgebung einfügten. Ihr Flaggschiff ist das 1988 auf der thailändischen Insel Phuket eröffnete Amanpuri.

Las Vegas reagierte damit, dass es familienfreundlicher wurde. Allein in den ersten elf Monaten des Jahres 1986 zählte die Hauptstadt des Glücksspiels über 14,2 Millionen Besucher. XXL lautete die neue Devise der Hotels. Der visionäre Kasinobetreiber Steve Wynn eröffnete 1989 das Mirage, mit 3303 Gästezimmern das größte private Hotel der Welt. Kostenpunkt: 0,5 Mrd. $. Und es war gleich ausgebucht.

Las Vegas präsentierte gewissermaßen ein All-inclusive-Angebot. Die Hotels erfüllten dem Gast jeden Wunsch, wie auf einer Kreuzfahrt. Da die Menschen im Alltag zunehmend gefordert waren, hatten sie hier ganz klar den Wunsch, dass man ihnen alles abnahm. Urlaub sollte schließlich Urlaub sein. Kein Wunder also, dass sich auch die Zahl der Passagiere einer Kreuzfahrt in die Karibik zwischen 1980 und 1990 von 3,8 Mio. auf 7,8 Mio. mehr als verdoppelte.

Daneben war auch in den 1980er-Jahren Tempo gefragt. Der Boom bei den Flugreisen verdankte sich nicht allein den Billiglinien, denn es gab auch immer mehr Privatjets, eine Art Familienkutsche der Superreichen.

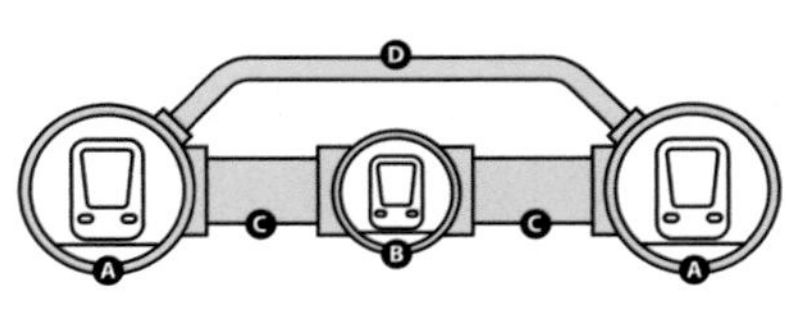

1986 Universal Studios' $6.5-million animatronic King Kong attraction ushers in new era in theme park design

Elektronisch gesteuerter, 6,5 Mio. $ teurer King Kong von Universal Studios läutet eine neue Ära der Themenparks ein

Le robot King Kong construit par Universal Studios pour 6,5 millions de dollars annonce une nouvelle ère dans le design des parcs d'attractions

1986 United buys Pan Am's Pacific Division for $715 million; expands service to Sydney, Australia, and 12 other Pacific cities

United erwirbt Pan Ams Pacific Division für 715 Mio. $ und bedient nun auch Sydney und zwölf weitere pazifische Städte

United rachète la division Pacifique de Pan Am pour 715 millions de dollars et étend le service jusqu'à Sydney en Australie et à 12 autres villes du Pacifique

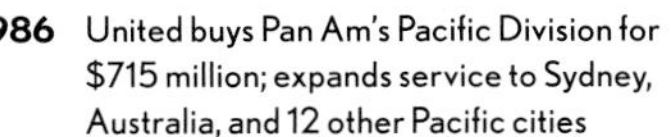

1988 Tunneling begins for "Chunnel" (English Channel tunnel) between Paris and London

Baubeginn des Kanaltunnels für die Verbindung Paris–London

Ouverture du Tunnel sous la Manche entre Paris et Londres

1988 Roughly 7 million tourists visit Mexico; almost 50% increase over two years earlier

Fast sieben Millionen Touristen besuchen Mexiko, doppelt so viele wie zwei Jahre zuvor

Environ 7 millions de touristes visitent le Mexique, soit une hausse d'environ 50 % par rapport à 1986

◂ Cunard, 1998

GEGEN ENDE DES JAHRHUNDERTS KAM IMMER WIEDER NOSTALGIE AUF. Daher hielten die Filmemacher ein Remake von *Sabrina* vermutlich für eine gute Idee, jene Kreation von 1954 mit Audrey Hepburn über eine bezaubernde Chauffeurstochter und zwei wohlhabende, doch sehr unterschiedliche Brüder. In der Fassung von 1995 wundert man sich, dass der eine Bruder, ein einflussreicher Geschäftsmann, um eine Reise nach Paris so viel Tamtam macht. Schließlich besitzt er doch einen Privatjet und lebt in New York, wo praktisch jede Stunde von den drei lokalen Flughäfen ein Linienflug nach Paris geht. Merkwürdig auch, dass er noch nie in Paris *war*.

In den 1990er-Jahren ein Flugzeug zu betreten war so, als würde man in einen Bus einsteigen – wenn auch weniger vergnüglich. Die eigentliche Beförderung verlief flott und äußerst bequem. Nach jahrzehntelanger Vorbereitung fuhren 1994 die ersten Hochgeschwindigkeitszüge durch den Eurotunnel. Mit 15 Mrd. Euro hatte man das Budget um 100 % überzogen, doch nun gelangte man in nur zweieinviertel Stunden mit dem Zug von Paris nach London.

Pauschalreisen förderten die Exklusivität des Topsegments, und Boutiquehotels waren umso gefragter. Ian Schrager eröffnete 1990 das Paramount in New York; dann zog er 1995 weiter gen Süden für einen 20 Mio. $ teuren Umbau des Delano in Miami Beach, eines Hotels der Streamline-Moderne von 1947; und 1996 hinaus nach Los Angeles, um das Mondrian am Sunset Strip aufzupolieren. Die Boutiquehotels fanden sogar in Paris Anklang. In der Stadt mit den erlesensten Hotels eröffneten die Costes-Brüder 1991 das Hôtel Costes, und es wurde zu einem der strahlendsten Orte in der „Stadt der Lichter".

Doch auch die Pauschalreisen nahmen weiter zu. Preiswertere Ausführungen der Boutiquehotels erschienen 1999. Die Starwood-Kette, Eignerin der St.-Regis-Hotels, lancierte die W-Hotels. Andre Balasz, Eigentümer von Topherbergen wie dem Chateau Marmont am Sunset Strip, eröffnete das erste Standard. Die Billigfluglinie JetBlue Airways wurde noch im gleichen Jahr angekündigt.

Und das Reisen verwandelte Las Vegas, während die Bevölkerung immer jünger wurde. Las Vegas war die am schnellsten wachsende Stadt der Vereinigten Staaten. Vor allem Ruheständler ließen sich hier nieder, doch das Durchschnittsalter ging deutlich zurück, nachdem Peter Morton 1995 das Hard Rock Hotel & Casino eröffnet hatte, das für jüngere Besucher zur beliebten Anlaufstelle wurde.

Die moderne Kunst und Architektur beeinflusste auch das Reiseverhalten. Kunstkenner verwandelten das spanische San Sebastian in ein Reisemekka, nachdem Frank Gehrys faszinierendes Guggenheim-Museum 1997 im nahe gelegenen Bilbao eröffnet worden war. In dem verschlafenen Schweizer Örtchen Vals öffnete 1996 die Therme Vals ihre Pforten. Der Entwurf von Peter Zumthor, der 2009 mit dem Pritzker-Preis ausgezeichnet wurde, sorgte für Aufregung – und eine Warteliste. Bedeutende Kunstausstellungen etwa in Venedig oder Kassel sowie große Kunstmessen in Basel und Miami wurden zum Pflichtpensum wahrer Kunstliebhaber.

Und dann gab es ein Ereignis von besonderer Symbolkraft: der Tod von Pamela Harriman, US-Botschafterin in Frankreich, während ihrer morgendlichen Schwimmrunde 1997 im Pariser Hotel Ritz. Pamela Digby Churchill Hayward Harriman war viel herumgekommen. Die einstige Debütantin aus England heiratete Averell Harriman, jenen Multimillionär und Diplomaten, der die Union Pacific Railroad kontrollierte und ab 1936 mit Sun Valley das erste Skiresort der USA errichtet hatte. Pamela Harriman, einstige Königin zahlreicher Atlantikfahrten, hatte sich gekonnt in eine Größe des Jetsets verwandelt. Ihren Tod fand sie jedoch im Ritz, der Grande Dame der Grandhotels, das noch vor dem 20. Jahrhundert, nämlich 1898, eröffnet worden war. Dies war mehr als der Tod eines Menschen, denn Harrimans Dahinscheiden steht für den Abschied von einer bestimmten Art zu leben – und zu reisen.

1989

1989 Steve Wynn builds Mirage in Las Vegas; largest private hotel in the world, with 3,303 guest rooms

Steve Wynn baut das Mirage in Los Angeles, mit 3303 Gästezimmern das größte private Hotel der Welt

Steve Wynn construit le Mirage à Las Vegas, le plus grand hôtel privé du monde avec 3303 chambres

1990 Cruise passengers to Caribbean more than double since 1980 – to 7.8 million from 3.8 million

Zahl der Teilnehmer an Karibikkreuzfahrten seit 1980 mehr als verdoppelt – von 3,8 auf 7,8 Millionen

Le nombre de croisiéristes aux Caraïbes a plus que doublé depuis 1980, passant de 3,8 à 7,8 millions

1990 Ian Schrager adds 1928 Paramount hotel to boutique empire, hiring Philippe Starck to reinvent it to be "Hotel as Theater"

Ian Schrager bereichert sein Imperium aus Boutiquehotels um das Paramount Hotel von 1928, das Philippe Starck in ein „Hotel als Theater" verwandelt

Ian Schrager ajoute l'hôtel Paramount de 1928 à son empire hôtelier et Philippe Starck de le relooker en « théâtre »

1991 Las Vegas theme hotels get "family friendly" with debut of Excalibur Hotel and Casino, world's largest hotel at opening

Das inzwischen „familienfreundliche" Las Vegas erhält Themenhotels wie das Excalibur Hotel and Casino

Désormais « familiale », la ville de Las Vegas accueille des hôtels thématiques tels que Excalibur Hotel and Casino le plus grand du monde lors de son ouverture

Marriott Resorts, 1989

► Hard Rock Hotel, 1999

L'AIRLINE DEREGULATION ACT VOTÉ EN 1978 MIT UN TERME À TOUTES RESTRICTIONS SUR LES ITINÉRAIRES LE 1ER JANVIER 1982. Cette année-là marqua la déréglementation des transports aériens sur le territoire américain. Les compagnies aériennes établies de longue date firent face à la concurrence féroce de nouveaux rivaux plus agiles et aux syndicats moins puissants. La décennie s'ouvrit avec *Y a-t-il un pilote dans l'avion?*, une parodie déjantée de tous les films jamais tournés sur les catastrophes aériennes. Parallèlement, People Express, un nouveau genre de compagnie aérienne sans chichi et à bas prix, commença à opérer à l'aéroport de Newark. A l'opposé du marché, la compagnie ultra luxe Virgin Atlantic Airways de Richard Branson se mit à assurer la liaison entre Newark et l'aéroport Gatwick de Londres en 1984, et devint rentable cette même année. C'étaient les transporteurs autrefois prospères qui rencontraient des problèmes. Par exemple, Braniff International Airways ferma en 1982. En fin de compte, neuf grandes compagnies jetèrent aussi l'éponge.

Au cours de cette période, un nouveau type d'établissement à l'ambiance intimiste mais élégante fit son apparition: le «boutique hotel». Les clients pouvaient choisir leur marque d'eau minérale, et même le genre d'oreiller sur lequel ils souhaitaient dormir. Tout commença quand Ian Schrager et Steve Rubell, anciens propriétaires du Studio 54, ouvrirent le Morgans Hotel à New York en 1984. Il était si chic qu'il pouvait se passer d'apostrophe. Cet établissement décoré par Andrée Putman changea la donne dans l'industrie hôtelière. En 1988, le duo renouvela la performance avec un succès encore plus éclatant, le Royalton, dont le moindre détail fut conçu par Philippe Starck. Son hall froid et sombre devint le salon le plus couru de New York.

Comme d'habitude, les plus fortunés étaient déjà passés à autre chose. Puisqu'à leurs yeux, les grands hôtels sentaient le moisi et les «boutique hotels» faisaient trop de chichis, des chaînes ultra exclusives et sensibles aux questions d'environnement commencèrent à faire parler d'elles, comme Aman Resorts. Ses petits hôtels somptueux mettaient en valeur leur environnement naturel. Amanpuri, son fleuron, ouvrit à Phuket en Thaïlande en 1988.

Las Vegas réagit en devenant une destination familiale. Plus de 14,2 millions de visiteurs déferlèrent sur la capitale du jeu au cours des 11 premiers mois de l'année 1986. Les hôtels y étaient désormais gigantesques. En 1989, le propriétaire de casinos visionnaire Steve Wynn ouvrit le Mirage, le plus grand hôtel privé du monde avec ses 3 303 chambres. Sa construction coûta un demi milliard de dollars. Et l'hôtel affichait complet.

Las Vegas offrait plus ou moins des vacances «tout compris». Le personnel de ses établissements répondait aux moindres attentes des clients, comme sur un paquebot de croisières. Le quotidien des gens était toujours plus surchargé, et afin que leurs vacances en soient vraiment, ils avaient clairement besoin qu'on prenne en charge tous les détails à leur place. Rien d'étonnant, donc, à ce que le nombre de croisiéristes mettant cap sur les Caraïbes fît plus que doubler entre 1980 et 1990, passant de 3,8 à 7,8 millions de passagers.

En dehors de ça, la vitesse avait aussi son importance dans les années 1980. En plein boom du voyage aérien, les compagnies bon marché devaient partager la vedette. Le jet privé devenait un moyen de transport de plus en plus utilisé, comme une sorte de voiture familiale pour les personnes extrêmement riches.

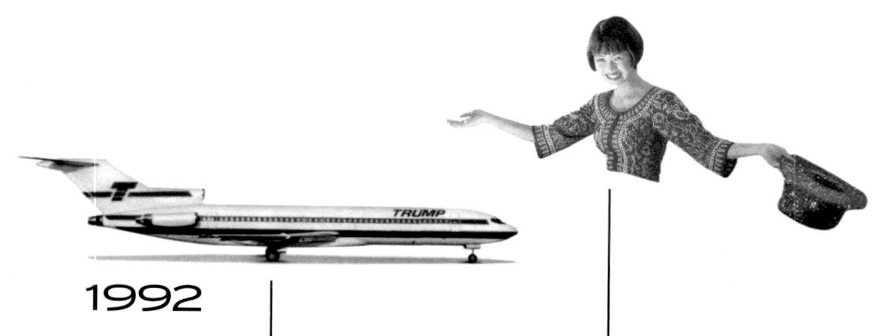

1992

1992 Donald Trump's shortlived airline, the Trump Shuttle, fails and stops flying

Trump Shuttle, die kurzlebige Fluglinie von Donald Trump, legt eine Bauchlandung hin und ist am Ende

Trump Shuttle, la compagnie aérienne de courte durée lancée par Donald Trump, fait faillite

1993 Madame Tussaud's wax museum installs "Singapore Girl," the Singapore Airlines stewardess, its first commercial figure

Das Wachsfigurenmuseum der Madame Tussaud präsentiert mit dem „Singapore Girl", der Stewardess von Singapore Airlines, seine erste kommerzielle Figur

Le musée de cire de Madame Tussaud présente la «Singapore Girl», symbole des hôtesses de l'air de Singapore Airlines

1995 Club Med changes from nonprofit association to for-profit limited liability company

Umwandlung des Club Med vom gemeinnützigen Unternehmen in eine Aktiengesellschaft mit beschränkter Haftung

L'association à but non lucratif Club Med devient une entreprise commerciale

1995 Hard Rock Hotel & Casino opens in Las Vegas, and demographics of Vegas visitors rapidly get younger

Eröffnung des Hard Rock Hotel & Casino in Las Vegas führt rasch zu einer demografischen Verjüngung der Vegas-Touristen

Avec l'ouverture du Hard Rock Hotel & Casino à Las Vegas, la moyenne d'âge des visiteurs de la ville chuta

Hard Rock
HOTEL
LAS VEGAS

H
C
Jenny

◂ Holiday Inn, 1998

QUAND UN SIÈCLE TOUCHE À SA FIN, LA NOSTALGIE EST SOUVENT À LA MODE. Voilà sans doute pourquoi des producteurs estimèrent qu'il serait avisé de tourner un remake de *Sabrina*, le film de 1954 avec Audrey Hepburn racontant l'histoire d'une charmante fille de chauffeur et de deux frères très différents. Dans la version de 1995, il est bizarre que le frère, un puissant homme d'affaires, fasse tout un foin à l'idée d'aller à Paris. Après tout, il possède un jet privé et vit à New York, où des avions de ligne décollent pour Paris presque toutes les heures depuis les trois aéroports de la ville. Il semble peu crédible qu'il ne *soit jamais* allé à Paris.

Dans les années 1990, monter à bord d'un avion revenait à prendre le bus, en un peu moins agréable. On pouvait voyager rapidement et tout confort. En 1994, après des décennies de conception, les trains à grande vitesse finirent par rouler à travers le tunnel sous la Manche. Le projet subit un dépassement de budget de 100 %, coûtant au final 4 650 millions de livres sterling. Cependant, les trains reliaient désormais Paris et Londres en deux heures 15 minutes.

Le tourisme de masse encouragea plus d'exclusivité sur le segment haut de gamme du marché, et les « boutique hotels » firent d'autant plus fureur. Ian Schrager ouvrit le Paramount à New York en 1990, mit cap sur le sud en 1995 afin de rénover le Delano – un hôtel moderne de Miami Beach datant de 1947 – pour un montant de 20 millions de dollars, puis partit à Los Angeles relooker le Mondrian sur Sunset Strip en 1996. La tendance des « boutique hotels » déferla même sur Paris, ville des grands hôtels par excellence. En 1991, les frères Costes inaugurèrent l'Hôtel Costes, aujourd'hui l'une des adresses qui a le plus d'éclat de la Ville Lumière.

Le tourisme de masse poursuivit toutefois son développement. En 1999, des versions moins chères des « boutique hotels » firent leur apparition. La chaîne Starwood, propriété des hôtels St. Regis, lança son concept W, tandis qu'Andre Balazs, propriétaire d'établissements haut de gamme comme le Chateau Marmont sur Sunset Strip, ouvrit le premier hôtel Standard. La compagnie JetBlue Airways, avec ses vols à prix discount, fut créée la même année.

Le marché du voyage transforma également Las Vegas quand sa moyenne d'âge se mit à baisser. Las Vegas était la ville qui connaissait la croissance la plus rapide d'Amérique, particulièrement pour les retraités. Néanmoins, l'âge moyen de la ville chuta quand Peter Morton ouvrit le Hard Rock Hotel & Casino en 1995. Des visiteurs plus jeunes en firent leur point de ralliement.

L'art moderne et l'architecture influencèrent également la façon de voyager. En 1997, les amateurs d'art transformèrent la ville espagnole de San Sebastian en Mecque du voyage dès l'ouverture de l'étonnant Musée Guggenheim de Frank Gehry près de Bilbao. En 1996, les Thermes de Vals s'installèrent dans un patelin suisse endormi. Le design de Peter Zumthor, qui remporta plus tard le prix d'architecture Pritzker, attira l'attention et généra une longue liste d'attente. Les grandes expositions comme celles de Venise en Italie et de Kassel en Allemagne, ainsi que les foires d'art contemporain de Bâle en Suisse et de Miami, devinrent des étapes incontournables sur le Chemin de Croix des pèlerins fanatiques d'art.

On peut presque considérer comme une métaphore le décès de Pamela Harriman, ambassadrice des États-Unis en France, qui mourut en nageant un matin dans la piscine du Ritz parisien en 1997. Pamela Digby Churchill Hayward Harriman avait roulé sa bosse. Cette Anglaise avait épousé Averell Harriman, diplomate multimillionaire qui contrôlait la compagnie Union Pacific Railroad et avait construit Sun Valley, la première station de sports d'hiver américaine, en 1936. Pamela Harriman, la plus belle femme de nombreuses croisières transatlantiques, s'était habilement reconvertie en membre éminent de la jet-set. Elle mourut néanmoins au Ritz, dans la « grande dame » des grands hôtels inaugurée avant le XXe siècle, en 1898. Dans une certaine mesure, ce ne fut pas seulement la mort d'une personne. La disparition de Pamela Harriman marqua la fin de tout un art de vivre, et de voyager.

1995 Airlines begin tests of video-on-demand to personal monitors at each seat

Erprobung frei wählbarer Filme, die auf individuellen integrierten Bildschirmen betrachtet werden können

Les compagnies aériennes commencent à tester la vidéo à la demande sur des écrans personnels à chaque place

1998 Starwood opens first W boutique hotel

Starwood präsentiert neue Boutiquehotels in Gestalt der W-Hotels

Starwood lance les « boutique hotels » W

jetBlue

1999 Plans for JetBlue, hip budget airline, announced

Pläne für JetBlue, einen sich cool gebenden Billigflieger, bekannt gemacht

Annonce des plans de création de JetBlue, une compagnie branchée

1999 Hyatt continues to favor towering, atrium-based design, developed by John Portman, with new Waikiki location

Hyatt favorisiert weiterhin das hoch aufragende Atriumhotel, wie es John Portman mit dem neuen Waikiki Hotel realisiert

Avec son nouvel hôtel à Waikiki, Hyatt continue à privilégier les tours construites autour d'un atrium, un design conçu par John Portman

HIGH PERFORMANCE

High Technology: We fly the Concorde between New York and Paris in just 225 minutes.
Efficiency: A leading record for on-time performance worldwide.
Cargo Leadership: One of the world's 3 largest cargo carriers.
Business Sense: We make your mileage count through our partnership in United's Mileage Plus.

AIR FRANCE

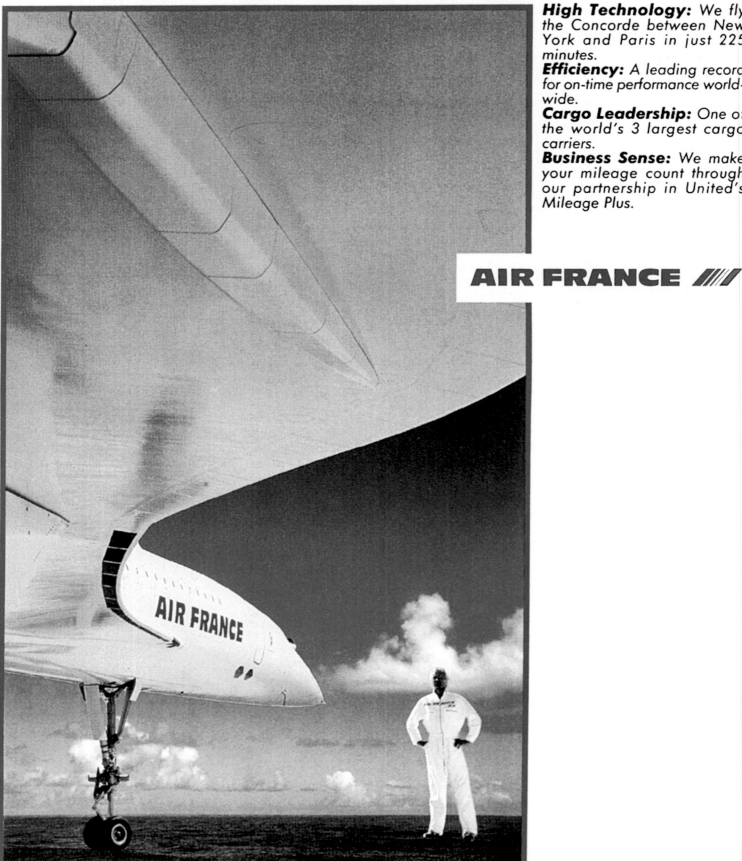

◂ Air France, 1985

The Concorde, a turbojet-powered supersonic transport, took three and a half hours to cross the Atlantic. You got there before you left. Britain and France subsidized the joint Air France–British Air effort. Air France commissioned the influential designer Raymond Loewy for the interiors. Regular, and expensive, service between the U.S. and Europe began in 1976.

Die Concorde, das Überschallverkehrsflugzeug mit Turbojet-Triebwerken, überquerte den Atlantik in nur dreieinhalb Stunden. Kaum gestartet, war man schon angekommen. Das Gemeinschaftsprojekt von Air France und British Airways wurde von beiden Staaten subventioniert. Air France beauftragte den führenden Designer Raymond Loewy mit der Gestaltung des Interieurs. Regelmäßige – und teure – Flüge zwischen den USA und Europa begannen 1976.

Le Concorde, avion supersonique à turboréacteurs, traversait l'Atlantique en 3 heures 30. Avec le décalage horaire, on arrivait avant même d'être parti. L'Angleterre et la France subventionnèrent ce projet commun entre Air France et British Airways. La compagnie française confia l'aménagement intérieur de l'avion au designer en vue Raymond Loewy. Les liaisons régulières, et onéreuses, entre les Etats-Unis et l'Europe commencèrent en 1976.

American Airlines, 1984

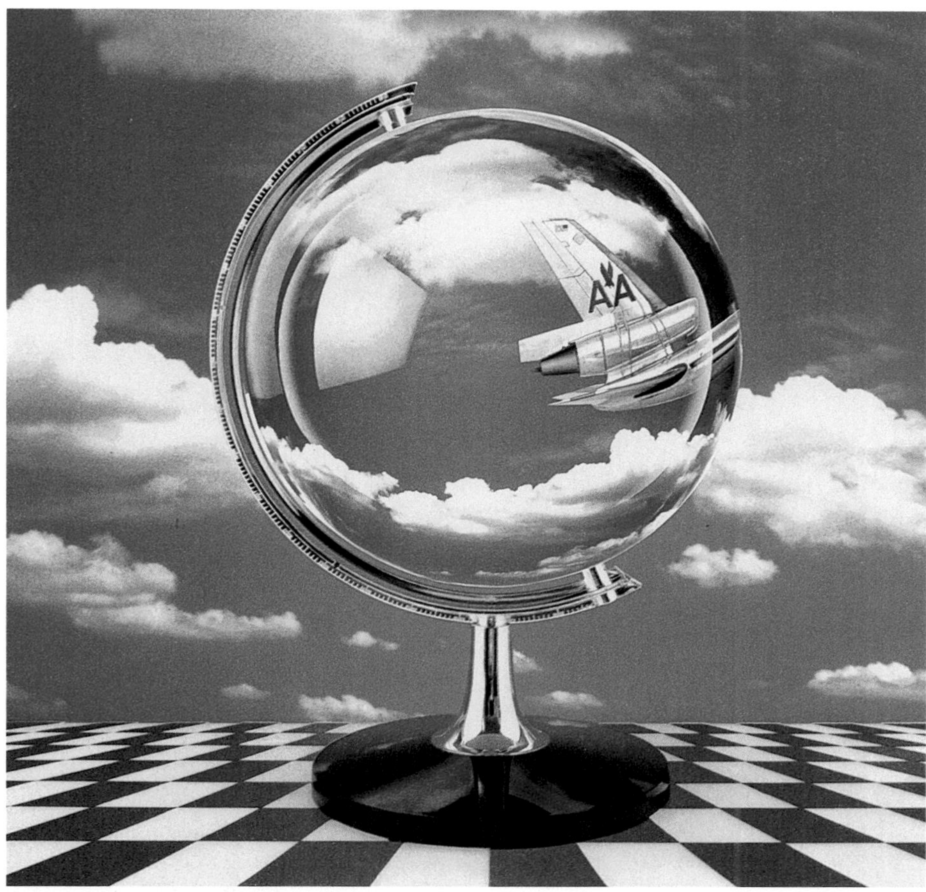

In a world of airlines, one airline has always been something special.

At first glance, all airlines may appear to be the same. But when you look closer, one airline offers you a special way to fly.

It's an airline so large it carries over 30 million people a year; yet so personalized, you can reserve your seat a year in advance.

It's an airline so committed to saving you time, you can get all your boarding passes for all your flights before you ever get to the airport.

It's an airline that's led the way by being innovative, not imitative. American Airlines. In a world of airlines, it's the one special airline that can make your trip something special.

366

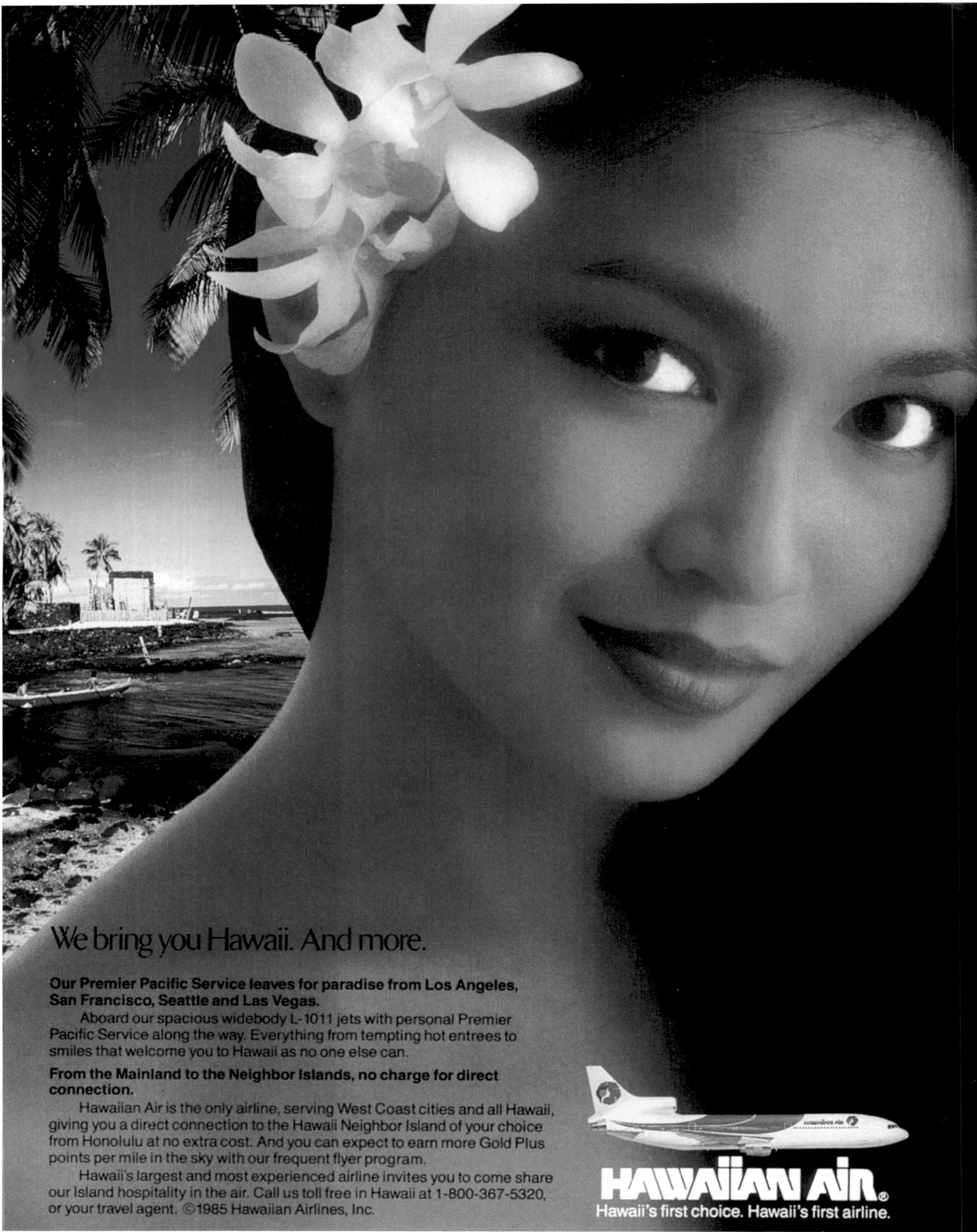

We bring you Hawaii. And more.
Our Premier Pacific Service leaves for paradise from Los Angeles, San Francisco, Seattle and Las Vegas.
Aboard our spacious widebody L-1011 jets with personal Premier Pacific Service along the way. Everything from tempting hot entrees to smiles that welcome you to Hawaii as no one else can.
From the Mainland to the Neighbor Islands, no charge for direct connection.
Hawaiian Air is the only airline, serving West Coast cities and all Hawaii, giving you a direct connection to the Hawaii Neighbor Island of your choice from Honolulu at no extra cost. And you can expect to earn more Gold Plus points per mile in the sky with our frequent flyer program.
Hawaii's largest and most experienced airline invites you to come share our Island hospitality in the air. Call us toll free in Hawaii at 1-800-367-5320, or your travel agent. ©1985 Hawaiian Airlines, Inc.
HAWAIIAN AIR®
Hawaii's first choice. Hawaii's first airline.

◂ Hawaiian Air, 1986

Singapore Airlines, 1998

The signature image of Singapore Airlines was its stewardess, the "Singapore Girl." Madame Tussaud's Wax Museum installed a figure depicting this Singapore Girl in 1991, the first commercial figure displayed there. The flight attendant uniform, a sarong kebaya, had originally been designed by the Parisian couturier Pierre Balmain.

Das Symbol von Singapore Airlines war ihre Stewardess, das „Singapore Girl"; es wurde sogar 1991 im Wachsfigurenmuseum der Madame Tussaud als erste kommerzielle Figur verewigt. Die Uniform der Flugbegleiterinnen, ein Sarong kebaya, wurde ursprünglich von dem Pariser Modeschöpfer Pierre Balmain entworfen.

L'image emblématique de Singapore Airlines était son hôtesse de l'air, la « fille de Singapour ». En 1991, le musée de Madame Tussaud en exposa même une statue de cire, tout premier personnage commercial présenté dans son enceinte. L'uniforme des hôtesses, le « sarong kebaya », avait été dessiné par le couturier parisien Pierre Balmain.

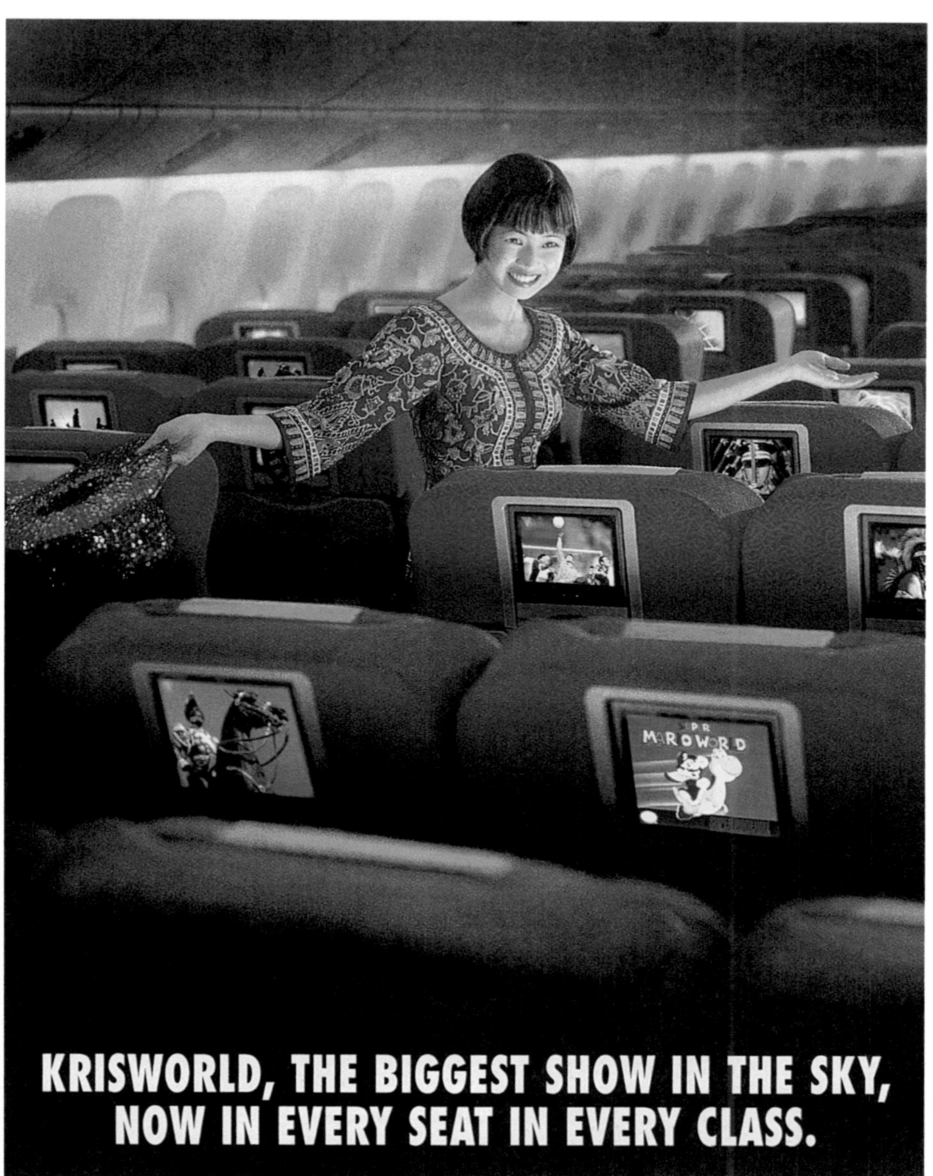

THE JOY OF COOKING.

In Palm Springs, lying by the pool, you can feel our warm sunshine soothe you. You can sense the calming influence of our dry desert air. Quickly and completely, winter's rough edges are smoothed.

And your mood turns golden right along with your tan.

Your most pressing decision will be what diversion to pursue next. Tennis, golf, bicycling. Shopping exclusive Palm Canyon Drive. Riding the Aerial Tramway. Dining, dancing, entertainment.

We have over 160 hotels for you to choose from. Some are intimate, others are grand. Some are economical, others quite luxurious.

So escape the gloom of winter and feast off the warmth of Palm Springs.

Palm Springs Convention and Visitors Bureau, Airport Park Plaza, Dept. 8603, 255 North El Cielo Rd., Suite 315, Palm Springs, CA 92262.

Send me your free Sunny Kit listing things to do and see and places to stay.

Name ______________________

Address ______________________

City ______________________

State ____________ *Zip* ________

Palm Springs
CALIFORNIA

For hotel referrals, phone toll-free 1-800-65-HOTEL (except Alaska). In California, 1-800-34-HOTEL. Ext. 603

◄ Palm Springs Convention and Visitors Bureau, 1985

Las Vegas Convention and Visitors Authority, 1981

Las Vegas Convention and Visitors Authority, 1982

L • I • F • E
ON • THE • BEACH

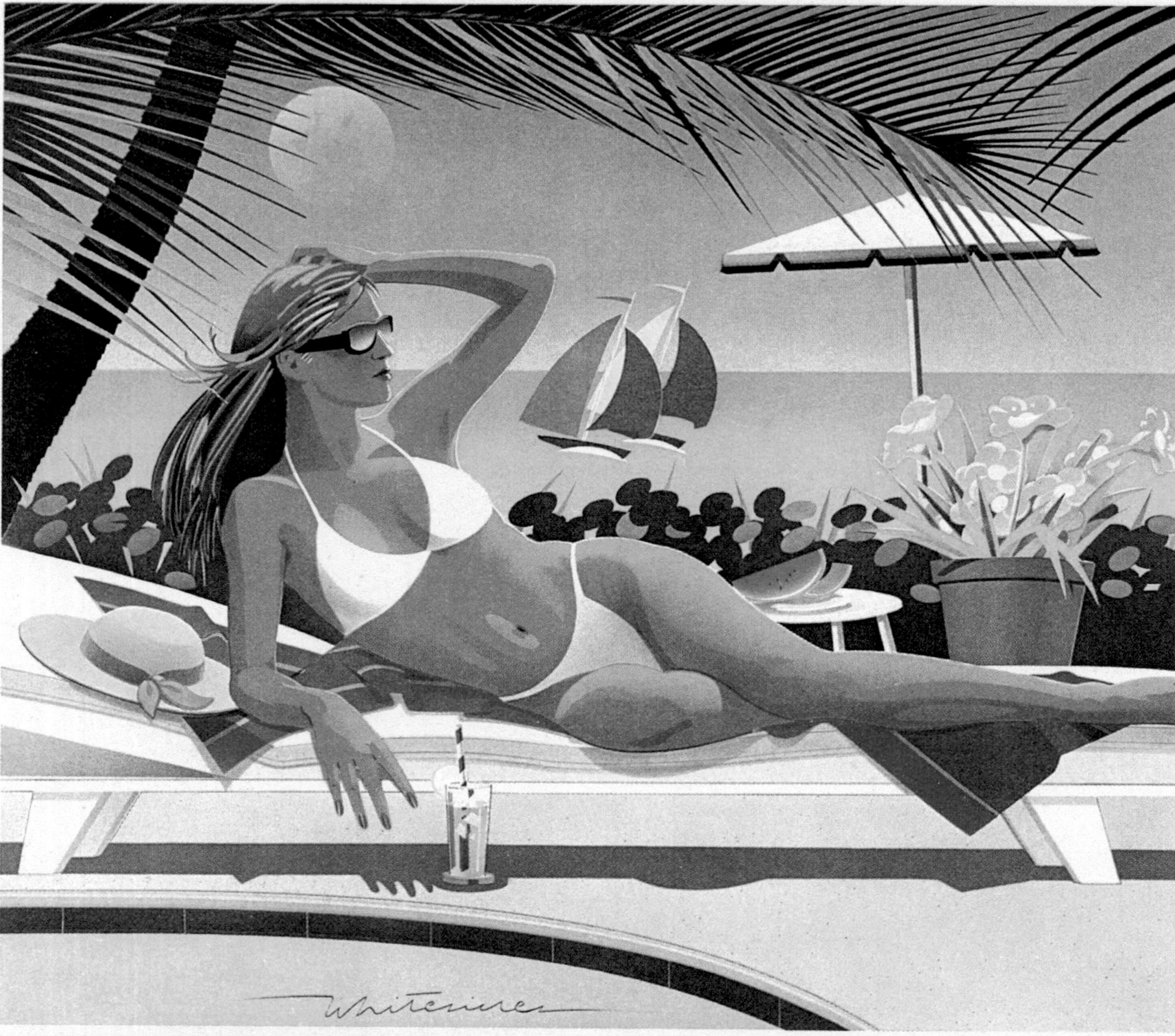

Life on the beach is ever so much better than life *at* the beach. The all-suite, all-luxury Alexander hotel is *on* Miami Beach. Recently, we have been transformed into one of the most tastefully exciting hotels in America. And when you dine, you'll dine at Dominique's, which is four-stars and for-gourmets. Or at Le Café for dining that's just as delicious, but more casual. When you add all our amenities, our service, our pool and our ocean, you'll know this. When you spend some small part of your life with us: you can do nothing. Gloriously.

For our free brochure or reservations, call 800 327-6121 or your travel planner.

THE ALEXANDER
ALL-SUITE LUXURY HOTEL
Elegance with a splash.

5225 Collins Avenue,
Miami Beach, Florida 33140

The Alexander Hotel, 1988

▸ Sunset Marquis Hotel and Villas, 1988

SMH
1200

IF WINSTON CHURCHILL WERE ALIVE TODAY
WHICH AIRLINE WOULD HE FLY TO LONDON

Virgin

VIRGIN ATLANTIC AIRWAYS. 747's MIAMI TO LONDON.
Take us for all we've got.

◄ Virgin Atlantic Airways, 1986

Most airlines that took off after the Airline Deregulation Act of 1978 were no-frills bargains. But Richard Branson, with his Virgin Atlantic Airways, was aiming for the prestige passenger. First-class seating was booked as "Upper Class" and included a limousine pickup. It was profitable in its first year—1984. A brave new world.

Die meisten nach dem Airline Deregulation Act von 1978 entstandenen Fluggesellschaften waren Billigflieger ohne Schnickschnack. Mit Virgin Atlantic Airways zielte Richard Branson hingegen auf den anspruchsvollen Passagier. Wer ein Ticket der „Oberklasse" buchte, wurde sogar per Limousine abgeholt. Virgin war gleich im ersten Jahr – 1984 – profitabel. Schöne neue Welt.

La plupart des compagnies aériennes créées après le vote de l'Airline Deregulation Act de 1978 proposaient des tarifs bon marché et un service sans chichis, mais avec Virgin Atlantic Airways, Richard Branson ciblait la clientèle de prestige. Le billet de première classe était appelé « Upper Class » et incluait un trajet en limousine jusqu'à l'aéroport. La compagnie devint rentable dès la première année, en 1984. Le meilleur des mondes.

Spain, 1989

Cultural travel surged in the 1990s, but, as this ad shows, it was blossoming in the decade before. Art lovers made pilgrimages to the Venice Biennale or Art Basel, in Switzerland. When Frank Gehry's Guggenheim Museum opened in Bilbao, Spain, in 1997, it became a cultural station of the cross.

Bildungsreisen verzeichneten in den 1990er-Jahren einen Aufschwung, doch wie diese Anzeige belegt, waren sie bereits in den Achtzigern ein Thema. Kunstfreunde pilgerten zur Biennale von Venedig oder zur Art Basel. Frank Gehrys 1997 im spanischen Bilbao eröffnetes Guggenheim-Museum wurde zu einer kulturellen Pilgerstation.

Si les voyages culturels explosèrent dans les années 1990, cette publicité montre qu'ils intéressaient déjà beaucoup de monde au cours de la décennie précédente. Les amateurs d'art partaient en pèlerinage à la Biennale de Venise ou au salon Art Basel en Suisse. Quand le Musée Guggenheim espagnol de Frank Gehry ouvrit à Bilbao en 1997, il devint une étape incontournable sur leur Chemin de Croix.

The Duchess of Alba
by Francisco de Goya.
Courtesy of
The Hispanic Society
of America, New York.

For once, view the works of the Spanish masters without flipping pages.

Goya. El Greco. Velázquez. Miró. Picasso.

From the pages of art books, their paintings have fascinated and inspired you.

Yet the printed page does not really allow you to see them. For what makes each a masterpiece is what it demands of the viewer: a personal relationship in which the work reveals itself layer by layer. Until finally, standing before it, you come to experience the full emotional and spiritual power the artist intended you to feel.

At the Prado in Madrid–and in many other museums throughout Spain–you will find hundreds upon hundreds of the world's greatest works of art. And you will recognize many from reproductions you have seen.

But as you fix your gaze on them you will recognize something else.

That you are looking at them for the first time.

The Prado. An extraordinary destination along your journey of discovery.

Spain

Everything Under The Sun.

United Air Lines, 1989

The 747 jumbo jet set passenger-capacity records when it took off in 1970, and held them for the rest of the century. With so many seats, price per ticket could be far lower. Travelers could jet off to exotic locales on the other side of the globe for a reasonable cost.

In der 1970 eingeführten Boeing 747 fanden so viele Passagiere Platz wie auch später in diesem Jahrhundert in keiner anderen Maschine. Derart viele Sitzplätze ermöglichten drastisch reduzierte Ticketpreise. Nun konnte man zu vertretbaren Kosten auch exotische Ziele auf der anderen Seite des Globus ansteuern.

Quand il décolla en 1970, le Boeing 747 explosa tous les records de capacité d'accueil de passagers et en resta détenteur jusqu'à la fin du siècle. Avec autant de sièges, le prix du billet diminuait considérablement. Les voyageurs pouvaient enfin s'envoler vers des lieux exotiques à l'autre bout du monde à des tarifs raisonnables.

► United Air Lines, 1989

國際
Showdown in Taipei.
Today's corporate warrior in Taiwan needs more than his own skills. He needs a fleet at his command.
The fleet of United nonstops to Taipei.
With more nonstops to Asia and the Pacific than any other airline, United lands you there ready for action. And each flight provides the best in international travel. Including, in First Class, sleeper seats and our exclusive Concierge Service.
United. Rededicated to giving you the service you deserve. Come fly the friendly skies.
UNITED
AIRLINES
Tokyo • Osaka • Hong Kong • Seoul • Taipei • Sydney • Melbourne • Beijing • Shanghai • Auckland • Singapore • Bangkok

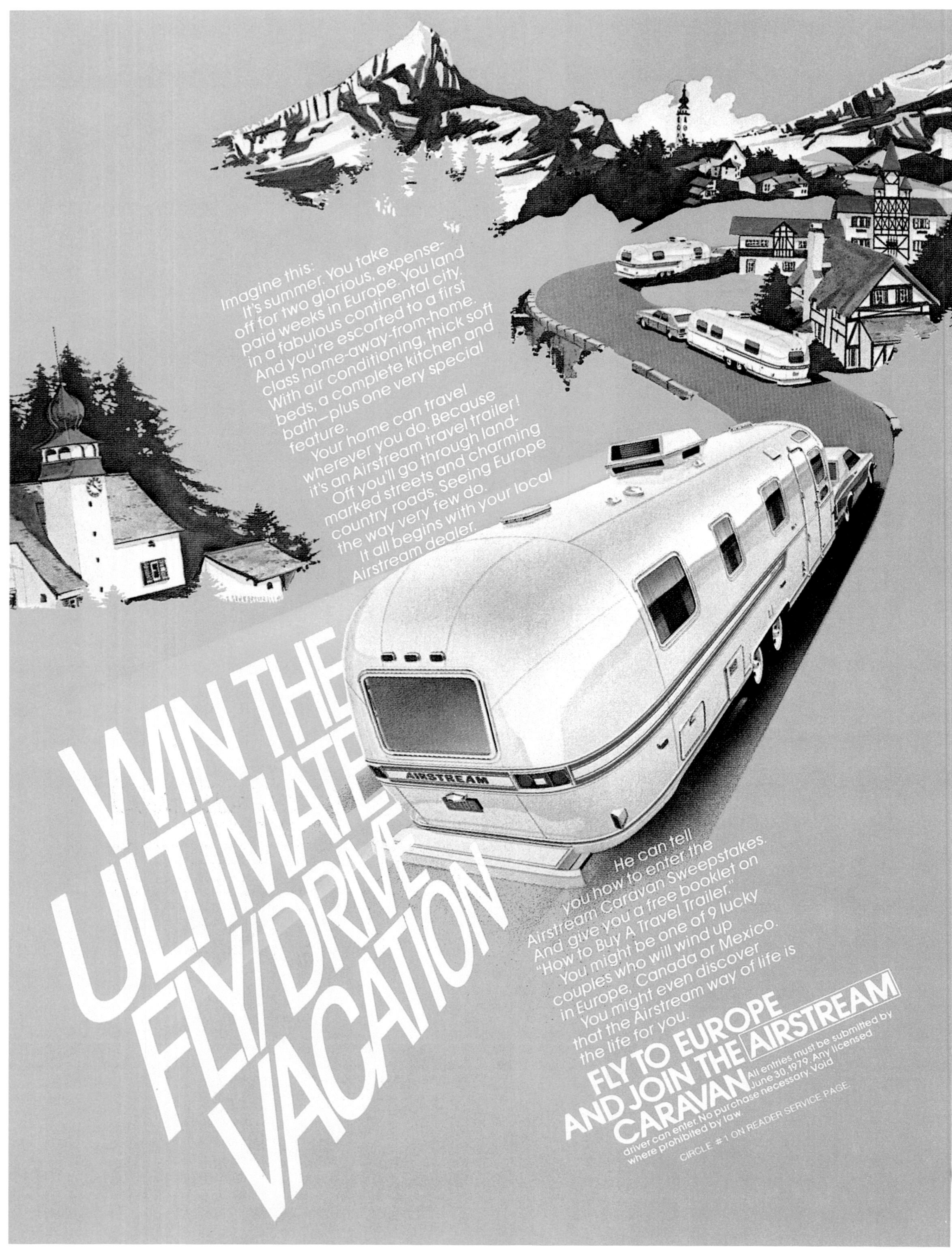

Imagine this:
It's summer. You take
off for two glorious, expense-
paid weeks in Europe. You land
in a fabulous continental city.
And you're escorted to a first
class home-away-from-home.
With air conditioning, thick soft
beds, a complete kitchen and
bath—plus one very special
feature.
Your home can travel
wherever you do. Because
it's an Airstream travel trailer!
Off you'll go through land-
marked streets and charming
country roads. Seeing Europe
the way very few do.
It all begins with your local
Airstream dealer.
WIN THE
ULTIMATE
FLY/DRIVE
VACATION
AIRSTREAM
He can tell
you how to enter the
Airstream Caravan Sweepstakes.
And give you a free booklet on
"How to Buy A Travel Trailer."
You might be one of 9 lucky
couples who will wind up
in Europe, Canada or Mexico.
You might even discover
that the Airstream way of life is
the life for you.
FLY TO EUROPE
AND JOIN THE AIRSTREAM
CARAVAN
All entries must be submitted by
June 30, 1979. Any licensed
driver can enter. No purchase necessary. Void
where prohibited by law.
CIRCLE #1 ON READER SERVICE PAGE.

◂ Airstream Trailers, 1980

Eurailpass, 1986

Budget airlines and super-cheap fares after the 1978 Airline Deregulation Act enabled ever more travelers to get to Europe. Once there, students or others with limited means discovered that Eurailpass offered an inexpensive opportunity to explore the Continent. Amtrak seemed even less inviting after Americans had sampled the trains in Europe.

Die seit dem 1978 verabschiedeten Airline Deregulation Act entstandenen Billiglinien ermöglichten immer mehr US-Bürgern einen Flug nach Europa. Dort angekommen, entdeckten Studenten oder andere Reisende mit begrenzten Mitteln, dass der Eurail-Pass sich hervorragend eignete, um den Kontinent kostengünstig zu erkunden. Nachdem die Amerikaner die europäischen Züge kennengelernt hatten, erschien ihnen die heimische Amtrak noch weniger einladend.

Le vote de l'Airline Deregulation Act en 1978 autorisant les compagnies aériennes à proposer des prix cassés permit à encore plus de passagers d'aller en Europe. Une fois sur place, les étudiants et autres voyageurs à budget restreint découvrirent le forfait Eurailpass, un moyen abordable d'explorer le Vieux Continent. Après avoir goûté aux trains européens, les Américains ne firent que dénigrer davantage leur compagnie Amtrak.

Eurailpass admits there may still be a less expensive way to see Europe.

Eurailpass gives you lots of ways to save money on European travel. With our Eurail Saverpass, for example, you get unlimited first-class rail travel in any or all of 16 European countries for only $199 per person.* That's less than $14 per day.

Of course, there is a way to travel around Europe that costs even less. If you like to pedal.

*Applies to 15-day pass, when three or more travel together. Other inexpensive rates are available for one or two people.

$199

EURAILPASS

Please rush me a *free* Eurailpass color brochure.

Name________

Address________

City________ State________ Zip________

Mail today to Eurailpass, Box Q, Staten Island, New York, 10305.

G00586

Universal Studios Tour, 1986

► Sea World, 1982

Sea World, like Disneyland, thrived as family vacations became ever more focused on amusing the children. Four UCLA graduates founded the marine zoological park in 1964, and it gradually evolved into a vast theme park with whales, dolphins, penguins, and amusement rides.

Wie Disneyland profitierte auch SeaWorld davon, dass es beim Familienurlaub zunehmend darum ging, die Kinder bei Laune zu halten. Vier Absolventen der UCLA hatten 1964 einen Meereszoo gegründet, der sich nach und nach zu einem riesigen Themenpark mit Walen, Delfinen, Pinguinen und Fahrgeschäften entwickelte.

Comme Disneyland, Sea World remporta un immense succès car les vacances en famille se concentraient toujours plus sur le divertissement des enfants. Fondé en 1964 par quatre diplômés de UCLA, ce zoo marin se transforma progressivement en un vaste parc à thème, avec baleines, pingouins, spectacles de dauphins et attractions.

San Diego's best
just keeps getting better.
Sea World is a living, changing place—
alive with new animals to meet and new ways to have fun
every time you visit. Shamu™ and his trainers constantly give
you the world's newest, most thrilling animal show.
You'll flip over our new dolphin show and this summer
"Up With People," direct from their Super Bowl appearance,
will lift your spirits with their new show. Bring your family
back to Sea World. It's a whole different world every day.
™

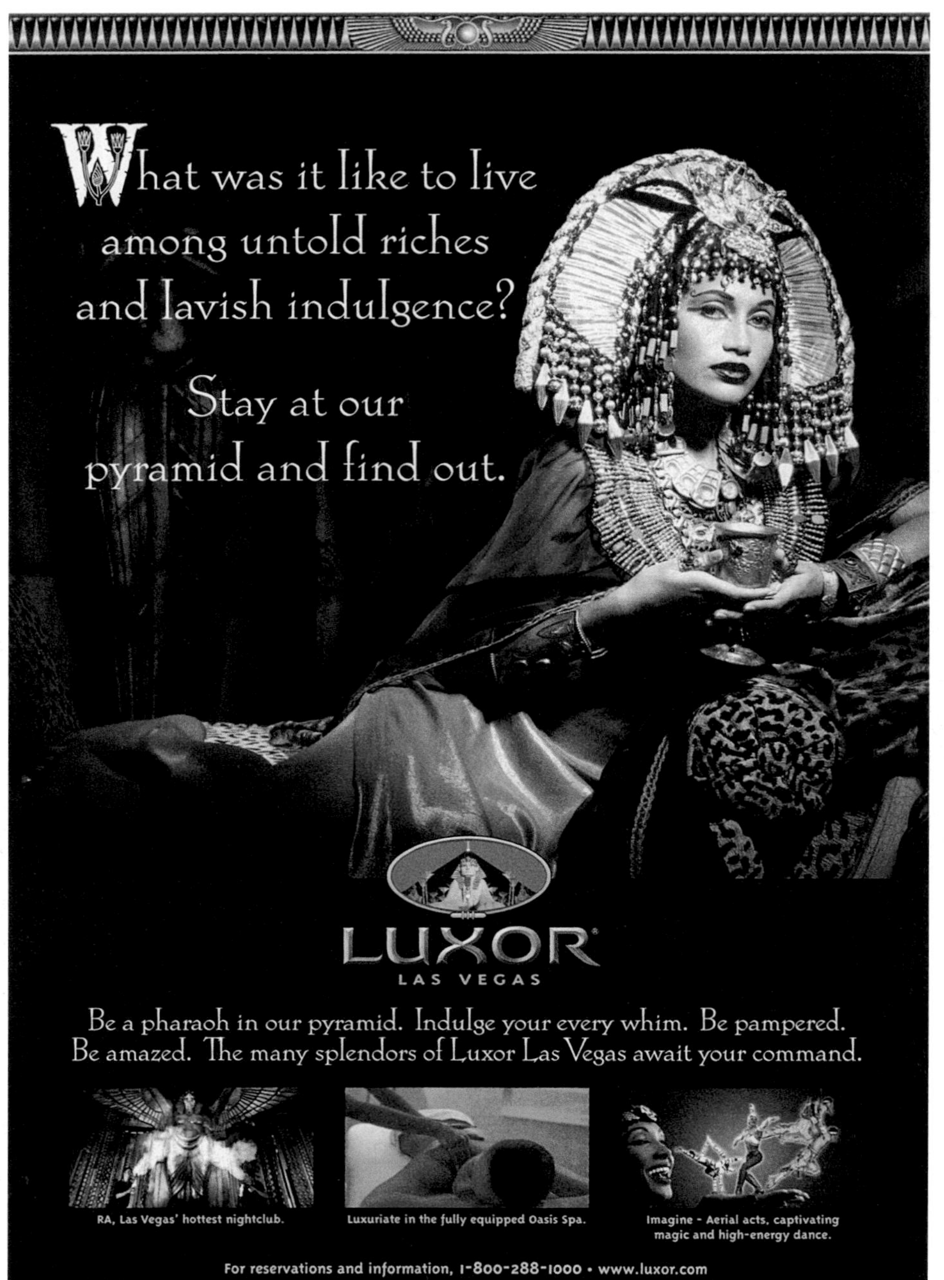

Luxor Las Vegas, 1998

Travelers could go around the world without leaving Las Vegas. Theme hotels boomed. You could be in ancient Egypt at the Luxor, in France at the Paris, in Manhattan at New York New York, in Italy at the Venetian, in Brazil at the Rio, in the South Seas at Mandalay Bay, in ancient Rome at Caesar's Palace, even in Camelot at Excalibur.

Eine Weltreise war auch möglich, ohne Las Vegas zu verlassen, denn die Themenhotels verzeichneten einen wahren Boom. Im Luxor konnte man sich wie im alten Ägypten fühlen, im Paris wie in Frankreich, im New York New York wie in Manhattan, im Venetian wie in Italien, im Rio wie in Brasilien, in Mandalay Bay wie in der Südsee, in Caesar's Palace wie im alten Rom und im Excalibur gar wie in Camelot.

Les touristes pouvaient voyager dans le monde entier sans quitter Las Vegas. Les hôtels thématiques explosèrent. Le Luxor vous emmenait dans l'Egypte des pharaons, le Paris en France, le New York New York à Manhattan, le Venetian en Italie, le Rio au Brésil, le Mandalay Bay dans les mers du Sud, le Caesar's Palace dans la Rome antique, et l'Excalibur au château de Camelot.

► Beverly Wilshire Hotel, 1981

Hotel
BEVERLY
WILSHIRE

Loosen up
the bonds of city life and unravel your problems on a Windjammer cruise. Surrender to the majestic ocean and enchanting ports of call. Let the currents guide you to peace of spirit, mind and body. Master the Windjammer knot and untie yourself from everyday hassles. Experience the real you.
Your share of the six day Windjammer adventure can be as little as $400.
For reservations only call toll free 1-800-327-2600.
Cap'n Mike, please send me a free Adventure Booklet in full color.
Windjammer 'Barefoot' Cruises

◄ Windjammer Barefoot Cruises, 1983

Club Med, 1988

Club Med started as a sort of a seductive vacation mixer, largely aimed at singles or lithe young couples. Club Meds opened around the globe during the 1960s and '70s, thriving on their image as hedonistic escapes. But by the '80s, despite this ad families were increasingly checking in.

Der Club Med bot zunächst so etwas wie eine verlockende Ferienmixtur, die vor allem Singles oder sportliche junge Paare ansprach. Die in den Sechzigern und Siebzigern überall auf der Welt eröffneten Clubs profitierten vom Image eines sinnenfrohen Refugiums. Ab den 1980er-Jahren fand der Club Med trotz dieser Anzeige auch bei Familien zunehmend Anklang.

Club Med se présenta d'abord comme un mix de vacances séduisant largement destiné aux célibataires ou aux jeunes couples libérés. La marque ouvrit des clubs dans le monde entier pendant les années 1960 et 1970, prospérant sur son image de refuge hédoniste mais au début des années 1980, et malgré le message de cette publicité, elle remportait un succès croissant auprès des familles.

►► Amtrak, 1983

A CLUB MED VACATION BEGINS WHERE CIVILIZATION ENDS.

Imagine, for a moment, nothing.

No clocks. No ringing phones. No traffic jams. No radios. No newspapers. No crowds.

Now imagine this. An island village where aqua seas brush dazzling white shores. Where lush green palms line wandering pathways. Where crystal blue skies change magically to golden sunsets.

Where you can indulge in everything from windsurfing, snorkeling and tennis, to afternoon classes in water aerobics or painting, to secluded moments on miles of sun-drenched beach.

Imagine not just three meals, but three gourmet banquets every single day. With freshly baked breads and pastries and free-flowing wine.

Where evenings are always filled with entertainment, dancing and a special atmosphere that turns new faces into old friends in moments.

If all this captures your imagination, drop by and see your travel agent or call 1-800-CLUB MED. It just may be the beginning of the end of civilization as you know it.

CLUB MED®

The antidote for civilization.™

Activities vary by village. © 1988 Club Med Sales, Inc., 40 West 57th Street, New York, NY 10019.

DTW
72-4394
DTW
PAS.270 (4-80) MADE IN U.S.A.

920
WR
MADE IN U.S.A.

STL
25-2222
STL
PAS.270 (4-80) MADE IN U.S.A.

SAT
05-9877
SAT

18-4
IA
PAS.270 (4-80)

GETTING THERE IS HALF THE FUN

FINISH

SELECTED INDEX

◂◂ Cunard, 1953

▸ Lockheed, 1955

Leadership demands constant achievement

20 Distinguished World Airlines

have selected

THE CONSTELLATION & SUPER CONSTELLATION

On every continent of the world leading airlines fly the famous Constellation. Today more people fly over more oceans and continents on the Constellations of these great airlines than on *any other modern airplane.* It is also the leader on the most traveled route, the North Atlantic. This successful operation by international airlines established the Constellation's record for dependable performance—leading to the development of the new Super Constellation, today's finest transport airplane. Altogether 20 distinguished airlines have selected the Constellation and Super Constellation. Whenever or wherever you travel, insist on the dependable service of these airline leaders.* If there is no local airline office, see your travel agent.

** Listed above on travel posters.*

LOCKHEED

AIRCRAFT CORPORATION · BURBANK, CALIFORNIA, AND MARIETTA, GEORGIA

BIBLIOGRAPHY

Blume, Mary. *Côte d'Azur: Inventing the French Riviera*. New York: Thames and Hudson, 1992.

Denby, Elaine. *Grand Hotels: Illusion and Reality*. London: Reaktion Books, 1998.

Flinchum, Russell. *Henry Dreyfuss, Industrial Designer: The Man in the Brown Suit*. New York: Cooper-Hewitt National Design Museum, Smithsonian Institution, and Rizzoli, 1997.

Fox, Robert. *Liners: The Golden* Age. Köln, Germany: Könemann Verlag, 1999.

Girard, Xavier. *French Riviera: Living Well Was the Best Revenge*. New York: Assouline, 2002.

Gygelman, Adele. *Palm Springs Modern: Houses in the California Desert*. New York: Rizzoli, 1999.

Hilton, Conrad. *Be My Guest*. Englewood Cliffs, New Jersey: Prentice-Hall, 1957.

Jodard, Paul. *Design Heroes: Raymond Loewy*. London: HarperCollins, 1994.

Krinsky, Carol Herselle. *Gordon Bunshaft of Skidmore, Owings & Merrill*. New York: The Architectural History Foundation and The MIT Press, 1988.

Lapidus, Morris. *Too Much Is Never Enough: An Autobiography*. New York: Rizzoli, 1996.

La Pietra, Ugo (ed.). *Gio Ponti*. New York: Rizzoli, 1996.

Loewy, Raymond. *Industrial Design*. New York: The Overlook Press, 1988.

Loos, Anita. *Gentlemen Prefer Blondes: The Illuminating Diary of a Professional Lady*. New York: Boni & Liveright, 1925.

Maddocks, Melvin, et al. *The Great Liners*. Alexandria, Virginia: Time-Life Books, 1978.

Melville, John H. *The Great White Fleet*. New York: Vantage Press, 1976.

Schönberger, Angela (ed.). *Raymond Loewy: Pioneer of American Industrial Design*. Munich: Prestel, 1990.

Sparke, Penny, and Felice Hodges, Emma Dent Coad, Anne Stone. *Design Source Book*. Secaucus, New Jersey: Chartwell Books, 1986.

Vaill, Amanda. *Everybody Was So Young: Gerald and Sara Murphy: A Lost Generation Love Story*. New York: Houghton Mifflin, 1998.

Varney, Carleton. *The Draper Touch: The High Life & High Style of Dorothy Draper*. New York: Prentice Hall Press, 1988.

Wharton, Annabel Jane. *Building the Cold War: Hilton International Hotels and Modern Architecture*. Chicago: University of Chicago Press, 2001.

Wilson, Richard Guy, Dianne H. Pilgrim and Dickran Tashjian. *The Machine Age in America 1918–1941*. New York: The Brooklyn Museum and Harry N. Abrams, 1986.

Zega, Michael E., and John E. Gruber. *Travel by Train: The American Railroad Poster 1870–1950*. Bloomington, Indiana: Indiana University Press, 2002.

► Braniff International, 1953

Frontispiece The Airlines of the United States, 1945

Images courtesy of: Amanresorts: Amanpuri (p. 27). Burton Holmes Historical Archive, www.burtonholmes.org: Burton Holmes (p. 9), Eiffel Tower (p. 11), Panama-Pacific International Exposition (p. 38). Charlie Brown, National Museum of History and Technology, Smithsonian Institution: RMS *Mauretania* (p. 37). Danubius Hotel Gellért (p. 42). Photograph by Ernest Lenart, courtesy Kathy Kohner: *Gidget* (p. 19). Georges Méliès: *A Trip to the Moon* (p. 33). Hard Rock Hotel (p. 361). Mandarin Oriental Hong Kong (p. 258). Nicholas Fasciano: RMS *Titanic* (p. 10), RMS *Lusitania* (p. 42). Nikolas Koenig: The Standard Hotel (p. 28). Parco dei Principi Grand Hotel & Spa (p. 258). The Queen Mary (p. 157). © Simon Fieldhouse: Peace Hotel (p. 18). Southwest Airlines (p. 25, 315). Starwood Hotels & Resorts Waikiki: Royal Hawaiian Hotel (p. 12, 64), Moana Hotel (p. 63).

The publisher would like to thank Craig Gaines, Doug Adrianson, Teena Apeles, Nicole Greene, and Mia Chamasmany for their invaluable assistance in getting this book produced.

To stay informed about upcoming TASCHEN titles, please request our magazine at www.taschen.com/magazine or write to TASCHEN, Hohenzollernring 53, D-50672 Cologne, Germany, contact@taschen.com, Fax: +49-221-254919. We will be happy to send you a free copy of our magazine which is filled with information about all of our books.

Hohenzollernring 53, D-50672 Köln, Germany
www.taschen.com

Art direction: Josh Baker, Los Angeles
English-language editor & project management: Nina Wiener, Los Angeles
Design: J. Tyler Flatt, New York; Marco Zivny, Los Angeles
Editorial coordination: Anne Gerlinger, Cologne; Ryann McQuilton, Los Angeles
Production: Jennifer Patrick, Los Angeles
German translation: Helmut Roß, Krenglbach
French translation: Claire Le Breton, Paris

Printed in China

ISBN 978-3-8365-1941-0

RIO
it's
BRANIFF
INTERNATIONAL AIRWAYS

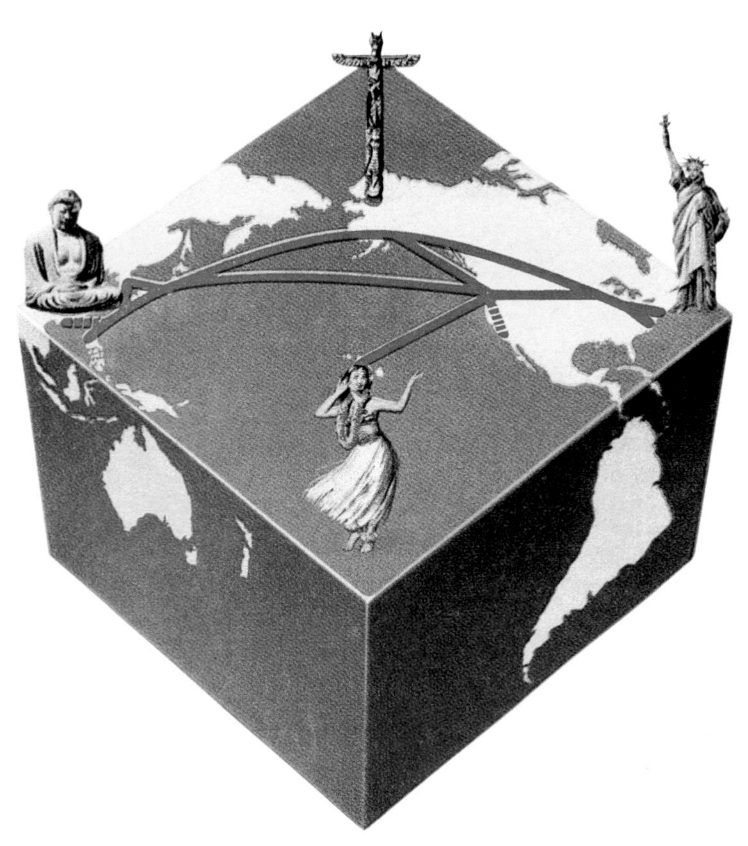

HOTEL MOUNT EVEREST DARJEELING
SLOW HALF FULL ASTERN STOP AHEAD SLOW HALF
TITANIC DISASTER GREAT LOSS OF LIFE EVENING NEWS
PARIS RITZ HOTEL
YELLOWSTONE PARK HOTELS
Chief
ROAD TO MOROCCO
WINTER SPORTS SUN VALLEY LODGE SUN VALLEY · IDAHO
Flamingo
Holiday Inn OF AMERICA
THE NATION'S INNKEEPER
PAN AM
PALM SPRINGS TRAMWAY
I ♥ NY
Hard Rock HOTEL
Virgin